A Symposion of Praise

A Symposion of Praise

Horace Returns to Lyric in *Odes* IV

Timothy S. Johnson

THE UNIVERSITY OF WISCONSIN PRESS

The University of Wisconsin Press
1930 Monroe Street
Madison, Wisconsin 53711

www.wisc.edu/wisconsinpress/

3 Henrietta Street
London WC2E 8LU, England

PA
6411
.J57
2004

5   4   3   2   1

Printed in the United States of America

Publication of this volume has also been made possible in large part through the generous support and enduring vision of Warren G. Moon.

Library of Congress Cataloging-in-Publication Data

Johnson, Timothy S.
    A symposion of praise: Homer returns to lyric in Odes IV / Timothy S. Johnson.
        p. cm—(Wisconsin studies in classics)
    Includes bibliographical references and index.
    ISBN 0-299-20740-4 (hardcover: alk. paper)
    1. Horace. Carmina. Liber 4. 2. Laudatory poetry, Latin—History and criticism.
    3. Lyric poetry—History and criticism. 4. Odes—History and criticism. 5. Rome—In
    literature. 6. Praise in literature. I. Title. II. Series.
    PA6411.J57 2005
    874'.01—dc22

                                                                2004025227

For Kathryn Renee Johnson

Contents

Acknowledgments ix

Abbreviations xi

Introduction xiii

1. Sympotic Horace 3

 Looking Back 3

 Levis et Gravis 6

 Parties and Politics 12

 Sympotic Horace's Epic Criticism 14

 Sympotic Horace Exiled: *Epistle* II.2 and *Odes* IV.1 26

2. *Encomia Nobilium* and Horace's Panegyric Praxis 40

 C.1 and 2: Great Expectations? Inventing

  Panegyric Discord 43

 C.3 and 6: The Poet among the *Nobiles* 51

 C.7: Panegyric and Politics, Putting Off Heirs 69

 C.8 and 9: As the Wor(l)d Turns, Praise and Blame 74

3. *Encomia Augusti,* "Take One" 94

 C.4: Epinikion[One] — The Panegyric Agon 95

 C.5: A Panegyric Tag[One] — All in the Family 114

4. Songs of Mo(u)rning   134

    C.10: Faces in the Mirror: Ligurinus, Horace,
        and Vergil   138

    C.11: The Phyllis Odes and the Comic Power
        of Shared Lyric   145

    C.12: Vergilius at the Symposion   158

    C.13: E/motive Song, The Art of Writing Off Lyce   167

5. *Encomia Augusti*, "Take Two"   181

    C.14: Epinikion^{Two}—Winners and Losers   182

    C.15: A Panegyric Tag^{Two}—"I Really Wanted To!" 198

Notes   215
Works Cited   279
General Index   301
Index Locorum   309

Acknowledgments

A scholar once whispered in my ear, "It can be hard to explain what you do for a living, when your art is no more than taking from one book and putting it in another." There may be more to this "art" than appears, but I am still sure that Horace would prefer that we simply read his poems. "Horace, if my art (reading) in any way detracts from yours I apologize. I was just not up to such a grand lyric task."

My reading of Horace owes mentors: Brent Sandy, Jane Phillips, Robert Rabel, G. M. Browne and his sharp critical eye, and foremost J. K. Newman, whose works on Alexandrianism and on the epic tradition are never far from mind. Other readers have commented and corrected at various stages of construction: Michael von Albrecht, Andrew Becker, Randall Childree, Jeff Fish, Kirk Freudenburg, Philip Hardie, Dan Hooley, David Konstan, Hans Mueller, Jennifer Rea, Alden Smith, Carol Staup, and Robert Wagman. I have learned much from their discussions and benefited from their friendship. A special thanks to Eleanor Leach and Michèle Lowrie, the readers for the University of Wisconsin Press, who generously offered their insights—not to mention the errors they prevented. All that remain, of course, are my responsibility. The Press has been the model of professionalism from Patricia Rosenmeyer and her kind interest in my project to the editors Raphael Kadushin, Erin Holman, and Jane Curran, without whom this manuscript would not have become a book.

Many have shown to me the best side of ἀκαδημία. My colleagues and friends in classics at the University of Florida have answered many requests for advice—Gareth Schmeling, Lewis

Sussman, and Mary Ann Eaverly more than their fair share. A grant from the Humanities Council (University of Florida) provided funding for work in Rome. Father Raffaele Farina (Vatican Library), Christina Huemer (American Academy at Rome), and Bruce Swann (University of Illinois) made available their libraries' fine collections. Friends at Baylor University, in particular William Cooper and Alden Smith (again), and at the University of Texas, David Armstrong and Tim Moore, have given invaluable support and encouragement. Janet and Tom Lane (and Bev) offered room and board to an itinerant scholar. I have been blessed with five brothers, all avid and witty readers (thanks to our mother). Deserving special mention are Galen, whose own scholarship inspired me, and Dwayne, who has taught me how, or at least how I would like, to live.

Animae dimidia meae — Pam, Love, if I had the talent to write an ode, it would be for you. To my daughter, Katie, I dedicate this book.

Abbreviations

ANRW	Temporini, H., and W. Haase, eds. 1972–. *Aufstieg und Niedergang der römischen Welt: Geschichte und Kultur Roms im Spiegel der neueren Forschung*. Berlin: de Gruyter.
A.P.	*Anthologia Palatina*
CIL	*Corpus Inscriptionum Latinarum*
EGF	Kinkel, G., ed. 1877. *Epicorum Graecorum Fragmenta*. Leipzig: Teubner.
FGrH	Jacoby, F., ed. 1923–58. *Die Fragmente der griechischen Historiker*. Berlin: Weidmann.
Gent.	Gentili, B., and C. Prato, eds. 1979, 1985. *Poetarum elegiacorum testimonia et fragmenta*. 2 vols. Leipzig: Teubner.
G.-P.	Gow, A. S. F., and D. L. Page, eds. 1965. *The Greek Anthology: Hellenistic Epigrams*. 2 vols. Cambridge: Cambridge Univ. Press.
IG	*Inscriptiones Graecae*
K.-H.	Kiessling, A., ed. 1884. *Q. Horatius Flaccus*. Berlin: Weidmann. Rev. by Heinze. Vol. 1: *Oden und Epoden*, 5th ed. 1908, 9th ed. 1958; vol. 2: *Satiren*, 6th ed. 1957; vol. 3: *Briefe*, 5th ed. 1957.
LGPN	Fraser, P. M., and E. Matthews, eds. 1987–. *A Lexicon of Greek Personal Names*. Oxford: Clarendon.
L.-P.	Lobel, E., and D. L. Page, eds. 1955. *Poetarum Lesbiorum Fragmenta*. Oxford: Clarendon.
N.-H.	Nisbet, R. G. M., and M. Hubbard. 1970, 1978. *A Commentary on Horace: Odes Book I*. Oxford: Clarendon,

1970. *A Commentary on Horace: Odes Book II.* Oxford:
Clarendon, 1978.

OLD   Glare, P. G. W., et al., eds. 1968–82. *Oxford Latin*
Dictionary. Oxford: Clarendon.

Pf.   Pfeiffer, R., ed. *Callimachus.* 1949, 1953. 2 vols. Oxford:
Clarendon.

PIR   Klebs, E., H. Dessau, and P. von Rohden, eds. 1897–98.
Prosopographia Imperii Romani Saec. I. II. III. Berlin:
Reimer.

PIR²   Groag, E., A. Stein, et al., eds. 1933–. *Prosopographia*
Imperii Romani Saec. I. II. III. 2nd ed. Berlin: de Gruyter.

PLG   Bergk, T., ed. 1843. *Poetae Lyrici Graeci.* 3 vols. Leipzig:
Teubner.

PMG   Page, D. L., ed. 1962. *Poeti Melici Graeci.* Oxford:
Clarendon.

RE   Wissowa, G., et al., eds. *Paulys Real-Encyclopädie der*
classischen Alterumswissenschaft. 1893–1980. 33 vols.
and 15 suppl. vols. Stuttgart; Munich: J. B.
Metzlersche; Druckenmüller.

SH   Lloyd-Jones, H., P. J. Parson, et al., eds. 1983.
Supplementum Hellenisticum. Berlin: de Gruyter.

TLL   *Thesaurus Linguae Latinae.* 1900–. Leipzig: Teubner.

W.   West, M. L., ed. 1971, 1972. *Iambi et Elegi Graeci ante*
Alexandrum Cantati. 2 vols. Oxford: Clarendon. 2nd
ed., 1989, 1992.

Journals are abbreviated according to the conventions of *L'Année*
Philologique. Abbreviations of the ancient authors derive from the
most recent editions of the *Oxford Classical Dictionary;* the *Oxford*
Latin Dictionary; and Liddell, Scott, and Jones, eds. *A Greek-English*
Lexicon.

Introduction

This is not a book on patronage. Horace tells us he is one in a circle of poets whose patron/s are the governing elite in the developing principate. He addresses the lead poem of his *Satires* and *Odes* I–III to Maecenas and follows the first ode with a praise poem to Augustus (c.2). He then honors Vergil, the senior poet who introduced him into the circle, with a propempticon (c.3) and follows it with a sympotic invitation to Sestius, the *consul suffectus* of 23 B.C. (c.4). After one love song (c.5) he addresses a *recusatio* to another poet who supported his entrance into the circle, Varius (c.6). By C.I.6 his coterie of friends from the trip to Brundisium (minus Plotius, *S.I.5*) are all present again. Horatian poetry embodies patronage (Ahl, 1984; P. White, 1993; Bowditch, 2001). Defining the qualities of Horace's patronage, its socioeconomic contexts and language, has important implications for Horace's poetic service or gift; nevertheless, as important as this is, it has left unexplored much of the contents of the gift. And in spite of Putnam's (1986) arguments for the merits of Horace's later lyrics, the one book (*Odes* IV), which Suetonius reports was commissioned by Augustus and is devoted to panegyric song, remains the least-studied Horatian poetry book. This book is about the contents of that gift, Horace's panegyric praxis in *Odes* IV.

When approximately five to six years after the publication of *Odes* I–III Horace accepted the commission of the *Carmen Saeculare* (17 B.C.) and subsequently continued to compose lyric *carmina* and cast these lyrics into another book of odes (13 B.C.), he undertook the vatic role of the *Romanae fidicen lyrae*. At least, this is how the poet represents his audience's perception of his later work

(C.IV.3.23). Although it would strain the limits set by Horace's literary environment to read back into his persona the modern sense of poet laureate and transpose his claim into an official title, there are major intersections between Augustan and modern literary/political contexts. Modern political theory has rediscovered the importance of story for forming and transforming shared ideologies (Sandel, 1996). The exchange of stories as the formative process of civic identity involves competition, a political agon. We can well ask about our own πολιτεία or *civitas*, "Whose story was it, is it, and whose will it be — that of the founding fathers and their antecedents, particular presidents and public leaders, the courts, congress, cultural movements, the people themselves with their ideals?" The same question, "Whose story is it or should it be?" can be asked of Horace's songs, and the answer is surely as complex, but I suggest a good beginning can be made by recognizing *Odes* IV as a unified collection, a book, and the Horatian panegyrist as its storyteller, who engages his audience in an interpretive dialogue rather than as an agent who persuades to any particular point of view.

An emphasis on persuasion reflects a bias for Ciceronian rhetoric. The great orator yields the stage reluctantly. Cicero follows the Aristotelian and Hellenistic rhetorical tradition, which posits praise and blame, the epideictic type (Arist. *Rh*.1358a36–1358b8; *demonstrativum*, Cic. *Inv*.1.7; *Part*.70), on propositions developed according to commonly admitted virtues and vices (ὁμολογούμενα ἀγαθὰ καὶ κακά; Isoc. *Helena* 11–15; Arist. *Rh*.1358b38–1359a5, 1362b29–1363a16; Nicol. *Prog*.48.20; Men. Rh. 368.1–8; Cic. *Part*. 71; Russell and Wilson, 1981: xix–xxiv). Cicero goes further. He nearly dismisses panegyric as a category of rhetoric because although praise, like senatorial reports and history, makes use of narrative and amplification, it needs no argument. Its proofs are naturally sustained by citing evidence, for panegyric the virtues a person practiced (*de Orat*.2.43–49, 65, 342–47; *Part*.71–72, 75–82). Cicero distinguishes the Roman tradition of praise from the Greek (*de Orat*.2.341), stating that the Roman has an unadorned simplicity based on the witnesses to a person's conduct. The orator may embellish or suppress particular aspects of a person's life (*Part*.73–74), but it stands to reason that there will be limits on what a *laudator* can say and remain credible to an audience that has witnessed the life praised (Men. Rh. 398.1–6). How much any intended audience may have observed or heard about the *laudandus* has implications for the speaker. Maintaining a reasonable degree of believability regarding the life lived is part of what Cicero means when he reasserts that panegyric admits only certainties and does not introduce points of debate (*Part.*71: *non enim dubia firmantur, sed ea quae certa aut pro certis posita sunt augentur;* see also Cicero's criticism of panegyric lies, *Brut.*62). Evidence aside, Cicero is perfectly willing to overlook such panegyric simplicity for himself. When he asks Lucceius to author his biography (*Att.*4.6), in particular his lead role in the Catilinarian conspiracy, without blushing Cicero urges Lucceius to exaggerate, ignore history, and go beyond the truth (*Fam.*5.12.2–4). He would do so himself, but autobiography makes braggadocio too obvious. Then again . . .

Far from avoiding and suppressing disputed propositions, Horace's praise exploits them. Consider a few Horatian panegyric plots. Horace celebrates Maximus's marriage to Augustus's cousin Marcia by praising the gentleman, over thirty years old and an old bachelor by Roman standards, for being a great lover (*C.*IV.1). Praise for Augustus's victory over the Sygambri, a triumph never technically held, should be led by the rather poor Pindaric imitator Iullus Antonius, while Horace stands back in the crowd and shouts traditional acclamations (*C.*IV.2). The epinikion for Drusus and Tiberius revisits an old scandal: Augustus acquired Nero's wife and his children. Augustus raised them well, and now Rome is in debt to Nero's sons, who savagely crushed the Rhaetians and Vindelicians as a lion attacks a helpless roe. Then Horace has Hannibal the liar praise Rome (*C.*IV.4). Horace praises Lollius, who lost Rome's standards, for being a great general (*C.*IV.9) and praises himself as a noble (*C.*IV.3). Augustus's patron deity Apollo is invoked as a violent god of epic vengeance, and then Apollo stops Horace from composing the martial praise he is ready to sing (*C.*IV.6; 15). These panegyric tensions or nuances (*dubia*) lie blatantly on the surface in the odes' plots, not just hidden in their details. Horace has neither followed the traditional guidelines transferred to Rome by Cicero and others nor set any precedent for Menander Rhetor's precepts for panegyric. He has taken another path, more Callimachean. The twists and turns of Horace's encomiastic plots, the variety of their poetic structures, and the complex allusive qualities of their narratives preserve a Callimachean spirit. In Callimachus the Nile sings

Sosibios's victories in the games (fr.384 Pf.), and locks of hair
(fr.110 Pf.), vowed by Queen Berenice for the safe return of her
husband, lament war and praise their lady's pledged steadfast
love in their own voice (Thomas, 1983). Callimachus did sing of
kings and battles and did so with an imagination not easily explained by rhetorical handbooks. Thus Alan Cameron (1995) assesses Propertius's praise elegy (4.6): "It is the fanciful, allusive,
asymmetrical style of Callimachean epinician that lies behind
the curious Propertian experiment. All that is lacking is Callimachus's saving irony and wit" (479; n.b. 476–83). Horace has
sustained the witty complexities in his encomia. When Propertius's praises are placed alongside Horace's, they are not so curious or experimental as supposed. It is certain that Plato as least
would have banished both Propertius and Horace and their
mimetic praise poetry from his city (*R.* 396b–d; 401b; *Lg.* 801e–2a;
829c–e; 957d–e). To be sure, Ovid, who would more fully exploit
the same imaginative multiplex panegyric strategy, would have
had to go.

    When Lowell Edmunds (2001) puts some final nails in the cof-
fin of authorial intention (viii), he does not excuse me from a question on whether the presence of disputed propositions (*dubia*) in
Horatian panegyric is different from the *aporia* that naturally
comes to the fore in negotiating sense with any literature. Fowler
(1997:24, 27; 2000:3–4) and Hinds (1998:48), I think rightly, position meaning in the moment of reception. What makes tensions in
Horatian panegyric different from those in hearing or reading in
general is not necessarily any clear evidence in the text of his
poems that Horace intended to include disputes, but rather that
other rhetoricians and panegyrists advise that disputes, especially conflicts that might impugn the character of the *laudandus*,
should be avoided. Perhaps what makes panegyric a dangerous
game is that disputes can never really be avoided (Bartsch, 1994),
and if this is the case, then I believe (just from the brief outline of
the above plots) that Horace takes on the panegyric hazards like
a daredevil. A panegyrist under a temperamental emperor would
not want Horace for his model nor would he want for his listen-
ers or readers, an audience Horatian praise had made sensitive to
the presence of disputes. Whether we call Horace's panegyric
"good" or "bad" depends on our own understanding of intention. We assume, too naively, that good panegyric means undis-

puted praise for the honoree. Horace models a more nuanced panegyric expression, more readily attributed to exilic Ovid (Barchiesi, 1994; G. D. Williams, 1994:154–68). Edmunds's supposedly safe concession, "Roman poets had intentions for their poems. A most obvious one is to please a patron (19)," may have limited value in appreciating the complexities of Horace's panegyric storytelling.

While dismissing the rule of intention, I would argue that a reading that discerns in Horatian panegyric an invitation to an interpreting community, that is the formation of praise through a complex of reciprocal voices, derives from impulses within the text and is not simply forced onto Horatian panegyric by the *aporia* of remote audience(s). Such *aporia* surely compounds the complexities of Horatian panegyric and may be confused, arguably so, with the disputes within the text; however, these disputes are also encouraged by the collective spirit of the panegyric. Horace's remodeling of Pindaric structures throughout book IV invokes the environment of the agon in which multiple participants (athlete, judges, audience, praise singers) comprise the event. Horatian panegyric in this short collection involves a wide range of communal experiences: weddings (c.1), triumphs (c.2), hymns (c.3, 6, 15), familial relationships (c.4, 5, 14), and laments (c.1, 10, 11, 12). The Dionysiac ritual symbolism, prominent in c.5 but always implicit in the poet's sympotic persona, places wine (poetry) inside the gathered revelers so that they are empowered through song to celebrate life's pleasures together. Thus the book's concluding invitation (c.15) is to communal song: *nos . . . canemus,* 'I' (the poet-singer) and 'we' (the poet's audiences). These communal moments of Horatian panegyric, the experiences in our living and dying that necessitate we come together and on some level incorporate individual expressions, position the internal and external audiences not as passive spectators but as active participants who create and re-create the events.

I borrow the dialect of modern public philosophy (sharing stories in the process of forming and maintaining civic identities) not only to shorten the distance between Horace's situation and our own but also to provoke a conversation on Horace's later poems that moves beyond intention, motivation, and the problem of sincere or insincere panegyric. This move, long suggested (Galinsky, 1975:210–17; Brink, 1982:532–33; Santirocco, 1995:225–29), has been slow to realize. Although panegyric poetry has received some renewed attention (MacCormack, 1981; Pernot, 1993; Bartsch, 1994, 1998; Whitby, 1998; Fantham, 1999) due to recent work on the later epicists, the application of panegyric modes of thought to *Odes* IV has maintained the assumption that praise and blame are mutually exclusive: the poet in total control of the creative and interpretive processes performs one act or the other. Consequently, Horatian panegyric has been oversimplified. In spite of Horace's consistent imaging of himself as the new and greater Pindar, exactly how he shapes and defines his panegyric persona is given short shrift compared to whether he reflects imperial interests. Many still view panegyric as a negative label, which offends us more than the poet, and approach *Odes* IV, via Suetonius, wondering why Horace wrote the book in the first place. Doubts about Suetonius's account that Horace put together *Odes* IV only because Augustus requested praise pieces for his sons have spread from Fraenkel (1957) throughout Horatian criticism, but there continues to be an overreliance on Suetonius and a disregard for the poet's own ambitions and creative passions even after the success of his *Carmen Saeculare.* Accepting imperial pressure as the prime motivation for Horace's later lyric immediately places *Odes* IV in a reactive posture and perpetuates the pro-/anti-Augustan debate. Some hear Horace's voice as authentic imperial praise, fervent or less so, with little consideration of what this implies about the poet's role in Roman society. Others read Horace as subversive without recognizing what might be at risk for a poet so well known and with such powerful patrons. As a consequence, there is still no clear unifying relationship between the so-called public (c.1–9, 14–15) and private poems (c.10–13). The private is still completely subsumed into the political so that certain poems are at best ignored and at worst confused.

Trends in literary theory often lead back to the same conclusions. Horace represses his voice; that is, the poet sacrifices independent expression to fulfill a public role and does his best under these circumstances (Oliensis, 1998). Some odes "sap" the sense of others so that the poet weakens his praise and renders it questionable (Lyne, 1995). Although such readings avoid the negative label of propagandist, they still heavily depend on presuppositions about authorial motivation. Others have tried to escape this quandary through metapoetics. The Callimachean and Epicurean aesthetic of the small or thin voice (Horatian *moderatio*) contradicts the persona required for praise poetry and makes panegyric impossible. The poet can never be believable in this role (Fowler, 1995; and to a lesser degree Lowrie, 1997:349–52). To be sure, Horace's poetry is about poetry, and as Lowrie's work has again proven, Horatian *techne* is often the point—not the only point, but a primary one. Putnam (1986) has well demonstrated that Horace is concerned to establish the role of the poet and the lyric poetic in Roman society. But is Horace's lyric so limited by encomium that poetic power can be reduced to an ability to immortalize the deeds of another? If this is the case, then Horace's lyric sympotic persona of *Odes* I–III is in full retreat in *Odes* IV. Horace's *Carmen Saeculare,* which presents the poet as the creator of its ritual magic (Putnam, 2000), announces the opposite: Horace's lyric has the power to give substance and form to civic identities. This is the impasse of *Odes* IV: either there is no credible Horatian imperial or Roman panegyric, or the poet is so completely an imperial panegyrist that he is little else.

One root cause of the dilemma (as Barchiesi, 1994, has already shown with Ovid; Habinek, 1998, with Augustan literature in general) is that the political and aesthetic have been so artificially divided that the lyric sympotic Horace and the panegyric Horace are too often completely disassociated. The failure to appreciate fully the irony of Horace's epic criticism and the diversity of the lyric tradition has led to the overapplication of this artificial division (when the poet is in a panegyric mode he has forfeited his independent lyric temperament). Studies on Horace have repeatedly, if inadvertently, communicated clearly the uncomfortable friction between the pleasures of Horatian drinking songs and imperial praise. It is so inconvenient that they together form the same lyric collection. But the poet has been so obviously deceitful. Horace is above all a sympotic poet, and his panegyric praxis is best understood as an expression of his sympotic persona from *Odes* I–III (chapter 1). Book IV does not stand independently from Horace's earlier lyric collection. From the first ode of book IV, Horace weds panegyric with his lyric sympotic persona. This is to say that Horatian panegyric depends on an invitation to community rather than a confrontational relationship of a poet facing an audience and attempting to persuade them to adopt a particular position toward a *laudandus.* We should also expect Horatian

encomia, like Horatian symposia, to be seriocomic. As such they
are prone to incorporate conflicting points of view and tone
(chapter 2). These tensions and conflicts provoke Horace's audience to become active interpreters, and as a result even the panegyrics for the imperial family do not offer easy resolutions between praise and blame or political and poetic power. Horace's
lyric praise requires and nurtures a collective interpretive process
that transforms panegyric into a vibrant communal activity
(chapters 3 and 5). The communal nature of Horatian panegyric
complements the expressions of lament and celebration prominent in *Odes* IV. The anguish expressed over the transience of life
is not so much an autobiographical sorrow over the poet's old age
but an individual's genuine emotive response to the episodes of
one's life consciously encumbered and significantly entwined
with the lives of others so as to necessitate and envalue individual expression (chapter 4). That is to say, Horace's panegyric is
sympotic.

To answer three possible criticisms — (1) I have not arranged
the book according to particular instances of the sympotic within
the encomia of *Odes* IV. Although this risks weakening the overall argument, it is more important to treat each ode as a whole and
not hinder the natural development of the book by rearranging its
odes out of turn. I have not been entirely successful in preserving
the book's linear order. The odes most affected are the *encomia
Augusti* (4–5, 14–15), which begin in the middle of the *encomia nobilium* and resume after the odes of lament (10–13). Therefore, I
have divided Horace's imperial praise into two chapters (3 and 5)
to preserve the book's chiastic structure. This division allows my
reading of the encomia to begin where Horace began, with the
praise of young nobles. (2) I have not attempted fixed distinctions
between "Horace, the poet's persona, the poet, the singer, and the
speaker" because Horace constantly blurs these distinctions so
that it becomes impossible to tell when he is wearing a mask and
when not. This confusion is part of Horace's fun. I will not ruin it.
(3) It is difficult to sort through and explain the details of Horace's
compressed lyrics with any brevity, especially since his later
songs interact so closely with his earlier work. Such attention to
complementary repetitions in Horatian song is a necessary task
and a large part of appreciating the music in Horace's lyric art.
Consequently, any book on Horace is forced to be Callimachean,

both fat and thin. Horace, I believe, would enjoy this compliment. He would still likely criticize my book for having too many words, but not too many words on literary theory.

I have tried in the notes to convey some sense of chronology for Horatian studies by generally citing authors according to the date of their earliest editions. For the reader's convenience I have referenced subsequent editions, which are commonly consulted, under their respective authors in the list of works cited.

A Symposion of Praise

1

Sympotic Horace

I stand amid the roar
Of a surf-tormented shore,
And I hold within my hand
Grains of the golden sand —
How few! yet how they creep
Through my fingers to the deep,
While I weep — while I weep!
O God! can I not grasp
Them with a tighter clasp?
O God! can I not save
One from the pitiless wave?
Is *all* that we see or seem
But a dream within a dream?
—*A Dream within a Dream,* Edgar Allan Poe

Looking Back

Whatever modesty he pretends, Horace never had a small voice. Horace enjoyed a productive literary career spanning almost thirty years of traumatic cultural and political change and incorporating four genres: *iambi, sermones, carmina,* and *epistulae.* He witnessed the decline of republican power, the expanding power of Rome over the East, the triumph of Octavian and the development of the principate, and the search for a unifying Roman identity to replace the hostilities of civil conflict. Horace, as he tells it,

began as an outsider, the son of a freedman who fought against
Octavian at Philippi. He became an insider, as Suetonius tells it, a
poet supported and befriended by Augustus's adviser Maecenas
and commissioned by Augustus to compose the hymn announcing a new age, the *Carmen Saeculare*.[1] Comprehending the breadth
of Horatian poetry and putting into context its politics have always been a large part of the intrigue in reading and assessing
Horace.

Any reading of *Odes* IV, especially any consideration of the
book's function as praise poetry, must confront the question of
change. What has the earlier Horace (*Epodes, Satires, Odes* I–III) of
the 30s to 20s B.C. to do with the later Horace (*Epistles, Carmen Saeculare, Odes* IV, *Ars Poetica*) of the 10s B.C.? Do the many transitions in the complex interplay between the poet, his cultural and
political landscape, and the varied generic expectations within
Horace's poetry books justify any search for continuity?[2] This is
where *Odes* IV begins. Horace in c.1 presents himself as an older
poet taking up again, at Venus's insistence, the lyrics he sang ten
years ago:

> Intermissa, Venus, diu
>   rursus bella moves? parce precor, precor.
> non sum qualis eram bonae
>   sub regno Cinarae. desine, dulcium
>
> mater saeva Cupidinum,   5
>   circa lustra decem flectere mollibus
> iam durum imperiis; abi
>   quo blandae iuvenum te revocant preces. (1–8)[3]

> [Interrupted for a long time, are you, Venus, starting your
> wars again? Spare, I pray, I pray. I am not as I once was under
> the dominion of gracious Cinara. Stop, sweet Cupids' fierce
> mother, bending a fifty-year-old now hardened to your soft
> commands: go away to where youths' flirtatious prayers in-
> vite you back.]

Porphyrio, Pseudo-Acro, and subsequent commentators have
recognized in the ode's plot (the poet's failure to resist the *bella
Veneris*) an allegorical statement that Horace is returning to lyric
poetry. Horace admits what he wrote on several occasions before,
that old age makes love battles inappropriate (C.III.15; 19.24; and

later *Epist.*II.2.55–57, 141–45) even for himself,[4] and by inference the writing of lyric love poetry. More than reluctant, Horace now declares that he is *durus*,[5] begs Venus to leave him alone with the emphatic alliterated anaphora *parce precor, precor*, and even offers Venus a substitute, the youthful Maximus. But Horace cannot resist Venus; he must return, over all his protest, to love poems. This is not the first time Horace has lost a battle with Venus, as his repetition of the beginning line from his ode to Glycera (*mater saeva Cupidinum*, 5; C.I.19) makes clear.[6] Horace could not resist Glycera, Lydia (C.III.9), or Chloë (C.III.26). Horace has only re-used a well-known plot and reapplied it as a metaphor for lyric composition.[7] Horace, far from ignoring *Odes* I–III, begins book IV by immediately acknowledging his absence from lyric and attempting some explanation for his return, especially since he had indicated that his earlier collection was so perfectly complete. The first word of the last ode of book III, *exegi* (I have finished), and the metaphor it introduces (a monument grander than pyramids) do not suggest a sequel.

Horace links *Odes* IV to his lyric past by plot, direct quotations, and common referents in language, but Horace is not content with a worn-out familiarity void of variation. *Intermissa*, the first word of his second collection, is resumptive and novel. *Intermissa* cannot be read as a synonym for *omittere* (to put aside), a rare and later usage,[8] but looking back it signifies the continuation of Horace's past lyric after a temporary interruption. *Intermissa* also invites new interest, since this is the only time that Horace uses the word, and he is perhaps the first poet outside of the comedians to do so.[9] There is much in book IV that is new. Beginning with the first word, Horace prompts his audience to look back to his earlier lyric books for comparison and forward to his new book in anticipation.

Horace's return to his previous lyric presents an essential methodology for reading *Odes* IV: Horace's present lyric is a repetition and variation of his past lyric. It is obvious, but often overlooked, that the most important background poems for *Odes* IV are *Odes* I–III. This is a self-reflective, introspective mode of intertextuality that gives book IV its intricacy and depth. Horace's memory of his earlier writings forces his audience back to discover the similarities and tensions of one ode with its prequels. When the second collection is isolated and studied as an

independent unit, it is easy to underestimate how readily and artfully Horace manipulates possible meanings. Each ode has an immediate (book IV) and secondary context (books I–III), both of
which enliven its sense. *Odes* IV cannot be hackneyed or simplistic panegyric — too much is happening in the background — but
against the backdrop of Horace's prior lyric personae it becomes
a complicated group of praise poems that provoke vigorous debate, evidenced from an early date.[10] The poet's and audiences'
recollections must constantly negotiate the interpretive space. In
this sense *Odes* IV becomes simultaneously individual and communal. The poet, people, leaders and heroes, insiders and out-
siders, come together to fashion their own unique song (*nos . . .
canemus*, C.IV.15.25–32). The interpretive process is expressed by
the very arrangement of the book: an inseparable blend of pub-
lic/private moments.

A diacritical methodology that subdivides the Horatian corpus
into distinctly public and private spheres, which at most form a
meaningful tension, still captivates much recent criticism, although common sense suggests that one's own living is not composed of such segregated experiences.[11] Even the rediscovered interest in metapoetics has not taken fully into account the
implications of a poet under patronage disavowing epic praise
poetry to become master of a new Roman lyric world, which is his
own (re)creation and to which he invites not only individual love
interests but other poets and the powerful who are (re)construct-
ing Roman society. That Horace presents himself as the *magister
bibendi* of this symposion is heavily invested with political (public) overtones.

What is the nature of Horace's sympotic world as he constructs
it in *Odes* I–III and to which he invites comparison? Horace's sympotic world is defined by paradox and illusion. The poet is running the game of bringing together opposites: the light and serious, parties and politics, the small (lyric) and grand (epic).

Levis et Gravis

Horace places every *carpe diem* command in *Odes* I–II within the
context of a drinking party, the symposion,[12] and although this
correspondence decreases slightly in *Odes* III (five *carpe diem* odes

[8, 17, 19, 28, 29] out of eleven sympotic odes), clearly *carpe diem* is a common feature of Horatian symposia, as it was in the Greek lyricists.[13] Such a consistent connection creates an association between the symposion and time; the symposion represents the present, which humanity can control, as opposed to the future and past, which are outside mortal province.[14] Horace's sympotic invitation is a summons to pleasures of the moment (*carpe diem*), made even more urgent by the certainty of death. Time is short. Come to the party.

The emphasis on human limitations and death as prime motives for accepting the invitation to enjoy life prevents sympotic poetry from being mere diversionary entertainment. There is more to Horatian drinking parties than the supposed lighter pleasures of wine, flowers, perfume, dancing, and lovemaking — Horatian symposia contain a variety of other serious themes. The brevity of life and certainty of death are the most frequent counterparts to sympotic pleasures (*C*. I.4, 9, 11; II.3, 11, 14), but they are not alone. Horace blends into the symposion a strong *Satiric* flavor: the equality of rich and poor (C.I.4; II.3, 14); the foolishness of worrying about tomorrow (C.I.4, 7, 9, 11); moderation and the dangers of drunkenness (C.I.18, 20, 27, 35, 38; II.3); the rejection of epic panegyric (C.I.6).[15] Sympotic pleasures cannot be separated from serious life issues because Horace intricately binds them together within his lyric structures by contrasting stanzas and interlacing patterns within the stanzas. The mix is more than a simple rotation from one ode that is light to another that is serious; the sympotic odes are a blend of both — their structure is best described as seriocomic.[16]

The leading sympotic odes of *Odes* I–II model the blend of the serious and comic as key to appreciating the structure and tone of Horatian lyric. Horace in his ode to Sestius (I.4)[17] contrasts the light-hearted pleasures of spring's return (stanzas 1–3) with the bleak finality of death (stanzas 4–5). Then in the poem's final moment Horace withdraws Sestius from his future home in the underworld and returns him briefly to the world of sympotic erotic pleasures, beautiful Lycidas (*nec tenerum Lycidan mirabere, quo calet iuventus / nunc omnis et mox virgines tepebunt*, 19–20). "Now" (*nunc*, 20) completes the anaphora of *nunc decet . . . nunc* (stanza 3).[18] The first "now" tells Sestius to put on garlands in response to the dance of the Graces and nymphs in honor of Venus; the

second "now" says to sacrifice to Faunus. What begins with a
dance ends in ritual death. Horace has loaded the present with seriocomic overtones. The repetition of *nunc* in the last line signals
that Sestius has the opportunity to enjoy love, but only for an instant. Death will come. The young Lycidas also is growing older.
Soon he will pass the age when he will be attractive to men, and
he will begin to arouse young women. Sestius has a brief moment
to act on his desires. Horace has so blended pleasures with the
pains of mortality that one hardly knows whether to be happy for
Sestius or not.[19]

Horace's refusal to write political praise poetry in C.I.6 reaches
its comic crescendo in the last stanza. Achilles' anger, wily Odysseus's journey home, Pelops's cursed descendents, the praise
of Caesar, Meriones covered in dust, and Diomedes powerful
enough to wound Aphrodite and Ares are all beyond Horace's
modest lyric (stanzas 1–4). Horace leaves praising these heroes
and Agrippa to Varius, a master of Homer's epic. Horace will sing
about drinking parties and lovers' battles:

> nos convivia, nos proelia virginum
> sectis in iuvenes unguibus acrium
> cantamus, vacui sive quid urimur,
> > non praeter solitum leves. (17–20)

> [I sing of feasts, I sing of battles, fierce girls with their
> sharpened nails fighting the boys; unattached or
> burning for some lover, as usual, I keep it light.]

The girls have their sharpened weapons drawn (*sectis*), but the
scratches that their nails may leave are harmless enough, only
marks from sexual games.[20] Horace's interlacing of the warring
parties (*proelia virginum . . . in iuvenes . . . acrium*) with their sham
weapons of war (*sectis unguibus*) figuratively surrounds the
young men with their *femmes fatales* and heightens the humor of
the comparison between epic battles and Horace's lyric warfare.
In the erotic battles of lyric no one is ever hurt badly, or are they?
It makes no difference to Horace whether he is embroiled in love
battles; his song will remain *leves* (light), the last word.

If the sympotic should be simply amusing, Teucer (C.I.7) errs;
he balances a reminder of his crew's exile (25–26) with the promise of Apollo's guidance (27–29). He recalls their sufferings (30–

31) before he invites them to forget with wine (31–32). Teucer's entire speech consists of seriocomic couplets and is evocative of Horace's advice to Plancus that reminds him that military duty keeps him away from beloved Tibur (19–20).[21]

Horace not only utilizes contrasting stanzas in the seriocomic structure of the *Soracte Ode* (I.9), but he arranges them in an interlocking pattern. Winter's freeze (stanza 1) is set against the warmth of an indoor symposion (stanza 2) and love games on the campus (stanzas 5–6). This contrast is interrupted by another seriocomic pair (stanzas 3–4), in which the poet orders Thaliarchus[22] to trust the future to the gods:

> permitte divis cetera, qui simul
> stravere ventos aequore fervido   10
>   deproeliantis, nec cupressi
>   nec veteres agitantur orni.
>
> quid sit futurum cras fuge quaerere et
> quem Fors dierum cumque dabit lucro
>   appone, nec dulcis amores   15
>   sperne puer neque tu choreas, (9–16)

[Concede all else to the gods; when they have calmed the winds fighting to the death the stormy sea, neither old cypresses nor mountain ashes are blown about. Avoid asking what will be tomorrow and credit yourself any day Chance will give, and, while young, do not disdain sweet loves or dances.]

Nature-images of violence and death portray the absolute control of the gods over mortality. Mortals are given only the present moment, and Thaliarchus must enjoy life's pleasures before they are lost to old age.

Horace duplicates this familiar *carpe diem* appeal in the sympotic invitation to Leuconoë (I.11), but changes the seriocomic balance within the principal arguments: divine control of the future, appreciating whatever time the gods allow, and taking advantage of the moment because time is short. Horace begins by directing Leuconoë not to speculate about her future in language similar to the commands given Thaliarchus (*Tu ne quaesieris . . . quem . . . / finem di dederint*, 11.1–2a; *fuge quaerere et / quem Fors dierum cumque dabit*, 9.13b–14a). Then the song turns to the present that Leuconoë does control, but compared to c.9 the comic tone is muted. Leuconoë enduring however many winters Jupiter sends (3b–6a) is not nearly as seductive as the dances, whispers in the night air, and giggles from the hidden nook, which Horace details over the last stanzas of c.9. By condensing the comic and weakening its contrast to the serious, Horace presents a more pessimistic outlook for Leuconoë. But passion can yet warm Leuconoë's winters. Horace tempers the pessimism in the concluding lines when he interjects pointed commands for Leuconoë to enjoy life (*vina liques; carpe diem*) into two expressions about the brevity of time (*sapias . . . reseces; dum loquimur . . . credula postero,* 6b–8). The coordination of the jussives indicates how closely Horace associates *carpe diem* and the sympotic. *Vina liques* and *carpe diem* have the same metrical value and thought: enjoy life, the poet's love, while winters last.[23]

C.II.3 is darker and even more personal. Horace names the song's addressee "Dellius bound to die" (*moriture Delli,* 4) and manipulates the seriocomic structure to maximize pessimistic tones. The ode appears perfectly balanced: a stanza pair, each on the common sympotic themes of moderation (1–3) and death (5–7), surrounding a central stanza (4) ordering the goods for a symposion. But Horace varies the seriocomic format within the stanza pairs. In the first he balances the serious and comic by offsetting life's pleasures and difficulties: there are good and bad circumstances (1–2), happiness is tamed by mortality (3–4), and there may be sadness as well as the joy wine gives (5–8). Then at the end of the song this careful balance vanishes. The comic is suppressed; everywhere Dellius faces death and separation from all that he loves. This shift is not a total surprise since the sympotic description that divides the stanza pair is far from carefree: flowers fade fast (13), and the party lasts only as long as the fates allow (15–16).

These carefully crafted structures disprove that the sympotic must always be light and exclude human anxieties. The Horatian symposion is *levis et gravis* (*nihil est ab omni / parte beatum,* C.II.16.27b–28).[24] When Horace burdens sympotic pleasures with weightier concerns of living and dying, he is not original. He is following generic convention, well established by the Greek lyric poets, both in his selection of themes and seriocomic structures. Greek sympotic songs commonly make death and the dread

people feel over their passing youth prime motivations for enjoying drinking parties—an argument Horace adopts with striking
similarity. For example, Horace's warning to Sestius that in the
underworld sympotic pleasures end (C.I.4.16–19a) echoes Theognis 973–78 (W.).[25] Horace sharpens his *carpe diem*/sympotic invitations with the satiric edge of *moderatio*, taking aim at Sestius,
Dellius (C II.3), and Postumus (II.14), who cannot escape death
because they are rich, and at Thaliarchus (I.9), Leuconoë (I.11),
and Quintius (II.11), who should leave their future to the gods.
Even here Horace is re-creating. Eliminate Horace's pointed
"you" from his advice to Thaliarchus, and again Theognis appears (1047–48 W.: νῦν μὲν πίνοντες τερπώμεθα, καλὰ λέγοντες /
ἄσσα δ' ἔπειτ' ἔσται, ταῦτα θεοῖσι μέλει; "Now let us enjoy drinking and beautiful songs. Whatever will happen in the future is the
gods' concern.").[26]

Drinking relieves life's cares, but Horace, just as the Greek
symposiasts, affirms the ambiguity of wine, that it is beneficial
and dangerous.[27] Too much wine loosens the tongue and wits, reveals secrets better kept, and promotes an exaggerated sense of
self-worth (C.I.13.10; 17.22–28; 18.7–11; 27.1–8; III.8.15–16).[28]
Theognis, whose symposia make much of moderation, recommends neither sobriety nor drunkenness,[29] and even Alcaeus and
Anacreon, known for their sympotic zest, acknowledge the dangers of excessive consumption.[30] Literary symposia do not exclude heavy drinking,[31] but consistently totally unrestrained behavior, especially violence, is incongruous with proper sympotic
custom, which Anacreon puts in no uncertain terms (eleg. 2.1–2
W.: οὐ φιλέω, ὃς κρητῆρι παρὰ πλέωι οἰνοποτάζων / νείκεα καὶ πόλε-
μον δακρυόεντα λέγει; "I am no friend of the man who, as he
drinks by the full mixing bowl, talks conflicts and tearful war). [32]

The influence of the Greek symposiasts goes beyond content to
structure. Horace is not inventing the seriocomic patterns for his
symposia; they are part of the tradition. Already the Greek lyricists made the comic give way to serious themes[33] or interrupted
the comic with the serious, as Phocylides does when he adds
the necessity for pleasant conversation into the call to drink
heartily.[34] More often the seriocomic is balanced by contrasting
pairs of lines, couplets, or sections; for example, Ion of Chios 27
(W.) divides nearly equally between religious ritual and sympotic
revelry.[35] Even Horace's more intricate seriocomic interlacing,

characterized by C.I.9, has antecedents,[36] the most striking being Xenophanes 1 (W.). Xenophanes sustains throughout his song a somber religious tone, beginning with the sacrificial setting (1–12) that portrays a very pleasant and sensual scene. The description of the altar (9–12) comes between the ample provision of food and the house filled with singing, dancing, and feasting, which in turn leads immediately into the religious duty of hymning the god (13–16).[37] Religious duty gives way to a discussion of moderation (17–23): an amusing picture of an old drunk barely able to totter home, followed by a progressively more serious moderate prescription (good memory, virtue, and the avoidance of discord), which climaxes in the piety of the last line, θεῶν <δὲ> προμηθείην αἰὲν ἔχειν ἀγαθήν.[38] Any degree of familiarity with such highly stylized seriocomic structures easily marks out Horace's imitation.

Parties and Politics

Seriocomic literary symposia mimic reality. The symposion was a mixture of ritual, hymning the gods and libations, serious forms of entertainment, such as the performance of poetry or philosophical conversation, combined with bawdy displays of buffoonery and the mayhem of the komic (κωμαστής) reveler carousing through the streets after the party.[39] Sympotic ritual encompasses the totality of human experiences, and because of its *sympathetic* depth, the symposion emphasizes a sense of kinship. Therefore, the symposion plays a communal role in society, symbolized not only in more obvious ritualistic customs but also in the banquet couch.

As early as the seventh century B.C. it had become Greek sympotic custom to recline on couches.[40] When the Greek aristocracy in the archaic period ceased to be defined by military function, the elaborate funerary customs that confirmed an aristocratic war status were gradually replaced with other iconographical symbols characteristic of the elite lifestyle—among them the leisure of the symposion pictured in the opulent banquet couch.[41] The banquet couch helps determine the size of the drinking party; with two on a couch, the average *andron* would hold between thirteen and thirty guests.[42] Subsequently, a limit is imposed on sympotic space. This creates the opportunity for a more intimate group in which the participants can be bound together by loyalties reinforcing their common cultural values. The prevalence of συν- compounds in sympotic poetry, especially Alcaeus, stresses the power of the drinking party to form and energize community. The community, however, is not necessarily society at large but the sympotic group, the *hetaireia*, which moves counter to society (in the case of Alcaeus, opposition to the *demos*).[43] The establishment of a subgroup within society lends the symposion a political dimension and gives it a sense of occasion, a moment in time to reinforce by ritual the ideologies and interests shared by the symposiasts. The symposion and politics share a natural affinity because of the dynamics between the sympotic group and its larger culture—precisely how will the more private sympotic group define itself against the public culture in which it also exists? Thus the symposion and, by extension, its literature fuse together private and public life. The symposion is inherently political.

Any interpretation of Horace must recognize the diversity of the symposion that is conveyed via its seriocomic structure. Extreme caricatures are bound to be inaccurate. Horace is not obsessed with death. Mortality in Horace's lyrics cannot be so personalized, since it is included in the sympotic poems, which account for most instances, as a convention of the motif.[44] At another extreme, if sympotic Horace's *tenue carmen* always advocates withdrawal from life's difficulties into a private realm, why do the last four poems of book I contain sympotic expressions just when Horace is closing out the book in grand fashion (a hymn to fortune, c.35; Numida's return from war, c.36; Caesar's victory over Cleopatra, c.37; orders for a drinking party, c.38)?[45] In fact, Horace often increases the seriousness of his themes within the context of sympotic poetry, actually blurring the distinction between epic grandeur and lyric compression. Dionysus leads Horace to sing of Caesar's immortal glory. Under the wine god's influence Horace will sing nothing small, humble, or mortal (C.III.25.17–18a).

Neither are all Horatian sympotic moments moderate, restrained behavior in a balanced seriocomic construct. Horace symbolizes Cleopatra's madness as drunkenness (C.I.37.10–11). The odes celebrating returns are marked by Thracian-like revelry (C.II.7.27b–28; I.20; 36; III.8; 14).[46] The comic disappears in the last sympotic ode of book II (c.14), when the poet warns Postumus that death will claim his riches, and his precious wine will wash the floor of his ungrateful heir. These exceptions produce a startling effect against the background of acceptable sympotic behavior portrayed throughout Horace's books. Cleopatra's madness, described as sympotic drunkenness, appears outlandish. When his earthly pleasures are destined to be squandered by his heir, Postumus's rejection of sympotic pleasures appears foolhardy. The poems to Sestius (I.4), Dellius (II.3), and Postumus (II.14), telling them that life is short, become progressively more cutting. C.I.4 ends in the world of sympotic pleasures, whereas II.3 spends the last three stanzas reinforcing the death sentence in *moriture Delli.* For Postumus there is no sympotic invitation, only the threat of an heir luxuriating in the wine of a forgotten testator. There is nothing trivial about the urgency of the sympotic invitation. Sympotic Horace's message is clear: Do not be another Postumus—join the party. Horace's sympotic invitations do not recommend a retreat into a private world of personal contentment. The sympotic Horace is a persona of initiation and engagement that invites individuals to share life together.

Sympotic Horace's Epic Criticism

Horace's epic criticism is one constant within the diversity of his poetry. Whatever turn his career takes, Horace never entertains the possibility of composing an epic. He will not be Vergil. A basic Horatian strategy for disassociating his poetic from the grandeur of epic heroism is the *recusatio* (his refusal to write epic-styled praise poetry), which he invests with allusions to Apollo's instructions to Callimachus (*Aetia* fr.1.13–30 Pf.) that the poet should keep the sacrifice fat (τὸ μὲν θύος ὅττι πάχιστον), the Muse slender (τὴν Μοῦσαν . . . λεπταλέην), and follow narrow paths seldom traveled (κελεύθους / ἀτρίπτους, εἰ καὶ στεινοτέρην ἐλάσεις), and to Vergil's topical addendum that the bucolic poet should not sing the battles of kings (*Ecl.*6.3–12).[47] Horace affirms the qualities of a thin poetic (the *genus tenue*), namely the personal voice of the poet (paths seldom traveled) and refined poetic compression (slender, narrow), and disavows the martial themes required for epic praise.[48] Horace heightens the comic tone of his *recusationes* by recommending another poet better suited for the task because his own talents risk belittling the *laudandus*. Horace would rather sing the pleasures of the drinking party. Horace draws the distinction: he is a lyric sympotic poet, not an epic praise poet.[49]

Horace's epic critique is plagued with paradox, just as it is in the Greek lyricists and Callimachus himself. The seriocomic structures of the Greek symposiasts imitated by Horace invest his lyric with the weighty themes of mortality, moderation, and politics. Callimachus's Lycian Apollo commands the singer to nurture a slender Muse but also to feed a sacrificial victim to be as fat as possible. Likewise, Horace's rejection of epic's high style and themes leads to their incorporation, and the *brevitas* of individual poems fades within the lengthy narrative scope of Horace's poetry books, when books are woven together with such an admirable degree of thematic intricacy and depth. Horace's lyric Muse is slender and very fat—a type of lyric that subsumes epic grandeur into its more intimate voice.[50] Augustus found this combination of short and fat too true to Horace's life not to be funny:

> habitu corporis fuit brevis atque obesus, qualis et a semet ipso in saturis describitur et ab Augusto hac epistula: "pertulit ad me Onysius libellum tuum, quem ego ut accusantem[51] quantuluscumque est boni consulo. vereri autem mihi videris ne maiores libelli tui sint quam ipse es. sed tibi statura deest, corpusculum non deest. itaque licebit in sextariolo scribas, quo circuitus voluminis tui sit ὀγκωδέστατος, sicut est ventriculi tui. (Suet. *Vita Horati*, Klingner)

> [Horace's build was short and fat as described by himself in the *Satires* and by Augustus in this letter: "Onysius delivered your little book, which I accept without faulting, however small a thing it is. I think that you are afraid of your little books being bigger than you. But what you lack in height, you make up in girth. And so although you write pint-size, the circumference of your scroll is well-rounded just like the distance around your belly."]

We can imagine Horace in the modest manner of the *recusatio* sending his book to Augustus with the Catullan-styled introduction, "Here is my little book; it is not much, just a trifle." Augustus is quick to see the literary fun in the book's body mimicking its author's. No matter how much Horace pretended his book was small, Augustus thought the scroll on which it was written was plenty fat. The contrast of Horace's little pint-size writings (*in sextariolo scribas*) and the plump (ὀγκωδέστατος) scroll reminded Augustus of their poet's or parent's physique — short and fat.[52]

Yet Horace's epic critique is more than an ironic method of defining one's own art by a conventional (given the extent to which Horace's lyric assimilates epic themes, I would risk artificial) contrast to another. The contrast that Horace draws between epicists and himself argues a political dimension; namely, Horace's epic criticism declares his sympotic persona free from the political constraints and biases involved in praising and pleasing patrons. Epic poets, not satirists and lyricists, concern themselves with the financial rewards and personal status earned by writing praise poetry. By incorporating epic into lyric Horace asserts his own command over his poetics while reclaiming epic, or at the very least attempting to distance the epic Vergil in particular, from the power of the patron.

A caveat — there is more in Augustan poets than the revolution in the principate and much in Augustan literature that does not appear to have any immediate interest with or for Augustus.[53] All the same, Horace's close association with Maecenas and Augustus does not make it easy to set aside the political context and the questions implied: Who were Horace's ancient audiences and were they as interested in the politics of the circle as Horace's modern audiences? Were the patrons sophisticated readers who envisioned a greater Roman literature, or was their approach simply utilitarian, an interest in creating a public image? How does any writer with political connections and personal interests overcome questions about credibility? What is the price of political dissidence? *Ne longum faciam:* Horace himself raises such questions at every stage of his writings.[54]

Horace's epic panegyric criticism and the stratagem of the *recusatio* were well developed before the publication of his lyrics. Horace begins with the other poet of *S.I.9*, whom Horace calls *ille*, some call the boor, and I will nickname nameless or pest. The neoteric pest of epic proportions openly questions or, in this case, encourages the satirist's ambition in working for his patron ('*Maecenas quomodo tecum?*' 43).[55] Horace and *ille* understand each other well for two poets who are casual acquaintances (*notus mihi nomine tantum*, 3). As he strolls down *Sacred Street*, Horace is in a Catullan mood pondering over his poems, or trifles (*nugae*), so intensely that he is unaware of anything around him (*sicut meus est mos, / nescio quid meditans nugarum, totus in illis*, 1a–2; cf. Cat. 1.3a–4: *namque tu solebas / meas esse aliquid putare nugas*). The other poet seems to read Horace's mind.[56] Before Horace speaks a word, that poet extends a Catullanesque greeting to match Horace's poetic trifles, 'sweetest in the world' (*dulcissime rerum*, 4). Horace responds in kind that he is doing 'nicely' (*suaviter*, 5) and adds the qualifier, 'as things are at present' (*ut nunc est*), a double entendre—for anyone who has caught that these common greetings are also specialized tags for the new poetry (*dulcis, suavis*)[57]—which lets the other poet know Horace has understood his greeting and is answering with the same literary jargon that is, or was, fashionable for a moment: *suaviter, ut nunc est* = I am doing nicely, which is how trendy poets talk for now. And trendy poets soon find themselves outdated. The satirist already sounds superior, and in saying "hello" he has tried to put the other poet in his place.

'Not to be a pest, but may I interrupt with a question? Is there enough detail in satire 9 to justify a connection to Catullus?' 'There is for me. Horace manages to suppress an iambic temper, but his audience can tell it is seething just below the surface, escaping every now and then when his unwelcome companion refuses to leave him alone (11–12, 20–21, 28–29). Catullus has similar plots: meeting his friend Varus's mistress, who asks Catullus personal questions about rewards from his patron (poem 10),[58] and being unable to escape a bad poet (poem 44). Then there is Horace concentrating on his trifles like they are something (cf. Cat. 1). Add in the words for Catullus's type of sophisticated short poetry (*dulcis, suavis*). Besides, if the word game is too obvious, part of the satire is lost—poets are not really ordinary people meeting on the street; they are a club; their talk is extraordinary, puzzling, often secretive.'

After this Alexandrian greeting game has established some association between the poets, nameless cannot accept Horace beating him at their word-game and walking away on unequal terms. He tags along and insists that Horace should know who he is because they are both *docti*, learned poets. With this title nameless (now definitely becoming a pest) begins to give away his true

poetics and intentions. As far as *ille* is concerned, his literary abilities qualify him for the same poetic circle as Horace and his
friends, the *docti amici* in the next satire (10.87). He would be as
valued a member of Maecenas's circle as Varius (22–23), a writer
of epic. Horace does not have his pest pick Varius out of thin air
as though any member of the circle might do for comparison. The
pest too has an affinity for lengthy epic, although he thinly disguises his temperament with Catullan language for short polished poems. The pest identifies himself as *doctus* like the long-
winded Cornelius Nepos, who writes the history of Italy into
three laborious books (Cat. 1).[59] What is worse is that the pest presumes, as Horace tells it (this is *Horace's* satire after all), that his
self-ass/umed literary prowess entitles him to the favors of Rome's
political elite—just like Horace. As the dialogue plays out, Horace gives the impression that such concern with status and rewards is the attitude of a bad epic poet specifically. When Horace's tag along declares his qualifications as a poet, Horace gives
him an abbreviated (lyrical) two-word introduction in formal
epic style (*incipit* placed before its subject *ille*, 21).[60] Further on Horace likens the pest's attempt to meet Maecenas to an assault on a
fortified city (martial themes; 41–43, 54–56), and by the last line
Horace, caught in the epic conflict, becomes the Trojan Hector
whom Apollo saves from self-destruction (78).

While Horace tries repeatedly to distance himself from nameless, the impertinent pest, tiring of hints, asks Horace straight out
for an introduction to Maecenas (43–60). You would think it easy
for Horace to dismiss a dramatic character who just happens to
bump into him on the street and who seems so obviously out of
step with the real dynamics between Maecenas and his poets. Horace tells the pest the way it really is with Maecenas. First, Horace
insists that Maecenas keeps his literary circle free from competitive conniving. Maecenas sees a person for who he really is and
accepts a person because of excellent character (48–50, cf. S.I.6.45–
64). Second, Horace defends himself. Such competition for personal recognition does not interest him. Each member of Maecenas's circle has a unique role (50–52).

Should we believe the satirist? Nameless does not. He answers
Horace with a lyric image of his own, an immoderate paraklausithyron (53–60).[61] Nameless admits that Maecenas's integrity only inflames his desire (*'accendis, quare cupiam magis illi /*

proximus esse'). When Horace teases back that, although Maecenas's defenses are strong, the pest's courage can win through (*expugnabis*), the pest, like an elegiac lover outside the door, swears that he will not abandon his quest (*'non, hodie si / exclusus fuero, desistam'*).[62] He will not give up (*'haud mihi deero'*), even if he has to bribe Maecenas's slaves to gain admission. The pest caps his profession of love with comic panache by corrupting a proverbial declaration of *moderatio* into a manifesto of harassment: life gives mortals nothing without great labor (*'nil sine magno / vita labore dedit mortalibus'*).[63]

The pest has a very different working definition for the *amicitia* of the patron-client relationship, one based on competition, victory, and claiming prizes. He approached Horace with a neoteric greeting, but his argument is epic. Horace presents a view emphasizing a spirit of cooperation, personal virtues, and shared friendship.[64] The pest's persistence shows that he does not buy Horace's argument (*magnum narras, vix credibile*, 52). The pest as audience fails to grasp or rejects, as I think is more likely the case given his cleverness, Horace's satiric persona of *moderatio*, which claims not to be motivated by common approval, popularity, or personal benefit. Horace never really manages to convince nameless that his relationship with Maecenas is different from what nameless supposes. The pest tastes his own medicine when a civil opponent finds him on the street, refuses to let him be, and demands his presence in court. Horace is only too glad to see the pest to the magistrate and tries to have the last laugh in the satire's final words, *sic me servavit Apollo*.[65]

Horace borrows Homer's τὸν δ' ἐξήρπαξεν Ἀπολλών ("Apollo took him away," *Il*.20.443),[66] describing Hector's rescue from Achilles, for the conclusion of his combat with the pest. Horace, true to the satiric and lyric modes, changes the impersonal epic third person (τὸν) to the first person of the poet (*me*) and intensifies the verb "took away" (ἐξήρπαξεν) to "saved" (*servavit*).[67] Horace becomes a Hector about to attack his greatest enemy, Achilles (the pest), and no doubt lose the fight until Apollo saves him. Therefore, while admitting that the pest's assumptions about Maecenas and his poets are impossible to ignore and difficult to disprove, Horace counters by having some satiric fun with genre. The nameless epic *doctus poeta* parodies the satirist in the neoteric exchange of greetings. The satirist responds by depicting

that poet's attempt to meet Maecenas as an epic battle, which that
poet changes back into a lyric trope, an exaggerated paraklausithyron. Horace ends the satire with a surprise epic parody:
Homer's Apollo saves the satirist teetering on the edge of his own
destruction. The satirist never wins the argument or the generic
game. Epic comes to his rescue. Satire 9 satirizes because it does
not offer a neat resolution to the argument behind the parodies
that the satirist has one idea of pleasing a patron (virtue and cooperation) and the epic pest another (competition and winning
rewards). I wonder whether we are more prepared to name the
satirist the victor in the literary-political agon than the satirist?[68]
Before we can decide, the drama ends, Apollo steps in, and the
satirist and nameless are gone. Thus Horace ends the satire short
of a well-drawn conclusion. He interprets his release from the
pest as divine intervention, a vindication of sorts, and claims to
have been rescued from this seemingly endless drama by an im-
probable *deus ex machina*, Apollo — the god of the lyre, Octavian's
guardian deity at the battle of Actium, the same god who warns
his poets not to sing of such battles (Verg. *Ecl.*6.3–12; *C.*IV.15.1–4).

   Horace has not easily brushed off nameless nor laughed off the
implications of his request for an introduction to Maecenas, that
there is an uneasy alliance between poetics and politics, and that
poetics may be, perhaps even must be, sacrificed for personal ambition. The satirist immediately introduces the same potential
conflict between a poet's loyalties and literary quality in *S.*I.10.72–
92. Horace insists that he is writing for a limited audience, Maecenas and his poets. "Few readers" (*paucis lectoribus*, 74) recalls
the "few men" of satire 9 (*paucorum hominum*, 44) whom Maecenas keeps around him, and Horace's regard only for the applause
of the knights narrows his focus to his patron, the knight Maecenas, right before he names the members of the circle (81–82). Horace is not writing for poetasters and the uneducated populace in
the cheap seats. Horace's iambic name-calling (*men moveat cimex
Pantilius aut cruciet quod / vellicet absentem Demetrius aut quod in-
eptus / Fannius . . . conviva*, 78–80a) shows his disdain for his critics, whom he disavows with an emphatic "not I" (*non ego*, 76).
When he calls Fannius a tactless dinner guest, he excludes him
and the whole lot of poetasters from his sympotic group.

   If nameless were listening, I doubt he would be convinced by
Horace's black and white declarations. Horace backs up his

claims that his ambitions are limited by actually naming the select few whose opinions he values (81–90). Horace does not hide his loyalties. He names his own circle first and places Maecenas at its center (81–82). Moreover, Horace realizes that he has not answered the question about the uneasy relationship between poetry, authority, and the poet's desire to please. Would it not be easier to ignore the wishes of the nameless crowd than close friends? Right in the middle of listing his friends the satirist stops and inserts a disclaimer: he has ambition on a leash (*ambitione religata*, 84). In s.10 there is no pest; the satirist on his own, right in the act of naming his literary friends, raises the question of ambition as a natural response to the political/poetic landscape in which he writes. Horace assumes or creates a skeptical audience who will wonder how to measure a poet's words, even if the audience is limited to the satirist and members of literary circles.

S.II.1 replays the last two satires of book I. Horace once more interjects genre into the question of poetry and patronage with the same intermediating modes of allusion and parody as in s.9 and limits his audience as in s.10. Again Horace's alleged audience, his critics, like the pest have rejected his moderate persona (1–4), some thinking his satire too spirited (*nimis acer*) and others finding it too limp and soft (*sine nervis*).[69] Like many lawyers facing a split jury, Trebatius advises the satirist to keep his mouth shut (*'Quiescas,'* 5).[70] When Horace responds this that would drive him to distraction (not to mention that poets, especially satirists, by definition cannot keep silent), Trebatius takes another approach: sing about unconquered Caesar (10–12a).

Horace interprets Trebatius's counsel as a recommendation to switch from writing dangerous satire to panegyric epic, which will earn rewards. The pest, no legal expert, could have suggested the same. Horace's response corresponds to the *recusationes* of the *Odes* and *Epistles*, specifically C.I.6, IV.15, and *Epist.*II.1.250–59. Although Horace desires to undertake the task (*cupidum*, 12b; cf. *volentem proelia me loqui*, IV.15.1b; *si quantum cuperem possem quoque*, II.1.257a), he is not up to the effort (*vires / deficiunt*, 12–13; cf. *nos, Agrippa, neque haec dicere . . . conamur, tenues grandia . . .*, I.6.5–12; *nec meus audet / rem temptare pudor quam vires ferre recusent*, II.1.258b–60).[71] Then to prove his incompetence with epic, the satirist polishes off his refusal with three Ennian lines, and not the bristling (*horrentia pilis / agmina*) Ennius at his best (12b–15).[72]

The weakness of Horace's disavowal of epic does not escape Trebatius, who counters that Horace could praise Caesar with satire just as Lucilius praised Scipio (16–17).[73] Satire does not exclude panegyric. Horace admits as much. In fact, he begins to repeat the creed of the pest ('*Haud mihi deero*' at the line end [17], the exact same position as *S*.I.9.56), but unlike the pest Horace tempers his confidence. If Caesar is stroked improperly, he can protect himself by kicking like a horse (19–20).[74] If writing satire is dangerous, epic is even more so. It is one thing to liken Augustus to a sensitive horse in satire and quite another to praise or blame in the weightier epic form.

Horace is resolute. He will continue writing brief *sermones* (*ne longum faciam,* 57) whether he reaches peaceful old age or dies young, is rich or poor, lives in Rome or suffers exile (57–60).[75] Floppy Horace (the pun on the meaning of his name *Flaccus,* 18) remains unflappable because he limits his audience — this time to only one, Caesar. In the end, Horace the satirist is willing to trust the horse Caesar to determine the difference between good and bad poetry, both legally, as far as libel is concerned, and aesthetically (83–86). Horace would have his audience believe that art wins out, not Caesar. If the verses are good and the abuse deserved (Horace asks), then (Trebatius answers) Caesar will dismiss the invective with a laugh.

Horace is keenly aware of how an audience may perceive his political/literary alliances and writes this as an integral theme into his poetry. Characters in the dialogues, patrons, the poets of the circles, the satirist himself, and the general anonymous audience all wonder to what extent *amicitia* between any patron and poet can influence literature. While Horace sensitizes his audience(s) to the difficult questions involved in the interaction of politics and poetics, he attempts to separate his poetic voice from political motivations by engaging in an artful dissimulation that sets up epic as the foil for lyric. Satire and lyric with their lighter tones and topics are safer than the serious martial themes of epic praise. Further, epic writers, as opposed to satirists and lyricists, are subject to the influence of financial and political rewards. For all the irony in Horace's epic disavowals, there is the implication (whether the satirist would have us really convinced or not) that satire and lyric escape the political ambition that tempts the epic poet.

Horace's most notorious example of an epic poet writing for rewards is Choerilus of Iasus, one of a literary coterie kept by Alexander the Great. Unfortunately for Choerilus, his surviving fragments are far outweighed by Horace's harsh criticism (*Epist*.II.1.230–44; *Ars* 357–60).[76] Granted, Horace is not so much concerned that Choerilus is an epic poet but a bad poet. Horace imagines Choerilus and his poems as a dysfunctional family. Choerilus has been a bad parent: his children, poems, are ill conceived (*male natis*, 233), poorly raised, and therefore ill mannered (*incultis*, 233). Choerilus as a scribe or musician? Choerilus repeats the same errors so frequently, like an incompetent copyist or a harpist who muffs the same chord (*Ars* 354–56), that Horace turns his name into a nickname for the inept poet (*sic mihi qui multum cessat fit Choerilus ille, Ars* 357). Ps.-Acro (on *Epist.* II.1.233) retells the tradition that Choerilus composed only seven good verses; Horace is surprised when he happens upon one or two. Even the venerable Homer begins to nod off at Choerilus's somnolent dullness, dramatized by Horace in the rhyming heavy assonance of the line endings, *Ars* 357–60: "that Choerilus . . . the same Choerilus . . . Homer . . . sleep." Horace is not finished. He rounds out his criticism with a comparison to the visual arts (361–65). Some art looks better at a distance, some up close; one in dim lighting, another well lit; in one instance a single viewing will suffice, in another instance ten viewings would not be enough. Choerilus clearly would be better at a distance, in poor lighting, and then only once. Horace does try to give Choerilus one excuse for being a bore: it is the law that sleep creeps up on a lengthy work (*Ars* 360). This may be the funniest reworking of the *dictum brevitatis* in Horatian poetry, Homer slowly falling off to sleep as the tale drags on. Choerilus could not help it; long books are naturally a yawn.

Horace's criticism, however, concentrates on one fault worse than all the others: epic Choerilus flattered for profit. Horace's opening words in each of the first three lines maligning Choerilus stress that he ingratiated himself to his patron and wrote poor verses for money (*gratus Alexandro . . . Choerilus . . . rettulit acceptos, Epist*.II.1.232–34). Choerilus debased the art of poetry to a mere occupation. In the hands of such poets as Choerilus, *epos* had become banausic, that is, by Aristotelian and Platonic definition, a low-based and enslaving mechanic (ἀνελεύθερον ἔργον), performed to earn wages (Arist. *Pol.*1258; 1337b4–22; *EN.*1107b, 1122a, 1123a; Pl. *R.*590c).[77]

By Aristotle's definition, banausic labor, including industrial education and money management, is characterized by immoderation, causing a loss of autonomy and self-control (ὑπερβολή as opposed to μεσότης, *EN.*1107b4–21; *Pol.*1337b12–15). Even the liberal arts become illiberal, if practiced improperly. For instance, banausia differs from munificence, not in the amount spent, but in the manner of the expenditure. There must be harmony, that is, the expense must fit the occasion. The deed can exceed but must not fall below the status of the recipient, and the motive for the expense cannot be personal recognition or profit, but the recipient's goodness (Arist. *EN.*1122a30–b; 1123a19–35; n.b. 1122b4–7). Any lack of harmony results in flattery (Pl. *R.*590a8–c). The Horatian *recusatio* as modeled in *S.*II.1 parallels the Aristotelian review of banausic labor and therefore distinguishes Horace's praise from flattery. Horace would have us believe that just because he writes for a patron does not mean that he is a literary day-laborer. He expresses concern that his gift be appropriate for the recipient.[78] Horace shifts attention to the worthiness of the recipient when he protests that his modest talents will not measure up to Caesar's greatness (12–15). Praise for Caesar must evince harmony: Horace worries that his praise may not be given at the right moment and may be rejected (17–20). Not Choerilus — the poetry/labor of illiberal Choerilus (*gratus Alexandro*) did not match the grand achievements of Alexander (*regi magno*) and was motivated by money and personal status. Choerilian epic was not art but a menial occupation.

What about Horace's own circle, the epic writers Varius and Vergil? Horace's immediate *apologia* for the excellence of their poems for Augustus (*Epist.*II.1.245–50) shows that Horace anticipates the question. He cannot deride the banausic Choerilus and avoid suggesting the same criticism for his *docti amici*. This is the brilliance of Horace's strategy: he has it both ways. Horace defends Varius and Vergil by praising Augustus. Horace places the question of whether Augustus's poets' praise is credible in the mind of Augustus and then reassures him of the greatness of his poets' work (245–50). Their literary labor is not banausic because the gifts Augustus awarded them were justified by the quality of their poetry and how well it represented Augustus's grand deeds.

Augustus knows the difference between good and bad poetry, which is to say, Augustus is superior to Alexander. Augustus is a more discriminating audience than Alexander, who did well choosing a painter, Apelles, and sculptor, Lysippus, but could not recognize the imaging value of poetry (*Epist*.II.1.214b–50a). Just as at the end of *S*.II.1, Horace trusts Augustus's literary judgment with the logical implication, of course, that bad poetry is symptomatic of a poor patron and good poetry of a good patron (Suet. *Aug*.89.3).

As soon as Horace finishes his *apologia* for Varius and Vergil he complicates it by completely disassociating his *sermones* from the suspect credibility of epic praise with a *recusatio* that ends the letter (250–70). Horace's strategy is familiar: he prefers epic's grandeur but claims his epic effort would be unworthy of the recipient, Caesar. Horace's feigned modesty appears to compliment both Caesar and his epic poets, but amusing as it is, it comes with an added bite. Neither Varius nor Vergil are a Choerilus, but Horace's *recusatio* underscores that he will still not associate his voice with theirs. Horace will not write epic praise, bad (Choerilus) or good (Varius and Vergil). What makes Horace's refusal so emphatic is not only that in respect to the overall argument it brings the epistle back to its beginning, when Horace would not wrong Rome by taking up Caesar's valuable time with a long poem (*longo sermone*, 4), making in effect the entire letter one ironic long panegyric *recusatio*, but that it contrasts Horace with the epic poets of his circle just after he defended them.

Three observations: (1) Horace's disavowal of epic is artificial, that is, it only calls attention to his utilization of epic themes, which was always characteristic of the satiric and lyric traditions. By specifying precisely what he will not write, Horace gives space to those themes. Horace's epic criticism, however, also strategically distinguishes and excludes. When sympotic Horace says he will sing about loves and banquets and leave political praise to the epicist, he activates a broader argument that his lyrics, like his *sermones*, are free from the rewards that entrap epic poets. The lyric to epic contrast is so much a part of Horatian symposia that if Horace were to disavow his sympotic persona, he would jeopardize his claim to this lyric freedom. (2) Horatian poetry constructs a critical audience: the patrons, poets in the circle, poetasters, and the audience at large. This may reflect cultural reality, but it is just as likely the creation of a satirist and lyricist who senses that dialogue between himself and imagined audience(s) is indispensable to his art. (3) As much as Horatian criticism suspects the epicists, it reclaims Vergil and Varius by distinguishing them from their banausic epic peers. Horace sets the stage for a further reassessment of Vergilian poetics in *Odes* IV, when he will associate Vergil with Horace's lyric persona, a voice motivated (he claims) by virtue and excellence, not rewards.

Sympotic Horace Exiled: *Epistle* II.2 and *Odes* IV.1

Has the sympotic poet left — for good?

> lusisti satis, edisti satis atque bibisti.
> tempus abire tibi est, ne potum largius aequo
> rideat et pulset lasciva decentius aetas.

> [You have played enough, eaten and drunk enough. It is time for you to leave, or youth, the better age for excess, will laugh at you, when you are drunk beyond the limit, and send you packing.] —Horace to Florus, or himself (at the close of *Epist*.II.2), just as he advised old Chloris (*C*.III.15)

Lucretius had said the same to anyone facing death: "Fool, why not retire from the banquet like a full dinner guest and with a calm mind secure a peaceful rest?" (3.938–39). But Horace's answer to Florus is more than an Epicurean lecture on the certainty of death. When Horace recalls Lucretius's image of the full banqueter, he necessarily involves poetics because he so reverses his former (old) sympotic persona that he places the lyric voice of *Odes* I–III in jeopardy. Horace for the first time refuses a sympotic invitation. Florus has been waiting for Horace to send the lyrics he promised, but Florus will go on waiting because it is time for the lyricist to leave the party or be run out the door. The lyric Horace has retired (*Epist*.I.1.10–19). Horace will not be Lucretius's fool. Unlike Chloris, the old lyric Horace has left before the young symposiasts started laughing.[79] Horace's repeated vocabulary from his ode to Chloris (*ludere, decet, lascivae, poti*) at the end of the epistle (*lusisti, potum, lasciva, decentius*) makes it impossible not to imagine the poet in her place. Sympotic invitations are no longer relevant for Horace. Yet, however reasonable Florus, or anyone listening in on the letter, may think Horace's excuse for not writing the verses, the poet has broken a promise. The lyricist has left the banquet with orders to fill still on the table.

Horace could not stay away from lyric. Less than three years after Horace told Maecenas and Florus that he would not write lyric (20–19 B.C.), he composed the *Carmen Saeculare,* and shortly after its success (17 B.C.) he began—if he had not already started—writing odes that would appear in a fourth lyric poetry book featuring panegyric as a principal theme. Although Horace in C.IV.1 returns to love lyric in a sympotic context, he does not recant his earlier renunciation of his sympotic persona (*Epist.*II.2). He again excuses himself from sympotic pleasures because he is too old. Horace's artful technique—his command of language, musicality, word order, and rhetoric—prove that his later poetry has all the lyric power of his earlier song in spite of his claim that he is not the poet he was. Since Horace has feigned poetic weakness so often before, he has prepared us to laugh off his comparison to his former powerful lyric persona as completely ironic, imitating the deceptively small voice of the *recusatio,* except that his turn to more direct panegyric in the course of book IV rankles because it clashes so dramatically with his epic criticism by which he distances himself from the complications of such poetry.

Horace's look back in c.1 immediately blends love and politics by describing his earlier life, when he fought Venus's battles (*bella*), with a metaphor of political domination (*sub regno Cinarae*). Horace was a poet under the authority of Love. Now Horace's rejection of his sympotic persona raises the question: if singing of Venus and Cinara brought lyric power, will the attempt to leave the goddess's realm result in lyric impotence? By the end of the book's opening song, Horace's attempt to escape Venus, sympotic pleasures, and lyric verses fails. Another love interest has replaced Horace's lost Cinara. Cinara's kind rule gives way to Ligurinus's hard rejection. Horace can hardly choke back his tears (33a–34). His voice falters into silence (35–36). C.1 seems an ending rather than a beginning. If, as I have argued, Horace with a fair degree of consistency (albeit incredulously) disassociates his lyric voice from the direct panegyric of ambitious epicists, my question, then, is whether Horace's explicit testing of his lyric voice announces a lapse into a univocal panegyric mode.[80]

Horace's look back creates a dilemma: to what extent should one read (not overread or underread) the constant reminders of Horace's earlier poetry and personae? Are two particular poems interrelated or not? This is without the other subtexts: Homer, Pindar, Sappho, Simonides, Bacchylides, Callimachus, Catullus, Vergil, Propertius . . . It is easy to gaze into the Horatian poem and see many reflections, in addition to one's own. Such layering is not just a challenge for an audience but also affects the poet. It would hardly be possible for a poet to predict how any audience might read one poem in view of another or for Horace to give any definitive shape to the interpretive space. And in this volatile interpretive environment Horace will write imperial encomia. The panegyrist's boldness borders on the Pindaric. The commission to compose the CS further complicates Horace's previous strategies. What plausible irony is left in a political *recusatio* from the celebrated poet of Rome? "I'm not up to such praise, but in fact you know I am, you've all heard my work." The hint of a *recusatio* in C.IV.8 takes on a more vivid nuance: "I do not have this power" (*sed non haec mihi vis*, 9). Who does have the power in the act of praising—the artist, the patron, the wider audience? Horace still has not resolved this primary question of his epic criticism, and now in c.1 he has disavowed the sympotic persona that he used to distinguish his poetry from the work of an ambitious praise poet. How much has the lyric Horace really changed?

At the risk of representing Horace as a thinly disguised *reconstructionist*, I suggest that Horace reshapes this complicated interpretive landscape by recalling his former lyric sympotic persona, disavowing it, and then immediately re-creating it. Horace allows the audience to witness the entire process so that he and the audience can together reconstruct the poet's sympotic lyric voice, which he had pretended in his epic criticism was so averse to praise poetry. Horace (re)writes the account of his early career for the last time in the same epistle to Florus (II.2):

> Romae nutriri mihi contigit atque doceri
> iratus Grais quantum nocuisset Achilles.
> adiecere bonae paulo plus artis Athenae,

scilicet ut vellem curvo dinoscere rectum
atque inter silvas Academi quaerere verum.   45
dura sed emovere loco me tempora grato
civilisque rudem belli tulit aestus in arma
Caesaris Augusti non responsura lacertis.
unde simul primum me dimisere Philippi,
decisis humilem pennis inopemque paterni   50
et Laris et fundi paupertas impulit audax
ut versus facerem; sed quod non desit habentem
quae poterunt umquam satis expurgare cicutae,
ni melius dormire putem quam scribere versus?
   Singula de nobis anni praedantur euntes.   55
eripuere iocos, Venerem, convivia, ludum,
tendunt extorquere poemata. quid faciam vis? (41–57)

[At Rome it was my fortune to be nurtured and taught how
much harm angry Achilles caused the Greeks. Good Athens offered a little more art, namely, that I be ready to discern the direct from the circuitous and to seek the truth among the sacred
wood of the Academy. But hard times drove me from my pleasant place, and the civic flood carried me untrained in war to
weapons poorly matched for the mighty arms of Caesar. As
soon as from these Philippi discharged me, humbled, with my
wings clipped and without the resources of my paternal home
and estate, fierce poverty attacked me so that I wrote verses; but
what amount of hemlock could suffice to purge me, now that I
lack nothing, if I were not to think sleeping better than writing
verses for pay?[81] The moving years are plundering from us
each and every thing. They have ripped away my laughs, Love,
banquets, jesting; they are working hard to wrench poems from
me. What do you want me to do?]

Horace had written autobiography before, and as before the poet
uses his life to influence the audience's perception of his poetics.
The letter presents multiple chronological vantage points for the
autobiography. The autobiography can be viewed starting at its
earliest time period (Horace's education) and looking forward
into the future from when Horace had not yet written his verses.
From this perspective the argument is apparent. Horace had to
write verses for money when he was young, but now that he is
older and has secured everything he needs, he should not be expected to do so. On the other hand, the epistle presumes an audience familiar with Horace's earlier poetry. Horace then can use

the past civil conflict, coupled with changes in the language he used to describe his lyric achievement in *Odes* I–III, to surprise and manipulate expectations. The audience will be negotiating a sense using both chronologies simultaneously, and the different time frames together complete a coherent argument. The poet writes for a patron; but while openly engaged in panegyric, he asserts an independent persona.

From the strictly historical perspective, this *vita Horati* is not very interesting, just information Horace has already disclosed: he was educated in Rome and Athens (41–45) and sided against Augustus at Philippi (46–49). After Philippi, Horace returned to Rome but found that he was reduced to poverty because the family property had been confiscated as part of the resettlement land for the veterans (49–52)—shades of the bucolic Vergil (*Ecl.*1; 9). Horace began to write verses for pay. Certainly the autobiography does not hide that Horace's poetic career involves the patronage of Augustus, and that Horace has political interests: the section opens with praise for Roman (Augustan) clemency in contrast to Achilles' unyielding anger. The praise, however, in a manner typical of Horace, is bounded by the realities of Augustus's military supremacy, marked by the line beginnings (41–48): *Romae . . . iratus (Achilles) . . . dura (tempora) . . . civilis (belli) . . . Caesaris Augusti.* All of this is thematic old hat.

What is distinctive about the autobiography is that at this stage in a lengthy poetic career (about twenty years) and well into Augustan rule, one might expect some expressed reconciliation to the Augustan achievement. Any conciliatory tone is missing and is replaced with a conqueror-subject matrix. The poet colors his history with Augustus with the language of military domination and exile (*emovere*, 46; *dimisere*, 49; *impulit*, 51; *praedantur*, 55; *eripuere*, 56; *tendunt extorquere*, 57). Horace places himself in an entirely passive position: it happened to me at Rome, Athens added, hard times drove me, the civic flood carried me away, poverty attacked me, the years are plundering me—leading to the exasperated, "What do you want me to do?" (57). And Horace's exile is in Rome, an inhospitable environment for a client of Bacchus (76–80). Horace's impatience at his exile turns caustic. He orders Florus, "Go compose the verses yourself!" (76). Horace could not have been more sarcastic. He compares Florus, (you and your song-filled verses, *versus . . . canoros*), to his own younger lyric persona, the songbird of C.II.20.15–16 (*canorus ales*, one of the few times Horace uses this adjective; cf. C.I.12.11; *Ars* 322). Horace, in the trappings of Rome, can no longer stand trying to manage his former lyric power. Florus will have to be the songbird.

Exile may seem to be interpretive hyperbole for Horace's situation, but Horace compounds his sense of displacement by reversing the confident images of his lyric achievement from the final odes of books II and III.[82] Horace's lyric flight had reached epic proportions (the lyric *tenui* is negated, *nec tenui . . . penna*, II.20.1–2), but after Philippi Horace's wings were clipped (*decisis humilem pennis*, *Epist.*II.2.50). The lyric Horace changes into a swan and leaves behind cities. Philippi sends him away humbled, not a powerful lyric *princeps* (III.30.12–13a), but a son who lost what wealth his parents had so that bold poverty drove him to write verses for his living. By encoding into his biography the image of an exile (trapped in Rome), Horace laments his loss and yet in the very act of writing refuses once again to write for profit. Horace asserts his lyric independence not from but within the act of praise.

Nevertheless, the plain statement that Horace became a poet for hire is most surprising compared to his other self-depictions. Horace never before offered that he wrote verses for money,[83] a banausic servitude that he criticizes in epicists. Why would Horace unveil this motivation so late in his career? Or if Lyne is correct and Horace was never so poor,[84] why would he put on a mask he has before stubbornly denied? Autobiography becomes poetics. This last biographical sketch overlays an epic versus lyric contrast in which Horace laments the loss of his lyric voice and resists the pressure he feels to fulfill any requests for additional verses. The poet has replayed this argument enough times that the pattern is beyond redundant: epicists concern themselves with meeting the demands of patrons, politics, and courting imperial favor; lyricists freely sing the pleasures of life.

The five lines (41–45) in which Horace recounts his education are divided by geography and poetics. Rome in first position (41) is contrasted to Athens at the end of line 43. At first glance, the first and second sentences run parallel, education at Rome (41–42) versus Athens (43–44), with the main clauses (41, 43) leading to the subordinate (42, 44). Horace unbalances this parallelism by continuing the adverbial noun clause of line 44 into 45. The structure becomes a bifold: two parallel thoughts contrasting what is learned at Rome and Athens are extended so that there is a central line (43), which defines what is meant by *ars, scilicet* being explanatory. Horace makes the pivotal moment of his education the art he learned at Athens.

Horace does not identify the Greek art until he names the Academy (45). At this point, the art Horace pursued at Athens obviously becomes philosophy, as one would expect since philosophy is so great a part of the Athenian achievement and was Horace's supposed occupation during his lyric retirement. In the process of touting his philosophical studies, Horace has some additional fun with his poetic. Exactly what Horace learned at Athens (*paulo plus artis,* 43) focuses attention on a lyric/epic contrast by juxtaposing the two code words *paulo* (lyric) and *plus* (epic). These simple words might appear insignificant, if Horace had not regularly used such tactics before and already introduced the question of genre in his assertion that at Rome he had learned how much angry Achilles could harm his people (41–42). Further, *bonae* could just as well modify *artis* as *Athenae* and would suggest the learning of a good poetic at Athens after the rejection at Rome of the epic theme of heroic anger. Horace is concerned with more than thematics (*iratus Achilles*), since he further explains *ars* as his preference (*vellem*) for the direct (*rectum*) over the circuitous (*curvo*). Horace, by aligning structurally verse 42 and angry Achilles with verse 44 (*curvo dinoscere rectum*), while obviously referring to the study of philosophy, suggests a reference to the other great epic character, the wandering Odysseus. The possible allusion to poetics in Horace's criticism of violent and wandering epic, taken with what immediately follows, that Horace is politically forced to leave Athens (now defined not only in a geographic but also poetic sense) and that he must resort to composing verses for a patron (52–54), makes it easier in this context of displacement, when Horace mentions the Academy, to recall Socrates' fight with the *demos* (perhaps even more Aristotle's exile) and what his search for the truth cost him. Horace is about to drink the hemlock himself (53).

Hard times drive Horace from his pleasant place (*dura sed emovere loco me tempora grato*). "Hard" has anti-lyric overtones (cf. C.IV.1.4–7), while *gratus* is one of Horace's favorite adjectives for sympotic pleasures. What would a move from a "pleasant place" be—his studies in Athens that Horace must give up because of civil war or poetically that he then and still now must respond to pressure to write verses? Caesar Augustus and Philippi would argue for the former. But the hostilities in the biography blend in with poetics: the outcome of the war, the confiscation of Horace's property, and the subsequent poverty that forced him to write for pay (49–51). Further, immediately after Horace's banishment from Athens he writes in praise of Augustus the two most epic lines in the entire section (*civilisque rudem belli tulit aestus in arma / Caesaris Augusti non responsura lacertis,* 47–48). *Responsura* (to answer back) is misplaced in meaning enough to suggest metaphor: Horace's arms are verbal and ill-matched to Caesar's physical, mighty arms. Horace's subordination of his own poetic ability to the greatness of Augustus's deeds both recalls and reverses the poet's earlier *recusationes* of *epos,* particularly when he recommended the Homeric Varius (C.I.6). Horace's autobiography and the *recusatio* of C. I.6 have several touch points. Both renounce the anger of Achilles and the wanderings of Odysseus and juxtapose lyric and epic code words to highlight generic tensions (*paulo / plus; tenues/grandia*). The playful lyric poet of the *recusatio,* however, who feigns humility, turns his refusal to praise into his tribute, and ironically denies his incorporation of epic themes, in this epistle becomes the conquered poet doing what he does not want and then not well enough. Horace is now a Varius but with a weak voice.

Up to this point (midline 52), Horace has so undermined his former claims to lyric greatness that he appears humbled enough to submit to the current pressure to compose verses. Horace is being a deceitful storyteller and building the suspense. Just when any self-possessed lyric voice appears to have been entirely banished, Horace with a jarring transition (*sed*) becomes defiant (52–54). Horace returns to the Academy and its foundations in the final determination of Socrates to drink down the hemlock rather than give in to tyranny. Horace alters the Socratic image to focus on his own failure if he should submit. The comparison is poignantly grotesque. Socrates judged that it was right and therefore better to drink the hemlock and sleep; the poet cannot imagine any amount of the poison that could clean out his system, if he thought writing verses for rewards better than death.

Horace's confidence quickly fades again in another reversal of

his sympotic persona (55–57). The passing years have done what
no mortal could do, steal away from Horace sympotic pleasures.
Laughing at the ridiculous behavior of lecherous old persons enjoying themselves at a sympotic revel is commonplace in comedy,
but any amusement here is muted by the change in Horace's previous lyric character. This situation is far from the immortality
Horace claimed for himself when he scolded the mourners at his
funeral (C.II.20.7–8, 21–24) and directly contradicts the poet's
power over time (C.III.30.1–7). Horace had been the one who invited others to symposia and chided any who were holding back.
Now old age has robbed him of his own sympotic world. What is
more, the years are attempting to twist out of him worthless little
poems. Horace's quick change from past to present intensifies the
injustice: old age has seized (*eripuere*) from me everything and
now is trying (*tendunt*) to rip from me poems I don't have the
power left to write.

The letter to Florus and C.IV.1 converge at this point. Horace
again uses his age to depict through metaphor his struggle
against returning to lyric poetry when he wishes Venus off to the
younger Paulus Fabius Maximus.[85] The poet's failure to rebuff
Venus should not be turned into metaphor so quickly that his
song's humor becomes obscured. Horace laces his epithalamium
for Maximus and his future bride, Marcia, Augustus's cousin,
with erotic innuendo. Horace creates within his plaint to Venus
the picture of himself as an older frustrated gentleman who has
not made love in the longest time, and now that he has the opportunity he fears that he cannot finish to his satisfaction or his
lover's. As Horace structures the first two verses (*Intermissa,
Venus, diu / rursus bella moves? parce precor, precor.*), *intermissa*
could modify the second word *Venus*. It is not until the second
verse, the ode's fifth word, that the actual noun referent for *intermissa* becomes clearer (*bella*). The sense of the whole allows that
both Venus and her wars have been interrupted. The word *venus*
commonly denotes lovemaking and either the penis or clitoris.[86]
Intermissa Venus taken together, a reflex reinforced by their juxtaposition, could suggest that someone has been interrupted in the
act of making love. Horace ends the first verse with a surprise
since the interruption has gone on for a long time (*diu*). The four
syllables of *intermissa* followed by the disyllabics *Venus diu* accentuate the pauses in the line and re-create the sensation of in-

terruption. Horace increases the sexual undertones in the second strophe with words of resistance to Venus that activate the sense of touch: hardness, softness, bending. The fifty-year-old is now hard (*iam durum*) and pleads with Venus not to bend (*flectere*) his hardness with her softness (*mollibus . . . imperiis*).[87] Horace has left just enough to the imagination. The old man has managed an erection barely and is scared that it will not last through the pressures of intercourse.[88] Of course, Horace is having some sexual fun at his own expense, appropriate enough on the occasion of a friend's approaching marriage. Old Horace is impotent compared to his friend, the Maxima (Venus).[89] The joke might have brought only nervous laughter because the poet's own metaphoric sexual anxiety may actually represent more closely the true mood of Maximus, the old bachelor soon-to-be-married into the most powerful Roman family.[90] Everyone can relax, though, and have a chuckle; everything will be fine; the poet has ordered Venus on to Maximus's house.

Laughter fades fast. The first two strophes illustrate well the seriocomic character of Horace's sympotic lyric. Seeing the sexual connotation connects the ode's beginning more closely to its conclusion. Horace's prayer against Venus is the frustrated cry of someone who has tried and failed to appeal to the young, sexually potent Ligurinus and who no longer has the heart for the pursuit. Horace's desperation takes on an equally serious nuance for the poet when it is read as an announcement that he is returning to lyric, because the metaphor, as did the autobiography in the letter to Florus, places Horace's previous lyric sympotic persona in crisis. Horace drastically alters his relationship to the symposion:

> me nec femina nec puer
>   iam nec spes animi credula mutui   30
> nec certare iuvat mero
>   nec vincire novis tempora floribus.
>
> sed cur, heu, Ligurine, cur
>   manat rara meas lacrima per genas?
> cur facunda parum decoro   35
>   inter verba cadit lingua silentio?
>
> nocturnis ego somniis
>   iam captum teneo, iam volucrem sequor

te per gramina Martii
     Campi, te per aquas, dure, volubilis. (29–40)   40

[Now neither woman, nor boy, nor a hope ready to trust
mutual affection, nor stout drinking contests please me, nor
temples bound with fresh flowers. But why, oh Ligurinus,
why does the tear choked back pour over my cheeks? Why
does my eloquent tongue midword fail in absolute disgraceful silence? I in my dreams now hold you captive, now I
follow you as you fly over the fields of the Campus Martius;
I follow you over the waters, hard one, I whirling round.]

Venus invites the poet, unlike in *Odes* I–III when the poet extends
every sympotic invitation, and now Horace refuses to attend, like
so many of those he invited before, but not because he is preoccupied; he is too old for the party. Old Horace emphatically punctuates his resistance with five negatives (repeated *nec*) over four
lines (29–32). The eroticisms of the symposion no longer please
him. Maximus is the warrior carrying Venus's standards and ex-
ulting over his beaten rival (16–18). Horace negates Venus's wars
as descriptive of his own life (*nec certare . . . nec vincire*, 31–32). The
lyric Horace has canceled himself out of his party. He is now outside of the sympotic world just like Lydia (C.I.25), Chloris
(C.III.15), Lycus (C.III.19), and Lyce (C.IV.13). Consequently, for
Horace *carpe diem* loses its validity. Horace's transfer of the temporal adverb *iam* (often used with *nunc* to support the *carpe diem*
argument, see C.I.4; 7.31; 9.2, 18, 21; 11.5; 37.1–2; III.29.17–21;
IV.7.1; 11.31; 12.1–3, 18) from himself to Ligurinus makes this
clear (7, 30, 38). As applied to Horace *iam* is negative: now Horace
is hard (*iam durum*) to Venus's soft commands and does not expect that his affections will be reciprocated (*iam nec spes animi
credula mutui*). Now only in his dreams Horace holds Ligurinus
(*iam captum*) or pursues him swift (*iam volucrem. . . te*) over the
campus.

     Horace closes with a personal lament (33–40). He does not ac-
cept old age with calm resignation. Horace has lost his hardness,
but Ligurinus, the object of his affection, is now hard (like the
elegiac *dura domina*), and no amount of pleading will win him.
Horace in frantic desperation cries, "why . . . why . . . why?"
(*cur . . . cur . . . cur*), a plaint that reverses the sympotic invitation
of C.III.19:

insanire iuvat: cur Berecyntiae
cessant flamina tibiae?
    cur pendet tacita fistula cum lyra?   20

parcentis ego dexteras
    odi. sparge rosas; audiat invidus
dementem strepitum Lycus
    et vicina seni non habilis Lyco. (18–24)

[It is a joy to go mad. Why do the blasts of the Berecyntian flute fail? Why do the pipe and the lyre hang on the
wall silent? I hate restraining hands. Scatter roses. Let
Lycus hear our mad uproar and be jealous, and the
neighborhood girl as well; she is no match for old man
Lycus.]

Previously the lyric poet played a frenzied symposiast (*insanire
iuvat*; cf. c.1.31, *nec . . . iuvat*), and his "why . . . why?" (*cur . . . cur*)
impatiently called for wilder celebrations. How greatly has the
poet changed from the assertive *magister bibendi* of *Odes* I–III. Horace faces a love that he would try to resist but cannot, and he is
brought to tears and nighttime dreams. Horace's own sympotic
world no longer appeals to him, and although he is its creator, he
cannot escape from it.

C.IV.1 is a masterful beginning. Through the verbal echoes of
his earlier poems in the opening stanzas and again writing an
erotic sympotic lyric, Horace bridges the gap in time between
Odes I–III and IV, but he also announces a new thematic direction
by his displacement from the sympotic world. The poet is now on
the outside; he is, however, struggling to reenter. This ode does
not redefine the sympotic, although in looking back over the
course of the book the eulogy to Maximus at the song's center
predicts a new frank emphasis on the blending of the sympotic
and panegyric. Initially c.1 leaves the audience wondering what
will become of the poet and his war with Venus. Will the disillu-
sionment continue, or will Horace restore his lyric sympotic persona to power?[91]

Compared to the lament of C.IV.1, only the beginning of the
book, the poet in *Epist*.II.2 sounds less broken. There the autobiography and the image of the old poet lack the poet's sexual frustration and his tears. *Epist*.II.2 does not leave Horace's lyric sympotic persona powerless, and neither will *Odes* IV: Horace pulls

apart and then rebuilds. This is his pattern. No sooner than Horace has displaced himself from the lyric world and its sympotic themes, he returns to the banquet (*Epist.*II.2.58–64). Horace turns *quid vis faciam?* from an expression of indecision into an *apologia* in a satiric mode with a priamel that brings the audience right back to Horace's earlier rhetorical structures (*S.*I.1; *C.*I.1). It is not the host's (poet's) fault that the guests (audience, patrons) can never make up their mind what to order. One wants lyric, another iambs, another satire. It is simply beyond the poet to please everyone's diverse tastes. Here is the old Horace again using a smile to disarm the potential danger of the truth. The movement of the epistle from the lyric poet's displacement to the recovery of sympotic laughter foreshadows the same re-creation of the sympotic world for *Odes* IV.

Horace has been all over the map—doubling back from the strong poet to the weak and back to the strong. In his autobiography Horace is on the move, topographically and poetically. He moves from Rome to Athens, his youthful rage carries him to Philippi, and from there he is dismissed back to Rome. The epic/lyric contrast, an Horatian tactic to assert his freedom from the banausic pressures of patronage, caves in to poverty in the aftermath of Octavian's victory when Horace frankly admits he wrote for hire. Autobiography and poetics merge. Horace, while unmasking his debt to patronage remasks with the face of an exile. The image of exile depicts the poet's distress, while it also makes a public and political declaration that the exiled was and may well still be a dissident. Exile by its very nature calls into question the justice of the exiling power or at least invites scrutiny. The exilic coloring of the autobiography, emphasized by Horace's language and the allusive destruction of his earlier lyric voice, allows Horace to reinvent a voice of resistance while he is in fact writing praise poetry. In spite of all his forced moves, Horace was not the one who ultimately changed. Horace puts Rome through a dramatic reversal. Rome was a nurse who taught Horace the dangers of epic anger, but changes into a city full of cares and labors that stifle poetic creativity (65–66).

When the poet protests that he is not the same as he was under the rule of Cinara (*C.*IV.1), we have been too ready to believe him and miss the poet's chuckle. The sympotic poet is exactly who he was, whether *sub regno Cinarae* or *Augusti* or *Romae*. Imperial praise does not limit his lyric power, and while defending his lyric, the sympotic Horace promises that his panegyric praxis, exemplified in *Odes* IV, will be just as allusive and elusive as he always was.

2

Encomia Nobilium and Horace's Panegyric Praxis

If you mention anything which does not apply to him (the *laudandus*) and which everybody knows does not apply to him, it not only seems unconvincing, but you will make yourself suspect for other occasions and you will have an uphill job with your audience. One must always concur with what is commonly admitted.
—Menander Rhetor: the propempticon (398.1–6)

Odes IV puzzles: Horace released this second collection ten years following *Odes* I–III and five after he quit lyric (*Epist.*I.1.10–19; II.2.52–64, 141–44).[1] Suetonius says Horace's return was prompted by Augustus, who requested/required (*saeculare carmen conponendum* iniunxerit . . . *eumque* coegerit . . . *quartum addere*) another book of *Odes*, as well as *Epist.*II.1.[2] Specifically, then, the occasions for Horace's lyric supposed propaganda/Augustan imaging would be the epinikia for Drusus (c.4) and Tiberius (c.14), and the odes praising Augustus (c.5, 15). I will state from the outset that I believe Horace's volte-face against writing direct panegyrics is more a matter of self-presentation and poetics than politics; although, as already argued, in Horace poetics and politics are not easily distinguished.[3] Horace's change of heart may be a parodied imitation of Vergil's reversal of his earlier Callimachean *recusatio* that resulted when he began composing epic. If parody is too strong to prove, certainly it is parallel. I consider Vergil's influence on *Odes* IV in chapter 5, but now

40

I would like to challenge Suetonius's biography, as commonly applied.

Even if Suetonius is credible and at least four odes were commissioned by Augustus, this hardly proves that the panegyric mode makes Horace's poetry inferior. This is precisely what much of the older scholarship assumes, and even recent studies have found it difficult to escape this prejudice, even though the Suetonian biography makes nonsense of book IV by forcing a bifurcation of the Horatian persona into public versus private and by ignoring that the Horace of the *Epistles,* some of which are roughly contemporary to *Odes* IV, is resistant, and argumentatively so, when facing the demands of patronage. Suetonius has been interpreted so that Horace simultaneously is (c.4, 5, 14, 15) and is not (the other odes) writing out of obligation, as if this would somehow affect the quality of the poetry.

It would be equally shortsighted to write off Suetonius as completely inaccurate and claim that book IV is not commissioned panegyric. Horace packs together in his shortest lyric collection more praise poetry than in any other of his poetry books. The chiastic arrangement of the corresponding pairs of imperial praise poems signals how prominent the epinikia/*encomia Augusti* (4, 5, 14, 15) are among the other poems. They are the conclusion of the entire book. On the other hand, if we accept the traditional view that the goal of panegyric is to persuade the audience that the deeds of the *laudandus* are worthy of immortal fame, in terms of poetics to convince the audience to adopt the interpretive perspective of the *laudandus,* then much of book IV is left out. Consider the odes to Ligurinus. And Horace does not name Augustus in c.1, and when he does in c.2 it is in the form of a *recusatio* addressed to Iullus Antonius. The odes addressed to Melpomene (c.3) and Apollo (c.6), exalting the poet's inspiration, frame the imperial praise poems (c.4; 5), and four odes (c.10-13), three to lovers and none with any apparent connection to imperial concerns, introduce the final two praises for Drusus, Tiberius, and Augustus. The poet throughout *Odes* IV sounds his own praises.[4] *Odes* IV leaves anyone expecting a collection of imperial encomiastic poetry wondering. I find it unfathomable—no matter how dull Augustus's literary sense may have been[5]—that such structural generalities would be unnoticed by a patron who requested a book honoring himself and was so concerned with his imaging.

Considering solely the primacy of the imperial encomia, we are left with either a collection awkwardly thrown together or with a dramatic limiting of the lyric persona in favor of imperial power. Poetic power becomes nothing more than an ability to secure immortal fame for others, or perhaps for the poet through his memorable praise, again for others. The lyric poet would play a supporting role at best. This is a full retreat from Horace's previous sympotic persona. In a metaphoric sense, the lyric persona of *Odes* I–III would remain in exile. I am not intending to stake out a middle ground between these opposing views. The puzzling incongruence of the book's structures and its public-private themes point to an intriguing panegyric praxis that champions the lyric poet as a leading voice in shaping civic identity and memory. The *encomia nobilium* do not support the caricature of the duty-bound poet, but a poet writing panegyric for the fun of it. Horatian panegyric offers a maze of artistic pleasure. In more formal literary terms, *Odes* IV is a panegyric story that keeps the audience not just guessing the outcome, but inventing it.

A lineup of the book's addressees serves notice that Horace's *encomia nobilium* are not fixed unchanging memorials. Paulus Fabius Maximus (c.1), Iullus Antonius (c.2), C. Marcius Censorinus (c.8), and M. Lollius (c.9) were among the young insiders forming around Augustus (20s B.C.), and at the time of *Odes* IV most of their political careers were ahead of them (only Lollius had been consul). Horace had little surety of their greatness, which makes panegyric risky for poet and *laudatus*. A politician's unpredictable legacy, enhanced by the volatility of the early principate, may make any praise undeserved. Horace does not cover over the challenge but designs his praises to emphasize the vulnerability of *laudator* and *laudatus*, and thereby to offer a critique of the praxis of panegyric. Horace does so by complicating the particular plots and details of the praise so that the resulting dissonance provokes the audience to consider the panegyrist-poet's craft. Throughout the *encomia nobilium* the complications increase, and the audience sees through praise and blame the panegyric process itself and how it directs collective memory, how a community's shared life becomes its history. The Horatian panegyrist is not a reactive recorder (a mere proponent or detractor), but an active inventor of a civic story shaping public discourse and self-image (ideology).[6]

C.1 and 2: Great Expectations? Inventing Panegyric Discord

To whom should Horace address his new collection? Maecenas, as before? Should the first poem address Augustus and acknowledge him openly as the preeminent patron? Horace's praise avoids the obvious. What about Sallustius Crispus (C.II.2), Maecenas's supposed political replacement? Moving him to first position might highlight Maecenas's withdrawal and potentially injure an old friend.[7] One of Augustus's favorites, not yet involved in intrigues or packing political baggage, would be safer. Fabius Maximus seems the perfect choice. He had distinguished himself by a military tribunate in Spain (26–25 B.C.) and quaestorship in the East (22–19 B.C.) but was still to hold the consulship (11 B.C.) or rival Tiberius.[8] Horace, however, with his encomium to Maximus, invents complication:

> tempestivius in domum
>   Pauli purpureis ales oloribus   10
> comissabere Maximi,
>   si torrere iecur quaeris idoneum.
>
> namque et nobilis et decens
>   et pro sollicitis non tacitus reis
> et centum puer artium   15
>   late signa feret militiae tuae,
>
> et, quandoque potentior
>   largi muneribus riserit aemuli,
> Albanos prope te lacus
>   ponet marmoream sub trabe citrea.   20
>
> illic plurima naribus
>   duces tura lyraque et Berecyntia
> delectabere tibia
>   mixtis carminibus non sine fistula;
>
> illic bis pueri die   25
>   numen cum teneris virginibus tuum
> laudantes pede candido
>   in morem Salium ter quatient humum. (9–28)

[More timely and swift on your purple swans you will parade in revelry to the house of Paulus Maximus, if you are

seeking to torch a well-suited passion. For Maximus noble
and winsome and outspoken in defense of anxious defen-
dants, and a youth of a hundred talents, far and wide will
carry your standards, Venus. And whenever he, more powerful, laughs triumphantly over the love tributes of a rich rival, he will erect near the Alban lakes your marble votive
statue under a citron roof. There you will breathe in plentiful incense and take pleasure in the combined music of the
lyre and Berecyntian flute and also the shepherd's pipe.
There twice daily lads and tender maidens will praise your
divinity and with white feet shake the earth in the triple beat
dance of the Salii.]

Maximus was a bachelor around thirty years old, about to marry
Augustus's cousin Marcia.[9] Horace humorously tailors his praise
to this occasion, as already observed: Horace praises Maximus as
a great lover. Horace also builds his eulogy so that its surprise
ending alerts his audience that this is not typical praise, even for
an aristocrat soon to be married. The only attribute befitting a
Roman nobleman that Horace ascribes to Maximus is that he is a
good lawyer (14).[10] After Horace wishes Venus off to Maximus's
house (9–12), Horace's praise becomes quite ordinary: panegyric
adjectives (*nobilis; decens,* 13) introduce Maximus's eloquence (14)
and suggest that the equally general *centum puer artium* refers to
military prowess (*late signa feret militiae tuae,* 15–16). Then "your"
(*tuae* = Venus) at the end of the verse changes what seems a standard encomium back into epithalamic praise: Maximus is a soldier in Venus's wars (17–18).[11]

Sympotic pleasures dominate Horace's praise for Maximus.
Horace's detailed description (four full strophes) of the sensual
ritual revelry (radiant swans, incense, music, singing, and Salian
dancing) in Venus's honor dramatizes the eroticism pervading
Maximus's home, while the future tense places the encomium in
the realm of imagination and reminds that the praise is fiction. As
Horace casts his character, Maximus does not neatly fit the stric-
tures of Augustan courtship and marriage. He may be an up-
standing noble, but the contrast of his character to the persona
adopted by the poet, one outside sympotic pleasures (29–32), implies that Maximus can still enjoy symposia (complete with a
woman or boy, flowers, and *merum*). Yet it is not necessary to
press any incongruity between the eulogy (the heroic lover) and

the occasion (marriage to Augustus's cousin) as entirely serious, and neither would I suggest that any humor is at the expense of the imperial house. Rather the joke is with the thirty-year-old Maximus. Maximus was likely not a verdant lover, and the poet's praise is a smile at the old bachelor who finally managed an impressive match.

Maximus is better off than the poet, an even older bachelor fighting and losing in Venus's wars (1–7, 30–40). The contrast between the bachelors muffles the humor directed at Maximus because it intensifies the poet's anxiety over his unrequited love. Nevertheless, treating the praise too seriously and lessening the disparity between Maximus's love life and the poet's epithalamic praise in some misguided effort to protect supposed imperial sensibilities ruin the contrasting reversal in the fortunes of the ode's two major characters: Maximus finally successful at love and the previously successful love lyricist unable now to charm his beloved. From the beginning of the book the seriocomic hyperbole in the panegyric alerts the reader that praise is poetic invention.[12] How seriously or literally should any praise be taken? Is Fabius really the *Maxima Venus* and the lyric poet *impotens*?

The panegyric humor of c.1 prepares for the poetic play of the *recusatio* in the book's first praise for Augustus, C.IV.2:

> Pindarum quisquis studet aemulari,
> Iulle, ceratis ope Daedalea
> nititur pennis vitreo daturus
>   nomina ponto.
>
> monte decurrens velut amnis, imbres   5
> quem super notas aluere ripas,
> fervet immensusque ruit profundo
>   Pindarus ore,
>
> laurea donandus Apollinari,
> seu per audacis nova dithyrambos   10
> verba devolvit numerisque fertur
>   lege solutis,
>
> seu deos regesve canit, deorum
> sanguinem, per quos cecidere iusta
> morte Centauri, cecidit tremendae   15
>   flamma Chimaerae,

sive, quos Elea domum reducit
palma caelestis, pugilemve equumve
dicit et centum potiore signis
    munere donat,   20

flebili sponsae iuvenemve raptum
plorat et viris animumque moresque
aureos educit in astra nigroque
    invidet Orco.

multa Dircaeum levat aura cycnum,   25
tendit, Antoni, quotiens in altos
nubium tractus: ego apis Matinae
    more modoque

grata carpentis thyma per laborem
plurimum circa nemus uvidique   30
Tiburis ripas operosa parvus
    carmina fingo.

concines maiore poeta plectro
Caesarem. quandoque trahet ferocis
per sacrum clivum merita decorus   35
    fronde Sygambros,

quo nihil maius meliusve terris
fata donavere bonique divi
nec dabunt, quamvis redeant in aurum
    tempora priscum;   40

concines laetosque dies et urbis
publicum ludum super impetrato
fortis Augusti reditu Forumque
    litibus orbum.

tum meae, si quid loquor audiendum,   45
vocis accedet bona pars et 'o sol
pulcher, o laudande!' canam recepto
    Caesare felix.

†teque dum procedit† 'io Triumphe!'
non semel dicemus, 'io Triumphe!'   50
civitas omnis dabimusque divis
    tura benignis.

te decem tauri totidemque vaccae,
me tener solvet vitulus, relicta
matre qui largis iuvenescit herbis   55
     in mea vota,

fronte curvatos imitatus ignis
tertium lunae referentis ortum,
qua notam duxit, niveus videri,
     cetera fulvus.   60

[Anyone who strives to rival Pindar, Iullus, trusts crafts-
man Daedalus's waxen wings and is fated to give his
name to the glassy sea. Like a river, rushing down from
the mountain and fed beyond its known bank by the
rains, so Pindar seethes and rushes measureless with
a deep-throated roar, worthy to be presented with
Apollo's laurel whether he rolls new words down
through bold dithyrambs and is carried on measures
freed from restraints, or he sings of gods or kings, the offspring of gods, who justly slew the Centaurs, who extin-
guished Chimaera's terrifying flame, or whether he sings
of those whom returning home the Elean palm exalts to
the heavens or of the boxer or the charger, and he presents them with a gift better than a hundred statues, or
mourns the young man stolen from his weeping bride
and extols his strength, spirit, and golden virtue to the
stars, and denies black Orcus these. Wind upon wind lifts
the Dircaean swan, Antonius, as often as it tempts a flight
into the cloudy heights; I, in the method and manner of
the Matine bee at work picking pleasant thyme around
many a grove and the moist banks of Tibur, I humbly
craft my elaborate songs. You, a poet of grander plectrum, will sing of Caesar, when crowned with the well-
won garland and ascending the Sacred Way he leads behind him the wild Sygambri; nothing greater or better
than this have the fates and kind gods given to the earth
nor will give, though the golden age of old return. You
will sing of the city's holidays and public games celebrated for brave Caesar's return and of the Forum bereft
of its contentions. Then, if I, joyous at Caesar welcomed
home, say anything worth hearing, the excellent part of
my voice will join in and I will sing, "O beautiful sun, O

worthy to be praised!" And while you lead on, once and
again we the entire citizenry will say, "Hail Triumph!"
"Hail Triumph!" and will offer incense to the gracious
gods. Ten bulls and ten heifers will fulfill your vows;
mine, one delicate calf who, just weaned from its mother,
grows strong feeding on plentiful grasses. His forehead
imitates the crescent fires of the moon at her third rising,
snowy white in appearance where he has a mark, otherwise tawny.]

Horace addresses Iullus Antonius, praetor in 13 B.C. and married
to Augustus's niece Marcella, but concentrates his praise on Augustus.[13] Iullus only plays the foil for the *recusatio* (*concines maiore
poeta plectro / Caesarem*, 33–34a). Antonius is better equipped to
praise Caesar. A *recusatio* in *Odes* IV does not have the same force
as in *Odes* I–III: the *CS* and its association of Horace's lyric with
Augustus's new age make Horace's claim that another is more
qualified to sing imperial praises overly trite.[14] The force of a *recusatio,* however, is not merely in the refusal but in its opportunity
for generic self-definition.[15] Horace, because of his repeated reliance on the *recusatio* to make his praise indirect, could expect his
audience to interpret critically any changes. Before in terms of
poetics the Horatian *recusatio* presented an opposition to epic, but
c.2 is a *recusatio* of Pindaric praise poetry. This shift introduces
Horace as Pindar's panegyric rival. Horace will use his disavowal
(the immoderately Pindaric Iullus is better at this sort of praise
than I) to set at odds the poetics of the *laudator* and the actual accomplishments of the *laudandus* and to demonstrate that panegyric excess belittles deeds.

Horace does not give Iullus a grand Homeric epithet as he does
Varius (*Vario . . . Maeonii carminis alite*, C.I.6). Instead, it is easy to
imagine Iullus's *Diomedeia* (twelve books like Vergil's *Aeneid*)
filled with a flooding torrent of Pindaric imitation, which Horace
effusively reviews in one long sentence (1–27a) and parodies in
the triumphant celebration near the song's end (49–52). The entire
structure is misconstrued Pindar,[16] a type of false epinikion: only
eleven lines of praise for Augustus (34–44), and at its heart a conflict between the ode's and audience's point of view. The ode's
dramatic situation has Augustus leaving for or still away in Gaul
(16–13 B.C.) so that from the perspective of Horace and Iullus,
Augustus's return and triumph over the Sygambri are future.

C.2 honors an event the poets only imagine will occur. It is a prophetic epinikion. By the time the ode was published, Horace's audience would recognize the hyperbole in Iullus's praise. Augustus, although honored greatly, chose not to celebrate a triumph over the Sygambri. Augustus set out for Gaul, but before he arrived at the front, Lollius had already vindicated his loss to the Sygambri.[17] Within view of such overstatement it is tempting, aided by the repetitious jingle of *maius meliusve* (37) and Iullus's larger lyre-pick (*maiore . . . plectro,* 33), to interpret "triumphant Augustus the greatest gift the gods will ever give though they restore the golden age" as an example of Pindar's unrestrained flood (37–40)—just the sort of panegyric Iullus might write.

The repetition of *concines* (Horace does not use such repetition lightly) suggests rather directly that verses 34–44 are Iullus's song, and there is little hope that Iullus could measure well the Augustan achievement with such Pindaric excesses as Horace's parody intimates he would incorporate. By contrast, when Horace finally adds his voice into the song (45–48), again with a touch of ironic self-deprecation (*siquid loquor audiendum*), it creates a dissonance, a conflicting decrescendo and crescendo between his conventional language of praise and the triumphal atmosphere. Unlike Iullus, Horace is only one of the crowd, singing a plain rendition of the soldier's *versus quadratus,* '*o sol / pulcher, o laudande,*'[18] the only direct praise in Horace's voice in the entire ode—traditional and short, an absurd exemplar for Pindar's rushing river. The exaggeration of the triumph becomes more apparent because Horace omits any martial praise typical for celebrating a victory and makes Augustus's primary achievement his return (42b–43, 47b–48).[19] The context of a Return Ode heightens the contrast between Horace's and Iullus's songs. A Return Ode anticipates less restraint. Horace's phrasing of the reason for the celebration, Caesar's return (*recepto / Caesare,* 47–48) recalls C.II.7 (*recepto . . . amico,* 26–28), when the poet's friend Pompey returned. Now Horace introduces Augustus's return with a picture of himself and others yelling out nondescript traditional praise. Then in the next verse Iullus returns to lead the procession to ecstatic but equally conventional cries of adulation, "*io Triumphe! . . . io Triumphe!*"[20]

Once Horace's seriocomic eulogy for Maximus dispels the notion that Horatian panegyric must be entirely serious and earnest, the poet's play with the precise panegyric tone of c.2 becomes harder to determine. Is Horace mischievously mimicking a Pindaric Iullus caught up in the celebration? Or are we to imagine the panegyrist eager to praise, but when he does, he relies on a traditional formula? Or is Horace happy to participate in the celebrations as one of the citizens with the excellent part of his voice (46)? This would bolster the *recusatio*. How serious or comic is this praise? The discrepancy in the ode's prophetic and historical perspectives plays into Horace's hands. It illustrates the conflicts inherent in panegyric when a poet is caught praising an achievement that never materializes, at least not as anticipated, or when a panegyrist allows his voice to soar to Pindaric heights.

Horace's *recusatio* shades the imperial encomium of c.2 and places his poetic at the center (25–32). The contrast appears black and white: the pretentious poetics of Pindar Iullus, the Dircaean swan, compared to Horace, the busy bee of Callimachean-Vergilian aesthetics. Then Horace elaborates on his "method and manner" with a collage of grand and slender combinations (29–32).[21] Horace as a bee is in a sympotic landscape, involved in the greatest labor, picking thyme around the Tiburtine groves (*grata carpentis thyma*[22] [*per laborem / plurimum*] *circa nemus uvidique / Tiburis*). The poet is small but fashions work-laden songs (*operosa* [*parvus*] / *carmina fingo*). In the metaphor of himself as the little bee from his native Mount Matinus, Horace surrounds the grand with the sympotic and then reverses and surrounds the slender with the grand. Here is the familiar paradox: Horace's poetry, even his panegyric, is fat and thin. Horace's praise can be Pindaric and Callimachean. Overlaying the text is the memory of C.II.20.13–16, when Horace metamorphosized into a swan more famous than Daedalus's Icarus. Horace never directly praises Antonius as "a Pindar"—*Antoni* and *Dircaeum cycnum* avoid (25–26) this—as he styles Varius "a Homer," because the real rival of Pindar, the Dircaean swan and Daedalus, is Horace.[23]

The point of Horace's *recusatio* and *komische Parodie* is that the Callimachean-Pindaric lyricist (Horace), not the effusive Pindaric Iullus, sings praise within appropriate limits. Therefore, Horace criticizes both epic and Pindaric panegyric, at least Iullus's imitation. Horace's classification of both Homer and Pindar as grand forms and his similar metaphors for each (flights and floods) do not necessarily reflect similar generic characteristics as much as a tactical shift to distinguish Horace's panegyric from the excesses of epic and Pindaric praise. Horace will not be a Homer and is the better rival of Pindar. Horace's praise only seems inferior (53–60). Horace compares his offering of one calf to Iullus's ten bulls and as many heifers, but Horace's calf is slender (*tener*) and growing vigorous (*iuvenescit*) from generous grazing (*largis . . . herbis*), another image of thinness and fatness. Lyric restraint lends vitality to praise (53–56; *iuvenescit* reverses the image of the old poet in c.1). The Callimachean aesthetic does not negate panegyric; its restraint gives praise life and strength.

C.3 and 6: The Poet among the *Nobiles*

Four odes intervene before Horace again addresses a young nobleman, and as the comparison with Pindar predicts, Horace's voice takes flight with two imperial praises (c.4–5).[24] But these panegyrics are pinned between two hymns to the poet's source of inspiration, to Melpomene (c.3) and her leader, Apollo (c.6). Horace within these hymns develops further his image as the grand lyric swan (C.II.20; IV.2). The poet's panegyric inspiration is not earthbound but heaven-sent; therefore, his praise is not directed to him by any human authority. The interdependence of c.3–6 establishes that the poet exercises a unique vatic function in Roman society as a manifestation of divine power.

Horace linked together Melpomene and Apollo only once before:

> . . . ex humili potens
>
> princeps Aeolium carmen ad Italos
> deduxisse modos. sume superbiam
> quaesitam meritis et mihi Delphica
> lauro cinge volens, Melpomene, comam. (C.III.30.12–16)
>
> [. . . from a humble beginning I became the powerful prince in shaping Aeolian song to Italian verse. Receive the pride I rightly acquired for my deeds and gladly wreathe my hair with Apollo's Delphic laurel, Melpomene.]

Horace is not just one leader among others (*princeps*), not when the preceding lines are so concerned with ritual power (*dum*

Capitolium / scandet cum tacita virgine pontifex, 8b–9; *regnavit*, 12).
Horace is affirming his preeminence in the lyric canon, a position
he envisioned at the start of the first collection (C.I.1.35–36). He realizes his vision and then some. Horace within the context of the
developing principate (Augustus established himself as the *princeps civium* particularly through the constitutional settlements,
27–23 B.C., dates roughly coincident with the writing of *Odes* I–III)
praises himself with an August tone. Given the status of the
Greek lyric canon, neither a metamorphosis into a lyric swan nor
the heights of the pyramids are any more ambitious or triumphant than Horace as an Augustus, a princeps, of the lyric
poets. These are the same self-portraits (C.II.20; III.30) Horace recalls in his fourth book (c.2, 3, 6).[25] Melpomene and Apollo, structurally enclosing the *laudationes* for Augustus and sons, set the parameters for imperial praise.

At first in c.3 the poet appears more reticent than in the epi-
logues of *Odes* II and III. The Muse's attentiveness and the poet's
thankful deference, represented in the anonymity of *quem* and
in the conditionals *si libeat* (20) and *si placeo* (24), give the ode a
solemn spirit:

> Quem tu, Melpomene, semel
>   nascentem placido lumine videris,
> illum non labor Isthmius
>   clarabit pugilem, non equus impiger
>
> curru ducet Achaico   5
>   victorem, neque res bellica Deliis
> ornatum foliis ducem,
>   quod regum tumidas contuderit minas,
>
> ostendet Capitolio:
>   sed quae Tibur aquae fertile praefluunt   10
> et spissae nemorum comae
>   fingent Aeolio carmine nobilem.
>
> Romae, principis urbium,
>   dignatur suboles inter amabilis
> vatum ponere me choros,   15
>   et iam dente minus mordeor invido.
>
> o, testudinis aureae
>   dulcem quae strepitum, Pieri, temperas,

o mutis quoque piscibus
   donatura cycni, si libeat, sonum, 20

totum muneris hoc tui est
   quod monstror digito praetereuntium
Romanae fidicen lyrae:
   quod spiro et placeo, si placeo, tuum est.

[Whom you have graced at birth, Melpomene, with your serene presence, Isthmian labor will not make him a famed boxer; a tireless horse will not lead him on to victory in Achaean chariot; martial art will not parade him to the Capitoline, a general wearing Apollo's laurel crown, because he smashed the angry, swelling threats of kings. But the waters flowing past fertile Tibur and the thick foliage of her groves will fashion him noble for his Aeolian song. The children of Rome, prince of cities, think I deserve a place in the beloved choruses of bards, and now I do not suffer criticism's envious bite. O Pierian Muse, who tunes the golden shell's sweet sound and who would easily give the swan's song even to voiceless fish if it should please you, it is entirely your reward that the passersby point me out as Rome's lyric poet; that I have the lyric breath and am so approved, if I am so approved, is your reward.]

These structural elements only thinly mask Horace's self-congratulatory tone.[26] This is the only hymnic address where Horace places the pronoun clause ahead of the vocative, and it does not modify the deity addressed. *Quem* transplants Melpomene from first position, and any sense of anonymity only emphasizes her displacement. *Quem . . . illum* is not all that general. Whom else but the poet would Melpomene bless from birth? Then there are the links to c.2 beginning with *labor Isthmius* (*laborem / plurimum*, 2.29–30). The priamel (3–9) so continues the Pindaric themes of c.2, in the same order of boxer, charioteer, and warrior (2.17–24),[27] that it is natural to assume that *quem . . . illum* is Horace before he names himself (15). The argument is the same as c.2—I am not Pindar; I surpass Pindar. Also the contrasting complement (*sed*) of the priamel pictures the same Tiburtine lyric landscape as the central panel of c.2 (30–32). The poet is still at the beginning and center of the song (9–16).

Melpomene is not completely upstaged. Her power is evident through the greatness of her poet, and a brief autobiographical moment reverses the entirety of Horace's unassuming satiric persona. The priamel denies that Horace has any claim to glory because of traditional aristocratic deeds (3–9); because of his Aeolian song he has become a nobleman (*nobilis,* the last word of the priamel and at the middle of the ode, 12). Horace's rise in status from the Horace of the *Satires* is remarkable, and Horace's allusion to C.I.1 does not allow the change to go unnoticed (*Romae, principis urbium, / dignatur suboles inter amabilis / vatum ponere me choros,* 13–15; *quod si me lyricis vatibus inseres, / sublimi feriam sidera vertice,* C.I.1.35–36). Before, Maecenas had honored Horace for his quality and character, while the citizenry refused to disregard his low birth. Now Horace does not seek the approval of a patron, because his lyric achievement has been recognized by the Roman race. The imagined onlookers of the *Satires* had envied and chided Horace because he dared to satirize others, although he lived beyond his social status (*S.*I.6.43–64; II.6.32–58); now their envy has subsided, and it is not the patron but those same citizens who count him among the love-filled choruses of the bards. Those who pass Horace on the street still point him out (*quod monstror digito praetereuntium,* 22), but their reason has changed—Horace is the Roman Pindar, *Romanae fidicen lyrae* (23). Horace transformed takes his place among the noble addressees of *Odes* IV. The ironic self-depreciation of Horace's lyric power in c.1–2 has been effectively countered.

Horace hymns Melpomene and then her master, Apollo (c.6):

> Dive, quem proles Niobea magnae
> vindicem linguae Tityosque raptor
> sensit et Troiae prope victor altae
>   Pthius Achilles,
>
> ceteris maior, tibi miles impar,   5
> filius quamvis Thetidis marinae
> Dardanas turris quateret tremenda
>   cuspide pugnax—
>
> ille, mordaci velut icta ferro
> pinus aut impulsa cupressus Euro,   10
> procidit late posuitque collum in
>   pulvere Teucro.

ille non inclusus equo Minervae
sacra mentito male feriatos
Troas et laetam Priami choreis   15
    falleret aulam,

sed palam captis gravis, heu nefas, heu,
nescios fari pueros Achivis
ureret flammis etiam latentem
    matris in alvo,   20

ni tuis flexus Venerisque gratae
vocibus divum pater annuisset
rebus Aeneae potiore ductos
    alite muros.

doctor argutae fidicen Thaliae,   25
Phoebe, qui Xantho lavis amne crinis,
Dauniae defende decus Camenae,
    levis Agyieu.

spiritum Phoebus mihi, Phoebus artem
carminis nomenque dedit poetae.   30
virginum primae puerique claris
    patribus orti,

Deliae tutela deae fugacis
lyncas et cervos cohibentis arcu,
Lesbium servate pedem meique   35
    pollicis ictum,

rite Latonae puerum canentes,
rite crescentem face Noctilucam,
prosperam frugum celeremque pronos
    volvere mensis.   40

nupta iam dices 'ego dis amicum,
saeculo festas referente luces,
reddidi carmen, docilis modorum
    vatis Horati.'

[God, you whom Niobe's children knew to be the avenger of a boastful tongue and whom the rapist Tityos acknowledged and whom Pthian Achilles nearly victorious over high Troy, greater than the other heroes, not your equal in warfare although he, the son of

sea-born Thetis, warring with his terrifying spear shook
the Dardan towers—he, like a pine struck by iron's bite
or a cypress uprooted by the East wind, fell forward flat
and laid down his neck in Teucrian dust. He would not
have shut himself in the horse, that false sacrifice for
Minerva, and deceived the Trojans caught up in their inappropriate festal day and Priam's court rejoicing in the
dances, but in the sight of all, vicious to his captives—
alas, a crime unspeakable, alas—he with Greek fires
would have burned speechless babes, even the unborn
nestling in mother's womb, if the father of the gods had
not been turned by your cries and the cries of charming
Venus and appointed for Aeneas's destiny walls built
under a better auspice. Lyric master teacher of melodious Thalia, you who bathe your tresses in the river Xan-
thus, guard the honor of the Daunian Muse, you Phoebus, smooth-faced Agyieus. Phoebus has inspired me,
given me the art of song, and named me poet. Best
noble-born lasses and lads, wards of the Delian goddess
who controls the fleeing lynxes and stags with her bow,
keep the Lesbian foot to the beat of my finger as you reverently hymn Latona's son, reverently hymn the Moon
goddess with her torch waxing, as she blesses the har-
vest and swiftly rolls on the sinking months. You will
soon be married and say, "I performed the song pleasing to the gods when the century was returning its festal days, I, learned in the verses of the bard Horace."]

Horace in c.6 continues the language of praise for his divine inspiration that ended c.3 (*fidicen . . . spiro*, c.3.23–24; *fidicen . . . spiritum Phoebus mihi . . . dedit*, c.6.25–30), but a prayer to Apollo as the
master teacher of the lyre automatically assumes political dimensions. After Actium and the dedication of the Palatine temple (31
and 28 B.C.), any prayer to Augustus's patron deity Apollo was
potential imperial panegyric. The poet's claim to be divinely inspired does not permit him to rise above the judgment that his
panegyric is bound exclusively to imperial interests.

Odes 4–6 are commonly politicized into a coherent plot line. It
had been over ten years since Actium, and Rome was secure, enjoying the Augustan peace. Horace's encomia no longer betray
any fear that civil unrest may return, as do his earlier imperial
panegyrics.[28] Although Augustus in c.5 is away from Rome, he is

in firm control. After years of civil war, the respite of peace is like a long holiday (c.5.29–40). Subsequently in c.6, the imperial panegyrist guides Augustan propaganda so that Augustus's Apollo mirrors the present peace and prosperity. The god loses his militaristic role as avenger and becomes the god of restoration and song. In short, Augustus is Apollo's emissary on earth, and Horace enjoys a particular status as Apollo's student bard. When Apollo empowers him to praise Augustan Rome, Apollo links the ruler and poet in a powerful juggernaut of imperial imaging. The circumstances of the ode's composition are taken to confirm this analysis. The ode's dramatic situation predates the performance of the *CS*. Horace anticipating this singular honor invokes Apollo's favor and encourages the chorus to make the most of their performance. Such a reading restricts the poet's boast of unending fame to his selection as the principate's spokesperson (41–44).[29] Any intimation that divine inspiration places the poet beyond imperial command, once Apollo is introduced, seems special pleading.

If the Horace of c.6 openly and without any rhetorical ploys embraces imperial favor and the glory of leading its praises, then this ode marks a watershed in Horace's career. The lyric Horace has so unmasked his patronage that there remains little if any room to interpret his song as a creative rather than reactive poetic agency. The *vates*, in spite of the emphatic *sphragis* that ends the ode (*vatis Horati*), has divested himself of his prophetic function, and consequently the ode becomes little more than the poet's affirmation of Augustan achievements. I do not mean to stigmatize patronage, when it was a strong fiber that helped hold together Roman society and was a benefit to the poet: the greater the patron, the higher his poet's status. Nevertheless, the typical portrait of Horace drawn from this ode focuses on the last four lines and the prestige that Horace gained by executing his commission without recognizing how his acceptance of this public honor would have affected his audience's perception of his work then and generations later. The poet of c.6 is keenly aware of the problem: in view of the *CS* a reader might assume after the grand imperial encomia of the last two odes that the poet has adopted the perspective of the divine Augustus. Horace, by addressing and re-creating the *CS*, alertly reasserts that this is not the case.

Admittedly, viewing c.6 as the culmination of the poet's praise for Augustus is a natural consequence of the sociopolitical environment of the late Republic, when it was common for political leaders to exploit their associations with a patron deity.[30] Octavian's devotion to Apollo began early and intensified until the god became the most potent political and religious symbol of Augustan Rome.[31] This is where c.5 and 6 begin. The parallelism in their opening addresses, specifically the repetition of the first words (*divis : dive*) and the vocatives *orte* (Caesar) and *dive* (Apollo), confirms what c.5 implies: Caesar's divine parent is Apollo. Horace amplifies Augustus's divinity by continuing in c.6 the images of light and day, the physical trait that father Apollo passed on to his son. Augustus's return will brighten the day (c.5.5–8); Horace names the sun god Phoebus three times in four lines (c.6.26–29). In the ritual celebrations that end each ode divine light is present in the drinking from sunrise to sunset, a complete journey of Phoebus across the sky (c.5.37–40), and in the dawn of a new age (c.6.41–42).

The symbolism of divine light, parallel to the *CS*, anticipates that the Apollo of c.6 will be a nurturing deity of restored Rome. What is shocking about the hymn is how quickly and thoroughly Horace replaces the Apollo of restoration and peace (c.5) with the Apollo of vengeance (c.6.1–24). An admonitory Apollo, although not without precedent in Horace, is not the poet's customary characterization. Apollo can be a symbol of restoration (C.I.7.21–32; III.3.65–68) or strictly admonitory (C.I.12.21–24; IV.15.1–4), but most often these traits are held in tension (C.I.21.9–16; II.10.17–20; III.4.60–68). Horace's Apollo is persistent in his dual roles. Horatian poetry shows no established pattern in which Apollo transitions from a state of revenge to restoration. Apollo is a simple duality: the same god capable of punishing the proud or healing the humble. Such contrasting powers compel the poet to invoke the god's blessing, pray for his protection, and direct his hostilities toward the enemy. Therefore, Apollo, god of war and healing, represents the conflation in Horatian lyric between the serious and comic and embodies the argument that the poet's lyre is strong enough to encapsulate epic's martial themes.[32]

Horace in c.6 leaves Apollo's nature unbalanced, devoting almost complete attention to the god's admonitory function against hubristic speech (1–20). Nowhere else does Horace so lavishly illustrate the avenging Apollo (on Niobe, Tityos, and Achilles).

Horace permits Apollo's part in the restoration of Troy, and consequently the Roman people, only four lines (21–24), and Apollo must share credit with Venus.[33] Neither does Phoebus's act of inspiring his poet (25–31) transition away from divine vengeance and violence. In the second half of the ode, Apollo's sister is also armed (33b–34). That Horace minimizes the god's role as nurturer makes the Apollo of c.6 quite different from Apollo in the *CS*. The *CS* asks Apollo to put down his bow; and although Apollo retains his weapon (34–35), by the end of the song the bow becomes one of the frequent images of light (2a, 9–10a, 23–24) that no longer threatens but promises healing (61–68). The *CS* balances the god's dual nature but leans decidedly toward a nurturing Apollo. He can be triumphant but should be generous to the vanquished (49–56), and since he granted Aeneas's escape, he should not fail to rebuild Rome's future (41–48). The Apollo of the *CS* has much more in common with the Augustus of c.5 than the angry Apollo of c.6.

Apollo's wrath against Niobe, Tityos, and Achilles brings to the forefront of Horace's hymn crimes of sexual violence against the individual and the consequences that these have for the family (1–8). Horace compresses into his lyric mythology the psychology of tyranny, the propensity to commit hubristic crimes of status that claim a position of domination to which the tyrant is not by nature or merit entitled. Niobe's boast that the number of her children proved her superiority to Leto did not just insultingly question Leto's authority; it also mocked the wound left by Zeus's rape and Leto's flight from the anger of his wife Hera. When Leto visited her son in Delphi, Tityos viewed her as an easy victim who had already been violated once, followed his father Zeus's example, and attempted to rape Leto again. Apollo answered his mother's cry, when her personhood, sexuality, autonomy, and physical well-being were threatened.[34] Achilles, whose lineage was not as high as that of Zeus born Tityos, would have annihilated the entire Trojan family, if Apollo had not intervened.

What might this have to do with Augustus, Apollo, and a *carmen saeculi referentis*? Horace places c.6 in an interesting position—published after the *CS*, the performance of which the ode anticipates. More specifically, the ode's form and occasion, a hymn to the gods of the new age, align it with the *CS*, but the recasting of Apollo makes it potentially corrective to the *CS* and c.5.

Isolating the ode within only one of its time referents, namely prior to the *CS*, causes undue accentuation, even fabrication, of a transition from a vengeful to peaceful Apollo. There has been a failure to account for the ode's angry militarism, particularly of the mythological exempla. An audience reading Horace's mythology back into the *CS* within an openly panegyric context could see Augustus through Apollo. As Apollo took vengeance on the enemies of his mother and triumphed in the restoration of his family, so his son Octavian avenged his father Julius Caesar and brought a new age of peace to his fellow Romans.[35] But since the Apollo of c.6 is so at variance with c.5 and the *CS* and since the ode's mythology casts the god in an admonitory role, the ode within the movement of the book has as much potential to restrain as expand the praise of c.5.

After Verg. *Ecl.*6.3–5, the first time in the Augustans that Apollo restricts martial praise poetry, the god rarely appears as a warning figure in Latin poetry.[36] It seems significant then in light of the opportune merging of Callimachean-Vergilian poetics with an Apollo who would have his poets sing of Rome's peace that Horace instead highlights Augustus's Apollo as a violent admonitory deity after two imperial praises, one being an epinikion (c.4).[37] After the poet comes as close to the adulation of a deified Augustus as any imperial praise (c.5), he introduces an Apollo who avenges the boastful.[38] What is more, the mythological trio are guilty of claiming equality to or even superiority over a god. Horace's pithy definition of Achilles' heroic dilemma (*ceteris maior, tibi miles impar*, 5) puts divine ancestry in perspective: gods procreate with mortals and produce other mortals lesser than themselves who must by their deeds achieve immortality — Augustus included (c.5.34–36; *Epist.*II.5–10). The only exceptions were Apollo and his sister. Horace's mythology vividly illustrates both that Augustus's divinity is of a different sort from Apollo's, since Augustus's divinity is dependent on the judgment of others (panegyric), and that exaggerated claims of divinity are dangerous.

It is possible at this point to draw some preliminary conclusions about Horatian encomia. Horace's praise does not fit the either/or of the pro-Augustan versus anti-Augustan dichotomy, which has been the mainstay of Horatian studies, especially regarding *Odes* IV.[39] I do not intend to argue that Horace simply subverts the imperial praise of c.4 and 5—the oppositional approach is far too easy—but to show how readily a Horatian praise ode supports either position. Horace constructs his panegyric to admit disputes (*dubia*) and conflicting viewpoints as is evident from the eulogy for Maximus, the *recusatio* to Iullus, the positioning of c.6 (its dramatic date versus publication date) and its mythological exempla. Consequently, Horace's panegyric praxis by its nature provokes debate. Such a patterning within the encomia permits the panegyric poet to explore the process by which praise is generated, to reveal the complex interactions among the *laudandus, laudator,* and the evaluations of the audience. By implication the Augustan ideology to which the praise poet supposedly reacts cannot be the sole possession of any one authority but is subject to the volatile climate of communal interpretation, the outcome of which cannot be predicted. C.6 constitutes such an interpretive event. The poet imagines his hymn as a choral performance that causes him to pray for Apollo's defense. C.6 as performance contradicts the notion of a poet who has withdrawn into community in order to abdicate his public role. Instead, the poet assumes the vital role of mediator between the various public sectors (*duces* and *cives*) that compose one political sphere. The panegyric poet creates the interpretive opportunity for ideas to be shaped into a shared cultural-political discourse and therefore is a co-creator of ideology rather than in a responsive position as a mere reporter. Horatian panegyric is a lesson in how poetics produces meaning.

Up to this point my discussion of c.6 has responded to the main focus of other studies, the relationship of Apollo to Augustan Rome. The conceptual unity of c.6, however, insists the song is primarily about Apollo and the poet. Disregarding the poet's prayer for divine aid and his defensive posture has pushed the poetics of c.6 aside, and the persistent reading of the ode within a specific historical setting (prior *CS*) has dissected it into two loosely connected halves. Horace faces two criticisms: [1] the transitions from addressing the god to the chorus (30–31) to a single chorister (41) are so abrupt that the hymnic prayer has little to do with the personal nature of the ode's conclusion, and [2] the mythological exempla (1–3) and the *intermissio* on the death of Achilles (9–24) do not support a coherent argument for both the hymn and address to the chorus.[40] The answers to these objections illustrate an artistry so intensely introspective that the poet's stance naturally shifts from a defensive to offensive posture: Horace again asserts within a panegyric mode the eloquent power of his lyric and his immortal fame as its director (χοροδιδάσκαλος).

The first objection proves easier to answer. Horace is imitating Pindar. Fraenkel, elaborating on Heinze (Kiessling and Heinze, 1908), cites Pindar's sixth paean as the model for c.6. The occasions and content of the two lyrics are similar (the poet anticipating a performance of his hymn to Apollo). The paean praises Apollo for the slaying of Achilles (78–91) and includes an abrupt transition from the poet addressing the god to instructing the chorus (121). Horace follows Pindar's lead and adopts the same general structure for his ode.[41]

Fraenkel's argument begins to reassociate the ode with the thematic progression of *Odes* IV. Horace in c.2 put himself forward as Pindar's rival and in c.3 his more accomplished successor. With c.6 Horace then demonstrates his command of a particular Pindaric hymn-form. Horace had done the same in *Satires* I when he backed up his criticism of Lucilius with a direct imitation of a Lucilian satire (s.4, 5). This is a case in point that it is possible to answer the criticism about Horace's *techne* in c.6 with structural paradigms common to the *Odes* without recourse to a specific Pindaric paean. Horatian odes often move swiftly from the general to the specific and personal within a single ode and from one ode to another. Such movement collapses the private versus public dichotomy, a boundary that is not as fixed in Horace as for the modern reader. For example, Horace waits until the close of C.I.1 to make himself the cap of the priamel. A hymn to Mercury (C.I.10) is followed by the *carpe diem* ode to Leuconoë (11), an ode praising Augustus (12), and then the poet's anger over a love triangle (13). C.III.14 turns quickly from a public ritual celebration of Augustus's return to a private party, presumably to celebrate the same occasion.[42] If Cairns is correct that the first half of C.IV.6 is the song to Apollo that the poet imagines in the second,[43] there is no shortage of such parallels in other Horatian hymns (C.I.32; IV.15)[44] and in the poet's sympotic invitations when the drinking party promised is depicted as ongoing in the same ode (C.I.17; II.7; III.19). Such poetic constructs are a consequence of lyric compression where the distinction between the present and future is blurred. The move from a hymn to its performance in c.6 is no more abrupt than transitions in other Horatian lyrics.

The second objection, that the violence of the mythology and the *intermissio* does not align with the occasion of the hymn's performance, the celebration for a new age of peace, is more complex. The traditional response is exclusively political: there is within c.6 a transition from the vengeful Apollo to the peaceful lyric Apollo who restored Rome and now inspires the poet.[45] Such a view reduces the violence of Apollo to a past and lesser interest in the ode (and attempts to rebalance what the poet obviously did not) so that the praise is forced to fit the constraints of a supposed imperial propaganda that after Actium sought to repress symbols of the past civil wars.[46] To return to metaphor: there was a movement away from the violent acts of vengeance displayed on the doors of Apollo's Palatine temple and toward the Altar of Peace. Horace's ode takes the opposite direction: the theme of vengeance (half the ode) reverses the standard chronology for Augustan imaging by lingering at the temple doors. This is a startling reversal in a book so intimately connected with monumental Rome and specifically the Altar of Peace. Any transition in the figure of Apollo from war to peace is diminutive and incomplete.

The unity of the ode cannot be found by subordinating the personal to the political (or the political to the personal) and ignoring that the ode is a hymnic prayer from the poet about a public occasion. The poem's private and public aspects are inseparable. Horace in his hymns does not always make specific requests, but here he makes two, both concerning his poetic: that Apollo defend his Italian Muse (27) and that the chorus guard his Lesbian lyric (35–36). The continuation of the ode's martial tone in both imperatives is telling (*defende; servate*). The lyric poet places himself in a defensive posture that requests the protection of a warring god and support from his followers. Horace in a battle of poetics musters the divine (Phoebus's inspiration) and earthly realms (human performance). The poet literally surrounds himself with his god (*Phoebus mihi Phoebus*, 29). Even here it has proven impossible to escape from the tendency to interpret the ode as strictly pre-*CS*, and consequently the battle has often been explained as the pressure Horace felt over going public. Horace is asking that Apollo by his divine inspiration and the chorus by their hard practice spare him public embarrassment. The sentimentality of the situation has a strong appeal: the humble poet nervously anticipating his official debut. The dramatic and extended description of Apollo's wrath and his victory over Achilles would indeed be excessive even for the most severe case of performance butterflies. A nervous poet does not fit the general boldness of Horace's lyric persona, certainly not this ode. The poet's prediction of success in the last strophe would require an extremely rapid metamorphosis in his attitude over the ode's second half. C.6 instead responds to the success of the *CS* and what official recognition would mean for the Horatian lyric persona. The battle is for Horace's lyric *ego*. Horace's acceptance of imperial commissions could well affect audience perception. Horace's feigned distance from weighty imperial concerns and policies that was much of his strategy for asserting his independent agency risks the credibility necessary to retain its seriocomic force, on which the *recusatio* of c.2 depends. Horace continues to clarify the identity of his lyric persona, especially after the sympotic disavowal of c.1. Is the lyric Horace the same or not?

Horace connects the direct addresses (1–8, 25–30, 31–40), the *intermissio* (9–24), and the *sphragis* (41–44) in structure and theme to form an *apologia* against the notion that direct panegyric has changed his lyric persona. First the *intermissio* supports Horace's prayer to the god and instruction to the chorus to preserve his lyric by setting out the generic breadth of his poetic, and then the *sphragis* champions the grandeur of Horace's contribution to the lyric tradition. C.6 is a microcosm of the Horatian poetry book, odes carefully crafted together, relating a trove of human experiences, defying generic boundaries, and ending with the poet reveling in his success. In spite of the familiarity of its argument and conceptual arrangements, c.6 is atypical of Horatian structures. The ode's eleven stanzas have no center, which is highly unusual for odes with an odd number of stanzas, and the poem resists any bipartite division. Instead, the symmetrical pattern is disrupted by a four-stanza insertion (9–24) and a one-stanza accretion (41–44). Horace is being Pindaric. If the *intermissio* and *sphragis* were removed, the symmetry would return (two direct addresses, twelve verses each: 1–8, 25–28; 29–40), but not completely since Horace inserts a third-person tribute to Apollo that delays the address to the chorus (29–30). Horace by this slight disruption ensures that the second-person addresses and third-person narratives remain inseparable. The song cannot be broken apart.

Although the *intermissio* is an intricate part of the ode's overall dynamic, it interrupts with syntactic violence the direct address and begins a movement and countermovement between the second and third person. In other words, the poet sets up a violent struggle between direct address and third-person narrative, which metaphorically supports the panegyric conflicts that he senses and then resolves in his address to the chorus. Achilles (9–24) temporarily usurps Apollo's place as the subject of the hymn, and the god recovers his rightful position only after killing his opponent. With Achilles' death, the direct address resumes (Phoebus regains control), but before moving on to address the chorus, the poet returns briefly to third-person narrative (29–30). Now, however, the distinction between narrative and direct address is blurred. The poet receives the answer to his prayer for Phoebus's help (29–30). It is as if he is reporting an imagined second-person address by Apollo: I inspired you and named you, poet. The conflation of narration and address continues in the poet's instructions to the chorus. The address to the chorus returns the deity (this time Diana) to the objective position but as an entity to be reverenced rather than challenged. The narratological rivalry between Achilles and Apollo is replaced by hymnic praise, the poet's song that makes his instruction to the chorus, if they obey, an address to the goddess (37–40). The poet's song resolves the structural conflicts he set in motion by blending together direct address and narrative, that is, inspiration and panegyric discourse. The ode's conclusion (41–44) comes with a bit of a jolt when the direct address to one female chorister gives the poem's final praise to the choirmaster. But his is not the vain boast of a Niobe, Tityos, or Achilles, because the poet's voice has already been placed in complete harmony with the god's. Horace is Apollo's prophet and the teacher of his lyre (*doctor*, 25 . . . *docilis*, 43). Consequently, a poem that begins as if Augustus will be so closely identified with Apollo that he will become divine ends instead with the poet more nearly so.

The song's defense of Apollo's/the poet's lyre incorporates the emotive nucleus of the sympotic *carpe diem* argument: the seductive party, the sexual tension of coming to age, and the brevity of life. The youthful Apollo bathes his hair in the river and teaches his song to Thalia, the beautiful Muse of festive revelry.[47] The seductive power of the moment matches the eroticism of Horace's invitations to Lyde and Phyllis to learn and share his song (C.III.28; IV.11). When Horace addresses the chorus, the virgin Diana has her bow bent. Her threatening posture suggests that she barely still restrains her human charges, the unwed choristers, who are on the verge of becoming the young married maiden who boasts of her lyric past. The Moon goddess marks how swiftly the months roll by (cf. C.II.11.10–11; IV.7.13). The sequence simulates scenes from any number of sympotic odes (I.17.13–28; I.38; II.3.5–12; 5.5–24; 7.17–28; 11.13–17), not least C.I.1.19–22, when the poet enjoys his day lazing beside a stream with a good wine.

Horace's sympotic lyre is not lightweight. Although this hymn contains no overt *recusatio* of *epos* — the admonitory Apollo does not intervene and change the poet's direction (see c.15) — the ode, as is typical of Horatian epic disavowals, does blend lyric and epic themes, specifically the inclusion of an epic battle within the sympotic world of the lyric Apollo. The violent *intermissio* displays the intertextual depth of Horatian lyric. The multiplicity of sources appears endless: Achilles' death by Apollo (Pi. *Paean* 6, which includes a contrary to fact condition that Troy would have been sacked if Apollo had not intervened; Hom. *Il*.19.409–14; 22.358–60) and the manner of Achilles' death, stretched out in the dust (Hom. *Od*.24.39–40) and fallen like a tree (Hom. *Il*.13.389–93; 16.480–86; Simon. fr.11.1–12 W.; Cat. 64.105–11; Verg. *A*.5.446–49).[48] Each intersection adds its own nuance to Horace's retelling, and therefore the *intermissio* is an eloquent apology for the marvelous capacity of Horatian lyric to look thin but be fat. This Horatian mythological narrative has been very well fed.

After the metaphor of the fallen tree, the intertextual dialogue narrows. In this way the metaphor represents a transition. Once Vergil's voice is heard, from then on the mythological narrative draws from the *Aeneid*. Horace's Trojan horse (*ille non inclusus equo Minervae / sacra mentito*, 13–14a; *votum pro reditu simulant* ... / *huc delecta virum sortiti corpora furtim / includunt caeco lateri*, *A*.2.17–19a), the ill-omened chorus (*sacra* ... *male feriatos / Troas et laetam Priami choreis / falleret aulam*, 14–16; ... *pueri circum innuptaeque puellae / sacra canunt*, *A*.2.238–39a), and the pleas of

Venus (21–22) owe more to Aeneas's storytelling than Demod-
ocus's.[49] The intertextual progression puts Vergil forward as
Homer's heir. Therefore, when Horace names the Muse Thalia
first before Phoebus, he is likely continuing his close interaction
with Vergil, specifically with eclogue 6 and the bucolic poet's
turned epicist's prelude to his earlier reinvention of the Callimachean dictum (*Prima Syracosio dignata est ludere versu / nostra
neque erubuit silvas habitare Thalea,* 1–2). Horace has called Vergil
on the ironic play of his *recusatio*. After sustained allusions to the
Aeneid, Horace's return back to Vergil's comic Theocritean Thalia,
who did not blush at rustic verses, challenges the implication of
Vergil's martial epic project — that for Horace Vergil's *Aeneid* con-
stituted a potential disavowal of Vergil's past poetic and its
strategies for asserting the poet's authority (such as the pretense
of the *recusatio*), both of which Horace refuses to abandon.[50] Horace's Muse once and for all is Apollo's lyric Thalia. Vergil's apparent reversal and Horace's resistance to any change are part of
the conflict behind his prayer to Apollo that the god defend the
glory of his poet's Daunian Muse and enhance the significance of
Horace's reference to his own Italian countryside (Daunus was
the mythic king of Apulia). Horace looks back across the *Aeneid* to
the bucolic, more lyric Vergil.[51]

Lyric Apollo and his poet Horace form one voice. When the
poet's *ego* speaks through the chorister (41–44), it adopts the role
of Apollo's priest and ends the ode in the same mantic voice that
Propertius develops in his praise for Palatine Apollo and Augustus (4.6.1–2, 5–10).[52] The *sphragis* is nothing less than Horace's
prophecy that his name will prove immortal. Augustus promised
to return to Rome (*redi,* c.5.4); Horace, after he dies, will return in
the performance of his songs (*reddidi,* 43). The supposition behind
Horace's instruction to the choir is that interpretation is part of
the ritual vatic process. Apollo, the teacher (*doctor*) of Thalia, inspires the poet-priest, who in turn teaches the chorister (*docilis*).
The combined choral performance of god, poet, and singer produces the poet's praise. The resulting panegyric is powerful religious ritual, the *carmen saeculare*.

The communal nature of Horatian panegyric should not be
taken to diminish the role of the poet nor detract from what a potent anomaly the arrangement of c.3–6 really is. It was not

uncommon for other Augustan and later writers (Vergil, Propertius, Ovid, Martial, Statius, Pliny) to revere their patrons as sources of inspiration or at least a support for their *ingenium*.[53] The closest Horace ever comes is C.I.1 when he says that Maecenas is his guardian (*praesidium*) and sweet honor (*dulce decus*). In c.3-6 Horace does the opposite: he surrounds the first duet of imperial praises with his own claims to be uniquely blessed by the gods and asks for Phoebus's protection, the very same god who destroyed the boastful. Horace's point could not be more definitively expressed. He is still Rome's divine prophetic voice, *vates Horatius.*

There is much in Horace's c.6 that is the same. Horace's effective modeling of Pindaric *techne* confirms that he should be enrolled in the lyric canon. The poet's reaffirmation of his sympotic persona reveals completely the ironic character of his disavowal of sympotic lyric (c.1) and introduces the *carpe diem* ode to Torquatus (c.7). Horace has not sworn off Venus nor will his old age lack Apollo's lyre (C.I.31.17-20). Apollo is dependent on his prophet for his voice — to make him come alive.[54] Inside the Palatine temple, in front of which the *CS* was performed, stood Apollo holding his lyre, mute, if it were not for the poets' songs:

> hic equidem Phoebo visus mihi pulchrior ipso
> marmoreus tacita carmen hiare lyra
>
> deinde inter matrem deus ipse interque sororem
> Pythius in longa carmina veste sonat. (Prop. 2.31.5-6, 15-16)
>
> [This marble statue opening its mouth to sing with its silent lyre seemed to me more beautiful than Phoebus in person. . . . Then between mother and sister the Pythian god himself, wearing his long robe, sings his songs.]

Horace and Propertius are on the same page. Horace breathes out his divine breath (*spiritum*) in c.8 and 9, when he rivals the immortality of the physical arts (8.13-15a), and breathes life back into Sappho (9.10b-12), just as Propertius gives the marble Apollo his song. Horace's lyric, a living monument sung and sung again, becomes the embodiment of cyclical immortal time (*saeculo referente*, c.6.42). Horace the panegyrist cannot be defined with regard to only the *laudatus* either quantitatively (the extent of the praise) or qualitatively (the poetic for the praise).

C.7: Panegyric and Politics, Putting Off Heirs

A. E. Housman's "most beautiful poem in Latin literature" can appear even more beautiful by comparison to its surroundings.[55] Among all the panegyric morass of *Odes* IV, c.7 has stood out as an oasis of Horatian artful pleasure, the lyric poet as he once was in *Odes* I–III:

> Diffugere nives, redeunt iam gramina campis
>   arboribusque comae;
> mutat terra vices et decrescentia ripas
>   flumina praetereunt.
>
> Gratia cum Nymphis geminisque sororibus audet   5
>   ducere nuda choros.
> immortalia ne speres, monet annus et almum
>   quae rapit hora diem.
>
> frigora mitescunt Zephyris, ver proterit aestas
>   interitura, simul   10
> pomifer autumnus fruges effuderit; et mox
>   bruma recurrit iners.
>
> damna tamen celeres reparant caelestia lunae:
>   nos ubi decidimus
> quo pius Aeneas, quo Tullus dives et Ancus,   15
>   pulvis et umbra sumus.
>
> quis scit an adiciant hodiernae crastina summae
>   tempora di superi?
> cuncta manus avidas fugient heredis, amico
>   quae dederis animo.   20
>
> cum semel occideris et de te splendida Minos
>   fecerit arbitria,
> non, Torquate, genus, non te facundia, non te
>   restituet pietas.
>
> infernis neque enim tenebris Diana pudicum   25
>   liberat Hippolytum,
> nec Lethaea valet Theseus abrumpere caro
>   vincula Pirithoo.

[The snows have scattered away, and now the grass is returning to the fields and the leaves to the trees; the earth is

changing her seasons and the subsiding rivers are flowing
along their banks. The Grace with the nymphs and her own
twin sisters dares to lead the dances naked. Do not hope for
immortality, warns the year and the hour that snatches away
the nourishing day. Zephyrs warm winter's cold, summer
heat tramples on spring and is sure to pass on swiftly as soon
as fertile autumn has poured out her fruit, and soon hiber-
nating winter runs round again. But swiftly moons repair
their absence from the heavens; we, when we sink down
where dutiful Aeneas, where rich Tullus and Ancus are, we
are dust and shadows. Who knows whether the gods above
will add tomorrow's time to today's total? Only what you
have spent on your own dear self will escape the greedy
hands of your heir. Once you die and Minos has passed his
righteous sentence on you, not your lineage, Torquatus, not
your eloquence, not your piety will raise you to life again. Indeed, not even Diana sets Hippolytus free from the darkness
of the dead, and Theseus is not strong enough to break his
beloved Pirithous free from Lethaean bonds.]

I will not to burden c.7 with a detailed structural analysis, since
I do not want to misrepresent the effect of the ode within the moments of book IV. C.7 is a panegyric pause, but as any persuasive
orator knows, pauses are stuffed with meaning. The task is to re-
connect the ode to its context through recognizing its unique
contribution to the collection. C.7 so thoroughly muddles the
boundaries of private and public, the poetics of *carpe diem* and
Realpolitik, that it is impossible to interpret the coming odes (10–
13) as some poorly executed Pindaric digression.

When *Odes* IV returns to the *nobiles* (c.7–9), the first addressee,
Torquatus, is strangely out of step with the book's other political
insiders. He is the only one of the nobles distinguished by a second address. In *Epist.*I.5 Horace invited Torquatus, a busy lawyer,
to set aside his clients' concerns and enjoy a drinking party. Horace casts Torquatus not as a political figure but as his friend. Although Horace tells us too little about Torquatus to substantiate
his identification as Manlius Torquatus, the son or grandson of
L. Manlius Torquatus (consul when Horace was born, 65 B.C.),
it is reasonably certain that this Torquatus never held political
office.[56] Torquatus, therefore, represents an older apolitical character compared to the young Maximus and Iullus, whose careers

were bolstered by marriage alliances with the imperial family. This is not an obscure point, but the beginning of the collection: one ode to Maximus, the soon-to-be-husband of Augustus's cousin, followed by another to Iullus, the husband of Augustus's niece. Torquatus is noticeably not in the family, a political outsider.

Why would Horace anchor *Odes* IV at its near center and introduce odes to Censorinus and Lollius with a *carpe diem* ode to a peer whose political career had not distinguished him among the *nobiles*? Certainly the ode breaks the panegyric mode of c.1–6. The person of Torquatus, the argument of the ode, and its prominent position in the collection prevent the conclusion that the poet routinely represents imperial interests. Only the most indirect panegyric leaves room for a Torquatus. And yet a *carpe diem* ode is particularly apt after the reaffirmation of Horace's sympotic lyric persona in c.6. For the poet to place a *carpe diem* lyric in a panegyric context after honoring Melpomene and Apollo for their inspiration is a remarkable statement of poetic authority. The poet will not push aside his lyric world and all that it implies from *Odes* I–III, including its epic criticism and formulaic aversion to praise poetry. Through c.7 Horace provides another instance of a persistent poetic *arete* that is the heart of the odes to Censorinus and Lollius (c.8–9).

Horatian poetics again lead back to the political background of *Odes* IV. Not far from view is the Horace of c.1 who disavowed his sympotic *carpe diem* world. Horace's reaffirmation of his lyric voice begins immediately: the sympotic landscape at the center of the *recusatio* (c.2), supported by divine inspiration (c.3, 6), culminating in a *carpe diem* ode (c.7). There is some change; Horace's *carpe diem* is not exactly the same. Missing throughout is any sympotic celebration of the type common in *Odes* I–III. Horace does not cap the *recusatio* of c.2 with a declaration that he will sing only of sympotic pleasures, as he did its counterpart in the first collection (I.6.17–20), but with a triumphal celebration for Augustus (42–60). C.6 sketches the argument for sympotic celebration, Apollo bathing his hair, the beauty of song and the transience of life, but there is no party, unless it is the celebration of the *novum saeculum* the poet claims as his own. C.7 appears the perfect traditional *carpe diem* argument—the transience of life portrayed by the changing seasons, the gods' control of the future, and the

permanence of death—but it alone of Horace's *carpe diem* poems
excludes any sympotic image.[57] Horace's omission of a sympotic
invitation to enjoy the present results in a more serious tone that
recalls the *carpe diem* warning to Postumus (II.14). Postumus is so
frugal he cheats himself out of any pleasures his riches afford. He
will bequeath his wine, sympotic pleasures, to an intemperate
heir:[58]

> absumet heres Caecuba dignior
> servata centum clavibus et mero
>   tinget pavimentum superbo,
>   pontificum potiore cenis. (25–28)

> [A more worthy heir will waste the Caecuban you keep
> under hundreds of locks and keys and will stain the
> pavement with your haughty wine, a choicer vintage
> than at the feasts of priests.]

Against all the expectations created by sympotic Horace's principle of *moderatio*, Postumus's heir is "more worthy" (*dignior*). In
spite of his extremely immoderate behavior (*absumet, mero . . . su-
perbo, tinget,* and *pontificum potiore*), the heir at least enjoys the
present with an immediacy befitting the shortness of life.[59] Frugal
Postumus, erring by excessive moderation, not only misses life's
pleasures but will join the greatest sinners, Geryon, Tityos, the
daughters of Danaus, and Sisyphus (7b–12).[60]

　　Inescapable death also awaits Torquatus; nevertheless, the pessimism of c.7 is not as penetrating as its prequel (C.II.14). Horace
draws out inviting scenes in nature and the renewal of seasons for
nearly half the ode (1–12), and although his descriptions include
a sinister side (summer trampling spring to death, 9b–10a), they
offer a more seductive beginning to the song than Postumus's
sacrifices failing to stop time's steady march. Heroes and kings,
Aeneas, Tullus, Ancus, and the bright judgments of Minos, not
tormented criminals, wait to welcome Torquatus. Horace's
change to a less menacing tone reflects the different addressees.
Horace does not represent Torquatus as a miser deserving censure, but Horace does jog his friend's memory by repeating the
advice from his earlier letter to him that it is insane to hold back
(like a Postumus) from life's pleasures for the sake of an heir:

Quo mihi fortunam, si non conceditur uti?
parcus ob heredis curam nimiumque severus
assidet insano. potare et spargere flores
incipiam patiarque vel inconsultus haberi. (*Epist.* I.5.12–15)

cuncta manus avidas fugient heredis, amico
quae dederis animo. (*C.* IV.7.19–20)

[What good is my fortune, if not to enjoy it? Being frugal and
excessively strict in order to look out for an heir is nearly insane. I
will start off the drinking and scattering flowers, and I do not care
if anyone thinks me thoughtless.]

[Only what you have spent on your own dear self will escape the
greedy hands of your heir.]

Horace shifts the focus from a father guarding his estate in order
to secure his son's future (*C.* II. 14; *Epist.* I.5) to the heir anxious to
inherit. Now the heir is not worthier but has grasping hands.

To return to the original question, the possible political dimensions of c.7—Horace begins the central panel of book IV with a
poem on the certainty of death from which neither Torquatus nor
epic Aeneas can escape. Only things not reserved for heirs escape
the consequences of mortality. By placing the eager heirs of c.7
among the encomiastic litany of young nobles, Horace conjures
up the impression of an older Augustus's concern and prepara-
tion for a successor.[61] What appears a private concern for Torquatus is for an aging Augustus and the Roman public Realpolitik.
Horace does not make this application a great stretch. The ode
could have ended well at verse 24, but Horace adds two intercon-
nected mythic exempla (told in present time) to make the point
(25–28). Hippolytus and Theseus together, an infamous story of
seduction, family rivalry, and misunderstanding with the most
tragic consequences,[62] summarize well for Augustus, his family,
and the *nobiles* around them the dangers of *ambitio* and of the intrigues surrounding great households, especially during transitions of power. The ode to Torquatus would find in the noble addressees of *Odes* IV a most empathetic audience.

C.8 and 9: As the Wor(l)d Turns, Praise and Blame

C.8 and 9 deserve special attention. They are the last of the *encomia nobilium* and the heart of *Odes* IV, marked out by their meters (Asclepiadean, c.8; Alcaic, c.9) that correspond to those of c.1 (Asclepiadean) and 15 (Alcaic). Although c.8–9 are at the middle of the collection, they represent extremes, as Horace tests the limits of panegyric propriety and impropriety — the first a generic set piece to Censorinus and the second a suspect encomium for Lollius.

C.8: Censorinus

Donarem pateras grataque commodus,
Censorine, meis aera sodalibus,
donarem tripodas, praemia fortium
Graiorum, neque tu pessima munerum
ferres, divite me scilicet artium   5
quas aut Parrhasius protulit aut Scopas,
hic saxo, liquidis ille coloribus
sollers nunc hominem ponere, nunc deum:

sed non haec mihi vis, nec tibi talium
res est aut animus deliciarum egens.   10
gaudes carminibus; carmina possumus
donare et pretium dicere muneri.

non incisa notis marmora publicis,
per quae spiritus et vita redit bonis
post mortem ducibus, [non celeres fugae   15
reiectaeque retrorsum Hannibalis minae,
non incendia Karthaginis impiae
eius qui domita nomen ab Africa
lucratus rediit] clarius indicant
laudes quam Calabrae Pierides; neque   20

si chartae sileant quod bene feceris,
mercedem tuleris. quid foret Iliae
Marvortisque puer, si taciturnitas
obstaret meritis invida Romuli?

ereptum Stygiis fluctibus Aeacum   25
virtus et favor et lingua potentium

vatum divitibus consecrat insulis.
[dignum laude virum Musa vetat mori]
caelo Musa beat. sic Iovis interest
optatis epulis impiger Hercules,   30
clarum Tyndaridae sidus ab infimis
quassas eripiunt aequoribus ratis,
[ornatus viridi tempora pampino]
Liber vota bonos ducit ad exitus.

[I would give bowls and pleasing bronzes readily, Censorinus, to my comrades; I would give tripods, the rewards of Greek heroes; and you would win not the least of the prizes, if I, of course, were rich in the crafts that either Parrhasius displayed or Scopas, both talented, the one in sculpting and the other in liquid paints, to fashion now a mortal, now a god. But I do not have this power; neither does your wealth nor inclination beg such dainties. You take pleasure in song; songs we can give, and we can name the value of the service. No, marble inscribed with public notices, through which good leaders regain breath and life after death, do not—not Hannibal's swift flight and his threats turned back, not the fiery destruction of impious Carthage—more effectively praise him who gained his fame by conquering Africa and returning home than do the Calabrian Muses; and if my pages should pass by your good deeds in silence, you would not gain the reward due. What would have become of the child of Ilia and Mars, if jealous silence blocked out Romulus's just rewards? The character and good will and song of powerful bards stole Aeacus from the Stygian waves and set him on the Isles of the Blessed. The Muse forbids that a hero worthy of praise die. The Muse blesses with the renown of heaven. Thus spirited Hercules partakes of the desired feasts of Jove; the sons of Tyndareus, bright stars, rescue sea-battered ships from the ocean's depths; Liber, his head adorned with green vine, brings vows to successful conclusion.]

The unstable text of c.8 and the resulting interpretive questions remain unresolved.[63] These difficulties are only compounded, however, by the presumption that the poem is an entirely earnest panegyric. Only the basic thesis is undisputed: poetry has the power to spare heroes an ignominious death. The poet destroys death's permanence, which dominated the previous ode, with nothing short of resurrection (*per quae spiritus et vita redit bonis / post mortem ducibus,* 14-15). Bards by their own character (*virtus*), blessing (*favor*), and word (*lingua*) can do what the goddess Diana and the hero Theseus could not (c.7)—defy death and rescue even Aeacus from the Stygian floods (25-27). Hannibal, P. Scipio Africanus, Hercules, and the Dioscuri, all saved by the Muse, overshadow Censorinus. The panegyric is the poem itself, a tribute for Censorinus theoretically to ensure his undying fame.[64] The encomium holds center stage, but Censorinus's deeds do not.

What is peculiar is the paradox that in a poem presenting the poet as the author of immortality, the gift of praise is so empty of any of Censorinus's accomplishments that it fails to be a lasting memorial. This is not the expectation created by the opening lines. The Pindaric priamel, passing by the heroic awards of the Greeks and the visual arts, makes poetry the greater gift.[65] Horace emphasizes this claim by litotes (*neque tu pessima . . . / ferres,* 4b-5a), the repetition of *munerum . . . muneri* (4, 12), and his rehearsal of historical and legendary heroes whom the poets immortalized (16-34). Poetry is a rich reward, and the poet is a full and generous giver, a meaning enhanced by the proximity of *pateras . . . commodus* (1) and the appearance of Dionysus at the end of the poem (34). *Commodus* is a loaded word. It appears in only one other ode, III.19.12.[66] In that symposion the poet plays a noisome *magister bibendi,* who orders the stronger of two wine mixtures (13-15a)[67] and meets any reluctance to join the party with vehement impatience (18b-22a). A 'generous' poet, then, anticipates an unrestrained encomium, but Censorinus vanishes.

Beyond the inference from the victory of the Scipios over Hannibal and the assumption that Censorinus has done some feat worthy of Horace's song (20b-22a), there is no reference to any of Censorinus's accomplishments: no mention about his praetorship (14 or 13 B.C.);[68] no hint of his illustrious family descended from the kings. The encomium is so generic that it is debated whether Censorinus is the younger Gaius Marcius or his father Lucius Marcius.[69] I would go further. This encomium is not designed to prevent obscurity. One could replace Censorinus with any number of young Augustans with some military experience, such as P. Cornelius Scipio, L. Domitius Ahenobarbus, P. Quinctilius Varus, or M. Messalla Appianus, without diminishing the poem at all.[70]

This nondescript praise makes the ode's main premise all the more perplexing. How exactly is such a praise poem a better gift than a sculpture or painting?[71] Horace raises the question when he offers the poem and commends its value, but then credits the solid arts with the same ability to give life to the dead (13–15). Horace makes clear with an emphatic *non* (13) that the superiority of poetry is never in doubt.[72] The immortalized Romulus, Aeacus, and then Hercules, Castor, Pollux, and Dionysus (21–34) by comparison dwarf Scipio and Hannibal, whose images and deeds are engraved in marble. The lyric Muse even immortalizes her own deity, Dionysus. Still Horace gives a good amount of space to the immortalizing power of statues by delaying for more than five lines (15–19) the crescendo of poetry's supremacy. S. J. Harrison's contention that lines 15–19 offer an epigraphic model that would be an integral feature of an honorary statue softens the contrast somewhat between poetry and the solid arts by arguing that even a fixed image needs words.[73] Harrison's explanation solves the difficult text but makes the question more pertinent—What distinguishes the excellence of the praise gift, poetry, from another praise gift, a statue with an inscription? Perhaps Censorinus liked poetry better (*gaudes carminibus*, 11)? This is a minimalist answer for a competition between poetry and the solid arts that occupies the entire ode.[74] Poems are not mute objects. They have the power of speech (*dicere*, 12) in contrast to silence when there is no poem (*sileant* and *taciturnitas*, 21 and 23), but Horace's direct reference to the power of the public inscription that accompanies the image and the detail he gives this inscription diminishes the distinction.

The solution depends on noting Horace's word choice in the opening condition, especially the sarcastic tone of *scilicet* (1–8). The sculptor Scopas and painter Parrhasius were renowned for their excellence (*sollers*)—their deficiency was not aesthetic. Their art lacked discretion. The compressed repetition of *nunc* depicts the flippancy of the painter and sculptor who at one time with the same craft fashion a man and then at another with no distinction to their art create a deity (*nunc hominem ponere, nunc deum*, 8). Horace distances himself and Censorinus from such nondescript panegyric. With a hint of the *recusatio* (*sed non haec mihi vis*)

Horace disavows his ability in the solid arts and refuses to treat his subjects so lightly (9–10). Certainly Censorinus is wealthy enough to commission such art, if he wanted; but Censorinus does not require such arts (*nec tibi talium / res est aut animus deliciarum egens*). Horace is complimenting Censorinus because he does not have the disposition (*animus*) to accept the indiscriminative standards (*deliciarum*) the other arts permit.

Again, *commodus* is a loaded word. It interjects the poet's vigorous sympotic persona from *Odes* I–III, which, as in C.III.19.18–22, energizes the power of lyric song and is essential for this ode and the second half of *Odes* IV, but *commodus* further suggests that the worth of an encomium depends on decorum. In the *Satires* Horace uses *commodus* for convivial pleasures, often when he is encouraging *moderatio* or narrating the conduct appropriate for a banquet (*S*.I.6.110; II.2.91; 8.75–76). In the *Epistles* the word is connected with encomiastic restraint, for the *laudandus* (I.1.36–40) and for the *laudator* (II.1.1–4).[75] The panegyric poet of c.8 is an active giver (*donarem, donarem, possumus / donare* all in first person, first position in their lines), generous and discriminating (*commodus*), which by contrast to the other arts is what makes his praise valuable. An encomium not only demands great deeds (*meritis . . . Romuli*, 24) but also virtuous poets to set them apart (*virtus . . . potentium / vatum . . . consecrat*, 26–27). This dual emphasis on the character of the giver (the panegyrist) and receiver (the *laudandus*) is evident in the ode's ritual conclusion that the Muse refuses to let a person deserving praise die (27–28), and that Liber ensures that vows taken succeed (34).

The two parts of the paradox, a nondescript encomium as an argument for the higher value of praise poetry, come together. This ode is more than praise for a patron; it is a critique of the craft and provides a negative model. Nowhere is this more clear than in the hyperbole of the apotheoses that dominate more than half the ode: the poet can immortalize the praetor Censorinus just as Romulus, Aeacus, Hercules, Dionysus. The poet had just done the same for Augustus (C.IV.5.33–36). Deification is certainly above the young noble's merits and is an example of how ephemeral panegyric could become, if a poet were hired to fashion *nunc hominem, nunc deum*.[76] *Muneri*, which punctuates the priamel (12), is not a synonym of metrical convenience for *donorum*. Horace uses *munus* for the poems and rewards that are the goods of patronage (*Epist*.II.1.246, 267). Behind *possumus . . . pretium dicere muneri* is the insinuation, we can set a price for our patronage. Horace's encomium separates Censorinus from those who would enjoy being praised even if it were only a business transaction. And the ironic fun is that Censorinus, if he welcomes the gift, must accept it on the poet's terms for what praise it offers. Horace's imagined gift exchange relies on the simple presupposition that a gift is most appropriate when it is deserved (*praemia* [3] . . . *dignum laude virum Musa vetat mori* [28]); and a gift is not a gift, if constrained. If it is, it is not a gift (*dona*) but a service (*munus*).[77]

C.9: Lollius

Richard Bentley: "Locus perdifficilis est, et varia hominum iudicia expertus." Bentley hesitates over the syntax that requires *consul* (39), *iudex* (41), and *victor* (44) to be appositional modifiers of *animus* (34). He preserves the lines and defends the metaphor with his customary barrage of parallel examples,[78] but his exasperation could apply equally to the entire encomium, namely that Horace's glowing praise of Lollius is so out of line with other ancient witnesses to Lollius's character and career:

> Ne forte credas interitura quae
> longe sonantem natus ad Aufidum
>   non ante vulgatas per artis
>   verba loquor socianda chordis:
>
> non, si priores Maeonius tenet   5
> sedes Homerus, Pindaricae latent
>   Ceaeque et Alcaei minaces
>   Stesichorive graves Camenae,
>
> nec, si quid olim lusit Anacreon,
> delevit aetas; spirat adhuc amor   10
>   vivuntque commissi calores
>   Aeoliae fidibus puellae.
>
> non sola comptos arsit adulteri
> crinis et aurum vestibus illitum
>   mirata regalisque cultus   15
>   et comites Helene Lacaena,

primusve Teucer tela Cydonio
direxit arcu; non semel Ilios
    vexata; non pugnavit ingens
        Idomeneus Sthenelusve solus   20

dicenda Musis proelia; non ferox
Hector vel acer Deiphobus gravis
    excepit ictus pro pudicis
        coniugibus puerisque primus.

vixere fortes ante Agamemnona   25
multi; sed omnes illacrimabiles
    urgentur ignotique longa
        nocte, carent quia vate sacro.

paulum sepultae distat inertiae
celata virtus. non ego te meis   30
    chartis inornatum silebo
        totve tuos patiar labores

impune, Lolli, carpere lividas
obliviones. est animus tibi
    rerumque prudens et secundis   35
        temporibus dubiisque rectus,

vindex avarae fraudis et abstinens
ducentis ad se cuncta pecuniae
    consulque non unius anni
        sed quotiens bonus atque fidus   40

iudex honestum praetulit utili,
reiecit alto dona nocentium
    vultu, per obstantis catervas
        explicuit sua victor arma.

non possidentem multa vocaveris   45
recte beatum; rectius occupat
    nomen beati, qui deorum
        muneribus sapienter uti

duramque callet pauperiem pati
peiusque leto flagitium timet,   50
    non ille pro caris amicis
        aut patria timidus perire.

[No, do not believe for a second that the words will die
that I, born near the far-sounding Aufidus, speak to be
sung to the strains of the lyre by arts before uncommon;
no, if first place belongs to Maeonian Homer, Pindar's
Muse is not hidden nor the Muse of Ceos nor the threatening Muse of Alcaeus nor Stesichorus's weighty Muse.
No, and time has not destroyed any playful verse Anacreon once sung; the Aeolian girl's love still breathes and
her sexual heat trusted to the lyre lives on. No, Spartan
Helen was not the only lover to burn, lust-struck at her
adulterer's dandy locks and gold covered clothes, and
his royal bearing and attendants, nor was Teucer the
first to fire shots from Cydonian bow; no, not just once
was Ilium assailed; no, mighty Idomeneus and Sthenelus were not the only heroes to fight battles worthy of
the Muse's song; no, bold Hector and fierce Deiphobus
were not the first to accept heavy blows while fighting
for their chaste wives and children. Many brave men
lived before Agamemnon, but all are weighed down by
death's long night, unmourned and unknown because
they lack a sacred bard. Once buried, unsung bravery
differs little from cowardice. No, Lollius, I will not pass
you over in silence without the praise of my pages, nor
will I allow black oblivion free reign to depreciate your
many labors. You have a practical mind, stable in both
promising and doubtful circumstances, an avenger of
deceitful avarice, and self-restrained with money luring
everything into its own control, and a consul not of one
year; but your mind, always a good and faithful judge,
has valued character above expediency and high-
mindedly has rejected the bribes of the guilty, and
through the opposing forces deployed victorious its
own armies. No, you would not be right, if you were to
call the rich man blessed. More rightly one earns the
name blessed who uses wisely the rewards of the gods
and understands how to endure hard poverty and fears
disgrace worse than death; no, the blessed man is not
afraid of dying for beloved friend or country.]

M. Lollius managed a brilliant political career.[79] As a young
man he administered the annexation of Galatia and served as its
first legate (25/24 B.C.); four years later he was sole consul during

a difficult time of political unrest (21 B.C.).[80] Lollius went on to serve his proconsulate in Macedonia (19/18 B.C.) and added to his military reputation by subjugating the Bessi, but he was not so fortunate in Gaul (16 B.C.). The Sygambri had arrested and crucified a number of Romans, whom they claimed to have caught in their territory. Not content with this outrage, they crossed west of the Rhine and ambushed a contingent of Roman cavalry. While in pursuit, the Sygambri happened upon Lollius and his forces, defeated them, and captured the Roman eagles. After Lollius regrouped, the Sygambri, who also may have heard that supporting troops were being dispatched, surrendered, returned the eagles, and gave hostages. Everything was settled when Augustus arrived later in the year. Augustus put Drusus and Tiberius in charge of the German campaigns, and Lollius returned to Rome.[81] In spite of the defeat, Lollius did not lose standing with Augustus, who years later (1 B.C.) sent him to the East as the adviser for Gaius Caesar when the nineteen-year-old assumed proconsular power. Then Lollius's career deteriorated. He was caught trying to influence Gaius against Tiberius and was accused of taking bribes from the Parthians. He died (or committed suicide) soon after.

Although the historians categorically censure Lollius for his military defeat and alleged treachery (Vell. 2.97.1–5; 102.1–4; Plin. *Nat*.9.118; Suet. *Aug*.23.1–3; Tac. *Ann*.1.10.17–19), Lollius's reputation may in fact be worse today than in antiquity. Commentators, as I just did, have so frequently cited these historians together that they have become a biographical indictment against Lollius's character. The historians, however, are suspect. Lollius's enmity with Tiberius made him vulnerable to Velleius's deference to the emperor.[82] A *novus homo*, who enriched himself by provincial rule and was rumored to have been in the pockets of the Parthians, fits Pliny's didactic moralizing. Tacitus and Suetonius are more difficult to dismiss. Setting aside any anti-imperialism, objectivity could prompt a historian to point out that the Augustan peace did not mean a complete lack of unrest in the provinces or in Rome; but other examples would be available without magnifying Lollius's loss into the bloody *clades Lolliana* and associating it with Varus's loss of three legions. Yet, however one may judge the individual credibility of the historians, it remains that for a Roman commander to lose eagles was a disgrace, no matter how quickly the standards were recovered.[83]

Especially relevant to c.8 is how closely Velleius and Pliny interact with the wording of Horace's encomium.[84] Velleius's *homine in omnia pecuniae quam recte faciendi cupidiore* and *plena subdoli ac versuti animi consilia* invert Horace's *animus tibi / rerumque prudens* (34b–35) and *rectus, / vindex avarae fraudis et abstinens / ducentis ad se cuncta pecuniae* (36b–38). Pliny turns Horace's *rectius occupat / nomen beati, qui deorum / muneribus sapienter uti* (46b–48) into *hic est rapinarum exitus . . . infamatus . . . muneribus* ("bribes"). Velleius further vilifies Lollius by contrasting the people's joy over his death to the mourning for Censorinus, a comparison directly confronting the sequencing of c.7 and 8 and the correlation of the two encomia. Velleius's Lollius was no Censorinus. Although there is some justification in light of such literary interplay to be wary of Velleius's Lollius and Censorinus, it would also be uncritical to dismiss the contrast as exaggeration by a later historian in a different context. Lollius had been a prominent public figure long enough when Horace wrote the ode, and certainly by the time his praise was published, to have earned a reputation; the public at large could readily know of Lollius's new wealth, his defeat, and Augustus's trip to Gaul. It is reasonable that if Horace's encomium, which emphasizes not just Lollius's administrative gifts but his moderate spirit and military prowess, provoked a direct counter from historians less than a generation later, its immediate reception would meet some skepticism.[85]

Discrediting Velleius has not ended the debate on how to read Horace's praise because it does not solve the primary problem: Horace chose to immortalize Lollius for his *virtus* with detailed directness, when he had shown in the ode to Censorinus that he could construct a nondescript encomium to avoid the difficulty.[86] Solutions divide into four categories: (1) The encomium is still general enough. Besides, Lollius is not the point, the poet is; (2) Horace may not have enjoyed the task of praising Lollius, but he did his best; (3) the encomium is an attempt to rehabilitate Lollius's reputation; (4) the poet's praise is a mock encomium indicting Lollius's moral turpitude.[87]

These answers tend to view the ode as an isolated unit and thus disregard how its content and structure accentuate the encomium for Lollius. In contrast to Censorinus, Lollius is not a typecast figure for idealized panegyric commonplaces. This is Horace's outstanding *encomium nobilium* in depth and length. No one outside the imperial family and Maecenas receives as high praise as Lollius in either collection. This comparison alone invites special consideration of Lollius's merit, and there is no escaping that part of Lollius's notoriety for the audience is that after recovering from a military setback he was replaced by Augustus's stepsons. Even if this poem were simply written to please Augustus by praising one of his favorites, Horace, as Lyne suggests, would "risk tactlessness" or at the very least an ambivalent response when he praises Lollius victorious in arms (43–44).[88] Interpreting Horace's song as only a general praise piece devoid of specific reference to Lollius's career would require an especially dull audience or a panegyric poet so perfunctory and unconcerned about his credibility as not to care about how anyone might react other than the patron. The ode's structure indicates otherwise: Horace includes disputes (*dubia*). Horace delays naming Lollius for over half the poem and places the extensive reaffirmation of lyric power in the lead, as if to take the immediate focus off Lollius, but the five-stanza encomium that closes the ode counters the effect. Further, since the power of the poet's lyric dominates the foreground of the ode, the virtue of the poet (as emphasized in c.8) gives even more weight to any praise that follows. Horace does not allow Lollius's character and deeds to escape notice.[89]

The encomium for Lollius cannot be properly understood without reference to c.8. Horace develops throughout the first seven stanzas of c.9 the précis of his praise for Censorinus (*gaudes carminibus; carmina possumus / donare et pretium dicere muneri*, 11–12). Horace begins by praising the permanence of poetic speech, which he accents with the pleonasm of *verba* and its juxtaposition with *loquor* (1–4). As the sympotic imagery at the opening and closing of c.8 predicted, c.9 now revels in the power of the poet's creative genius to transcend the boundaries of time with words. This song is no longer an amicable gift exchange agreeable to patron and poet, the pleasure of receiving and giving a poem. Horace commands. He tells Lollius not to believe for a moment that poetic power will ever end (*Ne forte credas interitura*, 1) and reaffirms his own lyric triumph (2–3) that closed the first collection: the poet born by the roaring Aufidus will not die (C.III.30.6–10). Horace by imitation resurrects Sappho, her passion and heat (*spirat adhuc amor / viuuntque commissi calores*, c.9.10b–11). Horace gives his breath to Sappho, and she in turn quickens his song. The relationship between the two lyric poets is reciprocal and vibrant. Statues with their inscriptions had some power to give life's breath to others (*hic saxo, liquidis ille coloribus . . . spiritus et vita,* c.8.7–14), but *color* and *calor* are not as close as their assonance suggests. Changing, living passions (*calores*), the lyric breath shared by poets, can never be reproduced by colors (*coloribus*) on any hard object. Subsequently, Horace's tribute to Ennius (c.8.13–20a) becomes conditional for Homer (*si priores Maeonius tenet /* *sedes Homerus,* c.9.5–6a), and given the power and ferocity of the lyric tradition Horace parades (*minaces, graves, lusit,* 6–12), the condition becomes more of a challenge disguised in Horace's small voice. Immediately Horace appears as a new Homer to demonstrate the immortal power of his poetic by rewriting an epic narrative into lyric (9.13–24).

Inanimate *artes* (c.8) give way completely to animating lyric (c.9). The poetic *ego* replaces the personified voice of Horace's pages, and Horace personally refuses to keep silent (*si chartae* *sileant,* 8.21a; *non ego te meis / chartis inornatum silebo,* 9.30b–31), because silence brings moral confusion. When he immortalizes human virtue, the panegyric poet performs a priestly function (*virtus . . . vatum . . . consecrat,* 8.26–27; *vate sacro,* 9.28). Sacred space requires virtue (character evident in meritorious conduct) from the panegyrist, who in spite of any pressure from a patron must exercise propriety (*commodus,* c.8), and from the honored hero. The poet, however, is preeminent since without his song moral opposites become confused: unsung virtuous action and absolute inertia die together (c.9.29–30a). Accordingly, both encomia praise the poet's and addressees' inner spirit (*mihi vis;* *tibi . . . est . . . animus,* 8.9–10; *est animus tibi,* 9.34), and the extended metaphor of Lollius's *animus* as *vindex, consul, iudex,* and *victor,* far from out of place, expresses the poet's understanding of virtue, that conduct either civil or military is an expression of one's inner-self.

The interface of the two odes presents a simple but critical thematic consequence. It hardly seems probable that Horace would write an encomium (with the epic Ennius at its heart) that champions the circumspect (*commodus*) poet of virtue and the necessity of meritorious deeds by the *laudandus* and then in a companion song with an enlivened dynamic lyric voice seriously use an exaggerated encomium to rescue a favorite of Augustus. If these two praise songs together make anything clear it is that encomia are not meant to protect broken virtue but to honor those distinguishing themselves beyond the limits of their humanity.

The solutions proposed for the encomium for Lollius share a questionable presupposition (or a particular reliance on the Suetonian Horace), that the occasion for the praise is the obligation of Horace's patronage. It was Horace's duty to praise, and therefore he either delicately bypasses Lollius's career through panegyric generalities and metaphor or attempts to distract the audience with his celebration of lyric power. Or, perhaps Lollius's reputation was not that bad yet and merited praise to some degree. Such theorizing produces a disjointed ode: the most prolonged and joyous expression of lyric's passion and power in the entire collection, for a Lollius. It is imperative not to ignore the pattern of Horace's *encomia nobilium.* Horace's praise openly engages complications so as to argue that human achievement and failures require praise to be a communal activity between a powerful sacred bard and an audience alert to interpret. Horatian panegyric does not avoid disputes (*dubia*); it stimulates audience interaction by encouraging multiple perspectives. Lollius offers the perfect case: a person whose (mis)deeds challenge the gift of immortality.

Through his lyric remodeling of Homer's epic and the structure of the encomium, Horace centers the ode on the ambiguity between praise and blame.[90] The second set of three stanzas (13–24), which completes the ode's first half, remembers the epic heroes of the Trojan War, but the silence of the ode is barely below the surface. There were adulterers, suitors, warriors, and the destruction of cities before Troy (13–24), but without a Homer they perished unknown. The argument implies the intrinsic value of song, since song preserves the memory of specific heroes as opposed to the unsung others. The negative *non*, the ode's predominant feature, repeated four times and coupled with the alliteration and anaphora of *sola . . . semel . . . solus,* enhances the sense of distance between the remembered and forgotten.

Horace is not merely listing disconnected snapshots of particular epic lives; his overlapping of the stanzas by the repetition of *-ve . . . vel* forms one continuous narrative.[91] Horace's choice of characters in his lyric Trojan War is not random. He moves with lyric swiftness from one combatant to the next, weaving the narrative together with subtle transitions. Teucer's Cydonian (Cretan) bow comes from Idomeneus's native land. The narrative covers the range of battle techniques: bowman (Teucer) to spearman (Idomeneus) to charioteer (Sthenelus). *Dicenda Musis proelia* (21), parallel to *dignum laude virum* (8.27) and recalling *proelia coniugibus loquenda* (4.68), lends a sense of lament that prepares for Hector and Deiphobus, as well as anticipating the pathos for the unmourned brave (25–28).[92] A Sapphic passion (10–12) breathes life into Helen. Horace's story is an erotic disaster of betrayal, exile, and murder rivaling any romance novel.[93] Horace provides the barest outline, but the familiar details are easily supplied. Helen is the dazzling and bedazzled mistress, seduced to abandon her home (*Helene Lacaene*). Her suitors, driven by passion and vengeance, fight to reclaim her, while her new brothers-in-law fight for her and the lives of their own wives and children. The affair is sordid enough that the chastity of the nameless innocents (*pudicis coniugibus puerisque*), who end the narrative, is not so much ironic as empathetic. What virtuous panegyrist would group the meritorious chaste into anonymous generic social classes, while extolling the notorious heroic others? It is left to the listener/reader to set the depth of the narrative details on which the poet is silent, that is, whether to imagine behind the general *pudicis coniugibus puerisque* the families of Hector and Deiphobus.[94] Andromache and Astyanax, as they are immortalized in their tender parting from Hector (*Il.*6), embody the narrative well. Helen is the only wife of Deiphobus named in the *Iliad*, but it is hard to accept that she could be the chaste wife for whom he fought. After Paris was killed, Helen was wed to Deiphobus, and she helped Menelaus murder him on the night Troy fell. Yet Horace makes Helen his lead character and Andromache remains unnamed. Poets' songs discriminate by immortalizing some and not others, and not all of their choices may find an approving audience.

Horace's narrative invites a dubious reading. Helen's guilt or innocence in the affairs leading up to the Trojan War was a well-worn topic. Horace plays both sides. The Helen of c.9.13–16 completes the seduction scene of *C.I.*15.13–15, the only other ode to name Helen, Teucer, and Sthenelus together.[95] In c.15 Paris sits in the bed chamber combing his hair and rehearsing his songs on the lyre. Helen plays a passive role, carried off by the shepherd Paris (1–2), taken in by his false promises of heroism (29–32). Paris bears all the responsibility for violating the laws of guest-friendship and the resulting calamity his treachery brings on his city. Horace's lyric in c.9 imagines Helen looking intently at Paris (as someone might view a breathtaking work of art), and although she still plays the responsive role, her passivity is replaced by the active state of her passions, *arsit . . . mirata.* Others bear the consequences of her insatiable desire, the Greeks who fought for her and the Trojans who suffered.[96]

Hector and Deiphobus only intensify the dilemma posed by the narrative—why some are remembered and others forgotten. Horace openly honors the Trojans so that their deeds rival those of the victorious Greeks. Commentators contrast the passive Trojans to the active Achaean heroes, but the Trojans, although in a defensive position, are not passive.[97] Horace emboldens the suffering Trojans with an active expression (*ferox . . . acer . . . excepit ictus*) and assigns them the most honorable motivation for fighting, to save their wives and children. In Horace's Trojan War, just as in Homer's, immortal glory is not based on the simple distinction of winning and losing, which might offer some consolation to Lollius. But Horace does not leave the heroism of the Trojans without complication. Horace does not name the greatest Greek warrior, Achilles, and makes this silence felt by the imbalance of Hector against the lesser Greek fighters and by pairing Hector with Deiphobus. Three times Achilles chased Hector around Troy, and it was not until Athena appeared to Hector in the guise of Deiphobus that Hector, challenged by the danger his brother risked when he ventured outside the walls, stopped running and faced Achilles (*Il.*22.226–246). Horace, with the hyperbaton *non . . . primus,* a separation of nearly three verses, and the juxtaposition and enjambment of *non ferox / Hector,* holds the narrative momentary suspended. Is Hector *ferox* or not?

Horace breaks the narrative when he ends the connecting pattern of *non . . . solus . . . primus . . . -ve . . . vel* (24), but thematically Agamemnon, strategically placed at the ode's center (25–28), crystallizes the compassion the narrative provokes for the unnamed (including the wives and children). Horace again leaves the quality of Agamemnon's reputation up to the audience. Agamemnon is the only hero that Horace does not praise directly by an epithet or as Teucer by a manner of fighting. The syntax implies that he also is *fortis,* but a lyric retelling of Agamemnon's passions of the type Horace has just illustrated with his lyric Trojan War leaves Agamemnon's case ambiguous at best. Horace's Sapphic Helen (10–16) sets the mood for remembering the disasters of Agamemnon's life: the curse of the house of Atreus.[98] Agamemnon killed his daughter, returned home with his captive mistress, and was murdered by his adulterous wife. Agamemnon is Idomeneus, Helen, and Deiphobus. Agamemnon is the center of attention, but many brave warriors (*fortes*) before Agamemnon died from memory because they did not have a Homer. The contrast between the remembered (Agamemnon) and the forgotten brave ends Horace's Trojan narrative with a violation of a fundamental supposition of justice: that meritorious conduct should result in reward, not loss. The brave were as deserving as Agamemnon, but they passed beyond the memory of even tears (*illacrimabiles*) and, as a result, suffered the worst fate a hero can endure, the loss of κλέος (*ignoti*). The singer has the power to prevent this calamity and restore the injustice of mortality. When he does, he becomes the sacred priest of Virtue.[99] Horace contextualizes panegyric in ritual and thereby requires that it be communal. The poet-priest must have an audience to engage and then in turn to enact the sacrificial rites, panegyric. Horace has included an audience as an indispensable participant in the formation and interpretation of immortal memory.

The argument is not that these heroes, the creations of a poetic tradition, are undeserving of their immortal fame, although nothing would of necessity prevent that conclusion, but that Homer's epic tale does not preclude Horace's lyric retelling and reshaping of the same events. Panegyric cannot be static. Horace's lyric narrative demonstrates that undying fame is the product of poetic invention and reinvention, which does not overlook the ambiguities of human experience. Nor is there a firm boundary between poetic memory (the Trojan War) and history (Lollius), each creating and influencing the other. Therefore, panegyric requires an audience to judge the ambiguities inherent in the merits and failures of a particular life remembered (Cicero: panegyric is established by testimony, *de Orat.*2.43–49, 65, 342–47; *Part.*71–72, 75–82). Panegyric, then, is not necessarily a reward to be coveted, since praise also risks blame.

The praise for Lollius is not merely tacked on to an encomium for Horace's poetics. The interpretive challenges in Horace's lyric

Iliad prevents a reductionist reading and prepares the audience to
engage and evaluate the poet's panegyric for Lollius. As the conflicts in the first narrative predict, Horace places a positive encomium for Lollius (35–44) within an introduction (30b–34) and
conclusion (45–52) that imply blame. The general meaning of the
introduction is undisputed: Horace intends to present Lollius
with the gift of immortality.[100] The personification of envious forgetfulness (*lividas obliviones*), which the poet will not allow to go
unpunished (*impune*) in its attempt to eat away (*carpere*) and blot
out Lollius,[101] transitions to the poet's priestly role as the
guardian of virtue (25–30a) and prepares for the extended metaphor of the encomium (35–44). Horace's pronouncement that the
absence of a singer can bury the brave and the cowardly alike in
forgotten tombs again recalls Pindar (*O*.10.91–92; *N*.7.12–13)[102]
and repeats the theme of c.8. (n.b. 21–22). Even if initially *labores*
were taken as the subject of *carpere* instead of *obliviones*, the general sense would remain constant: I will not allow your deeds to
be forgotten.

Horace does not leave this premise, that immortal memory
brings only blessing, as settled as supposed. Forgotten labors (*labores . . . carpere . . . obliviones*) for Horace's sympotic *carpe diem*
argument are a blessing, the chief pleasure of wine especially for
worn-out soldiers, such as Plancus (*C*.I.7.17b–21a) or Pompey
(*C*.II.7.17–23a).[103] Not only do the ups and downs of Lollius's
military career parallel the lot of these soldiers, but Horace builds
into the praise for Lollius the basic outline of the sympotic *carpe
diem* motif. The necessity of death in the press of unending night
(*omnes . . . urgentur . . . longa nocte*) brings to mind Horace's warning to Sestius (*iam te premet nox*, *C*.I.4.16a). The personifying attribute *lividas* lends an urgency that there must be some immediate
action (song) taken to counter the effects of death, as does the
modifier *invida* in *C*. I.11.7b–8. Then there is *carpere*. Pejorative denotations of *carpere* (to tear, wear away, destroy, harp at) are common in literature of the late Republic and Augustan period, but
not in Horace. Only once does Horace use *carpere* pejoratively ("to
pick on," *S*.I.3.21).[104] Add in the *carpe diem* theme of c.7 and the
sympotic beginning and ending of c.8. There is enough of the
carpe diem argument present in c.9 to see in the lines a negative
nuance, a reversal of Horace's sympotic rule that limited memory
is a blessing: "I will not allow your labors to be forgotten" be-

comes in the sympotic environment "There is no escape ever from your deeds." *Immortalis fama* is not for the soldier Lollius or any hero a completely comfortable thought.

The conclusion is more direct (45–52). Excluding blame from the end of the encomium requires one of two difficult assumptions or both. First, *vocaveris* must be an impersonal "one," which complements the subject of *ne forte credas* (1).[105] Perhaps *credas* may be read as a nameless "you," but after the extensive encomium praising Lollius and his Stoic character, the "you" has been personalized.[106] Second, if the poet is rehearsing the Stoic maxims by which Lollius in fact lives,[107] *vocaveris* implies that the voice of Lollius is speaking through the poet or that at least the poet is speaking directly for him. In either case, the voices of the *laudator* and *laudandus* become inseparable. This destroys the poet's lead role in panegyric because he would be giving his voice totally up to the *laudandus* and abdicating his sacred role. The notion is counter to the ode's entire thesis. The encomium does set Lollius up as a wise Stoic, but the direct address of *vocaveris* introduces a gentle correction that quickly becomes more stern. In Horace the Stoic sage never goes unchallenged (*S.*I.3; II.3). The encomium moves from *rectus* (36) to *recte* to *rectius* (46). The asyndeton (45–46) stresses Horace's switch from the second to third person: you would correctly call him blessed; (on the contrary) one would more correctly call. Lollius understands the blessed state as a negative, the lack of possessions, but the ode encourages him toward a more positive definition. Stoic life requires exercise (*exercendum*), and Horace specifies the regimen—sacrificial military valor.

Horace states the admonition against cowardice positively and negatively (50–52) and thus ties the conclusion to the end of the first narrative. The poet changes fighting for chaste wives and children (23–24) to courageously dying for dear friends and fatherland, a motivation applicable to the political responsibilities of the Roman nobleman. The noble who would not die for his people does not fit among the ranks of immortalized heroes. To help make his point Horace replays the language and theme of C.III.2 (*pauperiem*, 2.1 and 9.49; *dulce et decorum est pro patria mori*, 2.13 and *pro . . . patria timidus perire*, 9.51–52). Horace carries the alliteration of *pro patria* over to *perire* (*mori* in c.2), and the insertion of *timidus* between *patria* and *perire* places the focus at the end

of c.9 on the soldier's state of mind, *animus.* It is only a virtue that
has no knowledge of disgraceful retreat (*Virtus repulsae nescia sor-
didae*) that merits immortal reward (c.2.14–24): a painful reminder
for Lollius who, however inadvertently and temporarily, lost the
Roman eagles.[108]

Horace praises Lollius between the extremes. Horace does not
bury Lollius's failures beyond recovery, but forces them on the
memory. Neither is Horace's encomium an ironic attack. There
is no motive. Lollius had served Rome well. Neither praise nor
blame effaces the other. Horace allows both to stand side by side.
The resulting tension renders Horace's panegyric true to the life
lived: no one's history is a constant stream of success or failure. So
says the satiric Horace in a critique of the Stoic sage (*S.*I.3.68–
69a)[109] The ambiguities inherent in any human life are precisely
what makes this encomium difficult to read, and Horace uses the
conflict to draw the audience into the panegyric process. The conflicts within Horace's encomium for Lollius prompt the audience
to exercise their judgment about the merits and demerits of Lollius's life. Praise becomes a communal creation of the poet and
audience.

Conclusion

Through the *encomia nobilium* the poet presents his critique of
panegyric. Since Roman culture is not necessarily cynical of panegyric — a more modern predilection — Horace nuances his panegyric to invite the audience to evaluate the practice of praise, its
form and content. The sympotic environment of c.1 invests the
Horatian encomium with a seriocomic tone. The predicted triumph of c.2 exposes the dangers and limitations of encomium:
any praise once given can be belittled by a comparison to the past
or betrayed by future events. Then follow c.3–6 praising the
poet's divine source of inspiration, separating his poetry from
earthbound motivations or designs. C.8 and 9 test the limits of
panegyric: a generic hyperbolic set piece that fails to distinguish
the addressee in any meaningful or lasting sense versus a *laudatio*
that so risks opposition to the popular character and deeds of the
praised that it is directly challenged by later historians. Lollius
in the full scope of his merits and demerits is immortalized.

Throughout the *encomia nobilium* the poet is both panegyrist and a critic of panegyric, author and reader, and thereby models for his audience how they should engage his encomia. Part of the pleasure in reading Horatian panegyric is questioning the praise. Interpretation is the power of Horatian panegyric poetry, and the dynamic that ensures it will remain a vibrant part of a community's story. The twist of Horatian ingenuity is that the formative modeling of praise does not overload the panegyric genre with such negatives that it becomes weak. Horace does just the opposite. By changing the modality of panegyric from persuasion to the freedom of interpretation, Horace allows panegyric the flexibility to change with its society. Therefore, Horatian panegyrics are timeless not because they have the power to immortalize the *laudandus* as a particular type of hero, but because they adapt to the interpretive sensibilities of the audience. In this sense they belong to the present moment.[110] They constitute a sympotic experience.

3

Encomia Augusti, "Take One"

The imperial oration is an encomium of the emperor. It will thus embrace a generally agreed amplification of the good things attaching to the emperor, but allows no ambivalent or disputed features, because of the extreme splendour of the person concerned. You should therefore elaborate it on the assumption that it relates to things universally acknowledged to be good.
—Menander Rhetor: *Basilikos Logos* (368.1–8)

Menander's explication of Aristotelian/Ciceronian epideictic rhetoric does not reflect Horace's praise for the young nobles.[1] Horace admits ambivalent and disputed features (ἀμφίβολον καὶ ἀμφισβητούμενον), but will he alter his panegyric praxis to accommodate Augustus, at least for the commissioned poems? If he does, we would expect not just a greater accounting of Augustus's deeds but the suppression of anything contrary to what is commonly accepted as the good. If representing a triumph for Augustus within the seriocomic irony of the *recusatio* is an accurate predictor (c.2), Horace will not alter his panegyric strategy. Horace will remain the same.

C.4: Epinikion^{One} — The Panegyric Agon

Qualem ministrum fulminis alitem,
cui rex deorum regnum in avis vagas
    permisit expertus fidelem
      Iuppiter in Ganymede flavo,

olim iuventas et patrius vigor   5
nido laborum propulit inscium,
    vernique iam nimbis remotis
      insolitos docuere nisus

venti paventem, mox in ovilia
demisit hostem vividus impetus,   10
    nunc in reluctantis dracones
      egit amor dapis atque pugnae,

qualemve laetis caprea pascuis
intenta fulvae matris ab ubere
    iam †lactet† depulsum leonem   15
      dente novo peritura vidit,

videre †Raeti† bella sub Alpibus²
Drusum gerentem Vindelici; quibus
    mos unde deductus per omne
      tempus Amazonia securi   20

dextras obarmet, quaerere distuli,
nec scire fas est omnia — sed diu
    lateque victrices catervae
      consiliis iuvenis repressae

sensere quid mens rite, quid indoles   25
nutrita faustis sub penetralibus
    posset, quid Augusti paternus
      in pueros animus Nerones.

fortes creantur fortibus et bonis;
est in iuvencis, est in equis patrum   30
    virtus, neque imbellem feroces
      progenerant aquilae columbam.

doctrina sed vim promovet insitam
rectique cultus pectora roborant;³
    utcumque defecere mores,   35
      indecorant bene nata culpae.

quid debeas, o Roma, Neronibus
testis Metaurum flumen et Hasdrubal
    devictus et pulcher fugatis
        ille dies Latio tenebris,   40

qui primus alma risit adorea
dirus per urbis Afer ut Italas
    ceu flamma per taedas vel Eurus
        per Siculas equitavit undas.

post hoc secundis usque laboribus   45
Romana pubes crevit et impio
    vastata Poenorum tumultu
        fana deos habuere rectos,

dixitque tandem perfidus Hannibal:
'cervi, luporum praeda rapacium,   50
    sectamur ultro quos opimus
        fallere et effugere est triumphus.

gens, quae cremato fortis ab Ilio
iactata Tuscis aequoribus sacra
    natosque maturosque patres   55
        pertulit Ausonias ad urbis,

duris ut ilex tonsa bipennibus
nigrae feraci frondis in Algido,
    per damna, per caedis ab ipso
        ducit opes animumque ferro.   60

non Hydra secto corpore firmior
vinci dolentem crevit in Herculem
    monstrumve submisere Colchi
        maius Echioniaeve Thebae.

merses profundo, pulchrior evenit;   65
luctere, multa proruet integrum
    cum laude victorem †geretque
        proelia coniugibus loquenda†.

Carthagini iam non ego nuntios
mittam superbos: occidit, occidit   70
    spes omnis et fortuna nostri
        nominis Hasdrubale interempto.'

nil Claudiae non perficiunt manus,
quas et benigno numine Iuppiter
    defendit et curae sagaces   75
        expediunt per acuta belli.

[Like the winged emissary of lightning to whom the
king of the gods entrusted his rule over the wandering
birds, after King Jupiter had proven him a trusted servant in the rape of golden haired Ganymede: his youth
and sire's strength, ignorant as he an eaglet was of
labor, threw him from the nest, and now that the clouds
have withdrawn, the spring winds have taught him,
fearful though he was, unfamiliar flights; quickly vicious assault sent him down as an enemy upon the
sheepfolds; now the lust for feast and fight has driven
him on against the struggling serpents; or like a lion
just weaned from his golden haired mother's rich milk
when he sees a roe grazing unwary in the rich meadow,
soon to die on untested tooth: the Vindelici saw Drusus
bringing war upon them beneath the Rhaetian Alps—
The investigation into how they learned their custom,
handed on for all aeons past, to arm their right hands
with the Amazon axe I tabled, for it is unlawful to know
all—but their forces long victorious, ranging far and
wide, crushed by the strategies of the young hero,
learned how powerful is the mind, how powerful is the
character reverently nurtured at the home's sacred
hearth, how powerful is Augustus's paternal spirit for
Nero's children. The brave father the brave and the
good; horses and bulls reflect their sires' virtue, and
fierce eagles do not produce a gentle dove. Teaching
brings out inborn might, and correct training renders
hearts oak hard; whenever ancestral ways are forgotten, faults disgrace noble-born traits. What debts you
owe, o Rome, to Nero's sons the river Metaurus bears
witness and Hasdrubal defeated and that beautiful day
when the darkness fled from Latium, the first day to
laugh in life-giving honor since the dreaded African
galloped through Italy's cities as fire through pine trees
or Eurus through the Sicilian waves. Since then steadily
with every prosperous labor Rome grew full strength,
and the temples destroyed in the impious Carthaginian

War had their gods restored. And devious Hannibal finally said, "Stags we are, prey of voracious wolves, of
our own will pursuing, when it is a rich triumph to de-
ceive and escape them. This people boldly brought
from the ashes of Troy their sacral rites, beaten about
on the Tuscan seas, and carried safely to Ausonian cities their children and aged fathers, a people like an oak
on Mount Algidus, dense with dark foliage, which,
though hewn by double axes, through injuries and car-
nage draws sustenance and life from the very iron.
Stronger than the Hydra ever grew against Hercules as
he cut her body and anguished over being defeated,
and a greater portent than the Colchians or Echionian
Thebes bore. Sink it in the deep, it becomes more beautiful; wrestle it, to its own great praise it will overthrow
a tireless, previously undefeated opponent and wage
battles to be sung by wives. To Carthage no longer will
I send haughty messengers; all our hope and the fortune of our name died, died when Hasdrubal was
slain." Claudian power fails not in anything that
Jupiter's propitious will defends and that wise governance directs through the dangers of war.]

It is extraordinary how quickly the triumphant poetic *ego* evap-
orates between c.3 and c.4, and how convincingly Horace directs
the gaze through the opening similes away from himself and
toward Drusus. The comparison to Pindar, sustained since c.2,
only intensifies the poet's withdrawal of self into the epic-styled
similes. Pindar's eagles symbolize athletic strength and the
struggle of the agon (*I*.4.43–47; *P*.5.111–12) as does the Horatian
eagle, but in Pindar's praise eagles often represent the poet's *arete*
(*N*.3.76–84; 5.20–22; *P*.1.5–12). Horace plays with the possibility
that his eagle imagines his own grandeur. *Fulminis alitem* (line
1) recalls by direct repetition and assonance *mutor in alitem*
(*C*.II.20.10), when Horace transformed into the majestic swan.
With the memory of II.20 still fresh from the allusions of c.3, it is
tempting to assume that Horace's eagle is also the poet, but this
expectation does not survive beyond *rex . . . regnum* (line 2). The
poet of c.3 is a noble bard; he is not king (c.3.12b–15; *C*.III.30.12b–
14a). The eagle, whose maturation is guarded by Jupiter, is far
different from the poet on display in II.20 and III.30, whom
Melpomene guards from birth (c.3). In Horace's simile of the

eagle the poet disappears, and Horace confines the poetic *ego* to a digression (18–22), the relevance of which is obscure enough that many consider it un-Horatian.[4]

Strong competitors separate themselves from rivals. Horace is imitating Pindar, and yet not. He surpasses his predecessor with one of Pindar's own tactics, understatement for exaggerated effect. When Horace opens with a metaphoric proemium that by allusion to his lyric grandeur skips past the poet's *arete,* such a central theme in Pindaric lyric and Horace's IV.8–9, he magnifies his victory ode's apparent incomplete representation of the Pindaric model. Horace's epinikion has no hymn or prayer and lacks encomiastic detail. Before *Odes* IV reaches its midpoint, Horace foreshadows its conclusion: c.14–15 (a second epinikion for Drusus and Tiberius, followed by another encomium for Augustus) parallel c. 4–5 and supply the encomiastic details lacking. Splitting the two victory ode–encomium pairs draws the book into a panegyric ring composition. Like most Pindaric epinikia, *Odes* IV fits a chiastic outline. C.1–2 announce the Horace-Pindar agon and rehearse the credentials of the contestants much like a proemium. C.4–5—14–15 (A-A) frame two sets of four odes, each on the theme of the lyric poet's power, c.6–9 and 10–13 (B-B). This Pindaric patterning allows several important observations. Horace's rivalry with Pindar and his claim to have bested his opponent are a driving force within the book and complete Horace's claims in *Odes* I–III that he belongs at the head of the lyric canon. Consequently, the modeling of panegyric praxis is of paramount importance in *Odes* IV. Horace's imitation of Pindaric structures also explains why a book of fifteen odes lacks a precise center (c.8–9 are too similar to divide). Most importantly the book's structure suggests that the so-called private poems, 10–13, correspond to the encomiastic themes of c.7–9. The precise nature of this correspondence is the subject of chapter 4.

The aesthetic attraction in a chiastic pattern is that the ring remains hidden until its conclusion, in this case until the book's final ode. Meanwhile, the audience looks for complementary elements closer at hand. C.3–6 also comprise a Pindaric string. The prayer to Melpomene (c.3) serves well as a proemium on the poet's power. C.4 announces the victory, and c.5 fills out the praise for the victor's father begun in c.4. The string closes with a reinvocation (c.6) to the poet's inspiration, Apollo the god of the Muses.[5]

The invocation-reinvocation, framing the opening strophe-antistrophe of *Pythian* 1, illustrates how closely Horace imitated Pindar's proemia in the sequencing of c.3–6. *Pythian* 1.1–12 is Pindar's most extensive portrait of Jupiter's eagle, and although Pindar's docile eagle is the opposite of Horace's attacking lord of the sky,[6] the similarity in the eagles' titles (ἀρχὸς οἰωνῶν, 7; *cui rex deorum regnum in avis vagas / permisit,* c.4.2–3a) signifies that Horace had in view this particular epinikion. Given this precise referent, it is possible to see other parallels. Pindar opens by hymning the lyre, and by extension Apollo and the Muses (σύνδικον ... κτέ-ανον, 2), and closes the proemium with the same order, the charming shafts of the lyre, then Leto's son and the Muses (12). So Horace frames the epinikion/encomium (c.4;5) with praise for Melpomene (c.3) and a hymn to Apollo (c.6). C.6 also employs a dramatic occasion similar to *Pythian* 1. Pindar imagines that his victory song is just about to be performed (lines 1–2), as does Horace, and Pindar calls on his lyre to lead the singers (4) in much the same manner that Horace instructs his chorus to maintain his finger's lyric beat (35–36). C.3–6 are as inseparable as the lyre in the proemium of *Pythian* 1 is from the rest of its song.

Horace's epinikion includes a metaphoric proemium (1–16), victory announcement (17–18, 23–28), *intermissio* (19–22), gnome (29–36), historical/mythological narrative (37–72), and closing (73–76), all integrated by recurrence in sound and structure.[7] Excluding the proemium and narrative, there is an alternation of sections approximately one half the length of the other: an eight-line victory announcement is interrupted by a four-line digression; then follows an eight-line gnome, and the ode closes with a four-line *laudatio.* The proemium (16 lines) is roughly half the length of the narrative (36 lines). If the four-line digression were excluded, the verses of the smaller panels (proemium, victory announcement, gnome, and closing) would match the length of the narrative (16, 8, 8, 4 = 36). The digression is necessary to complete the rotation but can be removed, and the result is a more precise pattern. Whatever one surmises about the thematic relevance of the digression, it would require an extremely clever imitator to make such a precise insertion.

The proemium is a precise temporal ring composition moving from the present to the past and back to the present. We first glimpse the eagle as a powerful viceroy already entrusted by

Jupiter to rule the kingdom of the nomadic birds, because he has proven himself by capturing Ganymede in order to be his master's (ἐραστής) cupbearer. The second stanza flashes back to the eagle's birth and development. Horace carefully marks each stage with temporal adverbs (5–12): leaving the nest (*olim . . . propulit*), learning to survive (*iam . . . docuere*) and hunt (*mox . . . demisit*), and enjoying the sport of domination (*nunc . . . egit*). The simile reverts (*nunc,* 11) to its beginning. Horace connects the eagle's last assault with the rape of Ganymede by using the language of the banquet (*egit amor dapis atque pugnae,* 12). This bit of sympotic violence adds to the shocking horror of the eagle's attack. Like the drunken violent centaurs, the eagle is outside the boundaries of acceptable sympotic behavior.

The proemium is highly visual. The audience watches the maturation of an eagle, a powerful bird portrayed on coins, buildings, and military standards. The rape of Ganymede was one of the most popular subjects in art from the Classical to the Hellenistic and Roman periods,[8] and Horace could count on his audience being able to recall any number of models just as Plautus's Menaechmus could when he, a Ganymede look-alike, pranced about in his wife's robe (*Men.*143–146). Sight also provides a seamless transition to the conclusion of the similes and the victory announcement. Drusus is the eagle and the lion. The comparison is coordinated by the enjambed anadiplosis *vidit, videre* (16–17), which emphasizes the precision of the similes: just as one sees an eagle and lion attack, so the Vindelici see Drusus. *Videt, videre* are reinforced by *sensere* (25) so that the similes and Drusus waging war on his enemies and teaching them of his nobility form a single ekphrastic moment.

The proemium is also a musical. The assonance of the first line (*qualem . . . alitem* around *ministrum fulminis*) and the alliteration of the second (*rex . . . regnum*) set the rhythm. An overpowering recurrence of sound connects the second and third stanzas: ni*do,* ni*mbis,* ni*sus;* *verni,* *venti,* *paventem.* The assonance of the double "i" joins *demisit* and *vividus impetus* to *ovilia,* and by the oxymoron increases the empathy for the eagle's victims, whose living (*vividus*) attack slaughters the helpless no matter how the metonymy of sheepfold (*ovilia*) attempts to depersonalize the terror of "only the strong survive." The eagle's prey are not silent. From *demisit hostem vividus impetus,* an "e-i-i" pattern is repeated around the middle "o" of *hostem* that echoes the sounds of *mox . . . ovilia.* The sheep are bleating. And they continue to bleat during the eagle's attack on the hissing, striking snake (*reluctantis* d*racones . . .* d*apis . . . pugnae*).[9]

The comparison of Jupiter's eagle to Augustus's Drusus lays the thematic groundwork for the victory announcement and gnome. The eaglet becomes what he is by nature and training. He inherits his father's vigor (5) that thrusts him from the nest, but when nature totters on failure as the frightened eagle plummets to the earth, the winds teach the lesson of flight (7–9a). The eagle's life is a thematic preview of Drusus's, born a noble Nero but nurtured in the house of Augustus. The gnome (29–36) grows directly out of the comparison between the animal and human worlds (30–32) in which both lineage and education are necessary for success (29).

The real surprise of the proemium is that it does not end at line 12. The time sequence of the ring structure (present to past to present) has finished its course and anticipated the time sequencing of the entire epinikion: Drusus's victory (present), the glories of his ancestors (past), and the present and future greatness of the Claudian family. Horace has foreshadowed through the details of the simile the thematic concerns of ancestry and education, which recur in the announcement and gnome. The last word of the simile, *pugnae,* would transition well to Drusus's attack (*bella,* 17). Structurally the ode could have moved smoothly from the eagle to Drusus, but Horace extends the proemium with the emphatic repetition *qualemve* (13) to include a second simile. *-Ve* was last heard in *paventem,* and the trembling frenzy of anticipation fills the next episode. The simile again is highly pictorial (*intenta . . . vidit*), and Horace adds an emotional charge by setting the scene so that those looking in at the poem from the outside at a presumed safe imaginary distance are watching a victim who is not watching out for danger (not unlike themselves).[10] A young lion just weaned and boasting its new teeth creeps toward a small roe, away from its mother and lost in the pasturage of the meadow.[11] That she is about to die is the furthest thought from her mind. She is marked for death (*peritura*) before she sees the threat. The roe trembles with fear once she on a sudden has seen her peril, but we also tremble as we watch the cat slowly approaching its innocent prey. The lion-roe simile magnifies exponentially the pathos of the proemium. The ring of the first simile juxtaposes Ganymede and the snake capable of fighting back. The roe and her mother correct what may be a potentially misleading comparison by reminding that Ganymede too was caught unawares. Horace uses the repetition of color, *Ganymede flavo* (4) . . . *fulvae matris* (14), to prompt the association. However, the trauma in this second simile, unlike in the rape of Ganymede, is that there is no Jupiter responsible, only the inevitability of the lion's mastery. The lion and roe are innocents by nature, but all the same, mothers lose or lose control over their young. Young lions and roes will follow their instincts. The episode might be less disconcerting, if there were a divine hunter to blame.[12]

So Horace introduces the Vindelici to Drusus. The eagle carries Ganymede through the heavens for Zeus; Drusus wages war under the Alps for Augustus. The young eagle (*iuventas*) is appointed the ruler of the wandering fowl (*avis vagas*); Drusus in his youth (*iuvenis*) has restrained the wide-ranging Vindelician "flocks" (*catervae*). Horace leads his audience to interpret the details in the similes quite closely.

Drusus, however, does not hold the ultimate position of praise in the victory announcement. This belongs, in spite of all the attention given to nurturing Augustus (25–27), to the Neronian line (28). A less fearless panegyrist might have glossed over the innuendos and rumors that whirled around Livia's quick divorce, her marriage to Augustus, and Drusus's birth three months later.[13] Did Ti. Claudius Nero give Livia up willingly, or did Augustus (Livia) steal her (his) affections and then take her (leave Claudius)? Suetonius gives both opinions (*Aug.*62, 69; *Tib.*4). Was Drusus conceived through an illicit affair?—a matter for gossip.[14] Horace heads his epinikion straight into the tantalizing complications. A rapid dactylic movement (*in pueros animus,* 28) compresses together Drusus's and Tiberius's two families (*Augusti paternus . . . Nerones,* 27) and places center stage what was common knowledge, that Augustus's children were not his own. And then Horace constructs around this mixed lineage the gnome's main argument. An outstanding youth requires noble birth and sound training (29–33). The transition to the gnome and its structure carefully balances the value of birth and nurture. The nurturing parent (Augustus, 25–27), the corresponding pair of inherited *virtus* and acquired *doctrina* (29–39), then the heroic parents (the

Nerones, 28, 37–48; the Julian line, 53–56) form a ring that joins together the conclusion of the victory announcement, the gnome,
and the upcoming mythohistorical narrative. Within the ring Horace embeds a chiastic pattern: Augustus (education); the Neros
(noble birth); noble birth (29–32); education (33–36). Horace does
not allow the opening simile, as it plays out through the epinikion, to emphasize birth over education or education over birth.
This balance counters Pindar's emphasis on abilities granted by
nature, φυά (*O*.9.100a; *P*.8.44–45a), without discounting inborn
virtus. Upsetting the balance would give Augustus too much
credit, or the Neros too little, and would thematically divorce the
first half of the ode from the second, as well as discredit the his-
torical/mythological narrative that blends the two families together in the triumph of Rome.[15] The familial ideology in the
epinikion's praise teaches that victory does not belong to one individual. Augustus also is only a necessary part of the whole. The
grand Roman victory results from inclusion not exclusion.

Accordingly, when Horace continues the battle narrative (37–
48), he develops the inborn *virtus* of the Neros to complete the
ideology of the gnome (nurture, Augustus; nature, the Neronian
line). Horace extols C. Claudius Nero's victory over Hasdrubal
near the Metaurus River (207 B.C.), which sealed Hannibal's defeat in the Second Punic War. Horace fashions his praise as a direct address to Rome so that thematically the narrative enlarges
the argument of the gnome to the family of Roman citizens, who
owe their continued existence, moral recovery, and prosperity to
the *Nerones* (37). The Neros become the first parents of the Roman
family, a point Horace clarifies by verbal references back to both
aspects of the gnome, birth and nurture. The Neros brought Rome
back into the light. The Roman youths, like the young eagle, could
once again grow and prosper (*Romana pubes crevit*, 46; see *creantur*, 29). When war ended, the Romans rebuilt the temples and by
their pious devotion proved their character had been strengthened by training (*fana deos habuere rectos*, 48; *rectique cultus pectora
roborant*, 34). Another chiastic rotation outlines the familial relationships of the Carthaginian defeat: the Neros (37)—Hasdrubal
(38)—Hannibal (39–44)—Roman vigor (*pubes*, 46).

Horace's Hannibal (43–44), riding like a demigod through the
cities of Italy, sets the mood for the mythologizing of Roman history that culminates in Hannibal's mythic similes (57–68). Ho-

race's polished transition from *antiqua facta* to legend conflates the *laudator*'s role as historian and storyteller. Since Vergil's *Aeneid* the boundaries between legend and history, never precisely drawn, were thinner than ever. Horace begins his play with the linear progression of history when Rome's victory over the Carthaginians (39b–41) foreshadows Aeneas's flight from Troy (53–56), and then Horace brings Hannibal back to life and makes him speak.

Hannibal's speech (49–72[6?]) is the most distinctive feature of Horace's epinikion. It is a miniature of the ode's chiastic form (simile, 50–51a; praise for the victors, 51b–52; praise for their ancestors, 53–56; compound simile, 57–68). Hannibal opens with a simile from the same predator-prey imagery as the proemium.[16] Hannibal, casting himself as the weaker victim, preys on his audience's sympathies. The Carthaginian stags facing the rapacious Roman wolves force a sympathetic, even empathetic, look back at the roe in the meadows, no match for the hungry lion. But how deceitful (*perfidus*) Hannibal can be becomes clear as his argument unfolds and should lessen any pity that Hannibal's first words may have won. Hannibal acknowledges that the Carthaginians of their own volition chased after the wolves, when the greatest triumph any stag could win would be outrunning its pursuing foe (51–52). Hannibal reverses the roles of predator and prey so that his drama violates nature. Deer chasing after wolves is absurd. The tragedy of Hannibal is not dependent on the animal instincts of the earlier simile, but on willful recklessness.

Hannibal's hubris enacts the ideology of the gnome. When he retells the story of Vergil's Aeneas (53–57), it becomes obvious that Hannibal should have known better than attack a people who had learned to endure such calamity from their ancestors. Hannibal overlooked Rome's character passed down from generation to generation. Horace has Hannibal show that he has learned his lesson by incorporating the language of the gnome into Hannibal's *Aeneid*. *Gens . . . fortis* (53) echoes the gnome's *fortes creantur fortibus* (29). *Iactata . . . sacra* (54) for Vergil's *primus profugus iactatus* (A.1.1–3) underscores the sanctity of Aeneas's mission and reflects the religious vocabulary of the gnome (*rectique cultus, mores, indecorant*). The metrical balance of *natos, maturos, patres* with the almost imperceptible *-que* (55) sounds out the importance of the child-to-parent bond that *doctrina* and *mores* demand. Hannibal knows that Rome stood strong because of the Julian and Neronian lines.

Hannibal's other similes (57–68) continue to invert nature's norms. The Romans are like an oak tree that does not fall no matter how many times it is struck with axes, mightier than the Hydra that becomes stronger when cut, and a monster greater than men born from the ground. Together the similes are a prodigious string of ill-omened anomalies vividly expressing in one progressive mythic experience Rome's miraculous power to survive. Although the oak and the Hydra are both cut (*ilex tonsa,* 57; *Hydra secto corpore,* 61), they grow stronger (*ilex . . . ducit opes animumque,* 60; *Hydra . . . crevit,* 61–62; see *Romunu pubes crevit,* 46). The Colchian and Theban men are sown and rise from the ground just like an oak tree. Each simile adds a dimension to the whole picture of Rome's birth and regeneration.

Hannibal's mythology starts with what appears to be an image of Roman resilience, inspired by the trees in Pindar's *Pythian* 4 and Vergil's *Aeneid* 2.[17] Both these felled trees survive by changing form and location. Pindar's tree becomes fuel for the winter hearth or a support for its master's halls, and Vergil's Trojan ash tree will escape to build another city. As Putnam observes, Anchises continues the tree simile when he assures the Trojans that their strength stands oak-hard (*A.*2.638b–640).[18] Pindar may be behind the Vergilian simile and thus ultimately Horace's, but Hannibal's simile is more Vergilian. Horace's Hannibal, after giving his account of the *Aeneid,* repeats the weaponry (*ferro accisam crebrisque bipennibus,* 627; see *bipennibus . . . ferro,* 57–60) that brought down Vergil's ash tree. Hannibal sets up his unfelled oak to be a defiant opposite to Vergil's fallen tree, perhaps an enemy's tribute to Rome's indomitable spirit that might put a favorable spin on his own loss. No one could be expected to conquer such an oak-hard enemy.

A lie from *perfidus* Hannibal is hardly surprising. The resilient oak turns monstrous. Unlike the other trees suggested as models, Hannibal's Trojan oak never falls. There was one oak tree in the *Aeneid* that would not fall—Aeneas who did not give in to Dido however desperately she pled (4.438b–446).[19] Any tree that grows stronger from repeated wounds is *contra naturam,* and as Hannibal's similes turn more sinister the Roman tree seems more like Aeneas, too hard at its core toward its victims.[20] Hannibal barely suppresses his contempt. Horace last used *durus* to describe his failed attempt to withstand Venus's assault and Ligurinus's steadfast rejection (c.1.7, 33–40).[21] *Duris* (57) in the emphatic first position embodies the whole sense of the tree simile. Its juxtaposition with *ilex* intimates that the one thing harder than the axes is the tree itself. Hannibal was called cruel (*dirus*, 42), and now he is returning the insult, calling Rome hard-hearted (*dirus : duris*). And Hannibal's *ilex* is planted on the *Algidus Mons,* the northeastern group of Alban hills about nineteen miles southeast of Rome, known for its shady groves of holm oaks (C.I.21.6; III.23.9; Mart. 10.30.6; Sil. 12.536; Stat. *Silv.*4.4.16). Hannibal would have seen these trees on his march against Rome, when he crossed through the passes of Algidus (Cava dell'Aglio) on his way toward Tusculum and Gabii, eventually setting up camp within eight miles of Rome (Liv. 26.8–9). A holm oak on Mount Algidus not only symbolizes Rome's enduring might but reminds just how close Hannibal did come to capturing the city.

The liar Hannibal is not Rome's panegyrist, or is he? The end of his speech provides no final answer. The monstrosity of the similes makes it difficult to decide just how to read the whole sequence—an epinikion to Roman achievement or a backhanded attempt by a defeated foe to win a sympathetic response. Syntactically the similes more closely identify Rome with the tree (*ut ilex*) than the Hydra (*non Hydra*) and the supernatural men, but the repetition of *crevit* (*Romana pubes crevit,* 46; *Hydra . . . crevit,* 62) closes the gap. Hannibal (like the proemium) doubles the last simile: one group of dragon-men (Jason's armed warriors, 63) would have sustained the argument. The Spartoi (64) add the ultimate familial disaster. After their spontaneous birth from the earth they attack each other. Only five survive.[22] Civil wars threatened to ruin Rome as much, if not more, than Hannibal ever did. Hannibal's cap on the simile worsens the interpretive predicament (65–68). The general thesis supports the similes: Rome always endures and thrives. This is the pronouncement of a victory ode. The end of the tricolon is not so certain. Rome (her invincibility) is the proper subject of becoming more beautiful (65), throwing a strong opponent (66–67), and waging war (67–68), but defeated dead, not heroic victors, leave widowed wives to hymn their battles. These last three words (*proelia coniugibus loquenda,* 68) shift sympathy from the victorious Romans to the defeated

Carthaginians. Some emend *geretque ... loquenda* to make the tricolon end more triumphantly, but the entire stanza would have to be excised to improve the strange reversals in Hannibal's metaphor.[23] Rome fights back like a Hydra and dragon-men, a metaphor of heroic self-defense, but the notion of such monsters becoming more beautiful and winning praise (an epinikion) overturns the traditional myths. Horace's Hannibal's praise of Rome is restrained by the unnatural qualities of his mythic similes.

Hannibal closes in complete despair. His refusal to dispatch messengers back to Carthage picks up the undercurrent of disaster in *proelia coniugibus loquenda*. The only praise for the Carthaginians will be laments. Hannibal then laments Hasdrubal, which brings his speech back to Rome's moment of victory at the Metaurus River.[24] The epinikion's familial theme of birth and education has come full circle; for Hannibal it is a tragedy. He views his brother's death and his own defeat as the end of their ancestral line. With no noble lineage all hope dies (71–72a), which is summed up in the pathetic repetition *occidit, occidit*. Hannibal may not send back any haughty messengers, but his speech is exactly that since it attempts to win sympathy and restore some measure of pride by turning the aggressor into the wronged victim. Hannibal's panegyric is an exemplar of the stereotyped sophistic rhetoric that makes the weaker the stronger, and his deceptive spin on the Carthaginian invasion of Italy is highly persuasive. His praise rewrites Roman history with a particular slant. The ring structure has the effect of giving the Neros all the credit for Rome's victory. Once C. Claudius Nero defeated Hasdrubal, the war from Hannibal's point of view was over.

The last strophe returns to the proemium and encapsulates the gnome's thesis: great achievement depends on ancestry and education. Jupiter watches over the Claudians just as he did his eagle (73–75a), but their divine nobility is joined with a wisdom that guides them through the hazards of war (75b–76). The conclusion does not replicate the gnome exactly. Hannibal's speech has its effect. To borrow from Putnam's play on the simile of the tree, in the gnome "Claudian *vis* is grafted on to the tree of Julian *doctrina*, not the other way around."[25] Hannibal's speech reverses the gnome, and now Julian *doctrina* is grafted on to the tree of Claudian *vis*.

Horace's bold artistry—the visual depth of the opening similes, the imperial gossip behind the gnome, the compression of his-

tory and myth, the sophistic rhetoric of Hannibal's speech, the Ju-
lian-Claudian line that becomes the Claudian-Julian — should
end the criticism that Horace has written a perfunctory epinikion.[26] That such creativity is so evident in Horatian panegyric is
no small matter. From the beginning of book IV Horace has
engaged Pindar in a poetic agon to determine who gains the mastery in the praxis of praise. The athletic competition (the audience, athlete, and praise singer) overlays the interpretive environment of the Horatian epinikion so that there is more to the
poetic experience than the perspective of the winner. Horace's
epinikion draws the audience in as an active participant who not
only watches the poet-athletes compete, but in this literary agon,
where there is no defined finish line, serves as the judge for all
competitors, the *laudandi* and *laudatores.* Horace may attempt to
outdo his rival by serious imitation or parody, which can make
reading the tone of an ode difficult. For instance, the *intermissio* of
c.4 (19–22) could be a serious reflection of Pindaric style or a
mocking jab that exposes the weakness of his poetic *arete.* The
more skillfully Horace executes the imitation, the more he increases the possibility for disputes and expands the interpretive
depth of his praise.[27] Thus the *laudator* both competes in the agon
and draws the interpretive space for the viewer. As K. Crotty re-
marks, "the (Pindaric) epinikion is itself an action" where the poet
competes to win a prize of immortal fame. Horace is competing
for the prize, but unlike his opponent he does not attempt to win
by persuading the audience to adopt the viewpoint of the victorious athlete or warrior. He manipulates the differing points of
view to create an ongoing interpretive dialogue, that is, he reenacts the competition.[28] This is the most novel dimension of the
Horatian epinikion.[29] Horatian panegyric embraces the entirety
of the athletic event itself: the audience, the celebrant, and the
poet. The interpretive agon between these often competing vantage points produces the pathos, the outcome or experience of
the ode.

The imperial family could accept Horace's poem as a well-
executed praise ode in the Pindaric style and extract from it a sustained Augustan viewpoint. The simile of the eagle establishes a
chain of command within the family that is divinely sanctioned.
Augustus is the earthly Jupiter who trusts his son Drusus, the
eagle, to carry out his will, and when his commands are carried

out the result is a glorious victory over a troublesome enemy. The digression (19–22) proves how necessary it was to attack the Vindelici. They are not like the innocent roe. They had learned from one generation to the next to wield the cruel Amazonian axe (see *immanis Raetos*, C.IV.14.15).[30] Roman peace depends on imperial authority. The empathy in the poet's praise for those suffering in the face of Roman might agrees with the Augustan policy of leniency, and we should not needlessly invent an Augustus blind to the ravages of war. Anchises' shade looks past Aeneas and instructs the future Roman to manage the empire by sparing the submissive but finishing off the proud (Verg. *A*.6.851–53),[31] and Augustus preferred to spare rather than destroy, as long as it could be done safely (*RG* 3.1–2). The insolence of defeated Hannibal's speech proves that he merited destruction. The gnome with its anti-Pindaric emphasis on education transforms a rumored sexual scandal into an encomiastic moment that counters the violent reputation of the pre-Actian Octavian. In 39 B.C. Octavian married Livia and raised her children to be the future guardians of Rome. Octavian was the nurturing father (22–28) who would not allow Roman *mores* to fail (35–36). The historical/mythological narrative builds the epinikion into a grand panegyric finale. The victories of Aeneas's Troy and the Nerones unite the Julian and Claudian families into a divinely sanctioned powerhouse ensuring Rome's future.

   The epinikion can be read by a wider spectrum of experience. The ekphrastic similes place the audience in a position to judge the eagle and its attacks. The first three lines focus the audience on a courtly scene of Jupiter and his confidant, and they watch the eagle carry off Ganymede, attack sheep, and play-fight with a snake. The simile turns the audience's gaze progressively toward the victims. Then the praise singer adds the simile of the innocent roe so that the pathos of the image favors the prey. Consequently, the anadiplosis *vidit, videre* leads the audience to adopt the vantage point of the Vindelici as they see Drusus sweeping down on them in war. The audience is forced into an ekphrastic crisis (Drusus and the Vindelici are facing off against each other) whether to maintain the perspective of the prey or side with their own Drusus. Since the moment of decision does not occur until after the Roman audience experiences the attack from the viewpoint of its defeated enemies, the choice necessitates an uncomfortable acceptance of a personalized sense of weakness. The emotional conflict would be even more potent for those who had suffered as children or had parents who lost their fortune and lives to the victories of Octavian.[32]

If the viewpoint of the victim is felt strongly enough, the epinikion becomes potentially negative.[33] The anti-Pindaric emphasis on proper education in the gnome makes Augustus responsible for the behavior of his children. Instead of restraint Augustus taught them domination. The gnome takes on a strong didactic tone, and then the historical narrative reinforces the failures of the imperial house by praising the Neronian side of the family: Rome, what you owe, you owe to the Nerones (37).[34] Horace's Hannibal identifies the Julian line (53–56) with his monstrous images ending in an allusion to civil war (57–64), and it is the Claudian line that defeats him. Even the most general theme of Roman ascendancy fails in light of the ode's overall structure. The praise for the young Nerones and their ancestors, framing a gnome teaching that fathers raise sons like themselves, invites comparison between the victories of the present and the past. The comparison is not favorable. The ancestors drove out invading Hannibal, and now the sons of Augustus have invaded and beaten the Vindelici, a frightened roe, no match for their strength. The Roman Odes reach the same ending: each generation produces a lesser (III.6.33–36, 45–48).[35]

Where is the praise poet in all this? The panegyrist offers no simple resolution for the many competing interpretive vantage points. The panegyrist is not the judge, and the divergent viewpoints stand blended together so that as one position is argued, numerous objections come readily to mind. The panegyric can be read from differing perspectives depending on any number of unpredictable factors including political bias and personal experience (my own included). In this poem, as in all other poems in *Odes* IV, the personal is public. As is evident from the various manuscript readings in the last strophe, Horace's earlier audiences were as divided in their impressions about such panegyric as the modern reader. Augustus and his stepsons had won a grand victory, but the security of Rome had not come without a price. Here in Horace is the same Vergilian pathos that precludes a monochromatic reading of the *Aeneid.*[36]

The panegyrist facilitates the debate by the most curious and difficult features of the epinikion, the digression (18–22a) and conclusion of Hannibal's speech (74–77).[37] Horace first distinguishes the panegyrist's voice in the digression and then hides it again behind Hannibal. The digression comes abruptly. After Horace writes a metaphoric proemium that suppresses the poetic *ego,* then when the victory announcement is barely underway, he suddenly breaks the narrative with a strong disavowal in the first person. The disruption is just as startling as when Vergil's *cano* usurps the place of the Muse. Horace's emphatic *distuli* singles out the epinikion's *ego*: the panegyrist for an instant has come out of hiding. For these few lines he speaks directly to his audience, not through metaphor or another narrator.

The panegyrist still does not give any opinion that would help resolve the epinikion's tensions. The digression itself is thematically conflicted. Although the panegyrist does not know where the Rhaetians first learned to use the Amazonian axe, he places firmly in Rhaetian hands this most potent symbol of barbarism. If Romans did not know anything about the Rhaetians, and most probably did not, all they needed to know was that they were Amazonian. It is harder to feel sympathy for such legendary aggressors. Thus the digression rebalances the epinikion after the pity-provoking similes. The panegyrist, however, gives enough detail about the Vindelici to keep them from being dehumanized to the status of prey. These were parents who taught their customs to their children. The digression is rhetorically designed to stress the Vindelician success in passing on their culture from one generation to the next. The rhyming assonance and enjambment passes tradition (*mos*) on through the line and into the next (mos unde deductus per omne / tempus, 19–20a). Before the panegyrist presents Augustus as the parent and states the gnome that education strengthens birth, he describes parents who taught their children well, but taught savage violence. Horace does not allow tradition to stand as an undisputed good. The repetition of *mos-mores* and the sound of 19–20a in *utcumque defecere mores, / indecorant* (35–36a) color Vindelician practice with the failure of tradition. Certainly *mores* can die out and so fail; *mores* also in themselves can be deficient and when passed on from generation to generation lead to disaster. Nurture must be upright (*recti cultus*). Augustus passed on his *mores* to his sons, but could not their actions and the sympathetic view of the similes imply that he taught them to dominate the weak?[38] The panegyrist does not allow himself to be pinned down.

Perhaps I have been distracted and taken the digression too far. The digression is not really about the Vindelici, but the panegyrist's attitude toward research. He claims that for him to inquire into the remote past would be impious. *Nec . . . fas* contains a strong religious sanction. Here at last is the poet's *arete* that Horace passes over lightly with his imitation of Pindar's eagle. The panegyrist's virtue is silence. He knows there are limits to his praise that he should not exceed. The difficulty here is to determine just how serious is the panegyrist's refusal to command all the facts.

Horace defines the epinikion's *ego* by the language and character of the seriocomic sympotic persona of *Odes* I–III. The digression imitates two separate sympotic invitations. *Quaerere distuli* mirrors the command to Thaliarchus (*fuge quaerere,* C.I.9.13–16) and with *nec scire fas est omnia* replicates the beginning of the ode to Leuconoë (*Tu ne quaesieris, scire nefas, quem mihi, quem tibi / finem di dederint, Leuconoe,* C.I.11.1–2a). Such stockpiling of references to Horace's sympotic persona injects into the epinikion its basic poetic strategies. The sympotic panegyrist as opposed to the panegyric epicist does not want to take himself too seriously and is free from political interests. Horace is having some fun at the expense of more straightforward and pedantic—and therefore uninteresting and dry—panegyrists.[39] Be that as it may, of paramount importance is the sympotic temporality of the digression. The sympotic panegyrist divorces himself from the future and past. He is not operating from an omniscient point of view,[40] and he invites his audience to follow his lead. The epinikion as a sympotic expression is confined to the present moment; its pleasures are in the interpretive act of the moment. The poet does not carefully and covertly nuance his panegyric with disputed features (*dubia*) because he must disguise criticism to avoid offending imperial sensibilities; ambiguity and conflict are the pleasures of spinning a good panegyric yarn for the poet and his audiences. Declining a sympotic invitation can have serious consequences. Likewise, the attempt to remove the epinikion from the present, that is, to fix its interpretation, destroys the song's immortality because it jeopardizes its dynamic ability to grow with and influence its changing society.

After the praise singer openly declares himself in the digression, he hides behind Hannibal. Where does Hannibal's speech end and the praise singer's begin? The confusion centers on the song's last four lines, but the question applies equally to the entire speech. The treachery of Hannibal's speech is not entirely Hannibal's. The poet appears to have relinquished control to another narrator for almost half the poem so that Hannibal can distort praise for Rome into empathy for her defeated enemies. Yet throughout the speech the praise singer impresses on his audience that this particular Hannibal is his own creation. Hannibal has closely read Vergil's *Aeneid* and Horace—the beginning of this epinikion (especially the similes and the gnome) and other poems in the book as well (c.1, 8, 9). The effect is that Horace's old barbarian Hannibal sounds like a contemporary poet.[41] This game of text and subtext shows the audience how thinly the epinikion wears the mask of Hannibal. The audience becomes increasingly aware that the panegyrist is creating, not reporting. Further, it becomes entirely a matter of speculation whether the praise singer himself believes Hannibal or to what extent he anticipates that his audience will be persuaded by Hannibal.

The poet has not constructed a monochromatic praise either for or against the *laudandus* (Augustus) but a narrative that disrupts any attempt to resolve the epinikion into a single interpretive viewpoint. One of the best general descriptions of c.4 is W. R. Johnson's "amusing."[42] The panegyric puzzles are enticing. They invite the audience to come and share the interpretive experience of a song. This is precisely where Horatian panegyric is most sympotic.

C.5: A Panegyric Tag^{One}—All in the Family

> Divis orte bonis, optime Romulae
> custos gentis, abes iam nimium diu;
> maturum reditum pollicitus patrum
>   sancto concilio, redi.
>
> lucem redde tuae, dux bone, patriae.   5
> instar veris enim vultus ubi tuus
> affulsit populo, gratior it dies
>   et soles melius nitent.

ut mater iuvenem, quem Notus invido
flatu Carpathii trans maris aequora   10
cunctantem spatio longius annuo
    dulci distinet a domo,

votis ominibusque et precibus vocat,
curvo nec faciem litore dimovet,
sic desideriis icta fidelibus   15
    quaerit patria Caesarem.

tutus bos etenim rura perambulat,
nutrit rura Ceres almaque Faustitas,
pacatum volitant per mare navitae,
    culpari metuit fides,   20

nullis polluitur casta domus stupris,
mos et lex maculosum edomuit nefas,
laudantur simili prole puerperae,
    culpam poena premit comes.

quis Parthum paveat, quis gelidum Scythen,   25
quis Germania quos horrida parturit
fetus, incolumi Caesare, quis ferae
    bellum curet Hiberiae?

condit quisque diem collibus in suis
et vitem viduas ducit ad arbores;   30
hinc ad vina[43] redit laetus et alteris
    te mensis adhibet deum,

te multa prece, te prosequitur mero
defuso pateris et Laribus tuum
miscet numen, uti Graecia Castoris   35
    et magni memor Herculis.

'longas o utinam, dux bone, ferias
praestes Hesperiae!' dicimus integro
sicci mane die, dicimus uvidi
    cum sol Oceano subest.   40

[Child of the munificent gods, highest guardian of the Romulan race, you have now been away far too long. A
timely return you promised to the sacred council of the
fathers; now return. Return, munificent ruler, your light to
your homeland. For when your spring-like face has shone

on your people, the day passes more splendently and suns shine brighter. As a mother with every vow and prayer calls for her young man, whom, delaying across the waters of the Carpathian Sea, the Southwind with its jealous blast has separated from his sweet home longer than the span of a year, and does not turn her face from the curving shore, just so the homeland, smitten by faithful desires, longs for Caesar. For indeed the ox safely walks the fields, the fields Ceres and nurturing Prosperity nourish, sailors fly over the pacified sea, faith fears being found guilty, the chaste house stands undefiled by any disgrace, custom and law have vanquished filthy wickedness, children like their fathers bring glory to their mothers, guilt takes punishment for her companion. Who would tremble at the Parthian, who at the cold Scythian, who at the brood crude Germany births, if Caesar be well, who would concern themselves with war in wild Spain? Each spends his day on his own hills and weds the vine to the widowed trees; from there he happily returns to drink the wine and at the second course invokes you a god, honors you with many a prayer, with pure wine poured out from its bowls, and mixes your divinity with the household gods, as Greece remembers Castor and great Hercules. "O munificent ruler, would that you extend to the Roman West long festal days." This we pray, parched dry in the early morning; this we again pray, drunk when the sun sets beneath the Ocean.]

Compared to the narrative twists and turns of c.4, this *apotheosis Augusti* epitomizes direct panegyric that presents the monochromatic view of the *laudandus,* perhaps. What is so singular about this encomium is not the specific deeds by which Augustus merits deification, but the ode's form and occasion: a hymn prayed to Augustus while the princeps is still alive, written to celebrate his return from Spain (13 B.C.) but staged as if Augustus were still absent.

The hymn begins with a flourish. The opening direct address is doubled, the first stating the divine lineage (*divis orte bonis*) and the second the god's primary *raison d'être* (*optime Romulae / custos gentis*). The shift from *bonis* to *optime,* marked by a strong caesura, and their juxtaposition at the center of the first line indicate that the addressee has outdone his divine ancestors. As is common, the opening address is followed by a request that the deity (*bone dux*) return to its favored dwelling (3–16), and the triple *reditum, redi, redde* (3–5) add impassioned urgency to the plea.

Although the panegyrist has not yet named the hymn's honored recipient, there could be little doubt by the end of the second stanza that it is divine Augustus. *Divis orte bonis* reflects the familiar title *Iulii filius divi,* and solar theology played a prominent role in the deification of Julius and his chosen son: a comet appeared during the *Ludi Victoriae Caesaris* and was interpreted to be Caesar's deified soul; the sun dimmed for a year after Caesar's assassination; a comet appeared again near the time of the *Ludi Saeculares* (17 B.C.); Sol stood atop Apollo's Palatine temple; Augustus decorated Rome with obelisks originally devoted to the sun god in Egypt.[44] There is hardly any need to remember that Horace associates the *Iulium sidus* with Augustus (C.I.12.47) and in C.IV.2 praises Augustus with the shout '*o sol pulcher, o laudande!*' Horace punctuates the request for the deity's return with the climactic naming of Caesar (16), which leads directly to a rehearsal of the god's deeds (17–24). Then a banquet is held; prayers and a libation are offered to Augustus. The rite, as it is presented (29–36), does not distinguish between praying to the princeps' guardian spirit and directly to his person, or between the entities of the *genius, lares,* and *numen.*[45] The panegyrist uses a common metaphor taken from the mixing of wine at banquets to prevent the interposition of fine nuances. By custom the wine for the libation was unmixed and so pure (*mero,* 33), but this vinedresser in the performance of the ritual mixes the princeps' divine *numen,* a word reserved for the essence that constitutes divinity, with the Lares (*Laribus tuum / miscet numen*). There is no mistaking the powerful religious symbolism, nearly Dionysiac, of the prayers, wine, and divine presence of Augustus being all mingled together. The private banquet expands to a public celebration (37–40) and closes with an entreaty that the divine Augustus prolong the festal life of his people.[46]

Readings of c.5 by Lyne and DuQuesnay, both published in 1995, demonstrate what divergent interpretations such transparent panegyric can produce. Lyne finds direct panegyric of this sort so out of sync with the poet's previous more indirect imperial encomia that he thinks it belittles Horace's talents. To account for the discrepancy he returns to the Suetonian legacy that the ode was commissioned by Augustus, and Horace, out of obligation, coupled with his ambition to be "the court poet," took on the artistically risky task of public poetry. DuQuesnay defends the praise's "perfect execution." According to DuQuesnay, Horace's skill as a panegyrist is determined by how his poetry effectively contributes to the imaging of Augustus. Whether the poet personally agrees with the image he constructs is a moot point once he accepts the commission to write the praise.[47] If either Lyne or DuQuesnay are correct in their entirety, then the *encomium Augusti* of c.5 differs drastically from the rich polytonality of the panegyric storytelling displayed in c.4, and Lowrie would rightly conclude that the poet's lyric is suppressed in favor of an imperial voice as the book progresses.[48] There is no point in reduplicating the work already done,[49] but I would like to put forward an addendum to the conversation on c.5 by observing how this ode is more Horatian than previously noted, specifically in what ways it corresponds to other panegyrics in book IV and relies on common Horatian sympotic themes to affect the quality of Augustus's apotheosis so that it aligns with the panegyrist's emphasis on the power of the interpreting Roman community.

It is commonly observed that each epinikion is paired with a fuller encomium celebrating Augustus's achievements (c.4–5, 14–15), but the implications that one praise is incomplete without the other and that the encomia are an outgrowth of the epinikia have been denied or largely ignored. The Suetonian *Life* states only that Horace was commissioned to compose the *CS* and two epinikia, and adds that because of this Augustus compelled Horace to publish another book. It is an assumption that c.5 and 15 were commissioned in the same official sense as the epinikia and for this reason were paired with them. The poet's creativity in arranging the poems for a certain effect is a better explanation for the sequencing of the book than the obligations of patronage. If not, there would be no reasonable explanation for splitting the two pairs.

The epinikion relies on c.5 to supply the encomiastic detail that it lacks, and c.5 extends the epinikion's familial theme so that the encomium (c.5) becomes, as it were, a panegyric tag. Like Drusus, Augustus is a son (*orte*) who proved his lineage by guarding his divine father's people (1–2). When he is away, the people long for him as a mother for her absent son (3–16). The poet ties together the hymn's opening addresses, request, and simile with the etymological play of *patrum* (3), *patriae* (5), *patria* (16), which all would hold last position in their line except that *patria* loses its place to *Caesarem.* The rotation argues that Augustus has dual familial identities. He is a son to his fatherland and father to his people. The prosperous Italian countryside and society reverses the pessimistic prognoses of the Roman Odes[50] by reinforcing the gnome of c.4. Augustus nurtured his stepsons in his temple house (*nutrita faustis sub penetralibus,* 4.26); Ceres and Faustitas nurture (*nutrit,* 5.18) the land. Tradition and law (22), much like character (*virtus*) and education (*doctrina*) in the gnome, have vanquished impurity. Mothers have produced an offspring of the same noble character as their parents (23); therefore, the pronouncement about failed tradition (*utcumque defecere mores, / indecorant bene nata culpae,* c.4.35–36) changes to parallel praises (*culpari metuit fides,* 20; *culpam poena premit comes,* 24).[51] This again is the heart of c.4, that a generation's character is passed on and must be nurtured in the next.

The codependence of the two odes is problematic. When c.4 is read back through c.5, its panegyric seems to lose its ambiguity. Rome has benefited from Augustus's parentage. When c.5 is read through the narrative tangle of c.4, the effect is the opposite, especially when nothing indicates a change in Horace's panegyric persona. It would be hard for the panegyrist to suddenly alter his primary strategy and be straightforward, even if he wanted to be. The seriocomic nature of the poet's encomia in the book as a whole creates an atmosphere for second-guessing. Some might find a completely serious tone more persuasive for c.5 and conclude that the poet has finally written an aggressive imperial praise, although it is slightly late in the sequence (cf. C.I.2). More than a few, however, might raise a suspicious eyebrow, when in the middle of all the other panegyric disputes the poet has provoked, the *laudator* suddenly sings out a hymn to the god Augustus, divinized while alive on the earth (*praesens*). It is worth considering whether the song might be more than an elevated adulation of Augustus and his policies.[52]

The hymn to Augustus is the most stylistically elevated encomium in book IV. The diction (alliteration, anaphora, and assonance) that marks a highly formal panegyric style begins in the first line and continues relentlessly to the last. Many of these combinations are artfully done and contribute significantly to the pleasure and sense of the whole: as just mentioned, *orte bonis optime* and the repetition of *patrum, patriae, patria* along with *te . . . te* (33), the anaphora of the second-person pronoun conventional in prayers, together proclaim Augustus divine. Horace's language deepens the pathos in the simile of the mother waiting in frantic desperation for her son's return. Through Horace's explosive alliteration one hears the mourning woman drumming on her chest (*dulci distinet a domo*, 12), and she will not suffer anything to interrupt her pleading. *Votis ominibusque et precibus vocat* (13) forms an unbroken chiastic chain of alliteration, assonance, and elision that prevents the caesura and binds together the mother's vows, omens, and prayers. The rhythmic *quaerit . . . Caesarem* (16) links the searching homeland with the object of its desire. The parallelism of *enim* (6) and *etenim* (17) is the only syntactic argument that the hymn credits Augustus with Roman prosperity.[53] The doubled *dicimus* (38–39), when the panegyrist joins voices with the peasant, brings the conclusion back to the double direct address that began the ode, and *die . . . sol* (39–40) echoes the request that Augustus return (*dies . . . soles*, 7–8).[54]

Other recurrences are not so easily explained. DuQuesnay complains that the repeated *rura* (17–18) interjects an "unwanted" stress on work into the peaceful pastoral scene[55] or worse puns *rura . . . rura* equals *rursus:* Augustus should return back again (*rursus*) to his Italian countryside (*rura*). It would be easier to accept one of the suggested corrections, if there were no further examples of dissonant or exaggerated repetitions. The number of plosives (*bos . . . perambulat; pacatum . . . per . . . polluitur; domus . . . edomuit; prole puerperae*, 17–24) does not match the calm countryside or the harmony of the chaste Roman household. The chiastic alliteration of *culpam poena premit comes* seems to round off the verse-by-verse listing of Rome's moral recovery, but then the asyndeton presses on in a repeated question that runs another stanza. The question itself is a run-over, constructed as a tricolon crescendo[56] but extended with a fourth question (*quis ferae / bellum curet Hiberiae,?* 27b–28), anticlimactic since it follows the pacification of the German tribes who had caused Augustus's absence and by its length belongs between the shorter second and longer third elements. The prayer proper (33–40) begins with another chiastic alliteration, *multa prece . . . prosequitur mero,* and the whining of the prominent nasal "m" (*tuum / miscet numen; magni memor*) clashes with the peasant's joyous libation. To what purpose does the panegyrist make the joyous festal celebration of the final stanza hiss with so many sibilants (*longas . . . ferias; praestes Hesperiae; sicci; sol . . . subest*)? Although it may be pressing the argument too far to suppose that the repetition of sound, readily explained or not, occurring in almost every line pushes the hymn toward hyperbolic redundancy, certainly part of appreciating the ode's excellence lies in recognizing in its expression an unevenness between sound and sense, a dissonance evident in the other major components of the ode's composition: the stigmatic presentation of Roman prosperity replacing the hymnic narrative; the outstanding apotheosis of the hymn form supported by conventional praise; the use of lament to celebrate Augustus's return.

The emotive depth in the simile of mother Rome waiting for her son Augustus, which is conveyed by its unbreakable periodic structure (9–16), has proven universally appealing.[57] But the simile does not lead to a graceful lyric song on Rome's prosperity. Horace with little transition completely reverses his syntax. At the near center of the hymn he lists off for three stanzas a catalogue of the *res Romanae*, as if he is rehearsing a grocery-list outline and wants to make sure he does not leave out an item (17–28). This hyperparataxis in asyndeton is unparalleled in Horace's poetry.[58] Is this simply not Horace's best? If this were the case, the sudden and obvious shift from the simile to the list has produced an opposite effect, since it has created more interest in the ode. Collinge observes that the lines rotate between plain statements and divine abstractions, and wonders if the poet implies that Augustus is bringing everyday Roman life closer to an imagined utopia. For Collinge to be right, *Fides, Mos, Lex,* and *Poena,* as well as *Ceres* and *Faustitas* must all be divine abstractions—possible, but how probable?[59] Oliensis, following DuQuesnay, thinks these lines with their end-stops suited for choral performance[60] and yet such rapid-fire parataxis could result in a comic effect (nearly Plautine) when performed. The *CS,* written to be sung, offers nothing similar. It may be impossible to determine a precise reason for the listing. What is inescapable is that the panegyrist has ruined the direct statement of simplex panegyric by stressing syntactic brokenness at the precise moment he is enumerating the achievements of Augustus's Rome—one wonders (*dubia*).

The direct address to Augustus as the son of the gods and the hymn's elevated style lead the reader to assume that Horace is fashioning an extraordinary praise and that the encomiastic details will match. Actually this apotheosis is similar to those of Horace's contemporaries and his own earlier tributes, and there is much in its quality that falls short of the expectations set up by the hymn form. There was precedent for Horace addressing the living Augustus as divine.

Vergil illustrates how directly such attributions of divinity to a benefactor could be expressed. After Octavian granted Vergil's request to spare his father's land from the confiscations for the resettlement of the veterans (41 B.C.), Vergil's shepherd Tityrus praises his benefactor as a god deserving full sacrificial rites (*Ecl.*1.6–8). The point of the tribute is not that Tityrus necessarily believes that his benefactor is a god incarnate,[61] but that the attribution of divinity is the ultimate means of distinguishing benefactor from dependent (this is while Octavian is still struggling against Antony).[62] Vergil offers his poetry to Augustus through the metaphor of worship and asks Augustus to bless his work in the language of prayer (*G.*1.40–42). In the well-known proemium to *Georgics* 3, Vergil promises to fashion a poem into a temple for Augustus and lead a procession to sacrifice there in his honor.[63] Vergil's Anchises prophesies that Caesar will bring back Saturn's golden age and that the boundaries of his realm will exceed the stars, years, and sun (*A.*6.789–807).[64] Hercules and Liber never covered such territory. Caesar's star eclipses the constellations by increasing crops, deepening the color of the grapes, and securing prosperity: *Ecl.*9.44–50—a precursor to Horace's bucolic landscape (c.5).[65]

In Propertius's praise of Augustus, humanity and deity meld together. Propertius begins his epic-styled prophecy (*omina fausta cano,* 3.4.9) that Augustus will triumph over the Parthians by naming Caesar a god (*arma deus Caesar*). The elegy ends with two prayers to Augustus's patron gods: to Mars that he will exalt Caesar and to Venus that she will preserve forever her own offspring, the line of Aeneas, the son of god who will again found the golden age in Latium (cf. Verg. *A.*6.791–94a). When Propertius celebrates the victory of Actium (4.6), Apollo names Octavian the savior of the world (37) and dedicates his own bow to Caesar (37–40). Apollo joins Octavian's army. Apollo's speech runs for 18 lines, and then Propertius describes Octavian's victory over Cleopatra in only two paratactic lines (57–58). Divus Iulius breaks in and speaks only one line from his Idalian star, "I am a god; your faithfulness shows that you are my offspring" (60), a powerful pronouncement confirming his son's divine origin.

Augustus for his deeds merits immortality. Lucretius praised Epicurus with much the same argument: if Ceres, Liber, and Hercules had been declared immortal, then Epicurus, who eclipsed all others as the sun the stars, should receive the same honor (3.1040–44; 5.13–54). The attributes of the divine Epicurus, appear again in Vitruvius' praise for Augustus in the proemium to his *De Architectura.* Augustus's majestic divine mind (*divina tua mens et numen*) frees the Roman people and the senate from fear and continues to govern them with most excellent thoughts and judgments (cf. Lucr. 5.7–12; 6.24–28). Vitruvius expressly states what Caesar's star and Anchises' prophecy signify: Augustus holds imperial power by the divine right of kings.

Horace's *Augustus divus ex hominibus factus* in *Odes* I–III corresponds to the practice of his contemporaries in argument and in direct expression (C.I.2; 12; III.3). The poet puts forward a Caesar whose deeds demonstrate that he is the gods' divine regent. The apotheosis of C.I.2 is the dramatic opposite of C.IV.5. Instead of beginning with a direct address that honors Augustus's divine lineage, the poet poses the question, "Which god should the Roman people invoke?"

> quem vocet divum populus ruentis
> imperi rebus? prece qua fatigent
> virgines sanctae minus audientem
> 　　carmina Vestam?
>
> cui dabit partis scelus expiandi
> Iuppiter? (25–30a)
>
> [On which of the gods should the people call when the empire is collapsing in ruins? With what prayer should the holy virgins tire Vesta, completely deaf to their chants? To whom will Jupiter assign the duty of expiating wickedness?]

The interrogative chain is simultaneously an ascending and descending tricolon. The poet progressively elevates the religious

status of the subject: the people, the Vestal Virgins, and Jupiter
(25–30a). But while the first indefinite (*quem*) is without doubt a
god (*divum*), the status of *cui* is not as specific. *Cui* does not refer
precisely to an immortal, since it is a god's function to grant expi-
ation and the task of his representative, a priest and a sacrifice, to
enact atonement. The sacrifice is transformed into the divine
realm when it is accepted by the gods. In this sense *cui* is of a different nature from *quem divum:* mortal and potentially immortal.
The second question (*prece qua*) provides a transition between the
first and third by focusing on prayer, the act that transforms
the sacrifice (the mortal) so that it appeases the immortal gods.
The questions together ask which god should the people invoke
as their priest or sacrifice to remove their guilt. After calling on
Apollo, Venus, and Mars (Augustus's patron deities), the poet
settles on Mercury. As a divine messenger to humanity he can
bridge the immortal and mortal worlds and become the divine
and human solution to the poet's questions. The poet proposes
that Mercury take on mortal form and become the avenger of
Caesar (*vocari,* [43] repeated from *vocet* in the first question [25]).
Naming Caesar introduces the prayer that the entire ode anticipates—only two stanzas long (45–52), but unmistakably redi-
rected to Caesar. Read as a title that belongs properly to Caesar's
adopted son who took vengeance on his father's assassins, *Caesaris ultor* collapses the distinction between Mercury and Octavian. Thus the prayer addresses the metamorphosized Mercury,
Octavian the messenger of the gods on earth.

     This prayer is as direct an honorary apotheosis as c.5, but the
apotheosis is reversed, an anthropomorphosis. Caesar is not a
mortal who becomes a god, but a god like Mercury who for a time
appears in human form. Therefore, the prayers become complementary opposites. The panegyrist of c.5 asks that Caesar return
home to his people, while in c.2 he prays that Caesar will delay his
return home to the heavens (45–46). Octavian is, as it were, on
loan to the people, temporarily human but more properly divine,
which is why the god Caesar will consent to stay among the Romans only if he receives proper honors (c.2.47–50). Both Octavian
(c.2) and Augustus (c.5) are *divus praesens*—all the more startling
in c.2, if only because it is earlier.[66] As surprising as it may be, Augustus receives a more direct praise in the second ode of the first

collection than he does via the *recusatio* in the second ode of the last collection.

Horace uses the same basic organizing principle for the apotheosis of C.I.12. Again the apotheosis becomes the reply to a series of questions, which lead through a priamel form to the final praise of the ode's two great divinities, Jupiter and Caesar. Horace opens with a line from Pindar's praise for Theron, another interrogative tricolon crescendo moving in a very straightforward manner from man to hero to god (τίνα θεόν, τίν' ἥρωα, τίνα δ' ἄνδρα κελαδήσομεν, *O.*2.2; *Quem virum aut heroa lyra vel acri / tibia sumis celebrare, Clio? / quem deum?* C.I.12.1–3a). Horace's questions seem to outline the process of apotheosis by which a mortal through heroic deeds earns divinity, but the categories (man, hero, and god: an apparent clear progression) are neither fixed nor stable. Before the poet balances these three introductory stanzas of questions with another three stanzas at the end of the ode that supply the answers, he runs through two lists of *laudandi:* gods (13–32) and heroes from the founding of Rome down to the ode's present (33–48).[67] Both catalogues resist easy characterization and illustrate the fluidity between the categories of divine and human. The poet leads the audience to think that he will move through the gods in descending order according to their status. Jupiter is first with no second, Athena comes closest, and so on. Horace, however, crosses the strict boundaries between the Olympians and divinized heroes when he places Liber, who belongs with Hercules, Castor, and Pollux, ahead of both Diana and Apollo.[68] The listing of heroes appears to move chronologically from Romulus to Numa and then Tarquinius, but Horace breaks the chronology at Cato. To maintain the chronology Camillus (ca. 400 B.C.) would come after Tarquinius; Fabricius and Curius, heroes in the war with Pyrrhus (281–275 B.C.), before Regulus (ca. 250 B.C.). Surely no conventional list for apotheosis in the Augustan period would be likely to include the Tarquin kings regardless of how they had expanded Roman rule.[69]

What we have learned from Horace's panegyric praxis advises against explaining away any incongruence. The catalogues work well on the general level of the priamel: here is a group of gods worthy of praise and another of Rome's historical *laudandi,* but now I am praising specifically the highest Jupiter and the Caesars

who outshine all the other lesser lights (46a–48). Yet a close look
at the specifics brings out a dissonance that prepares the audience
for the ode's ultimate volte-face. The poet earlier in the song pointedly denied that anything or anyone was like or second to Jupiter
(*unde nil maius generatur ipso / nec viget quidquam simile aut secun-
dum*, 17–18). Then when he returns to praise Jupiter after the priamel, the poet asks him to rule with Caesar as his second (*tu se-
cundo / Caesare regnes*, 51b–52). The switch from no second at all
to a Caesar second only to Jupiter effectively enrolls Caesar in the
canon of the gods after Jupiter but before Athena. Caesar eclipses
all other gods and heroes except Jupiter himself. Jupiter is in
charge of the sky and Octavian the earth. To emphasize his praise
Horace switches from the optative (*regnes*, 52) to the emphatic future (*reget*, 57). Horace leaves no doubt about Jupiter's supremacy
(*te minor*, 57). The anaphora of the hymn form belongs exclusively
to Jupiter, and whereas Caesar governs the earth with an even-
mannered administration, Jupiter shakes Olympus. Nor is Jupiter
confined to the heavens. In spite of the fact that Caesar rules the
earth, it is still within Jupiter's province to enter Caesar's realm to
punish impiety with his thunderbolts. There is no hint at all of any
potential conflict between the two deities. Jupiter's actions support his just divine regent.

C.III.3 locates Augustus back in heaven:[70]

> hac arte Pollux et vagus Hercules
> enisus arcis attigit igneas,
>   quos inter Augustus recumbens
>   purpureo bibet[71] ore nectar; (9–12)

> [Because of this quality Pollux and wandering Hercules
> in their struggle attained heaven's fiery citadels, and
> Augustus will recline at the banquets with them and
> drink nectar, his lips stained purple.]

Augustus propped on his elbow and enjoying a symposion with
Pollux and Hercules is not nearly as surprising as how he won
the right (*hac arte*). Augustus deserves his place among the gods
because he is so resolved on moral excellence that he would have
the confidence to withstand the thunderous collapse of Jupiter's
heaven (6–8). Jupiter striking with lightning his own earthly
emissary is a preposterous notion for Horace's audience to imag-

ine, and no one after reading c.12 would do so on their own, but if Augustus is the relentlessly just man behind the generalized *iustum . . . virum* (1) that is the very scenario the poet proposes. It is an astonishing conditional suggestion, all the more because Horace reminds his audience of the cooperative relationship between Jupiter and Caesar by replaying the language from the end of c.12 (*Iustum et tenacem propositi virum . . . quatit . . . nec fulminantis magna manus Iovis,* 1–6; *tu . . . quaties . . . mittes / fulmina,* C.I.12.58–60).[72] The poet by a direct comparison to c.12 has expanded Augustus's power over his earthly realm by making him its moral governor. In the fullest sense, both by military and moral superiority, Horace praises Augustus as Jupiter's winged regent of lightning (C.IV.4.1).[73]

That Horace composes a hymn (c.5) deifying Augustus before his death is hardly extraordinary after the apotheoses of *Odes* I–III. Every Horatian *apotheosis Augusti* makes Caesar an incarnate deity (*praesens*). It is more appropriate to wonder why in a later ode, in a hymn so indebted to the tradition of praising Hellenistic kings, there is comparatively so little of the cosmic Augustus. Without argument Horace's adaptation of the Ennian account of Romulus's apotheosis, when combined with the address *optime Romulae custos gentis,* harmonizes with Augustus's portrayal of himself as the second Romulus:[74]

> Pectora . . . tenet desiderium; simul inter
> Sese sic memorant: "O Romule, Romule die,
> Qualem te patriae custodem di genuerunt!
> O pater, o genitor, o sanguen dis oriundum!
> Tu produxisti nos intra luminis oras." (*Ann.*105–109 Skutsch)

> [For so long desire has held their hearts . . . together as one they recount: "O Romulus, divine Romulus, how excellent a guardian for your country the gods bore you! O father, o parent, o blood sprung from the gods! You have brought us forth to dwell within boundaries of light."]

However, despite the harmony between the two portraits, it should also be observed how much Horace pares down Ennius's panegyric rhetoric. Horace removes the emotive anaphora (*O Romule, Romule*) and withholds the name of the god (16). He folds the exclamatory *qualem . . . custodem di genuerunt* back into the

direct addresses and completely deletes Ennius's ascending tricolon (*O pater, o genitor, o sanguen*). Horace quiets, or at least post-
pones until the simile of the mourning mother, the mob-like
frenzy of the Roman people bereft of their leader. Horace replaces
the Romulan nation's exasperated cries with the repeated demand
that Augustus return (*reditum . . . redi . . . redde*). For most of the
second strophe Horace recapitulates a standard formulaic praise
from Hellenistic panegyric, that the *laudandus* has turned night
into day (Ennius' *Tu produxisti nos intra luminis oras*).[75] Then Horace changes the image ever so slightly. Augustus's presence
makes the day more welcome; he does not bring Rome out of
complete darkness (7a–8). Augustus intensifies the light; he does
not eclipse the sun or stars. Likewise, Horace concludes Augustus's great achievements with a standard prayer for his safety (*incolumi Caesare,* 27), and Augustus equals but does not surpass
Hercules and Castor (35–36). This is still great praise but with a
carefully muted tone.

These details complement the unique plot of this particular
apotheosis. The conventional effect for an attribution of divinity
is to separate out the *laudandus* from his citizen peer group by the
most basic distinction; they will die, but the *laudandus* will not.
The drama of this hymn, however, is all about Augustus rejoining
his citizens. This particular apotheosis embeds Augustus more
than ever within his community. The divine child Augustus has
taken on the responsibility for another's family (*Romulae / custos
gentis*) and in fulfilling his obligation makes himself answerable
to Rome's other fathers, the senate (*pollicitus patrum / sancto con-
cilio*). The interdependence of familial ties makes any separation
intolerable. Horace turns to word pictures. The chiastic tendency
of encomiastic language imagines Augustus within the boundaries of his native land in spite of his absence (*tuae, dux bone, patriae,* 5). While Augustus is away, Rome is just not Rome, and Augustus belongs to his homeland. Such reciprocity informs the
simile that follows. Augustus, again the child, should return out
of duty to his anxious motherland, who can never rest until her
son returns.

To review, Horace's mix of competing nuances in the ode's language, structure, and form—the discord between sound and
sense; the staccato rehearsal of Augustus's achievements; a slight
muting of the imagery typical in an apotheosis—explains how di-

vergent interpretations are likely. One reading emphasizes the
stresses within the panegyric apotheosis (such as the lack of a connected narrative in the hymn) and invents a cautious poet, while
another represses all dissonance and finds a poet reveling in commissioned praise. Reconstructing the mood of a panegyrist is always highly speculative. More to the point, restricting this hymn
to the perspective of adulation and how effective it is or is not dismisses what the song has to say about what was to become a primary symbol for imperial power, apotheosis. Further, it risks belittling the song's emotive quality so powerfully portrayed by an
eight-line simile (20 percent of the whole) of a mother praying for
her son missing and presumed dead, an image that must reflect
Rome's genuine fear about the death of Augustus, especially
when she was institutionalizing so much of her power in one
person.

Whether by happenstance or because Horace was informed of
advance plans that would be implemented whenever Augustus
succeeded Lepidus as pontifex maximus, c.5 was published during a critical juncture in the development of the imperial cult.
Praying to the emperor's *genius* as opposed to his person was always a razor-thin distinction, and the difference was about to become more obscure. Lepidus finally died (13 B.C.), and Augustus
took up the office in March of the following year (12 B.C.).[76] Convention required that the pontifex maximus live in his public
house in the forum. Augustus refused. He instead made the public house part of the complex for the Vestal Virgins and declared
public a portion of his private house on the Palatine. In that public domain of his own house, only a month after taking office, he
dedicated a shrine to Vesta, including the sacred palladium and
eternal flame. Rome now worshipped Vesta, the Penates of the
state, the *Genius Augusti,* and the *Lares Augusti* in the same place.
Augustus had symbolically combined the worship of the state
and his own person by the conflation of public and private space
(Ov. *Fast.*4.949–54).

The advances of the ruler cult provide empathetic insight into
the interest such a hymn would have for the panegyrist and his
audience. Horace publishes this hymn at the precise moment of
the transition to state-promoted ruler worship, and when a question faced Horace's contemporary audience as dire for them as for
the Romans of old who lost their first ruler Romulus. Augustus

had been away before years at a time and then returned to great celebration, but there would soon be a time when his absence would be permanent. Then what? What would happen or should happen when a person dies who is by public acclaim indispensable to the existence of the state? The drastic shifts from lament to joy constitute the hymn's pivotal tension, and the dissonance in the hymn is a means by which Horace can embody in the text the unsettling emotion of fear and lament in the middle of a celebration for Augustus's return.

When Horace brings the klētikon (a formal request for someone's return)[77] in the first stanzas (1–16) together with the unrestrained drinking celebration (29–40) characteristic of his Return Odes,[78] he puts into play a dramatic plot parallel to the sympotic invitation. In effect the hymn asks Augustus to attend the party that will be held in honor of his return and to stay with his people so that the celebration lasts. Keeping with the scenario of the reluctant guest, the panegyrist tries to lure Augustus home with familiar sympotic enticements: the pleasures of spring (17–20), the prosperity of the Roman home (21–24), and peace (25–28).[79] The staccato parataxis builds through this list of pleasures an almost overpowering sense of Rome's prosperity and at the same time inserts an element of disruption into the land because the master Augustus is gone. The whole presents an argument as compelling as any other sympotic invitation that Augustus should return and enjoy his party.

Nowhere does the hymn indicate that Augustus has returned or will return for a certainty. The hymn leaves the question open whether Augustus hesitates of his own volition or whether another force beyond mortal control prevents his return. On the one hand, Horace reminds Augustus that he had promised a prompt return (3), and the quick repetition of *reditum, redi, redde* conveys the panegyrist's impatience—if the return is not already *non maturum*, time is running out.[80] On the other hand, the circumstances for Augustus's delay in the simile are more doubtful (9–16). The Southwind, an unpredictable outside power, has prevented the son (Augustus) from setting out for his home. He could not be responsible for the delay. The son, however, is not entirely passive; he is the one delaying (*cunctantem*, emphasized by hyperbaton and its leading position in its line). The ambiguity arises from the placement of "longer than a year" (*spatio longius annuo).* If the comparative is taken with *distinet* (12), then most likely the gale kept the young soldier from sailing during the navigable time of the year and he was forced to spend the next winter;[81] but, if *iuvenem . . . cunctantem* (11) governs the comparative,[82] then the young man delayed his return and now the Southwind is keeping him pinned down. Either reading seems perfectly plausible, and neither comforts. Augustus delaying his return or some other force keeping him from his people are both frightening for Rome.

The plot's similarity to a sympotic invitation both intensifies the longing for the absent Augustus and places him on the outside, threatening the viability of the banquet. When Horace honored Augustus's earlier return from Spain (24 B.C.), he praised Augustus for creating the opportunity for celebration (C.III.14.13–16). Now apparently the person whose presence within the drama of the hymn makes the party possible has not arrived and may not. The sympotic Horace on no other occasion makes the drinking party contingent on the acceptance of the invitation. The party goes on with or without the person invited. Without a return in c.5 there can be no homecoming celebration, only unfulfilled desire, and loss is the dominant mood of the klētikon. Mother Rome continues to wait longingly for her absent son. Horace does not put enough detail into the simile to allow reference to a specific source.[83] There is no need. A mother's hope for her son's return from military duty often goes unfulfilled. After the civil wars, the Romans did not need metaphor to tell them this; they had experienced such anxiety and loss many times over. The preceding Return Ode (III.14.9–10a) calls to ritual silence the mothers and wives who are rejoicing over the safe return of their men, but the immediate context of *Odes* IV is more pessimistic. Pindar's poems lament husbands snatched away from their wives (2.21–22), and spouses are left to sing their dead husbands' praises (4.68)

Augustus did return. One could object that such a sympotic rendering of the hymn requires a complete suspension of the historical occasion. Horace's audience, who were enjoying the festivities or would, of course, remember them, knew Augustus had come home. Horace plays the dramatic perspective (Augustus absent) against the historical occasion (Augustus returned) to intensify the crisis of separation. Staging the joy of Augustus's glorious reception via this plaintive klētikon forces the imagination to revisit the pain and fear that Augustus's absences caused. The historical and dramatic perspectives together take the hymn through the cycle of absence, return, and then absence remembered. Horace mutes any revelry with the prospect that separation from her princeps is part of the pattern of Roman life and, with an aging princeps, death. Augustus had been gone before and would be gone again.

The ode does not end in lament nor Augustus's physical return. The transition between the lament of the klētikon and the unrestrained drinking at the end of ode does not require superimposing the physical presence of Augustus from the historic occasion onto the dramatic, that is, the audience need not have in the back of their minds the return of Augustus safe and sound at home for the structure of the poem to work.[84] The tension between the dramatic and historical viewpoints argues against fixing the poem too rigidly in one moment of time. To insist that Augustus's return in 13 B.C. must be the sole defining motivation for the ode's joy misses the climactic moment of the hymn form and apotheosis, and as a result cheapens the vitality of Roman religious ritual. The only person who actually returns is the peasant vinedresser (condit quisque diem collibus in suis / et . . . hinc ad vina redit laetus, 29–30a).[85] When he comes out of his field after spending his day mending the vines (a fine pastime for the symposiast of Odes I–III, repairing the goods that provide for livelihood and the banquet), he reconstitutes community through the power of the wine in ritual libation (see the symposiast's advice to Varus, C.I.18.1–4). When the vinedresser pours the libation and invokes the god Augustus, through his prayer Augustus unbounded by any distance or manner of separation, even death, does return (praesens), and the celebration spreads from the rustic's private house to the public banquet. The vinedresser averts the crisis of separation by wedding Augustus permanently to sympotic celebration through ritual. The people are dry (sicci; see siccis, c.18.3 above) in the morning, but by night they are drunk (uvidi). They have escaped their cares through the ritual of wine and found once more communal celebration. The peasant has taken on the function of the sympotic lyricist in the earlier Return Odes, but the change in person is minimal, because the peasant's prayer is the poet's own magical carmen (dicimus . . . dicimus, 38–39). Augustus's return here is dependent on the power of language, as ritual, to represent and create reality. The poet's words of praise fuse the earthly with the divine realm and protect the Roman people from the pain of mortality.[86] The poet is priest.

The argument of the ode focuses on the transition from lament to joy that the hymn effects. Augustus is summoned. The citizen-peasant enacts a powerful ritual moment by which Augustus though absent rejoins his people. Horace's hymn to the divine Augustus should not be taken merely as rhetorical hyperbole. The conventional panegyric apotheosis translates the human to the divine sphere and by that act of sanctification separates a person so honored from the human world. By contrast, through the hymn form and invocation, the Augustus of c.5 becomes inseparable from his people even after death. The panegyrist emphasizes the power of the peasant, the Italian countryside, and its people bonded together in communal celebration. Within the social circumstances of the developing ruler cult (13/12 B.C.), such a reversal in the literary convention of the apotheosis is no minute detail. The panegyrist is interpreting Roman imperial ritual, and the imbalance he incorporates into his praise forces the question—Where does the power for Rome's continued prosperity lie? The power lies with the pastoral vinedresser making a libation. The encomium turns divinization around or at the very least accentuates a different note so that it becomes for the sake of the other (the stability and wholeness of Rome past and present) rather than a lesser rite of self-glorification. We do not have here a reticent poet nor a poet sounding the party line. His praise also does not counter the Augustan image or imperialism. It transcends these boundaries by investing the simple country folk with the creative ritual needed to restore brokenness: libation, which is the poet's panegyric song.

4

Songs of Mo(u)rning

I have my books and my poetry to protect me. . . .
and a rock feels no pain and an island never cries.
—"I Am a Rock," Simon and Garfunkel (1966)

A primary structural enigma of book IV has always been c.10–13, a chiastic run of two erotic imprecations (10, 13) enclosing two sympotic episodes (11, 12), which disrupts the panegyric movement of the whole. These poems appear without any encomiastic elements and return to c.1, resuming its mood of lament. There is no need to search for the poet's voice and wonder why it may have vanished, because, as in c.1, Horace casts the *poetae persona* as a dramatic character. The poet confronts Ligurinus a second time (c.10), and his stammering tongue finds the words that failed him (c.1.33–36), words filled with harsh invective. The first person dominates c.11 from the first two words *est mihi* to the seductive invitation of the final strophes. It is the poet's wine, house, garden, and love. C.12 repeats the conclusion of c.11: a first-person address (*non ego te meis / immunem meditor tingere poculis*, 22b–23; cf. 11.33–34a), a compound imperative (*pone . . . et . . . misce*, 25 and 27; cf. 11.31, 34), and then a gnomic principle (*dulce est desipere in loco*, 28; cf. 11.35b–36). The gods of c.13 have answered the poet's prayers and brought old age down to curse Lyce, who in her youth exhaled love (*spirabat amores*) and blew the poet's mind (*me surpuerat mihi,* 19–20). In comparison to the rest of the collection the poet's self-references overpower.

C.10–13 stand out but not unexpectedly, since the first ode of the collection combines the first-person voice of the poet, love interests, and encomium. Labeling these poems "private" and treating them as if they were "the other poems" of book IV ignores how c.1 blurs boundaries between personal and public. Still c.10–13 continue to receive minor attention. This neglect persists over an obvious dilemma: when the poet presented the collection, he made any "private" themes public and did so within the context of panegyric song. If Fraenkel is correct, and the careful chiastic arrangement of the poems confirm his opinion, that *Odes* IV is the most finely arranged poetry book of the Augustan period, then bracketing 10–13 as a private lyric expression related tangentially to the political panegyrics defies sense, especially when the poet politicized genre in his earlier poetry. C.10–13 must be part of the poet's public imaging.

One popular option is to play the public and private against each other. The question here is whether the private becomes subordinate to the public or the public to the private. Lyne interprets the private as the poet's means of diminishing the importance of the public: to use Lyne's term, the private "saps" the public.[1] Oliensis reads the poet's shift from invective to praise as a matter of self-preservation under the dominion of Augustus. Horace, like old Lyce, is a survivor and refuses to die young like the beautiful Cinara (c.13).[2] By both accounts the private poems are on some level anti-encomiastic. Less popular have been Fraenkel's and Putnam's attempts to reconcile 10–13 to the collection.[3] Fraenkel's explanation is simple: Horace has returned to the theme of the aging poet (c.1). Fraenkel does not elaborate on the connection between encomium and a senior poet, but clearly *laudator* and *laudandus* share a motivation in the writing of panegyric, securing immortal fame. Putnam concentrates on the aesthetic power of song. Sappho lives again (c.9) through the lyric poet, and after his death so too will his praise. I would like to bring Fraenkel's aging poet and Putnam's lyric aesthetic together and explore the possibility that c.10–13 convey the essence of Horace's panegyric praxis through the theme of lament, and that the poet uses this theme to push the book toward a resolution in the

last panegyric couplet (c.14, 15), when the poet and audience/
community join their voices together.

Although Roman burial customs range from depersonalizing
mass graves to simple rites for the poor to the extravagance of
state burial, lament cuts across social stratification. Every lament
for the common poor or noble rich assumes the intrinsic value of
the person mourned and is therefore one of humanity's earliest
forms of encomium.[4] When wailing Roman women and men in
ancestral masks paraded with their dead through the streets, the
private expression of grief found an audience. Mourning in Rome
was a public event in which the individual was put on display
so as to model and effect the community's ideologies.[5] Roman
funerary ritual brought the grieving family out of its house and
back into contact with the citizen body, thereby ensuring a communal dimension to lament.[6] Laments are as subject to interpretive conflicts as other encomiastic forms, since laments can be
both overheard praise and staged praise simultaneously: the
painful cry mourning a loss, unrestrained by the presence of an
audience, and a professional display of societal conventions that
effectively shields the individual at a moment of public vulnerability. Subsequently, residual in lament is the same ambivalence
that pervades other panegyric modes. That Horace has included
a sequence of poems dominated by lament (10–13) becomes significant not for their private voices—we may or may not find in
them the poet's unique interests as a private individual—but for
their public interest. When the poet gives a public forum to grief,
the earliest societal context for encomium, he asserts the power of
praise to shape communal values and its capacity to overcome
life's deepest pains. The laments of c.10–13 rely on a poetics of
community, which is most characteristic of Horace's panegyric
praxis.

Lament is a natural emotive reaction to a perceived loss and
therefore changes the responsive position of the audience. Persons engaged in lament, although they may instinctually conform
their lament to known and therefore readily understood societal
conventions, do not depend on an interpretive audience to invest
their cries with meaning. That is to say, lamentation does not
derive its initial impulse and sense from the perception of the
audience but from the emotional state of the mourner.[7] Yet those
hearing a lament are not passive.[8] Public mourning intends to

generate an empathetic bond with its audience so strong that the audience identifies itself with the mourner so that the resulting sense of community overcomes any brokenness caused by the loss. Audience and speaker merge as one voice. In this sense tears constitute an invitation issued by the grieving to what Thomas Greene calls a "catharsis of passion."[9] It is a dangerous situation: the audience may accept the invitation and become lost in the mourner's all-consuming pain.

Dido's suicide illustrates well the communal power of lament. After an audience has heard Dido's bitter plaints against Aeneas, her mourning atop the pyre for her own loss, and has witnessed Anna's sobs while she embraces her dying sister, the empathy for Dido's plight has become so strong that it is nearly impossible to leave Dido behind and sail on with Aeneas. The simple transition to Aeneas's continued voyage jars abruptly, "meanwhile. . ." (*interea medium Aeneas iam classe tenebat, A.*5.1). Moving to the other extreme, there is the risk that an audience, like the immovable Aeneas, may find a lament illegitimate and decline the invitation, which locks the participants in irresolvable conflict. When Aeneas meets Dido in the underworld he adopts her lament, "Whom do you flee?" (*quem fugis?* 6.466; cf. *mene fugis?* 4.314), but the rock-like Dido flees into the shadows. Aeneas held his course (*tenebat*), and so did Dido (*tenebat*). She kept her eyes fixed on the ground and refused to acknowledge Aeneas's tears (*illa solo fixos oculos aversa tenebat,* 6.469). Neither would identify with the other's lament, a symbolic enactment of the Carthaginian Wars.[10] The *Iliad*, however, finds resolution in mourning when Priam's lament for Hector reminds Achilles of their common humanity (*Il.*24.476–551). For this reason laments often create a pivotal moment, a *krisis* in narrative structures, which propels the story to its conclusion and can either transcend or erect boundaries dividing poet, mourner, and audience. Will the participants embrace and find a common experience in their humanity or not, and then what will result? Tears unite Achilles and Priam but forever divide Aeneas and Dido. There is, of course, doublespeak in my use of audience. The lament is heard by the characters within the story and overheard again by later listeners/readers, who are also invited to embrace the passions of the lament.[11] Whether they do or not depends largely on the aesthetic power of the song, which is precisely the pleasure: song provides a shared experience through which individuals can negotiate community. This again is Horace's sympotic panegyric praxis.

C.10: Faces in the Mirror: Ligurinus, Horace, and Vergil

O crudelis adhuc et Veneris muneribus potens,
insperata tuae cum veniet †pluma† superbiae
et quae nunc umeris involitant deciderint comae,
nunc et qui color est puniceae flore prior rosae

mutatus, Ligurine, in faciem verterit hispidam, 5
dices, 'heu,' quotiens te in speculo videris alterum,
'quae mens est hodie, cur eadem non puero fuit,
vel cur his animis incolumes non redeunt genae?'

[O you cruel still and still powerful in the tributes of Venus, when the feathery down has come and caught you unawares in your haughtiness, and the hair, which now waves over your shoulders, has fallen, and now your complexion, which surpasses the bloom of a red rose, changed, Ligurinus, has turned into a bristly face, you will say, as often as you look in a mirror and see yourself another person: "Ah me, the vision which I have now, why did I not have it in my youth; or why do my cheeks not come alive again with their passions?"]

C.10 offers an excellent lesson in the poetics of Horatian lyric: thin (only C.I.11, 30, 38, and III.22 are as short), but with depth, just like the image in a mirror. For the first time Horace pictures someone looking in a mirror, but it is not the first time that he has created mirror images, when characters have been made to face themselves in corresponding poems (Helen, C.I.15–IV.9; Phyllis, C.II.4–IV.11; Quintilius, C.I.24–Ars 438; Lyce, C.III.10–IV.13; Lycus, C.I.32–III.19; Torquatus, Epist.I.5–C. IV.7). The reflections cast are not always this simple. Mirrors as metaphors in Horace contain multiple images; for instance, Maecenas and Augustus (C.I.1; 2) and the poets, Horace and Vergil, whose poems continually reflect each other so that the image of one is incomplete without the other (neque quis me sit devinctior alter, S.I.5.42; et serves animae dimidium meae, C.I.3.8). In c.10 the poet stands Ligurinus before a mirror to force him to imagine his future by comparing the image that is projected to the portrait of old Horace (C.IV.1).

While Ligurinus sees his old age in Horace's present, we see reflections of old friends, Horace and Vergil, through recollections
of *Eclogues* 2 and 5 and Horace's language of *animae dimidium
meae*.

Horace names Vergil ten times (*S*.I.5.40, 48; 6.55; 10.45, 81;
C.I.3.6; 24.10; IV.12.13; *Epist*.II.1.247; *Ars* 55), but what Horace
says about Vergil is tantalizingly sparse. We hear that Vergil
introduced Horace to Maecenas (*S*.I.6.55; 39–38 B.C.),[12] and that
the two traveled together to Brundisium as members of Maecenas's coterie (*S*.I.5). Horace greatly admired the bucolic Vergil
(*S*.I.10.44b–45) and, as is generally agreed, modeled the structure
of his first poetry book of ten satires on the bipartite division of
Vergil's book of ten eclogues.[13] From beginning to end the Horatian corpus resounds with Vergilian echoes. This level of interaction is enough to reasonably conclude that Vergil and Horace
own leading voices among Augustus's poets, and yet the lack of
verifiable evidence about their personal lives has left enough
room to speculate whether their relationship was purely professional or their friendship always close.

The consensus that the two colleagues remained friends is beginning to weaken under the pressure of the irrepressible conflicts in the odes to Vergil (I.3, 24; IV.12).[14] Even the precise sentiment of *animae dimidium meae* seems less secure. In the "*animae
dimidium meae* ode" (*C*.I.3), after a short prayer to the ship that it
bring Vergil safely to Greece and back (1–8), Horace lashes out for
the remainder of the song against the impious audacity of seafar-
ing. This rapid and extended shift in focus has caused different
readings of the singer. Is he a prankster tacking a diatribe onto a
propempticon for rhetorical show, a mourner carried away with
a bitter lament against the invention carrying off his friend, or a
literary critic turning sailing to Greece into a metaphor for Vergil's turn to epic, a dangerous Gigantic venture (37–40)?[15]

In Horace's *consolatio* to Vergil upon the death of Quintilius
(I.24), Horace appears to empathize with Vergil (7–11). Then with
no other transition except the repetition of the second-person pronoun to add punch to his point, Horace calls Vergil's mourning
empty (*tu frustra pius, heu, non ita creditum / poscis Quintilium deos*,
11–12). "You in vain pious" could have struck hard with an antiheroic sting against the poet at work composing the epic of pious
Aeneas. Vergil's loss is not the same as when Horace lamented

being temporarily separated from Vergil (*navis, quae tibi credi-tum / debes Vergilium*, 3.5-6a). The gods do not owe Quintilius (*non ... creditum*) to Vergil like some passenger entrusted to a ship.[16] Vergil's song, if it were more alluring than Orpheus's lyre, cannot bring the dead to life (13–14; *non me carminibus vincet nec Thracius Orpheus, Ecl.*4.55). Horace closes by instructing Vergil on the appropriate limits for grieving with a *consolatio* from the *Aeneid*. Aeneas, distraught over losing his ships to the Trojan women's torches, ponders abandoning his journey. Nautes consoles him: "Whatever fortune one faces, it must be overcome by endurance" (*quidquid erit, superanda omnis fortuna ferendo est, A.*5.710). Now Horace tells Vergil that grief is hard, but whatever cannot be changed, patience makes lighter (*durum. sed levius fit patientia / quidquid corrigere est nefas*, 24.19–20).[17] It is time for Vergil, like Aeneas, to sail on.

In the last ode to Vergil (IV.12), Horace invites his friend to a drinking party but not without reminding Vergil that he is dependent on patronage (*iuvenum nobilium cliens*, 15) and demanding that he quit his profiteering (*rerum pone moras et studium lucri*, 25), Horace's conventional charge against epic writers (see Horace's Epic Criticism in ch.1).

Such negatives contradict the sentimentality often expressed about the poets' friendship; nevertheless, the powerful interaction of their poetry supposes a relationship of continued interdependence and mutual respect, if not genuine admiration. Horace's incorporation of lament and poetic differences into his poems to Vergil fashions them into a more complex symbol than the typical epic/anti-epic interpretation allows. Neither *alter poeta* (*S.*I.5.42) nor its companion *animae dimidium meae* (*C.*I.3.8) offers a simplistic metaphor equating friendship with similarity. Agreement in poetics need not be at the heart of a literary friendship, and criticism is not necessarily antagonistic or sarcastic. The wonder of music sustains itself through a symphony of competing and repeating sounds just as the songs of Mopsus and Menalcas on the death of the master singer Daphnis, with which Vergil concludes the first half of his *Eclogues* (5), converge to form a single encomium of lament and apotheosis.[18] The shepherds' songs are not the same but still are interdependent. Mopsus's lament by itself would end in the death of the bucolic singer Daphnis and more tragically in the collapse of the bucolic tradition into a written, and consequently more fixed and limited, form (13–15a).[19] Menalcas's song reinterprets the lament as an apotheosis that renews oral song and immortalizes its musicians (56–73), but his song first requires the reality of a death and the lament of the divine poet before any apotheosis becomes possible. Such competition has no single winner who dominates rivals, and therefore the shepherds complete their contest with a gift exchange (85–90), a ritual of community. The senior poet passes on his pipe, his songs, to the younger, and the younger gives in exchange his shepherd's crook, a symbol of strength and rescue. Thus poetic traditions live on and gain immortality: one singer becomes from another (*alter ab illo*, 49), which is the essence of Horace's *animae dimidium meae*.

Alterum / animae dimidium meae has a rich literary history making it difficult to identify a precise source for Horace.[20] Callimachus (fr.400 Pf.; epigr.41 Pf.), if his two fragments are read into one, and Meleager (Mel. 81 G.-P.) use the theme in a propempticon, which comes the closest to Horace's C.I.3.[21] These fragmentary bits reduce the motif to a lament over separation from a beloved and fail to explain the competing poetics within the Horatian odes. As sources they have proven deceptive since they have obstructed the search for an impulse closer to Horace that might provide further insight. *Alter ab illo* from the songs of Mopsus and Menalcas would serve as a better parable for Horatian song and its fusion of competing forms and genres into a single lyric whole. Horace has left specific markers to eclogue 5: adopting the bipartite structure of the *Eclogues* for his *Satires* I; naming Vergil for the first time in the fifth satire and calling himself *devinctior alter*; naming Vergil again in the *Satires* at verses 45, 48, and 55, the frame for the interlude of the fifth eclogue (45–55; *alter ab illo*, 49) and the verses of the interlude where the older poet Menalcas praises Mopsus as a divine poet (45), says that he has the voice of the master (48), and where Mopsus returns the compliment (55); inviting Vergil to a symposion with the verse, *adduxere sitim tempora, Vergili* (c.12.13; Menalcas: *quale . . . saliente sitim restinguere rivo*, 46–47). But if Horace had left none of these pointers, the poems to Vergil would still make it obvious that Horace's vision of *alterum / animae dimidium meae* reaches beyond a mere sentimental expression of friendship to include poetics, the power to make one song from divergent voices. The two poets' voices are not the same; Horace will not be another Vergil, in particular an epic Vergil. However, like Menalcas and Mopsus, Horace without Vergil leaves the song incomplete. The interdependence of their songs, in fact, is so close that on any given occasion it can be hard to determine which poet owes what to the other, that is, in terms of the metaphor, which poet is the other's half. In spite of *meae, dimidium* defies exclusive possession; each must possess the other.

What has *animae dimidium meae* to do with Horace's Ligurinus? The mirror of the poem reflects more than one face: Ligurinus, Horace, and Vergil. Ligurinus casts the foremost reflection. The ode has a heavy concentration of temporal pointers all anchored in the present (*adhuc,* 1; *nunc,* 3; *nunc,* 4; *hodie,* 7), but the first, *adhuc* (still), presupposes a past that diverts attention back to c.1. It is as if the story of Ligurinus's rejection of the poet has continued playing in the background, while eight odes have intervened, and suddenly breaks in again with disruptive force. The situation has been remarkably static. Venus has still not left the poet alone; as in c.1 Horace has tried to resist, claimed to be hardened, but in fact is not. Ligurinus, to the contrary, has proven himself so persistent in his rejection that Horace calls him cruel and powerful, a dangerously hurtful combination. To make matters worse, Venus favors the young boy. In the words of the poet, Ligurinus has been blessed with Love's gifts (*Veneris muneribus potens*) and stands triumphant, as did the younger Maximus (*et, quandoque potentior / largi muneribus riserit aemuli,* 1.17–18). Horace has started Ligurinus laughing and in the opening verse has made Ligurinus such an obdurate beloved that one wonders whether Horace might play the same dejected character of c.1, who in silence could hardly choke back his tears (34).[22] Horace's tongue does not fail him now. He reels off an invective, one continuous sentence, in one of the most complex meters, fifth Asclepiadean, without a stammer, only a slight pause after *hispidam* and before *dices*—just enough to make sure Ligurinus has time to think over what is said.

The poet, perhaps hoping Ligurinus will recognize the inevitable loss of his youthful charms and relent, forces him to face reality, and the poet is not gentle. Horace attempts to shake the youth by causing a dramatic collision between his present and future.[23] The interlacing rhyme *et quae nunc . . . nunc et qui* crystallizes attention on Ligurinus's present beauty, which has given him a brash confidence and made him forgetful of his mortality. The future will have the victory. The frame of the second verse (unexpected and arrogance; *insperata . . . superbiae*) contradicts the frame of the first (cruel and powerful; *crudelis . . . potens*), and the present tenses, which are seemingly so emphatic, are subordinate to the future tenses within the temporal clauses (*veniet, deciderint, verterit*). Ligurinus's future lament (*dices*) controls the whole. Ligurinus's blindness will bring him pain when his confidence cheats him and old age catches him unawares. Bluntly put, the boy will not be able to keep his hair where he wants it: off his face and on his head. Horace intensifies the calamity by his use of uncommon words for sensual effect: feathery down (*pluma*) will appear on Ligurinus's face, his cascading (*involitant*) hair will fall, and the color of his cheeks more crimson than the budding rose (*puniceae*) will change (*mutatus*). *Mutatus*, the midpoint of the song, condenses the poet's argument to a single word, "changed"—no one stays forever young. Then the poet completes the ring of his argument by returning back to facial hair. A feathery soft beard would not be so bad, but Ligurinus's complete metamorphosis ends in a prickly old man's beard (*faciem . . . hispidam*) that would scratch a lover's smooth skin.[24]

Now the poet turns Ligurinus toward a mirror. The unnatural shock of the ode is that Ligurinus does not see the reflection he expects, but another unrecognizable image peering back, an *alter*. The chiastic separation of *te* from *alterum* saves the surprise for the end of the verse. Whose image Ligurinus sees hides in the words the poet puts into his mouth: *Ligurine . . . heu . . . cur . . . cur . . . genae*, c.10.5–8; *cur, heu, Ligurine, cur . . . genas . . . cur*, c.1.33–35. Horace has retained the structure and vocabulary of his lament for Ligurinus so that literally his words become Ligurinus's.[25] Ligurinus becomes the old scorned lover of c.1. Horace in a sense looks at Ligurinus and says, "See my face; you're it. What's happened to me will happen to you." While the poet has stood Ligurinus in front of the mirror, Horace has stayed standing behind him so that Horace's image peers back at Ligurinus. Ligurinus has seen the future in another person's present, and by this conflation of time Horace has made Ligurinus's future demise certain.

Another image dimly casts its shadow onto the poem and into the mirror. Pseudo-Acro and commentators since have noted that

O crudelis names by title Vergil's second eclogue ('*O crudelis Alexi,
nihil mea carmina curas?'* 6—one could switch *Ligurine* for *Alexi*
and have a working title for c.10). In eclogue 5 Menalcas gives
Mopsus the pipe that knows this same song, eclogue 2 (*Formosum
pastor Corydon ardebat Alexin*, 2.1; *Hac te nos fragili donabimus ante
cicuta, / haec nos 'formosum Corydon ardebat Alexin'*, 5.85–86). Horace by specific markers to eclogue 5[26] and reference to the title for
eclogue 2 has replayed in c.10 the gift exchange at the conclusion
of eclogue 5 and thus reenacted the powerful immortality of the
poetic tradition. Here Horace is the younger poet performing the
song that was passed on to him by a senior poet Vergil. Horace
adds a penetrating note of sorrow when he includes in his/Lig-
urinus's lament the language of *animae dimidium meae* (*alterum . . .
animis incolumes*, 6–8; *animae . . . alter*, S.I.5.41–42; *Vergilium . . .
reddas incolumem precor*, C.I.3.6–7).[27] Thus the process of aging
(Vergil's death) is repeating itself in the present (Horace) and will
repeat itself again in the future (Ligurinus). Ligurinus, Horace,
and Vergil cast their images on the mirror of the ode, and no
amount of mourning can erase their reflections (*tu frustra pius,
heu . . . poscis Quintilium*, C.I.24.11–12a). Therefore, the lament
carries particular force because the poet has experienced the
truth: death is inevitable, friends die.[28]

A ship set sail carrying Horace's friend Vergil to Greece (19
B.C.). Vergil never arrived. He fell ill, returned quickly, and soon
died. C.I.3 and its expression of *animae dimidium meae* were composed and published too early to refer to Vergil's last voyage, but
if that angry propempticon when written was metaphor, then the
greatest irony in Horatian poetry, a tragic twist beyond any poet's
control, is that life made that metaphor reality. To be sure in c.10
a biographical lament overlays the conventions of Hellenistic epigram, and it is intriguing that here we catch a glimpse of a poet
altering the interpretation of one of his earlier poems to make it fit
more closely his life experience (thereby giving us another ancient precedent for what has been often thought a contemporary
model for how poetry is conceived and read);[29] but the poetics
involved comprehend more than the irresistible fates. Horace,
lamenting the death of a master singer, sings Mopsus's song that
ended with the poetic tradition in crisis. The death of a poet, such
as Vergil or Horace, represents a serious communal loss. Imitating Mopsus's example, Horace brings Vergil back to life for his

audience through his own poetic imagination; nevertheless, just like in Mopsus's song, the sorrow of lament still dominates. As of yet in c.10–13 there is no Menalcas to sing a corresponding triumphant apotheosis for the master poet Vergil. This must wait until Horace's c.12.

C.11: The Phyllis Odes and the Comic Power of Shared Lyric

> est mihi nonum superantis annum
> plenus Albani cadus, est in horto,
> Phylli, nectendis apium coronis,
>   est hederae vis
>
> multa, qua crinis religata fulges;   5
> ridet argento domus; ara castis
> vincta verbenis avet immolato
>   spargier agno.
>
> cuncta festinat manus, huc et illuc
> cursitant mixtae pueris puellae;   10
> sordidum flammae trepidant rotantes
>   vertice fumum.
>
> ut tamen noris quibus advoceris
> gaudiis, Idus tibi sunt agendae,
> qui dies mensem Veneris marinae   15
>   findit Aprilem,
>
> iure sollemnis mihi sanctiorque
> paene natali proprio, quod ex hac
> luce Maecenas meus affluentis
>   ordinat annos.   20
>
> Telephum, quem tu petis, occupavit
> non tuae sortis iuvenem puella
> dives et lasciva tenetque grata
>   compede vinctum.
>
> terret ambustus Phaethon avaras   25
> spes et exemplum grave praebet ales
> Pegasus terrenum equitem gravatus
>   Bellerophonten,

semper ut te digna sequare et ultra
quam licet sperare nefas putando   30
disparem vites. age iam, meorum
    finis amorum

(non enim posthac alia calebo
femina), condisce modos amanda
voce quos reddas; minuentur atrae   35
    carmine curae.

[I still have left a full jar of Alban wine nine years old;
I have, Phyllis, in my garden parsley for weaving
crowns; I have an abundant supply of ivy to tie back
your hair and set off your dazzling radiance. My home
laughs with the shine of finest silver; an altar bound
round with sacred leafy boughs desires to be sprinkled
with the blood of a slain lamb. Every hand busy hur-
ries, here and there run the servants, boys and girls
mixed in together; flames flicker, whirling aloft their
sooty smoke. Yet so that you know for what joyous
occasion you are invited, you must celebrate the Ides,
the day dividing April sacred to maritime Venus, a
sworn religious day on my calendar and more sacred to
me than my own birthday, because from this day my
Maecenas figures the increasing stream of his years.
Telephus, a young man beyond your reach but whom
you pursue, has fallen captive to a young girl. She is
rich and sensual and holds him enchained with welcomed bonds. Phaethon burned alive frightens greedy
ambitions and winged Pegasus's refusal to bear the
earth-born horseman Bellerophon offers a weighty example to strive always after what is worthy of you and
to avoid the mismatch by declaring it unthinkable to
dream beyond the limits. Come now, last of my loves —
for after this I will not burn for another woman — learn
with me measures to sing back with your lovely voice;
black cares will lose their power as we sing.]

    The poet spoke with a firm voice to Ligurinus and reaffirmed
the brokenness and alienation of C.IV.1, affecting every moment
of time — past, present, and future. This dissolution invaded the
poetic tradition, and while the poet has some power to recover

Vergil through the revival of a memory, *o crudelis*, which is the slightest power of encomium, the power to heal or negotiate any sense of community is not in c.10. Will Horace, the lyric *vates*, be only a memory, or will the remembering of his poetry have the power to influence societal identity and values? Just when the sympotic panegyrics of *Odes* IV have established once more the poet's powerful lyric, c.10 places the sympotic persona back in crisis. Now the feathers of Horace's metamorphosis into a swan have become a symbol of aging and death, the imagined beard on Ligurinus's old face. The poet's persistent self-glorification and his own apotheosis through his poetry distinguish the unique depth of the poetic crisis in c.10, which in turn reveals the full strength of its reversal in c.11 when the poet suddenly bursts onto the scene possessed of all the sympotic pleasures and intent on seducing the younger Phyllis. The potent lyric poet of the symposion once again immediately returns full strength, just as he did after his first lament for Ligurinus.

Like the two addresses to Ligurinus, the odes to Phyllis are a matched set. The first (II.4) has received the most attention, and yet it remains an incomplete story without its companion ode.[30] The main characters, the poet and Phyllis, have lived on; only Xanthias has dropped out of sight, as might be expected from the poet's clever usurpation of the lover's role at the end of the ode. After the lament in the ode to Ligurinus, it is easy without a look back at C.II.4 to exaggerate the sadness of c.11 and underestimate the power of shared song over the losses that living brings:[31]

> Ne sit ancillae tibi amor pudori,
> Xanthia Phoceu; prius insolentem
> serva Briseis niveo colore
>   movit Achillem,
>
> movit Aiacem Telamone natum   5
> forma captivae dominum Tecmessae,
> arsit Atrides medio in triumpho
>   virgine rapta,
>
> barbarae postquam cecidere turmae
> Thessalo victore et ademptus Hector   10
> tradidit fessis leviora tolli
>   Pergama Grais.

nescias an te generum beati
Phyllidis flavae decorent parentes;
regium certe genus et Penatis   15
    maeret iniquos.

crede non illam tibi de scelesta
plebe dilectam, neque sic fidelem,
sic lucro aversam potuisse nasci
    matre pudenda.   20

bracchia et vultum teretesque suras
integer laudo; fuge suspicari
cuius octavum trepidavit aetas
    claudere lustrum.

[Do not let your desire for your handmaid put you to
shame, Xanthias of Phocis. You are not the first. The
slave girl Briseis with her snowy white complexion
excited arrogant Achilles; the shapeliness of captive
Tecmessa excited her master Ajax, the son of Telamon;
and the son of Atreus burned for a prisoner maiden
right in the middle of his triumph, after the barbarian
troops fell to the Thessalian victor and Hector slain
handed over Troy's citadel, more easily taken, to the
war-worn Greeks. For all you know, blonde Phyllis's
rich parents will bring you, their son-in-law, honor.
Certainly she comes from royal stock, and she mourns
her unjust Penates. Do not imagine that one you love
has descended from the low common class and do not
imagine that she so true, so averse to profiteering,
could have been born to an immodest mother. Innocent, I praise her arms and face and smooth calves; stop
suspecting me since my age has sped past forty.]

Horace's fun with Xanthias is a play on genre. The conventional comic plot, not specified until the fourth strophe, goes like
this. A young Roman noble, Xanthias of Phocis, falls in love with
a slave girl and pursues her with some minimal degree of secrecy
from any who might disapprove. The conflict resolution occurs
when it is discovered that the young woman, Phyllis, is actually
an aristocrat who was captured or lost and sold into slavery at too
young an age to remember her high lineage. The plot is beyond
trite, but Horace's Xanthias of Phocis, as unlikely as it might be

with that name, has not seen his Plautus. His ignorance results in an inversion of the familiar comic plot: instead of pursuing his love without any embarrassment and with every trick imaginable, Xanthias, like the old noble *paterfamilias*, is ashamed. Now to translate the plot into the poetics of the ode: Xanthias represents an anti-lyric or tragic/epic type; Horace's *carmen* recovers laughter and in the process illustrates the power of lyric over its epic/tragic rivals.[32]

The poem divides into equal halves along generic boundaries, epic/tragedy in the first and comedy in the last. Horace, however, does not wait to begin his comic parody of epic. He tongue-in-cheek lists three exempla whom the noble-minded Xanthias can imitate: the greatest epic warriors. Loving a slave girl should not shame even the most heroic-minded Xanthias, if Achilles loved Briseis, Ajax loved Tecmessa, and Agamemnon burned for Cassandra. Horace's careful ordering—Achilles, Ajax, Agamemnon, Achilles (*Thessalo victore*, 10)—could not have been better designed for optimal tragic effect, and it requires little imagination to expand his lyric brevity. When Achilles lost Briseis to Agamemnon, he withdrew from the war and would not return no matter how many Greeks perished. Ajax took Tecmessa captive, a war prize from her father, the king of Phrygia, and Tecmessa comforted Ajax after he went mad in his rage over losing his bid for the armor of Achilles.[33] While the city of Troy burned, Agamemnon burned for Cassandra, and he took her back to Argos as part of his victorious plunder, where he was then murdered by his vengeful wife.[34] The temporal marker (*postquam*) leads back to the end of the *Iliad*, the death of Hector, and the destruction of Troy (9-12). Within this cyclical movement the poet places the tragic fall of the women in a progression of increasing violence, which ultimately removes their identity (*serva Briseis; captivae . . . Tecmessae; virgine rapta*, the nameless Cassandra). The well-known tragic circumstances of the epic models, emphasized within the poet's list, turns Horace's advice farcical. If Xanthias could be like these heroes, should he want to be? "Xanthias, consider Achilles and Briseis (but you know what happened there); then there is Ajax and Tecmessa (you know how that turned out); Agamemnon and Cassandra (you know how that ended)." Horace has made epic implode into comedy, and the line between comedy and tragedy may not be as distinct as Xanthias supposes.

He should have thought about his own name, Xanthias. The color yellow exploits the generic parameters of comedy and epic, and Horace plays on the confusion to quickly sketch the character of his addressee. After the command not to be ashamed of an ill-matched love, the audience is well prepared for a noble Roman name, but instead they hear/read Xanthias, a common name for a slave in Greek comedy (Ar. *Ra.; V.; Ach.*243; *Av.*656).[35] The name makes nonsense out of the first verse, because who could possibly care so much about one slave in love with another.[36] Horace immediately begins to elevate the name by adding a geographical epithet (*Phoceus*),[37] but the name receives no epic coloring until the fourth verse, when the most famous epic blond of all appears on the scene. The outlandishness of a Xanthias-Achilles, two characters from opposing genres sharing the same poetic stage, shows noble Xanthias for who he really is—a pretentious snob pretending to be what he is not. Xanthias of Phocis behaves more arrogantly than *insolens* Achilles.

Xanthias would be better off a slave. In the erotic comic world slaves control masters, a message Horace encodes into the exempla with an artful manipulation of word and sound.[38] Horace places the enjambed synchysis, *movit Achillem / movit Aiacem*, within the larger chiastic pattern of the names, *Briseis . . . Achillem . . . Aiacem . . . forma Tecmessae.* As a result, the slave girls, both subjects, surround their captors, while at the same time the anaphora of *movit,* as well as the rhyming alliteration of the heroic pair (*Achillem . . . Aiacem*), stresses the male heroes' objective status. When the poet juxtaposes *captivae* with *dominum* (6), the combination comes with an ironic edge, since Horace has through his song created a metathesis: the women have enslaved their enslaving masters with desire. Desire turns self-destructive. Horace reverses, and makes Agamemnon the actor. Agamemnon burns with a fire as deadly as the flames of Troy, a comparison Horace helps Xanthias imagine through the alliteration and assonance of *arsit Atrides . . . barbarae.* One need, however, note only the parallel placement of the verbs in asyndeton to understand the tragic dangers of love for epic heroes: "she moved, she moved, he burned-up" (*movit . . . movit . . . arsit*). The sequence ends with Hector making it easier for the tired Greeks to capture Troy (11–12). The lyric poet has his laugh since epic heroism defeats itself.[39] Such a detailed analysis hazards ruining the comic effect Horace masterfully achieves, but it is worth the risk to see the process by which Horace implants one opposing genre inside others, in this case comedy within the most dire circumstances of epic and tragedy. The later song to Phyllis will end on precisely this comic note (*minuentur atrae / carmine curae*).

After three stanzas of covert appropriation of genre, Horace openly declares his comic game and alerts Xanthias of Phocis to the possibilities, that Phyllis's parents may be rich royalty and his slave girl a displaced princess like Briseis, Tecmessa, or Cassandra. The poet displays a sophisticated appreciation of comic and tragic design. Horace turns tragedy into comedy by inverting the comic. The principal verbs (*nescias . . . crede*) start the reversal and maintain its force to the conclusion. The sharp transition to comedy depends on *nescias*.[40] A typical *fabula palliata* reaches it resolution when the characters recognize the truth about someone's identity; Xanthias's tragic circumstance could become comic through a broken recognition scene. Xanthias can pretend he does not know Phyllis's lineage and believe that she really is an ill-starred royal. Horace's Xanthian comedy works because of willful ignorance. Xanthias, like any good audience, must engage in a little self-deception for his own pleasure and imagine (*crede*) that the comedy will work out well for him because of the virtues of the characters involved, himself and Phyllis. Since the presupposition about nobility, that a noble stands out from the masses and that noble parents reproduce noble offspring, must be true, Xanthias of Phocis could not have possibly chosen to love a woman from the lowest class, and Phyllis, loyal and opposed to filthy profit, could not descend from a shameless prostitute.[41] This emphasis on character is nothing short of comic raillery laced with mocking sarcasm.[42] The poet for three strophes has poked fun at the hypocrisy of Xanthias's noble snobbery, and although it might be tempting to take the poet's praise of Phyllis a little more seriously and therefore think the poet chivalrous, if it is not clear from the exaggerated *certe . . . sic . . . sic* that his is not genuine epithalamic praise, then in the last stanza everyone learns what kind of lady Phyllis really is.[43] Still, the audience, including Xanthias, can imagine what they will.

The invitation for Xanthias to risk a little self-delusion places Xanthias in a dilemma of tragedy versus comedy. If Xanthias accepts the comic possibilities, he is probably gullible enough also to believe the poet is the real *senex* of the comedy and the sexuality of his praise for Phyllis is completely innocent. *Integer* implies that the poet has never touched Phyllis.[44] Should he be trusted? The preceding comic inversions give away that she and the poet are about as "untouched" as Xanthias is Achilles. The last four verses moan with sensual passion ("a, u, au") and the carryover of these sounds from *teretes suras* to *suspicari* makes the poet seem suspect. If he has not enjoyed Phyllis yet, he could win her with his passionate song. Which role should Xanthias play, the tragic or comic? In the tragic world he will know Phyllis's true identity and must put aside his shame, but if he should, he would become enslaved just as the other epic heroes. In the comic world the yellow Xanthias can keep his noble airs, and Phyllis can be his princess, but the princess would then be in love with someone below her,[45] and Xanthias must risk losing her to a more seductive rival. Horace's fun is that the pretentious Xanthias loses face either way. Whether epic, tragedy, or comedy, the lyric poet wins.

Horace puts his character through a similar downfall and reversal within a sequence of interrelated odes (II.4, IV.1, 11) as sharp and complete as the transition Xanthias must experience between the two halves of C.II.4. The close interplay between the two addresses to Ligurinus suggests that a similar correspondence between the only two odes to a Phyllis is likely, but Horace has also left precise temporal markers to correlate these three odes. Only in II.4 and IV.1 does Horace cite his age according to the five-year cycle of the *lustrum;* in the first he is around forty and in the second about fifty. The Alban wine Horace proposes to share with Phyllis (IV.11) has survived into its tenth year.[46] The age of the Alban wine equals the difference in the dramatic dates of II.4 and IV.1, ten years. Horace has given his audience a chance to see how the lyric poet has fared through this cycle of time.[47]

The poet in II.4 claims to be too old to be a serious rival for Phyllis's affections; this, however, is playful irony, and the poet may win the girl, if Xanthias is not careful. In essence the poem celebrates the seductive comic power of the poet's lyre. Then after ten years Horace swears off Venus and sympotic pleasures. He is too old, and Venus is better off spending her time on a younger ward (C.IV.1). Suddenly in c.11 the poet's alienation from the festivities of Venus vanishes, and his relationship to the sympotic reverts to the familiar pattern of *Odes* I–III. The poet once again seductively tempts a girl to join him for an intimate celebration, not just any girl but the younger Phyllis. The poet shifts from 'too old for the young Phyllis, but not really' (II.4) to 'too old for the young Ligurinus, or anyone else, and rejected' (IV.1; 10) to 'the seducer of the same younger Phyllis' (IV.11). The reversal is so pronounced that the poet's advice to Phyllis against pursuing a youth not her match (11.21–32) appears curious and would be outright hypocritical except that Horace acknowledges that for him also the opportunities for love will soon end. Here a full appreciation of the comic nature of the poet's lyric in II.4 becomes important. Horace can assume a comic persona in one poem and a tragic in another without the necessity of any dramatic connection. But in a sequence in which the first ode focuses on the comic inversion of the tragic, then in the second there occurs a tragic displacement of the poet's sympotic lyric voice, and in the third he recovers the earlier sympotic persona, it is more reasonable that the third ode represents a restoration of the lyric poet's power rather than a further pessimistic explication of its loss.

   C.11 systematically reverses all the negatives of Horace's sympotic disavowal. The poet's pleas that Venus leave him alone seem an aberration as he now invites Phyllis to a party of the sensual type that he had sworn off (c.1.29–32). Compared to the ephemeral dreams and mirrors in the odes to Ligurinus, the song by which the poet attempts to seduce Phyllis emphasizes sympotic goods the poet has in hand. No lad or lass, no wine, no garlands change to Alban wine (1–2), Phyllis radiant with her ivy-bound hair (2–5), and the bustle of the household girls jostling with the boys (10).[48] The poet cried and Maximus laughed (*potentior . . . riserit*, 17–18), but now laughter returns to the poet's house (*ridet argento domus*, 6). The scene's opulence (sparkling silver) and green lushness (garden, parsley, ivy, and vines—compatible with the name Phyllis, "leafy") prove that Horace really does not need to send Venus off to a younger man. The poet is in command, pursuing the girl of his affections, and although she is reluctant to accept his invitation because she wants Telephus, whom another possesses (21–24), the love triangle does not daunt the poet lover (25–31), nor is there any hint that he will fail to win her. His first word (*est*) marks his confidence in the present, the impact of which is increased by the anaphora, *est . . . cadus, est . . . apium, est . . . vis*; no longer does the poet wistfully look back to his past (*non sum qualis eram,* 1.1–4) or ahead to a future of rejection (c.10). This song revels in an erotically charged atmosphere not to be denied. Symbolically the lovers are already bound together. For the first time, the sympotic invitation emphasizes garlands: *apium, hedera,* and *verbenae*. The parsley and ivy for Phyllis's hair come from the poet's own garden, and as soon as Phyllis's hair has been bound (the symbolic act for lyric composition), the poet makes the inanimate live: the personified house laughs, and the altar becomes a lover bound with chaste leafy boughs and desiring the consummation of sacred rites.[49] On the altar of Venus, lovemaking and ritual sacrifice share the same sacral vocabulary (*castis / vincta verbenis avet,* 6b–7).[50]

The poet's song is not exclusively light, and therefore it cannot be considered as simply a restatement of the comic inversions of C.II.4 and treated as if the poet's displacement in C.IV.1 never occurred. The serious moments are not new but are those common in the sympotic odes of books I–III and the addresses to Ligurinus: the transience of human existence (11–20; 31–34) and *moderatio* (21–31). The poet allows darkness to creep into the preparations for the festivities of Venus. The dirty smoke from the wavering light invades the otherwise bright atmosphere (*sordidum flammae trepidant rotantes / vertice fumum,* 11–12). Horace regularly uses *trepido* in contexts about mortality, which includes a reference to his age in the other ode to Phyllis (*cuius octavum trepidavit aetas / claudere lustrum,* 23–24).[51] Any doubt remaining that the smoke suggests mortality is removed by the dark imagery for Horace's last love affair in the final strophe (*non . . . calebo; atrae . . . curae*)[52] and by the warning given to Vergil to be mindful of the black fires (c.12.25–28). The flickering flames and black smoke dim only two lines in the brilliant jubilation of the first three strophes, but against the radiant surroundings they cast their shadow even more deeply over the poet's announcement that the party is to celebrate Maecenas's birthday. The metaphor has a certain kind of dark humor that can be enjoyed between friends, but it is only a little more subtle than stringing up black crepe paper to celebrate a fiftieth birthday party. "Parsley garlands, Phyllis, are used in mourning" (line 3; *ut Linus . . . apio crinis ornatus amaro,* Verg. *Ecl.*6.67–68).

After naming Phyllis (line 3), Horace spaces throughout the

first half of the poem second-person verbs (*fulges,* 5; *noris, advoceris,* 13) so that the song, while rehearsing the preparations for the party, stays focused on her. Phyllis too has grown older and fallen victim to desire: she loves Telephus, but has been rejected. Even though the hyperbaton (*Telephum, quem . . . vinctum*) includes Phyllis within the lovers' triangle, the contrast of *petis* with *occupavit* makes clear just how far she has actually been closed out: Phyllis is chasing Telephus, but another girl has already seized him as an army might take control of a conquered territory.[53] The poet may have avoided Xanthias's term *ancilla* in order to make Phyllis more comfortable, but he implies it here; Phyllis the *ancilla* has lost out to a young rich sensual rival. Horace's assessment of the situation alters the seductive metaphor of the ivy and the chaste boughs entwining Venus's altar. Phyllis, her name the very image of the binding vines, has met her match, and another girl has bound her Telephus.

The poet shows his comic wit by lightening the mood with the weightiness of two tragic mythological exempla arguing for *moderatio.* Phaethon's demand to drive the chariot of the Sun, his divine father, left his lover, the Ligurian king Cycnus, mourning his death until the king was transformed into a swan. Horace put a feathery beard on Ligurinus (c.10.2, *pluma*) to remind him of Cycnus's grief and persuade Ligurinus to love while still young. The poet also has some fun punning on *grave . . . gravatus* (26–27): Pegasus finding Bellerophon too weighty, when the hero tried to fly to the heavens, offers a weighty example. As it stands here in c.11, the grandeur of Horace's mythmaking adds comic distance between the lofty hopes of Phaethon and Bellerophon, and Phyllis's more down-to-earth act of pursuing a lover beyond her reach. The poet appends to these two exempla some typical advice against overstepping life's boundaries from other *carpe diem* odes, particularly to Leuconoë (*ultra / quam licet sperare nefas putando,* 29b–30; *scire nefas, spem longam reseces,* C.I.11.1,7; *dum licet,* C.II.11.16, IV.12.26). Someone outside looking in can only speculate whether a person in Phyllis's situation would fully appreciate the humor.[54]

The dissonance among the lighter and more serious aspects of c.11, all intersecting in one moment, differs from the comic/tragic inversions of the first Phyllis ode, and these distinctions more than anything else define the singular quality of the resolution achieved as the poem draws to its conclusion. The poet introduced the comic plot to Xanthias with the suspension of belief (*nescias*), but he begins his own invitation to Phyllis with understanding (*noris*, 13). The first Xanthias and Phyllis comedy was predicated on pretense. This invitation to Phyllis with all its jubilant seductive appeal stems from the acceptance of life's tragedies since Horace wants her to know the exact circumstances of the occasion. It is Maecenas's birthday; another year has past; Phyllis should give up her ill-matched desire and become the last of the poet's loves before it is too late for them both.[55] The lyric poet's celebration encompasses all of life, its joys and pains, which in this song, unlike the false comparisons of Xanthias to epic heroes, are genuine shared experiences. No character in this ode acts in isolation. The poet considers Maecenas's birthday more solemn than his own. The poet, too, grows older. Phyllis could not win her beloved Telephus nor could the poet win the younger Ligurinus, and for the poet youth continues to have its allure because he again sings his love to a younger woman. The advice that he gives to Phyllis applies equally to himself. The characters' lives and desires are all bound together in one song. By this sense of community the ode finds its positive resolution.

Horace sets aside sympotic metaphor, and for the first time it is not the wine that removes cares but the responsive songs themselves.[56] The shared experience of lyric song cuts tragedies down to size. *Minuentur* (35) should not be read in its weakest denotation of only diminishing but not removing. The mathematical connotation of *minuentur* with *modos* sets up a much more positive quantitative equation. As the pair measures out their songs, the cares are cut back until they are tiny and insignificant (*minutae*).[57] The song that Horace will teach and share with Phyllis has power to heal the hurts of time, a triumph predicted by the wine's survival (*superantis* used here for the first time of longevity, 1) and by Maecenas's control over his own years (*ordinat annos*, 20). The careful wording of the final stanza is remarkable. Horace mixes the song among the cares (*minuentur atrae / carmine curae*) and sets the first and last words of the verses in contrast (*femina, voce, carmine* versus *calebo, atrae, curae*). The first (woman, voice, song) relieves the pain of the last (burning, black, cares). The only other time Horace uses *condisco* is in C.III.2.3, where it stresses the labor that a young soldier must exert to endure poverty. In c.11 the word connotes a shared experience (attested only later in Apul. *Fl*.18.142). Others may have their favorites. For me these are the most beautiful and bittersweet persuasive verses ever sung: *age iam, meorum / finis amorum / (non enim posthac alia calebo / femina), condisce modos amanda / voce quos reddas.* They compel beyond resistance. Through rhyme the poet-musician personifies love in Phyllis's voice and physically unites himself with his beloved through their song (*meorum . . . amorum . . . modos amanda*).[58] The lyric poet's sympotic persona has not failed nor has he lost the enjoyment of the present moment; the sympotic has instead been revealed as an invitation to the joys and power of shared song. In turn the poet attains a new level of authority. He is the teacher of the song who also benefits from the performance of his audience. The same could be said for Horatian panegyric.

I have not forgotten Maecenas's birthday. Once before Horace reminded his patron that their lives were inseparably entwined:

> Cur me querelis exanimas tuis?
> nec dis amicum est nec mihi te prius
>   obire, Maecenas, mearum
>   grande decus columenque rerum.
>
> a, te meae si partem animae rapit   5
> maturior vis, quid moror alteram,
>   nec carus aeque nec superstes
>   integer? (C.II.17.1–8a)

> [Why do you take away (*ex-*) my soul (*animas*) with your complaints? It is not the gods' will (*amicum*) nor mine that you die before me, Maecenas, the great honor and support of my being. Ah, if an inopportune violence seizes you, part of my soul (*animae*), how could I, the other half (*alteram*), go on living, neither beloved as I was nor surviving whole?]

Maecenas, like Vergil, is Horace's other half,[59] and Horace honors Maecenas's birthday as his own, placing this final tribute for his literary patron-friend at the center of c.11, an erotic lyric celebrating the healing potential of sharing songs, that is, the pleasure of the poetic circle. The inclusion of this tribute as a central motivation for just such a song tells much about Horace's panegyric

praxis: the power of praise resides in the unification of the private
and public and in the common experience a truly responsive song
creates.

C.12: Vergilius at the Symposion

Iam veris comites, quae mare temperant,
impellunt animae lintea Thraciae;
iam nec prata rigent nec fluvii strepunt
    hiberna nive turgidi.

nidum ponit Ityn flebiliter gemens   5
infelix avis, heu, Cecropiae domus
aeternum opprobrium, quod male barbaras
    regum est ulta libidines.

dicunt in tenero gramine pinguium
custodes ovium carmina fistula   10
delectante deum cui pecus et nigri
    colles Arcadiae placent.

adduxere sitim tempora, Vergili;
sed pressum Calibus ducere Liberum
si gestis, iuvenum nobilium cliens,   15
    nardo vina merebere.

nardi parvus onyx eliciet cadum
qui nunc Sulpiciis accubat horreis,
spes donare novas largus amaraque
    curarum eluere efficax.   20

ad quae si properas gaudia, cum tua
velox merce veni; non ego te meis
immunem meditor tingere poculis,
    plena dives ut in domo.

rerum pone moras et studium lucri   25
nigrorumque memor, dum licet, ignium
misce stultitiam consiliis brevem.
    dulce est desipere in loco.

[Now spring's companions, which settle the sea, the Thracian winds drive full the sails; now neither are the grassy
meadows stiff with frost nor do streams roar swollen with

winter snow. The bird of misfortune, ah, the eternal
shame of the Cecropian house, builds her nest while she in
tears mourns for Itys, because maliciously she took revenge on barbaric royal lusts. Shepherds on the soft grass
watch over their fat sheep and play songs on their pipes,
the delight of the god who takes pleasure in the flocks and
black hills of Arcadia. The change of seasons has brought
thirst, Vergil; but if you, client of noble youths, long to
drink down draughts of Freeing Wine pressed at Cales,
earn your wine with nard. A small onyx box of nard will
lure out a jar reclining in Sulpicius's storerooms, rich in
granting new hopes and with the power to wash away bitter cares. If you are to enjoy these pleasures with any
speed, come quickly with your pay. I for one do not intend
to wet you down with my cups for free, as if I were some
rich man in a stuffed house. Put aside life's delays and
your pursuit of wealth and remembering the black fires,
while you are able, mix temporary foolishness in with
your discretion. Sweet it is to play the drunken fool for a
moment.]

C.IV.12 repeats the most familiar sympotic plot from books
I–III.[60] Again the poet invites to a symposion a person so en-
tangled in daily business that there is no time to enjoy a drinking
party (13–16, 25). Wine is the cure for cares (17–20), and the appeal
to forget life's troubles (21–22; 25–28) finds its immediacy in the
transience of human existence, conveyed in seasonal imagery (1–
12). The ode's seriocomic structure utilizes both contrasting stanzas (Procne mourning for Itys, strophe 2, between the arrival of
spring and the peaceful bucolic countryside, strophes 1, 3) and interlacing word groups (*misce* introducing *stultitiam consiliis
brevem*, 27). The song's content and form are so familiar that un-
detected an editor could paste it back in *Odes* I–III and use it to invite any number of Horatian characters, except that here the addressee is (a) Vergilius.[61] Nowhere else does Horace invite his
poet-friend to a drinking party, but his presence now both affirms
the permanence of song through the poet's power to revitalize a
poetic tradition after the death of a master singer and solidifies
the unity of the Horatian symposion and panegyric.

The identity of Vergilius is at the center of the ode (strophe 4)
and critical debate that has produced vehement opinions, if not

always well-reasoned arguments. The question should not be omitted, though it has been,[62] not only because Horace waits until such a prominent position to name his addressee, but if Horace does invite the poet to a drinking party in a collection published after Vergil's death, then the resurrection cannot be unintentional and without impact on the meaning of the ode and thematic direction of the book.

Vergilius non poeta condenses to three objections. (1) The majority of manuscript titles identify Vergilius as some unknown businessman. (2) An invitation to a dead person is an absurdity. Even if the ode were written when Vergil was alive, it is unlikely that an invitation, rendered so remote, would be included in the fourth book.[63] (3) Horace addresses Vergilius as a dependent client and charges him with chasing after profit. Speaking so bluntly of the poet's banausic profiteering is demeaning, and publishing such a caricature after his death is unacceptably rude.[64] Fraenkel, the most influential supporter of this view, warns against turning Horace into a "monster of callousness."[65]

Against Fraenkel (and others) can be set no less than Bentley, whose identification of the *nobiles iuvenes* assumes that Vergilius is the poet, and since the publication of Bowra's article (1928) support for the poet has steadily grown.[66] *Vergilius poeta* has three arguments. Echoes of Horace's other poems to Vergil (I.3; 24) and of Vergil's own poetry (*Eclogues; Georgics*) form a progression beginning in the first verse and developing throughout the first three strophes to the unveiling of the addressee Vergilius in the fourth.[67] Even if a reader misses the Vergilian influence on the *infelix avis* (Orpheus's song [*Ecl.*6.78–81] and lament [*G.*4.511–15]), it would require complete unfamiliarity with Vergil's bucolic song not to see the Vergilian landscape (strophe 3) where Horace names Arcadia for the only time.[68] Second, the pattern of *Odes* IV is to reserve the central stanza for a eulogy. Would a greedy ointment merchant really fit alongside Maximus, Maecenas, and the Neros?[69] Although Horace regularly delays naming his addressee, in only three other instances in the *Odes* does Horace wait until the central strophe: Maecenas (I.20; III.8) and Vergil (I.24). How likely would it be that IV.12 addresses an unknown lesser friend? Third, nine other times Horace mentions Vergil, and his identity is unquestioned (*S.*I.5.40, 48; 6.55; 10.45, 81; *C.*I.3.6; 24.10; *Epist.*II.1.247; *Ars* 55). If Horace did not mean the poet, it would be difficult to prevent his audience from making this assumption, especially in a context loaded with Vergilian language.[70]

But what of the objections raised against the poet? Bowra's response to the manuscript evidence is that it is derivative. For example, two Paris manuscripts (7971, 7974) have the ascription *ad Vergilium quendam unguentarium*. *Quendam* Bowra interprets as an open admission of ignorance and *unguentarium* a weak deduction from verses 17–22, as in other cases *mercator* is from *studium lucri* (25) and *medicus* from some contortion of *iuvenum nobilium cliens* and *curarum eluere efficax* (15, 20). Ps.-Acro identifies Vergilius as a *negotiator*, but Porphyrio assumes he is the poet. The manuscripts and scholiasts show signs of long-standing debate.[71] Moritz offers some light by suggesting that this is not a historical invitation, requiring that the ode be written when Vergil was alive.[72] Reality is not a poetic requirement, as critics are quick to acknowledge regarding the winter scene of C.I.9 or any number of Horatian lovers. In fact, there is nothing (outside of the insistence that the occasion at least be a historical possibility rather than poetic imagination) that would preclude the ode from being written after Vergil's death. Instead, the mournful tone of strophes 2–3 argues that Vergil was dead, and the nightingale's cries and black hills of Arcadia reveal Horace's tears for his lost friend.[73]

There are no signs of lament in the first strophe. Horace begins by reworking the seasonal imagery from the odes to Sestius (I.4) and Thaliarchus (I.9) to give this sympotic invitation a hopeful start. In both c.4 and 12 spring has arrived, but Horace intensifies the warmth of spring in c.12 by using dual negatives, as in c.4, to melt the snowy landscape of Mount Soracte, c.9 (*Solvitur acris hiems grata vice veris et Favoni, . . . ac neque iam stabulis gaudet pecus aut arator igni, / nec prata canis albicant pruinis, c.4.1, 3–4; nec iam sustineant onus / silvae laborantes, geluque / flumina constiterint acuto, 9.2b–4; iam nec prata rigent nec fluvii strepunt / hiberna nive turgidi, c.12.3–4*). The spring thaw predicts that winter's chill (death) will have no hold over the poem, and accordingly the prominent anaphora of *iam* (c.12.1, 3) focuses on the present with the same energy as the ode to Phyllis (c.11). Horace leads his audience to assume through these similarities that c.12 also will develop into a sympotic lyric seducing some lover or urging another to enjoy life's pleasures,[74] but Horace delays the sympotic invitation for two strophes. Strophes 2–3 could be removed and *adduxere sitim tempora, Vergili* (13) would carry on the familiar sympotic plot after the spring thaw (1–4). Horace holds any hopeful expectations in suspense.

At strophe 2 the mood quickly turns black. The nightingale, the metamorphosized Procne, mourns the death of her own son, whom she served up as a feast for her husband Tereus because he violated her sister Philomela.[75] Procne's endless mourning, which Horace effectively conveys with a compressed tricolon (*flebiliter gemens* / *infelix*, 5–6) reminiscent of Vergil's lament for Quintilius (*flebilis occidit,* / . . . *flebilior*, C.I.24.9–10a), equals the immoderation of the crime and her vengeance. *Heu* (6) is especially empathetic, acting as a monosyllabic stop before the rhythmic *Cecropiae*. The poet pauses over the moan, a human cry from the once woman, now animal. By giving the metamorphosized mourning bird back a human voice, Horace captures the depersonalizing nature of Tereus's assault against the women and draws the human audience closer in to the bestial world of the tragedy. The sigh performed well would leave the audience wondering whether *heu* is Procne's cry alone or also the poet's sigh as he joins his voice to the lament.[76] Therefore, the Vergilian bucolic scene of shepherds lazing in the soft grass and piping their songs is introduced by a reminder of eternal mourning and ends in the black hills of Arcadia, hemmed in by dark symbols of death in the previous ode (*sordidum . . . fumum*, 10–11; *atrae . . . curae*, 35–36) and death's black fires in the last strophe (*nigrorum . . . ignium*, 26). Horace has followed up each springtime scene with an opposing representation of death and shadow, which by contrast intensifies the darkness like black paint on a snow-white canvas.

Horace does not break this dark mood immediately. He waits one verse. His address to Vergilius continues the metaphor of lament since thirst is a common symbol for death (*adduxere sitim tempora, Vergili*, 13).[77] Finally, when Horace names Vergil, he makes good on the hopeful renewal that the changing seasons promised with the simple transition, *sed* (14). The sympotic invitation pushes the lament for Vergil in the last Ligurinus ode one step further: Horace will recall not just Vergil's song but the poet himself back to life. Such a resurrection might seem to be extreme symbolism, but it reflects the Dionysiac power of the symposion to renew all life. Wine (equated with sympotic song in c.11)[78] is ritually potent; to drink *Liber* is to ingest his liberating power. Appropriately the symposion is where absent friends return and acquire new life (C.I.20; 36; II.7), and therefore the dead friend Vergil in a sympotic context is most aptly addressed as if he were alive. As deep as the lament is, so complete is the poets' victory over death: the prefix *ex-* dominates the verbal elements of the fifth strophe (*eliciet, eluere, efficax*); the power of wine to erase bitter cares (*amaraque / curarum eluere*) parallels the language of song's triumph over death in the last lines of C.IV.11 (*minuentur atrae / carmine curae*); and for the first time in any Horatian sympotic invitation the addressee instead of being warned against excessive hope is told that wine renews hope.[79] In this sense Horace's song to Vergil is like the rustic's invocation to Augustus that ensures the princeps will remain a significant part of Roman life even after death (IV.5.29–36) and like Menalcas's song that placed Daphnis among the stars (Verg. *Ecl.*5),[80] and yet Horace makes the apotheosis of his friend Vergil more earthy and tangible by inviting the master singer over to his house for a drink.

Perhaps Horace's sympotic invitation sounds too common, and it becomes hard to accept that he is addressing the great Vergil. *Iuvenum nobilium cliens* and *studium lucri* cause most of the hesitation and raise doubts about the friendship of the two poets, as have the earlier odes to Vergil (I.3; 24). If it were not for the addresses to Ligurinus, Horace's criticism here of Vergil would be harder to read. Horace's incorporation of the *animae dimidium meae* theme into c.10 confirms that Vergil was a close colleague—and Vergil's death, I am convinced, lies behind the plaintive introspective mood of c.10–12—but poet-friends do not have to have the same song. Mopsus and Menalcas competed, and their songs formed a harmonious whole. This is the appropriate paradigm for Horace's and Vergil's poetry: competing voices so closely interrelated that they form two halves of the whole.[81]

Answers have tended to extremes. On one hand, the friendship could have had its difficulties, and the reluctance to accept this is the source of the entire problem in c.12. Horace may have intended to be insulting.[82] On the other hand, *cliens* is an accurate enough term for the poet-to-patron relationship, which in Vergil's case included such key figures as Varus, Agrippa, Pollio, Maecenas, and Augustus. Recalling such associations is far from insulting.[83] *Studium lucri* is more difficult, since it is typically pejorative,[84] which leads to the most common assessment: Horace was only kidding. This is the playful banter exchanged between friends.[85]

These either/or answers disappoint. Nowhere does Horace intimate that Vergil is anything but a friend, unless Horace's criticism of Vergil's epic poetics is interpreted personally, and to develop such a notion on the basis of the controversial c.12 is critical suicide, especially given the Vergilian echoes to *animae dimidium meae* in the Ligurinus ode. Horace's sympotic invitation may be amusing sarcasm between friends, but Putnam still complains that playfulness is one thing, carping at a dead friend is quite another.[86] Scholarship seems in a predicament. It would work out well if Vergilius were the poet, but the result would seem to turn Vergil out of Horace's good graces or Horace into an insensitive caviler.

The real problem, then, is not the identity of Vergilius—the evidence overwhelmingly favors the poet—but that there has been no explanation for Horace naming and addressing the poet in the manner he does. The original question, "Just who is Vergilius?," must be rephrased. Why would a sympotic invitation with such similarities to the sympotic odes of books I–III be included in *Odes* IV and name as its addressee Rome's most prominent poet now dead?

The inability to even raise this question results primarily from the failure to consider Horace's invitation to Vergil in relationship to its predecessors (the other sympotic odes and earlier odes to Vergilius, C. I.3; 24), and thereby determine how it contributes to the book's encomiastic program. *Studium lucri* loses its shock in view of Horace's typical sympotic invitation. Vergilius is reluctant to come to the party, and one should expect Horace in such circumstances to call *carpe diem* in strong terms, just as he does with Sestius (C.I.4.13–20), Dellius (C.II.3.13–28), Quintius (C.II.11), and Maecenas (C.III.8.25–28; III.29.5, 9–12).[87] This is not to argue that Horace's blunt references to Vergil's client status and his pursuit of rewards (banausia) can be explained merely as gentle ribbing. Blatant accusations of poetry for profit are Horace's standard complaint against the epicists (S.II.1.10–15), the charge he levels against Choerilus for ingratiating himself to Alexander (*Epist*.II.1.231–244).[88] Horace's invitation is overtly critical of Vergil's epic poetics, as are the earlier odes to Vergil. C.12 fits the pattern: lament coupled with competitive criticism. The black Arcadian hills are only a part of the whole. Horace calls Vergil a client, while he claims that he has become noble for his Aeolian song (C.IV.3.10–12). The crying for Itys recalls the lesson in the fall of Phaethon from the ode to Phyllis (11.25–26). In Euripides' *Phaethon* the nightingale mourns for Itys: μέλπει δ' ἐν δέν-δρεσι λεπτὰν / ἀηδὼν ἁρμονίαν / ὀρθρευομένα γόοις / Ἴτυν Ἴτυν πολύθρηνον.[89] Horace with a neoteric-styled allusion to Phaethon, as he did with the image of Daedalus (C.I.3.34–35), hints that Vergil also should have confined himself to stricter limits, less weighty than the epic *vates*. Vergil should have stayed away from the air and sea and kept his feet on solid ground.

This is much more than banter to offset lament.[90] The epic criticism of Vergil fits within the panegyric framework of book IV. Vergil is a poet with patrons, Rome's highest powers. Horace has invited to his party none other than a poet laureate of Rome, now known for his national epic, and also for the first time demands that his guest bring a gift. Horace does not mention this in passing but goes on for three of the seven strophes (13–24). Without Vergil's gift of nard there is no party. Repeatedly in book IV poetry is a gift or payment. Horace receives his poetry as a gift from the gods (IV.3.17–24; 6.29–30) and applies commercial terms to writing for patrons (IV.8.9–12, 21–22). The metaphor, gift equals poetry, transforms Vergil's nard into a poem that he must bring to share at the symposion. [91] Spikenard (νάρδος) could be used to flavor wine (ναρδίτης, Dsc. 5.57). If this was the use Horace intended for Vergil's gift (which produces better sense from the nard enticing out the wine jar, 17), then the metaphor, nard for poetry, is all the more appropriate. As nard sweetens wine, so Vergil's poetry will heighten sympotic pleasure.[92] Sympotic pleasure, more powerful than death, comes from sharing songs just as in the Phyllis ode.

C.12 illumines the central concern of the entire book: creating a lyric civic discourse. The sympotic invitation in which Vergil must buy his way in with a poem links the sympotic theme with public praise, the most likely gift that a *iuvenum nobilium cliens* would bring.[93] There will be praise songs at Horace's symposion, but the *Aeneid*'s fierce battles and expansive style will not capture the sympotic moment of the lyric poet. There are serious generic qualifications behind Horace's tribute to Vergil. The mourning for Itys and the pastoral landscape (5–12) recall the bucolic Vergil (*Ecl.*6) and bring to mind once again the *genus tenue*.[94] The epic Vergil does appear, but in the macabre black fires (*nigrorum . . . ignium*, 26) that suggest the funeral pyre of Dido (*atris ignibus*, *A.*4.384) and the Trojan War dead (*ignibus atris*, *A.*11.186). The death image is nearly obligatory in sympotic *carpe diem* poetry, but here it has wider generic implications, since it allows the poet to tactfully urge his friend to put aside the mournful epic themes that occupy him and join in the pleasures of lyric song. The poem ends with the command to Vergil to enjoy the moderated madness that in the Greek lyric tradition was the key to inspired poetic composition (27–28).[95] C.12 unravels the Vergilian *recusatio* of epic praise poetry (*Ecl.*6), but in exactly the opposite way that Vergil's writing the epic *Georgics* and the national myth of the *Aeneid* had done. The sympotic Horace is arguing that encomium should be fit to the lyre and at the same time that the lyre avoids the banausic pressures of patronage. Accordingly Horace's lament for the bucolic Vergil and his invitation to the epic Vergil join Horace's sympotic lyric persona and encomium tightly together just before the climactic c.14–15, the remaining exempla of imperial praise poetry in the lyric mode. Horace thus in his panegyric lyrics expresses the full breadth of Apollo's admonition: Horace has kept his muse thin (lyric) and fed the sacrifice to be as fat as possible (panegyric as shared song). The lyric-panegyric combination lies behind the paradoxical metaphors in the first strophes. The winds temper the sea but strike the sails full (*mare temperant, / impellunt animae lintea Thraciae*, 1–2; *impellunt* sounds heavy on the first syllables of the verse), and the keepers of fat sheep sing their songs on fine grass (*in tenero gramine pinguium / . . . ovium*, 9–10a).[96]

C.12 exemplifies Horatian encomium: it is simultaneously private and public. Horace mourns the loss of his poet-friend in the most graphic of images, the groaning of a mother for her dead son, and pays Vergil the compliment of a lyric competitor on the public stage interacting with the powerful legacy of Vergil's bucolic to epic poetry. I would have loved to have heard Vergil's responding song.

C.13: E/motive Song, The Art of Writing Off Lyce

The poet has been in a nostalgic mood (c.10–12). A second poem
to an old flame again presenting the poet's empathy with common weaknesses and illustrating his use of song to heal human
brokenness would round off his more personal laments and set a
tone of restoration that would make a smooth transition to the final two poems praising the Augustan peace. Horace breaks the
sequence: "The gods have answered my prayers, Lyce; you, Lyce,
are turning into an old hag":

> Audivere, Lyce, di mea vota, di
> audivere, Lyce: fis anus; et tamen
>   vis formosa videri
>   ludisque et bibis impudens
>
> et cantu tremulo pota Cupidinem   5
> lentum sollicitas. ille virentis et
>   doctae psallere Chiae
>   pulchris excubat in genis.
>
> importunus enim transvolat aridas
> quercus et refugit te, quia luridi   10
>   dentes, te, quia rugae
>   turpant et capitis nives.
>
> nec Coae referunt iam tibi purpurae
> nec cari lapides tempora quae semel
>   notis condita fastis   15
>   inclusit volucris dies.
>
> quo fugit Venus, heu, quove color, decens
> quo motus? quid habes illius, illius
>   quae spirabat amores,
>   quae me surpuerat mihi,   20
>
> felix post Cinaram notaque et artium
> gratarum facies? sed Cinarae brevis
>   annos fata dederunt,
>   servatura diu parem
>
> cornicis vetulae temporibus Lycen,   25
> possent ut iuvenes visere fervidi
>   multo non sine risu
>   dilapsam in cineres facem.

[They have heard, Lyce, the gods have heard my vows, the gods, Lyce. You are becoming a crone, and yet you still agonize to seem pretty, and you play at love games, and you drink shamelessly, and with a wavering song you, drunk, harass sluggish Cupid. He keeps watch over Chia's lovely eyes, she a learned lyricist. He, with contempt, wings past the withered oaks and flees full flight from you because your yellow teeth, because your wrinkles and snow-white hair have turned you ugly. Neither now do Coan purple nor costly jewels bring back to you time, which the fleeting day has forever shut away in familiar records. Where has Venus fled, alas, or where your complexion, where your graceful moves? What do you have left of her, of her who was exhaling, inhaling passions, who had stolen away my very self from me, who next to Cinara was my favorite and a famed beauty with winsome charms? But to Cinara a short life the fates gave, sure to preserve Lyce for ages until she equals the times of an old crow so that lust-filled suitors can call on you and laugh heartily in your face at your torch disintegrated into ash.]

No other ode demands a more abrupt transition from its preceding poems than the abusive c.13. Its vitriolic spirit proves impossible to mistake, hard to laugh off, and difficult to contextualize. Previously when playing the jilted lover, Horace attacked indirectly with a moralizing tone of superiority, warning his rival that faithless Pyrrha would soon abandon him too (C.I.5.5–12), and teasing Lydia that Telephus would eventually prove false (C.I.13.13–16). The poet's erotic descriptions of the lovers and confession of jealous rage revealed the hypocrisy of his good riddance attitude: "Venus, I'm hanging up my love weapons. But wait—won't you rouse Chloë one more time!" (C.III.26). The poet clearly hoped his songs would win his lovers back, not just triumph in their demise.[97] For all lovers time is quickly slipping away, but Horace more often used *carpe diem* to persuade the reluctant (Leuconoë, C.I.11; Tyndaris, I.17; Neobule, III.12; Lyde, III.28), and when he did turn the pain and wrinkles of old age against the rejecting lover, it was an imagined future allowing them the opportunity to change their minds and accept love

(C.I.25; III.10; IV.10). C.13 savages its curse by contrast, opening with a theatrical repetitious outburst, more common in Catullus or Edgar Allan Poe, that drives the singer's hostility upon his desired who rejected his charms.

Horace's return to the iambic tone of his earlier work cuts sharply against the persona he assumes in the other love odes of book IV — the old man past the time for love. The old poet could never be taken very seriously. As much as he appeared to withdraw from the games of Venus, the power of his love lyrics betrayed the irony of his songs. But now with c.13 the ironic cleverness becomes an obvious sham. The supposedly scorned old poet turns against the rejecting Lyce and completely switches the theme of old age from a point of comic irony and empathetic persuasion to an abusive weapon just at the moment in the book when it would be the hardest to overlook, since he has prominently paraded the persona of the aging poet during c.10–12. "Ligurinus, you're going to regret refusing my love. You'll end up old like me" (c.10); "Phyllis, I'm old, and you're not any younger either. Let's make this my last love" (c.11); "Vergil, forget your epic and return to a lyric celebration at my house" (c.12). These are songs by a vulnerable poet urging acts of love and exerting the power of lyric over brokenness in the human condition. In this sense the sequence has been overtly introspective, sensitizing the audience to the character of the speaker: his humanity that he shares with them. The poet's appeals in c.10–12 aimed at closing any gap between singer and audience so much so that Phyllis and Vergil were invited to sing songs in return. The intrigue of a Horatian invitation is that its drama remains unresolved, the responding song or answer unwritten. It is left to the secondary audience to imagine whether the invitation was effective. What might be the content and tone of the response? Does Ligurinus remain cruel, Phyllis bound to another, and Vergil beyond the reach of sympotic lyric? Could the poet's laments be rejected, and what might the consequences be? Since Horace clearly alters the singer's empathetic persona, it is worth exploring how this playing off of the poet's persona against itself twists the mood of the book just before its close. Whatever subtleties c.13 includes, the cursing of Lyce illustrates the hazards of resisting lyric song. Jilted lover-singers are dangerous. Their fury can explode, and before the rejecting lover realizes, another younger and more beautiful beloved, like Chia, will end up as the favored companion-singer.

Horace does not fix the exact dramatic setting for c.13, although the love games and lyre playing suggest a drinking party. The singer may have recently seen Lyce at a party and been struck by how unkind the years had been. The plot is clear enough. The singer fell in love with Lyce, she rejected him, and in his anger he cursed her with a loveless old age similar to the threat made against Lydia (*in vicem . . . anus*, I.25.9a).[98] Now his curse is coming true, and he allows us to see through his song the transformation of Lyce into a pitiful figure trying to be the beautiful seductress but looking ridiculous. This song about Lyce is curse fulfillment. For Phyllis and Vergil lyric transcended time, offering them another chance to enjoy love and return to the symposion. Since the ode to Phyllis, the effects of time had been suspended. Now at c.13 the poet still controls time but uses it against Lyce, and in effect claims both the power over time to heal (Phyllis, Vergil) and the power through time to destroy (Lyce).

The move from the triumph of lyric over time to the manipulation of time against a rejecting lover introduces between c.10–12 and c.13 a fundamental shift, which cannot be reconciled by any amount of pity, empathy, or regret that has been read into the cursing of Lyce. The aging beauty is a well-worn theme in the Hellenistic epigram,[99] but Horace's unmitigated anger and abuse against the aged Lyce have made him seem most uncivil,[100] especially when he complains so bitterly about Ligurinus rejecting old Horace (IV.1; 10). Most avoid putting Horace in this position by drawing a sharp distinction between the song's first and second half: the poet's jubilant mood changes after the fourth strophe to an introspective reflection that he, too, is subject to the ravages of time (dramatically depicted in the pathetic interrogative series *quo . . . heu . . . quove . . . quo . . . quid . . . quae . . . quae*). Thus the poet softens his invective with a touch of humanity. The swift passing of time (14a–16) is too universal in Horace's *Odes* to refer solely to Lyce.[101] When Horace remembers that the once beautiful Lyce held Venus's power over him (19–20), he forces himself to look back to his youth when he lost his beloved Cinara to the brief years (22b–23). Horace's song becomes not curse fulfillment nor even so much a lament for Lyce as with Lyce, and as such is another example of shared song modeled in the invitations to Phyllis and Vergil (c.11; 12).[102] Such a reading, however tempting, complicates the ode's thematic coherence: Horace, after his most graphic and triumphal rejection of a female antagonist since the most potent of his iambics (*Ep*.8; 12), suddenly with *tempora* (14)[103] becomes sentimentally introspective, only to snap out of it after his memory of Cinara (24) just in time to polish off his song with the meanest of threats. Young suitors will look up Lyce only to scoff at her, a burned-out flame (25–28).[104]

Quinn and Lyne preserve the ode's thematic consistency by sentimentalizing the song into a soliloquy, a private meditation, in which the rejected lover sees how his curse comes to its brutal fulfillment and now feels sorry, even guilty, because Lyce at present looks so ridiculously disgusting next to young beautiful Chia. The opening repetition is the poet's distressed cry at what his curse has done, and the third-person *Lycen* (25) gives away that the poet is talking about Lyce and not to her.[105] That Horace imagined his song as a soliloquy (or that we could) is certainly possible, although neither the direct address to Lyce nor the third person compel us to imagine either that Lyce must be listening or that the poet must be alone. The poem allows either scenario. Naming Lyce in the third person could aim at depersonalizing her, which would lead into the objectifying metonymy of her as a burned-out torch.[106] What is at question is the song's tone. Whether Lyce is listening or not, does Horace draw the ode more as a song of a prophetic poet jubilant because his prayers against Lyce have been granted or as a regretful apology?

An empathetic singer has become orthodoxy primarily because it resolves so neatly several difficulties: Horace escapes the charge of thoughtless inhumanity; the friction between a gloating curse over an old hag and the poet's laments about his own old age disappears; and the song gains the satiric flavor of self-criticism since Horace repudiates the consequences of his anger.[107] Nevertheless, representing Horace's introspective old poet as a consistent characterization without dramatic shifts creates greater inconsistencies than it resolves. In c.11 and 12 Horace has just declared the power of the lyric poet to overcome time, but then according to the sentimental view he immediately reverts back in c.13 to lamenting his own weakness. If so, this nostalgic lament right at the close of the book cancels any claims that

Horace's lyric can transcend human limitations and effectively represents the ultimate failure of Horatian lyric to triumph in the present, which would be a total collapse of the sympotic persona so central to Horatian panegyrics. Instead of *Odes* IV progressing from the poet's paradoxical rejection of his sympotic world to his restoration through the power of shared song, thus affirming the vitality of his panegyrics, the book would become anticlimactic since Horace would again be the poet of c.1 except that now he would have accepted with philosophical resignation that he, the lyric poet, has no more power to transcend the pains of life and death and to enjoy the pleasures of the present than the rest of humanity.[108] The poetry book would be rendered internally incoherent. *Odes* IV would undermine much of *Odes* I–III and the representation of the poet as life's *magister bibendi,* while at the same time it reaffirms in c.2.27b–32 his lyric sympotic persona and echoes in c.3 Horace's celebrations of his timeless lyric achievement.[109] This can hardly be correct. It contradicts Horace's numerous reassertions of lyric power, destroys the very premise of panegyric that the poet rises above the limitations imposed by time, and specifically makes no sense out of the poet's pronouncement in c.13 that his words had the power to create Lyce's present circumstances.

The poet is not angry with Lyce because, unlike himself, she refuses to act her age, and he is not lamenting a once beautiful courtesan who should have stopped plying her trade long ago. Horace cursed Lyce because she turned down his invitation to love (an act against the poet's lyric power).[110] Her rejection places her in opposition to Horace's poetics and therefore subject to the denunciation of the lyric poet. The poet's rejection of Lyce is in proportion to her rejection of his song and its power to heal. The curse is triumphant, intensely concentrated, and consistent. It extends from the opening of the song to the end with no empathetic parenthesis (14–24). Horace aims the full arsenal of his previous love lyrics and their themes against Lyce so that he writes her off as the principal antagonist of book IV, the quintessential anti-lyric character. The book is not anticlimatic but progresses thematically from the lyricist's lament over lost youth (c.1; 10) to his power to heal life's losses through shared song (c.11; 12) to a warning in the example of Lyce against rejecting his invitation to join in his song (c.13).

In the parallel threat against Lydia (C.I.25),[111] it was impossible to know whether she had personally rejected the singer or other callers, since Horace generalized the only first person into a stock plaint fitting any locked-out lover (*'me tuo longas pereunte noctes, / Lydia, dormis?'* 7–8).[112] Horace adopts a different strategy with Lyce. In the first and fifth strophes, both distinguished by concentrated anaphora of an elegiac quality, the poet puts himself forward.[113] The song begins with the preeminence of an angry poet. By rotating "gods" (*di*), the third element of the repetition (*audivere, Lyce, di*), into first position (*di / audivere, Lyce*), Horace creates an intricate interlocking sequence ([a, b] c, c, [a, b]) which locates at its center the singer's prayer (*mea vota*), spit out in a violent staccato mono/disyllabic combination, *di mea vota di*. The gods' presence physically envelops the singer's vow. As soon as the repetition ends at the middle of the second line, the abrupt mono/disyllabics return in synchysis to specify that the prayer was malevolent (*fis anus et tamen*). Horace through sound and word order clearly emphasizes that his vow is the active agent transforming Lyce into an old hag, and the conjunction *et* extends the curse so that all of Lyce's troubled behavior results from the singer's prayer. Horace has constructed an elegiac repetition[114] that expresses pride in the attack rather than empathetic regret. Horace has also managed the anaphora so that the verbal element (*audivere*) remains in emphatic first position (1–2). The act of being heard reverses the poet's previous experience with the Lyce of C.III.10.[115] When he, the rejected lover, was pleading with Lyce before her door, he asked if she heard the door creaking and trees howling (*audis*, III.10.5–8).[116] Lyce left him outside. *Audivere, audivere* changes the question "Do you hear?" into an emphatic declaration that although Lyce did not listen, someone did. The poet has the gods' ear, a claim that he punctuates with the syllable *di*: *au[di]vere* is immediately recalled in its subject, the gods (*di*), and is echoed in the prominent "i" sound of the curse itself (*fis anus . . . vis . . . videri*). Favored by the gods, the poet controls time by his words and uses this power to curse Lyce.

The poet's anger resounds nonstop until Lyce dissolves into ashes in the last verse. The ill-tempered sound of a repeated *f-s*, which added venom to the judgment against Lydia's rejection of love (I.25: *fenestras*, 1; *prius . . . facilis*, 5; *anus arrogantis / flebis*, 9–10; *flagrans*, 13; *matres furiare*, 14; *aridas frondes*, 19) and Chloris's refusal to retire from love's games (III.15: *famosisque laboribus*, 3; *desine funeri*, 4; *filia rectius*, 8; *flos purpureus rosae*, 15; *faece tenus*, 16), reveals the disdain that fills the singer's curse (*fis anus . . . vis formosa videri*, 2–3). The sound of attack disappears momentarily while Cupid lights on Chia's cheeks, and returns slightly when Cupid flies past Lyce (*transvolat aridas / quercus et refugit te*, 9–10a) and the swift day closes in on her (*notis . . . fastis / inclusit*, 15–16a). Then Horace begins the second series of anaphora with the same *f-s* hiss (*fugit Venus*, 17) and builds the sound of the curse through the last two strophes. The heaviest concentration occurs in the comparison of Lyce to Cinara just when the singer is supposedly becoming introspective and sentimental (*felix post*, 21; *facies? sed*, 22; *annos fata*, 23; *visere fervidi*, 26; *cineres facem*, 28). The consistent repetition of the serpentine *f-s* does not match an apologetic lover.

In this angry mood Horace turns his most favored lyric topics against Lyce: the abuse of the aging lover, the symposion, the propempticon, and the paraklausithyron—all in rapid succession, and each designed to write Lyce out of Horace's lyric world for good. Listing physical deformities is a regular feature in attacks on lovers in the Hellenistic epigrams,[117] and yet only once since his iambs has Horace done so (Barine, C.II.8). He reserves this special treatment for Lyce—yellow teeth, ugly wrinkles, white hair (10–12)—and her situation is far uglier than that of Barine, Lydia, or Chloris. Barine's supposed (*si*) demise (*dente si nigro fieres vel albo / turpior ungui*, 3–4) does not efface her radiant beauty on which the ode ends. Lydia and Lyce are the only hags (*anus*) in the *Odes*, and as already noted, Horace links them closely by the similar sounds in the curses leveled against them, (Lydia) *anus . . . flebis* : (Lyce) *fis anus*. Still the difference between the curses is as striking as their similarity. Lydia's ruin is a future probability. The vivid progressive present "becoming" (*fis*) makes Lyce's aging an ongoing process and sets her transformation right before the eyes of her audience. It is a monstrous scene from which the audience cannot turn away by thinking that the future curse may not come true.

While she is undergoing this tragic metamorphosis into the ugly, Lyce exhibits the human tendency of trying to hang on to youth. Like Chloris, she insists on attending parties and playing the rival of younger women (5–8). Horace takes the criticism against Chloris (*nec flos purpureus rosae / nec poti vetulam faece tenus cadi*, C.III.15–16) and sprinkles it throughout his attack on Lyce. Both are drunk (*poti : pota*, 5); the allure of their purple garments is gone (the repeated negative *nec . . . nec* and *purpureus : purpurae*, 13–14); both are old women (*vetulam : vetulae*, 25);[118] both through metaphor disintegrate into disposable remnants, Chloris in the wine lees and Lyce into cinders. Clearly these repetitions remind the listener/reader that old Chloris and Lyce have much in common, but by comparison the attack on Chloris is tamer and leaves more to the imagination. Beyond Chloris casting a dark cloud over the love games (5–6), most of her conduct must be inferred from the behavior of her daughter. There is no description of Chloris's appearance and nothing specific about how she fails at her seductive ploys. Lyce is maligned in direct lurid detail for over two strophes. She sports at parties, drinks immodestly, makes a fool of herself singing, and fails to arouse flexible or sluggish desire (*cupidinem / lentum sollicitas*, 5–6a). The sexual inference is plain enough, especially since desire is not definitely personified as Cupid until he lights on Chia's cheeks (6b–8). The sight of Lyce can no longer give any man an erection no matter how hard she works.[119]

Lyce's situation is hopeless. Her beauty has faded, and she has no inner qualities, no song to recommend her as does the learned lyricist Chia. And this song does not encourage her like Lydia to open the creaking door more often and does not advise her like Chloris to go home and take on the duties of a matron; the angry singer does not hold open such possibilities. Instead, Lyce's continued attempts at seduction end in a horrible reality that Horace's song parades in the parallel *vis–videri–visere*. Lyce wishes to be seen as pretty (*vis–videri*, 3), but when the young men come to call (*visere*, 26), it is only to laugh at her ruin.

No wonder the youths laugh. Lyce is a total failure as a symposiast. As argued in ch.1, Horace's sympotic persona is a serio-comic construct, blending the sympotic summons, *carpe diem*, and its pleasures with death, politics, literary ideals, and self-restraint (*mediocritas*). These themes are indebted, as Horace is proud to claim, to the Greek lyricists.[120] Drinking alleviates life's anxieties, but the songs of the sympotic poets reveal that wine can be a dangerous gift. Wine can possess the person, steal away wits, give away secrets, induce acts of arrogance (Alc. 358 L.-P.; Anacr. 356b

PMG; Thgn. 475–478 W.). Symposia can include heavy drinking, but reckless and certainly violent behavior conflict with accepted sympotic custom.[121] Horace over the next three strophes (4–16) manipulates meter, language, and the ode's dramatic circumstances to stress Lyce's deviance from proper sympotic conduct and subsequently her seclusion from sympotic pleasures.

There are only four drunken women in the *Odes:* Damalis (I.36), Cleopatra (I.37), Chloris (III.15), and Lyce. Damalis, a hard-drinking Thracian prostitute, celebrates Numida's safe return from the wars in Spain. Her revelry is as expected for a Return Ode. Cleopatra is so drunk on delusions of her own fortune that she has unlimited hopes (10b–12a), a strongly anti-*carpe diem* sentiment.[122] Even she sobers up enough, after losing all but one of her ships, to recognize Caesar's might and to choose a courageously noble death (12–16, 21–32). Lyce is a shameless drunk, *ludisque et bibis impudens* (4). The cadence of this glyconic line with the elision *que-et,* which pauses slightly on the third heavy syllable before rapidly moving past "you drink" and then slowing again at the next heavy syllable (*im-*) to emphasize the negative shameless, accentuates Lyce's lack of self-control.[123] Her drunkenness is void of any sympotic inspiration that the Dionysiac poet is privileged to enjoy; she has filled herself with wine, and yet her song, lacking Bacchus's spirit, trembles.[124] Again Horace uses sound against Lyce: shameless Lyce (*impudens,* 4) leads to unfavoring Cupid (*importunus,* 9). Thus Cupid resists Lyce's song because of her immodest conduct and flees from her to the beautiful Chia, whose name and talent exudes desire—Chia, the tastiest wine and a lyricist learned in seduction.[125] Horace further intensifies the horror Cupid feels at Lyce's attempt to summon him and his total desertion of her by a series of verbal prefixes (*ex-cubat; trans-volat; re-fugit,* 8–10).[126]

The curse places Lyce in the opposite predicament of Horace in the propempticon of c.1. The old poet begged Venus to leave him alone, and to secure some peace from the goddess he offered a younger substitute, Maximus. Even then the lyric poet could not escape Venus. Venus may have been cruel, but not so cruel as to reject the poet. His lyric song remained strong, which added irony to his claim of weakness. Lyce pleads for Cupid's presence. Cupid leaves. For Lyce there will be no more chances at love, no restoration such as the poet may enjoy with Phyllis (c.11). The situations for the two old lovers, the poet and Lyce, as Horace has constructed them are too disparate to allow much room for empathy between the two.

Once more Horace uses rhyme to transition to the next motif directed against Lyce, the paraklausithyron (13–16).[127] Cupid has beat a hasty retreat (*refugit*, 10), and Lyce can do nothing to lure him back (*referunt*, 13). Horace casts Lyce as a rejected lover attempting to seduce a beloved with the very types of gifts, expensive clothes and jewelry, that she likely received from lovers calling at her shut door.[128] The words are carefully chosen to wound deeply. The anaphora neither (*nec*) this gift nor (*nec*) that gift, along with an adverbial intensifier for the present (*iam*, 13), only reminds Lyce that in her youth she did not have to resort to such bribes and shows Lyce's frustration as she tries one rejected gift after another. Then Horace gives a sense of finality to Lyce's rejection by switching the logical object of Lyce's love quest (*referunt*) from Cupid to "times" (*tempora*), which effectively limits Lyce's desire and desirability to her past. Lyce's past life, when Cupid attended her, has been enclosed (*inclusit*) and hidden away (*condita*) inside the Roman archives (*fastis*). *Inclusit* and *condita* are common technical vocabulary for documentary writing, storing away events and names deserving to be remembered permanently.[129] Horace pairs the words here so that they write young Lyce out of active memory. Inclusion in Rome's famed (*notis*) records should secure immortal glory for Lyce; the oxymoronic juxtaposition, however, of *notis* and *condita* reminds Lyce of what is often the case, that old records (her sexual charms) quickly become curiosity pieces forgotten by all but the lore masters—for instance, her anti-sympotic peers (L. Aelius Lamia, C.III.17; the antiquarian, III.19), whose searches into genealogical oddities lock them away from sympotic pleasures, which, incidentally, Horace represents by the antiquarian's ignorance of Chian wine.[130] The insult to Lyce is devastatingly personal. Only dated antiquarians could ignore Chia and love Lyce. The panegyric poet transforms a primary method of Roman praise and fame, being mentioned in calendrical records, into a permanent emblem of Lyce's despair and fractured psyche.[131] Horace has the *fasti* mimic a door locking old Lyce out from her younger self, who has been shut inside (*inclusit*).[132] Again the threat made against Lydia that she would find herself forever locked in behind her own door becomes Lyce's reality — only worse: Lyce is simultaneously shut in and shut out.

Horace could have stopped the attack right here (16), and the ode's plot would be complete. Lyce rejected the poet whose curse against her was heard by the gods, and therefore Cupid abandons Lyce. The god refuses to hear her pleas. Horace does not end the song; he begins a second barrage against Lyce that hardly pauses for breath over twelve verses until Lyce lies on the floor in a cinder heap, the dirty climax of her fiery passions. The song does not transition to a more even-tempered view that none can escape old age; it achieves a great measure of its angry emotional intensity when the lyric poet doubles his attack after he had already written off the cursed Lyce perfectly.

The interrogative tirade of the fifth strophe — the first question "where" (*quo*) balanced by a second question "what" (*quid*); where repeated around an exasperated sigh (*heu*, 17) and again at the beginning of the next verse (18) to create the neatly matched anaphora of the first word in each of the strophe's verses (*quo . . . quo . . . quae . . . quae*); the emotive and immediate repetition of *illius* enclosed in the middle — mimics elegiac lament and therefore could suggest a change in the rejected singer's mood from anger to empathy.[133] Relying only on form can be misleading, especially in a song that takes as a major theme the illusory nature of outward appearance, physical beauty. The form is actually part of the singer's attack. He appears to adopt a sympathetic mode and then upstages it. The poet just finishes stating plainly that Cupid has fled (*refugit*, 10) from Lyce, and then he turns suddenly to ask her where has Venus fled (*fugit*)? Redundancy mocks. Everyone except Lyce knows that Venus has fled to Chia. Further, the singer imagines for Lyce one final cry. Until he specifically mentions himself at the end of the strophe, the questions could easily be imagined as a plaint Lyce might cry when she realizes her past beauty can never be recovered. The first time the poet cursed Lyce she became Lydia's future (*fis anus*). When the poet restates the curse in rhetorical questions, now Lydia becomes Ligurinus's future. Horace allowed Ligurinus to still possess Venus's strength (*Veneris muneribus potens*, c.10.1b). His complexion is more lovely than a crimson rose (*color est puniceae flore prior rosae*, c.10.4b). All this beauty Ligurinus will lose, and soon he will see in the mirror an other old self (*alterum*, 6). Horace's questions about Lyce follow the same order as his description of Ligurinus's beauty with much the same language so that his threat against Ligurinus becomes Lyce's reality. Desire (*Venus*), complexion (*color*), and graceful moves have left Lyce. She did not merely lose them; they fled. The doubled remote demonstrative (*illius, illius,* that other woman) transforms Lyce into an other self, estranged from the person she once was.

Lyce's loves are past, particularly her love with the poet (19–20). Horace's choice of past verbs focuses on Lyce's present impotence. In book IV Horace reserves *spirare* for inspired poetic power, and this is the only time that he uses it in a past sense (*spirabat*; cf. C.IV.3.24; 9.10; *Epist.*II.1.166). The lyricist Sappho long after her death lives to inspire and light erotic fires.[134] Lyce's seductive spirit did not last; she is out of breath, dead while still alive. Now Horace switches to the past perfect (*surpuerat*). The effect is hardly empathetic. The rather abrupt change in tenses makes clear to Lyce that although she had some lyric inspiration, it vanished.

Cinara (21–25) is not a nostalgic journey down *Memory Lane*. She, like Chia, reinforces Lyce's demise. Horace's first three words about Cinara (*felix post Cinaram*) emphasize that she was a love against whom even the youthful Lyce could not compete. Only after Cinara was gone could Lyce capture Horace with her charms, which were entirely physical. *Notaque et artium* (parallel to *ludisque et bibis*, 4) at the end of verse 21 for an instant plants the expectation that young Lyce was known for arts of seduction that complemented her prettiness, but *gratarum facies* immediately disappoints that expectation. Lyce's pleasing arts were only the beauty of her face, which always fades. The singer stands Lyce right next to the sexually potent Chia as evidence that external beauty never lasts, and he implements the same strategy of comparison at the end of the song by the indelicate rhyme of *facies* : *facem*. Lyce's torch (*facem*), her beautiful face (*facies*) by the association created with the rhyme, collapses into ashes. The elision of *dilapsam in cineres* creates a graphic word picture of Lyce's fall into the ash pile. Cinara's name offers Horace a chance for a verbal game of abuse not to be resisted: Lyce is no Cinara — she only comes close — she becomes *cineres*, ashes. Given this level of abuse in the comparison of Lyce to Cinara, it is reasonable to conclude that Horace misses Cinara primarily because Lyce treated him so badly. Kind (*bona*, c.1.3) Cinara would not have done so. Horace's memory of Cinara seems motivated by anger over being rejected by the lesser Lyce, and not by the universal lament that we all age.

The attack ends (26–28) where it began, with another allusion to the threat against Lydia (I.25.16–20). The two curses include parallel litotes in their final scenes when the young men show their contempt for the aged courtesans: (Lydia) *non sine questu*, 16; (*iuvenes*) *multo non sine risu*, 27. In the end the poet allows Lydia a voice. It may be only the bitter voice of lament, but Lydia is at least left with enough will to protest her rejection. The poet assigns Lyce no distinct voice of her own; her lament (stated as the poet's own words, 17–19) is replaced with the laughter of the youths who come as spectators to witness her ruin.

Horace does not allow his laments to become merely senti-mentalized empathy expressed through the persona of a retiring old man. Horace renders lyric lament, as he does his other pane-gyrics, more nuanced and even dangerous, since his laments (to Ligurinus, Phyllis, and Vergil) are incomplete without the nega-tive view provided through the cursing of Lyce, namely that the poet embraces and heals those who will accept his invitation to enjoy lyric song but rejects with certain finality anyone who refuses. Sentimentalizing the cursing of Lyce and consequently Horace's persona of the old poet has done much to blunt the cut-ting edge of Horace's later lyric. Horace would have created a very different expectation, if he had introduced the final two im-perial praises (c.14–15) with a pathetic nostalgic look back by a poet succumbing to the passing of time rather than a command-ing poet in control of time, heard by the gods, and cursing Lyce, the embodiment of anti-lyric expression. The preeminence of the poet's will in the cursing of Lyce is incompatible with a retiring poet about to set aside the triumph that he claimed for his lyric achievement. Horace leads the way into c.14 and 15 with such a dominant and powerful lyric voice (restoring and cursing) that he counters any notion that he is in the process of abdicating the poet's vatic role. In writing off Lyce, the poet in fact writes her in, not into his sympotic world but into the memories of his audi-ence. Lyce gains immortality of a tragic quality. Horace's lyric tributes can have a disconcerting, dangerous double edge.

5

Encomia Augusti, "Take Two"

Arma virumque cano . . . "Arms and the man I sing . . ."
—Vergil, *Aeneid*

Nine odes intervene between the epinikia to celebrate Drusus's
and Tiberius's victory over the Germanic tribes in 15 B.C. (c.4,
14)—over half the book. The repetition of odes of the same type
for the same occasion in tandem with parallel imperial encomia
(c.5, 15), a repetition unprecedented in Horace, like a recurrent
musical theme throughout a symphony, brings the book up just
short of its conclusion and returns the reader to a reconsideration
of imperial panegyric. Such re-presentations sensitize the audience to the qualities of the theme (the similarities or variations
in the praise), the discovery of which is the primary pleasure of
music and what makes song worth hearing again. Horace, by separating the epinikia-panegyric pairs, prevents repetition from
becoming rote duplication, since he has enriched the context by
the themes of the intervening songs: the power of the lyric poet
and the political dimensions of his sympotic *carpe diem* invitations
(c.6–7), the vanity of indiscriminate praise (c.8) and the interplay
of praise and blame (c.9), the poet's triumph over time through
shared lyric (c.10–12), and the final shutting of the door on Lyce
(c.13). Horace through these *carmina* has taught the audience to be
alert to panegyric complications and to expect a poet on the edge:
confident to face human frailty and overcome it through the lyric

experience, prepared to attack and destroy the one who refuses his lyric invitation. Horace has claimed more than that the poet-*cliens* is an indispensable worker for the patron because he has the power to immortalize the patron as the patron wishes, or pays. The Horatian panegyrist plays a vatic role; the poet forges the panegyric agenda, setting out the quality of the praise (its mode, lyric, and its content both positive and negative) and calling together a community to join in creating and re-creating Roman identity and values. The Horatian panegyrist is both inspired and inspiring. Like Sappho (*spirat,* c.9.10) he inhales and exhales (*spiro,* c.3.24) power through his lyric song.

C.14: Epinikion^Two — Winners and Losers

> Quae cura patrum quaeve Quiritium
> plenis honorum muneribus tuas,
>   Auguste, virtutes in aevum
>   per titulos memoresque fastos
>
> aeternet, o, qua sol habitabilis   5
> illustrat oras, maxime principum?
>   quem legis expertes Latinae
>   Vindelici didicere nuper,
>
> quid Marte posses. milite nam tuo
> Drusus Genaunos, implacidum genus,   10
>   Breunosque velocis et arces
>   Alpibus impositas tremendis
>
> deiecit acer plus vice simplici;
> maior Neronum mox grave proelium
>   commisit immanisque Raetos   15
>   auspiciis pepulit secundis,
>
> spectandus in certamine Martio,
> devota morti pectora liberae
>   quantis fatigaret ruinis,
>   indomitus prope qualis undas   20
>
> exercet Auster, Pleiadum choro
> scindente nubis, impiger hostium
>   vexare turmas et frementem
>   mittere equum medios per ignis.

sic tauriformis volvitur Aufidus,   25
qui regna Dauni praefluit Apuli,
    cum saevit horrendamque cultis
        diluviem meditatur agris,

ut barbarorum Claudius agmina
ferrata vasto diruit impetu   30
    primosque et extremos metendo
        stravit humum sine clade victor,

te copias, te consilium et tuos
praebente divos. nam tibi, quo die
    portus Alexandrea supplex   35
        et vacuam patefecit aulam,

Fortuna lustro prospera tertio
belli secundos reddidit exitus,
    laudemque et optatum peractis
        imperiis decus arrogavit.   40

te Cantaber non ante domabilis
Medusque et Indus, te profugus Scythes
    miratur, o tutela praesens
        Italiae dominaeque Romae.

te fontium qui celat origines   45
Nilusque et Hister, te rapidus Tigris,
    te beluosus qui remotis
        obstrepit Oceanus Britannis,

te non paventis funera Galliae
duraeque tellus audit Hiberiae,   50
    te caede gaudentes Sygambri
        compositis venerantur armis.

[What care of the Fathers and the Quirites will, Augustus, with the honors you fully merit, immortalize your virtues through titles and commemorative records wherever, O highest leader, the sun lights the inhabited world? The Vindelici, unschooled in Roman laws, recently came to know you and how mightily you wield Martial power. For with your soldiery Drusus fiercely, beyond like retaliation, threw down the Genauni, a warring people, and swift Breuni, their citadels built on the awe-inspiring Alps. The elder Nero soon joined the hard battle and under your blessed auspices defeated the

monstrous Rhaeti; a spectacle in the contest of Mars because of the great destruction through which he ex-
hausted hearts devoted to a noble death, almost like the
unmastered Auster troubles the waves when the chorus
of Pleiads splits the clouds, he was quick to harass the
enemy's cavalry and to charge his roaring steed through
the middle of the fires. So the taurine Aufidus rolls on
and flows past the realm of Apulian Daunus, while it
raves and plots horrific flood for the cultivated lands, as
Claudius with a full-scale assault crushed the barbarians' ironclad battle lines and strewed them on the
ground, mowing down both front and rear, he victorious without a loss—you supplying your troops, your
strategy, your divinities. For to you, on the very day
suppliant Alexandria threw wide her harbor doors and
empty palace for you, fifteen years to the day, good Fortune has led back a favorable end to the war and has
granted the desired praise and honor by the fulfilling of
your commands. You the Cantabrian unconquered before and the Mede and the Indian, you the nomadic
Scythian admires, O incarnate guardian of Italy and
lordly Rome. You the Nile, concealing the sources of her
waters, and the Danube, you the swift Tigris, you the
beast-laden Ocean, roaring about the distant Britons,
you the land of Gaul, fearless in the face of death, and
the land of hard Hiberia hear; you the slaughter-loving
Sygambri, their weapons laid aside, worship.]

The basic frame of the ode combines the chiastic structure of the
earlier epinikion (c.4) with the hymn form of c.5.[1] There is no need,
however, to wait for the hymn form of c.14 to develop[2] to suspect
that an imperial praise repeating within the first verse the thesis
of the earlier hymn (the longing of the senate and Roman people)
with what could pass for an epitomizing title (*Quae cura patrum
quaeve Quiritium*) might likely repeat its form. Horace creates the
primary ring by splitting the hymn (1–6, 41–52) with an aretalogia
(7–40) incorporating mythologizing similes to illustrate the power
of the victories,[3] which in turn are presented in a chiastic series
(Augustus's, 7–9; Drusus's, 10–13; Tiberius's, 14–32; and Augustus's, 33–40). Horace unifies the whole with the same breathless
movement that characterized the opening seven-strophe period
of c.4. The ode's thirteen strophes divide into only three periods,
the first lasting six strophes. The only other pauses occur at verses

9, 34, 40, and 44, but all but one occur within structural components (the aretalogia for Drusus, the aretalogia for Augustus, and
the closing of the hymn). The only break corresponding to a shift
in elements is at verse 40, when the poet returns to the hymn form.
Reading c.14 would strain the breath of the most highly skilled
Roman orator. There is space for only one full breath near the end
of the ode. Pindaric praise has returned full strength: hymnic elements (1–6; 33–35; 41–52), the victory announcement and aretalogia (7–40), mythologizing similes (21–32), and a gnomic reference
(*didicere*, 8; cf. *doctrina*, c.4.33–36). The major structural difference
lies in the narratives. The poet has replaced Hannibal's speech,
which provided a wealth of ambiguity, with the most sustained
militaristic imperial encomium in all his poetry. Indirect praise
through a secondary narrator has seemingly become direct.

It has become popular to read c.14 as a direct encomium in
which Horace as panegyrist effaces his own voice and sets aside
any panegyric dissonance (*dubia*).[4] At issue is not the poet's independence because effacement can be an ironic act of rebellion
if, when the poet fades from view, all that is left is insipid praise
that has little force to hold attention, let alone immortalize (c.8).
What is at issue is the character of the poet's encomia. Any effacement of the poet's voice would represent a momentous shift
near the close of the book, since it would cause a collapse of Horace's panegyric praxis, which requires the interaction of the poet,
audience, and *laudandi*. In the literary commotion over the presence or absence of a poetic *ego* within an epinikion that shows a
remarkable degree of creativity, the simplicity of the plot stands
out. Horace begins with a question that challenges the Roman
people's ability to praise Augustus sufficiently and then puts forward an epinikion-hymn that fairly directly suggests that the
poet can do what the people cannot. In the course of the hymn the
poet presents the deeds of the victors in a rather lengthy narrative. All the players then are present, the Roman citizens, the poet,
and the *laudandi*. An appropriate question would be what is the
relationship between the characters involved? How does the
epinikion stimulate interaction among the interpretive players?
The poet in the process does not efface his persona but the
epinikion, that is, the opening question puts into play the appro-
priateness of the epinikion's praise. If the traditional modes available to immortalize the greats of Rome will not suffice for Augustus, how does the epinikion offered measure up?

There can be no question that the epinikion assigns the victory and the honor gained through it entirely to Augustus. The Vindelicians learn from Augustus what he could accomplish with the power of Mars (7–10). The aretalogia for Drusus and Tiberius are wholly dependent on Augustus. The panegyrist attributes (*nam*) Drusus's victory to Augustus's power (*milite . . . tuo*, 9), and after he pronounces Tiberius victor (32), he gives over the victory to Augustus with the hymnic tricolon, *te copias, te consilium et tuos / praebente divos*. Augustus supplied the army, the stratagem, and his auspices. Anaphora and assonance reinforce the sons' subordination. Augustus possesses the might of Mars (*Marte*) and passes it on to Drusus (*milite . . . tuo*) and to Tiberius (*in certamine Martio*, 17). The repetition *nam . . . tuo* (9) . . . *nam tibi* (34) ties Drusus's and Tiberius's recent victories to the battle Augustus won against Cleopatra, when his boys were only twelve and eight years old. Their recent victories resulted from the greatest of Augustus's past victories working itself out in the present. Like Hannibal (c.4), the Germanic tribes should have taken a lesson from the past and realized that resisting Rome would have dire consequences, since fifteen years to the day before their defeat suppliant Alexandria opened her doors wide for the mighty Augustus (34b–40). The honor that the epinikion grants to Augustus agrees with his new constitutional position.[5] Augustus alone embodied the imperium and therefore rightly was the sole sovereign of the Roman armies. The auspices were to be taken in his name and by right the triumph belonged to him. The poet's epinikion on this level routinely expresses the power of the offices that the Roman people had lauded on Augustus (*plenis honorum muneribus*, 2). If the *laudator* questions whether these are sufficient praise to match Augustus's worth (1–6), his praise must be more than a confirmation of the honors that the people had already granted.

The epinikion aims to immortalize Augustus wherever the sun surveys inhabitable lands. The dual direct address imitates that of c.5, a combination of divine and human titles (*Auguste : divis orte bonis* [14.3 : 5.1]; *maxime principum : dux bone* [14.6 : 5.5]), and thus continues the hymn to deified Caesar. The epinikion wraps the hymn form around the aretalogia so that Augustus's divinity envelops the praise, and the panegyrist augments the hymn form throughout with the language of the divine. *Tuos / praebente divos* (33–34) recalls *divis orte bonis*, and therefore implies that Augustus lent his son the support of his own divine lineage. And after the ritual return of Caesar through the rustic's invocation (c.5), *o tutela praesens* (43) must mean more than Augustus has returned from war. Once again his divinity on earth (*praesens*) is for the welfare (*tutela*) of the Roman people. Instead of Augustus's return only brightening the day (c.5), the boundaries of his immortality rival the sun's domain. Augustus rules over peoples and rivers of the North, South, East, and West. The hymn metaphorically names Augustus the son of Apollo. All nations worship him,[6] and the catalogue at the end of the hymn records their homage with the progression, wonder (*miratur*, 43), obedience (*audit*, 50), reverence (*venerantur*, 52).

The divine Augustus controls time. The ode follows a typical chronology for ring composition. It begins in the present (the hymn), moves back to the recent past (Augustus's/Drusus's victory, *nuper*, 8), and turns back toward the present (Tiberius's/Augustus's victory, *mox*, 14). Yet before completing its cycle back to the present, the chronology reverts back to the more remote past (*quo die*, 34), the day Alexandria surrendered. The past glory of Augustus returns in the present victories of his children so that it transforms their victories into an expression of his past. The past and present are conflated. By contrast, the power of the sympotic *carpe diem* invitation is that the present stands alone. Consistently in *Odes* I–III Horace makes the sympotic a symbol of the present moment and lends his call to *carpe diem* urgency by placing the past and future beyond human control.[7] An obsessive love for mastering the obscure details of heroic genealogies causes the antiquarian to miss sympotic pleasures.[8] An antiquarian has no lyric power. He is as useless (*taces*) as the pipe hanging quietly on the wall by the silent lyre (*C.III.19.8, 20*). The future captivates Leuconoë. The sympotic poet orders her to accept whatever length of life Jupiter has assigned. To search into the future violates divine law (*nefas, C.I.11.1–6*). The past cannot be changed, the future cannot be predicted, and thus the only moment a person can claim and enjoy is the present. All else belongs to the gods. No mortal, except the poet,[9] can transcend the temporal limitations of the present. Augustus, therefore, demonstrates divine power when he blends together the past and present. The only question is whether Augustus also has power over the future, a question the panegyrist will address in the next ode.

The divine Augustus empowers his sons and in turn receives the full honor when they defeat Rome's enemies. The placement of *tibi* before the temporal clause beginning *quo die* (34) allows the pronoun to function as the secondary object with *patefecit* and in hyperbaton with *reddidit* and *arrogavit:* "Alexandria opened up for you, Augustus, Fortune returned favorable victories for you, Augustus, and assigned the praise and glory to you, Augustus." Drusus and Tiberius only carried out to the letter the orders they were given (*peractis / imperiis,* 39–40). As the sons of Augustus they enacted their father's divine will. Thus the constitutional position of Augustus extends the Roman ideology of *paterfamilias* to a national scale. In this way Drusus and Tiberius through their subordination to father Augustus reenact the premise of c.4, that the behavior of sons expresses their parents' character. If the panegyrist gives a "stark, factual" depiction of the war, then what image of Augustus does his sons' aretalogia draw?[10] Since the sons' actions are an expression of Augustus's will, their conduct in the war gains center stage. Without the three strophes of the closing hymn their victories would hold center position between two pairs of framing strophes, and in contrast to c.4, where the terseness of the victory announcement attracted attention, the narrative of the Neros' attack on the Rhaetians constitutes the praise's principal action and takes up nearly half the poem.

Throughout the aretalogia the poet keeps alive the question begun in the earlier epinikion (c.4) about precisely how the Caesars manage violence against their enemies. The poet amplifies what seems to be a straightforward victory announcement (10–16) by encoding into the narrative his combined retelling of the Titanomachy and Gigantomachy from C.III.4.41–68.[11] Drusus hurls down the giants, the Genauni and Breuni, from their citadels set high in the Alps (*arces* . . . impositas, 11–12; cf. III.4.51–52: *fratresque tendentes opaco / Pelion imposuisse Olympo*). Tiberius dislodges the Titans, the monstrous Rhaeti (immanisque *Raetos* . . . pepulit, 15–16a; cf. 4.42b–44: *scimus ut impios / Titanas* immanemque *turbam / fulmine sustulerit caduco*). The Horatian battle story comes complete with the whistling and crashing of lightning in the sibilants and plosives in the last lines of each strophe (*Alpibus impositas tremendis; auspiciis* pepulit *secundis*). The brother giants Otus and Ephialtes lose;[12] the brothers Drusus and Tiberius win. Horace transforms the interrogative tricolon mocking the impotence of the giants (quid *Typhoeus et* . . . *Mimas, sed* quid . . . *Porphyrion* . . . quid *Rhoetus* . . . *Enceladus* . . . possent, 53–

58a) into a singular declaration of Augustan mastery (*Vindelici didicere nuper,* / quid *Marte* posses, 8–9a). The entire scene of Drusus and Tiberius overthrowing their mythic insolent assailants likens Augustus to a Jupiter presiding over earth's rebellious nations.

Applying mythological battles to Octavian and Antony (C.III.4) is one leap of the imagination; Drusus, Tiberius, and the Rhaetians (even given the mountainous terrain) necessitate quite another. When at the end of the aretalogia the panegyrist combines the victories over Antony and Cleopatra and the German tribes together as one victory, he invites a comparison of the earlier Titan/Gigantomachy with this later version and opens himself up to the speculation that he has gone a little over the top and exhibited the Pindaric excess he assigned to Iullus Antonius (C.IV.2). Horace shows he is conscious that his audience may suspect his mythic embellishment by qualifying the first simile for Tiberius's heroic power with *prope,* "well almost" (20), but even before this qualification he adds to the myth a more indirect restraining element. The Giants and Titans were not the only immoderate warriors; Drusus does not deliver a measured response to their rebellion (13), but overly fierce (*acer plus*), he goes beyond simple recompense (*plus vice simplici*). Drusus's reaction counters the earlier Titan/Gigantomachy when Jupiter justly punished a hubristic revolt. Drusus's intemperate violence hazards placing him outside the benefits of the gnomic conclusion of III.4.66–67a (*vim temperatam di quoque provehunt* / *in maius*) and risks ignoring the warning to any king who forgets there is only one Jupiter powerful enough to defeat Giants (C.III.1.5–8, 14b–16).

The mythology of the victory announcement introduces two extended similes honoring Tiberius (17–32). The first word, *spectandus,* puts Tiberius in the same ekphrastic position as his brother Drusus in the first epinikion, and at the outset these similes on Tiberius appear less circuitous than those of c.4. The panegyrist places up front the identity of the person behind the metaphor (*maior Neronum,* 14; Drusus is named after the similes, c.4) and *spectandus* immediately signals that Tiberius is the primary point of reference. There is no manipulation (*vidit* / *videre,* c.4.15–16) of the audience so that they identify with the Vindelicians and see Tiberius as their assailant. Instead, a purely Roman point of view introduces a quantitative exclamation for the audience's consideration, "With what great destruction did Tiberius wear down the hearts of his enemies!" (19). The quantitative force of the exclamatory question matches the characterization of Drusus as *acer plus vice simplici* and continues to focus attention on the extreme violence of the conflict, about to take on epic proportions.

In general, the two similes work together to imagine Tiberius as an epic warrior whose anger rivals Achilles and Aeneas. Such panegyric parallels the hyperbole in Drusus and Tiberius, sons of the earthly Jupiter, hurling down from the mountains the Titan Rhaetians and Giant Genauni and Breuni. But then the panegyrist with the single word *prope* (20), which is placed right before the first simile and therefore sets the tone for the whole, restrains the grandeur of the epic similes before they start.[13] If Horace were writing prose, *prope* would give little pause. To qualify a metaphor in prose is common enough, but in poetry and epic praise, where the hyperbole of a simile is customary, it is an absurdity.[14] With *prope* the *laudator* goes outside of convention and qualifies his own praise—Tiberius is like, but not really—and therefore the panegyrist begins his encomium by first alerting the audience that they are likely to find some impropriety in the similes.[15] But impropriety of what sort? Do the similes fall short of Tiberius, or does Tiberius fall short of the similes? If a reader thinks the former, the effect of the epic similes is even more exaggerated. The Southwind does not even measure up to Tiberius. Such hyperbole should make it obvious that the similes cannot be read for historical detail and gives the entire epinikion a strongly fictitious flavor, especially for an audience already affected by the mythic texture of the praise. If the latter, then Tiberius does not really measure up to the epic conventions. Either way Horace has complicated the praise. In *prope* the panegyrist has inserted his own voice, just as he did in the digression of c.4, with a wonderful degree of subtle sophistication.

Tiberius typifies the enraged epic hero, swifter than winds, eager to attack, riding a fierce steed, and fiery (20–24). Horace recycles the same basic elements from his description of the invading Hannibal (a horsed warrior, wind, and fire, c.4.42–44), but for Tiberius he intensifies the action through the verb forms at the beginning of verses 21–24 (*exercet, scindente, vexare, mittere*). The language in Horace's portrait of Hannibal and Tiberius is ultimately reminiscent of Vergilian epic heroes possessed by *furor* and ready to avenge the wrong committed against them. The Ausonians harness their snorting steeds (*ille frementis / ad iuga cogit equos,* A.7.638–39b). Aeneas calls for his raging horses (*equos . . . frementis,* 12.82), prays for success (*da sternere corpus,* 97; cf. *stravit humum,* c.14.32), and, shooting fire from his eyes, rages like a bull spoiling for a fight (cf. *sic tauriformis . . . Aufidus,* c.14.25). Turnus watches wounded Aeneas retreat from the ranks and pushes the battle forward. He spurs on his furious horses (*furentis . . . immittit equos,* 12.332–33; cf. *frementem / mittere equum,* c.14.23–24), which fly faster than the Southern and Western winds (*ante Notos Zephryrumque volant,* 12.334) into the middle of the fight (*media inter proelia,* 337; cf. *medios per ignis,* c.14.24). Except for *prope,* the panegyrist's Tiberius would be right at home among the heroes of the Iliadic *Aeneid.*

True to the poet's word (*prope*), readers have been dissatisfied with his portraiture of Tiberius. The incongruity between the high-blown epic rhetoric and the border wars against the Rhaetians, including Horace's substitution of *ignis* for the more traditional *proelia,* has caused some speculation that Tiberius actually did have to ride through the fires of battle, as if the metaphor might be more acceptable if its last three words were closer to reality. The Titan/Gigantomachy, the Southwind, the Pleiadian chorus, and the imagery of the epic warrior have pushed the narrative far beyond a purely historical occasion.[16] Collinge, while defending his identification of the Vergilius of C.IV.12 as the poet, concludes that other odes would have shocked Vergil more, "especially 14."[17] Collinge does not explain what in c.14 might have surprised Horace's colleague, but it is amusing to imagine the laugh Vergil may or may not have enjoyed over Horace applying Vergil's epic language so freely to the rather unpopular Tiberius.

The first simile is tame compared to the second, a compound allusion within an inverted metaphoric frame. The epinikion fills Tiberius's onslaught with the wrath of Achilles and Aeneas. Both Quinn and Putnam view Tiberius through Catullus's Achilles, who also mows down his enemies and lays out their bodies like a reaper (Cat. 64.353–55).[18] The shared imagery and language suggest a relationship between the two texts, and placing the anger of Troy's greatest enemy into Tiberius complicates the praise since Achilles' wrath, a powerful symbol of excess for a lyric poet, lends a nearly heinous negative overtone to the character of Tiberius. Horace's hymn to Apollo (c.6) portrays Achilles as plotting against the Trojans the very same atrocities that the

Rhaetians had, in fact, committed, killing their enemies' children—even those still in their mothers' wombs (C.IV.6.17–20; Cass. Dio 54.22; Str. 4.6.8). If Tiberius is like Achilles, the comparison erases the distinction between the barbarity of the Rhaetians and the violent retaliation of the epic Tiberius, another Achilles.[19] At Rome Horace had learned during the civil wars how much harm an angry Achilles had brought on the Greeks (*Epist.*II.2.41–42).[20] Excessive anger tends to self-destruction, and Achilles in the end destroys himself.[21]

Yet it is questionable whether Achilles is the primary referent for Tiberius. In spite of the Greek-styled compound (*tauriformis*) that begins the metaphor, the simile remains thoroughly Roman: the Aufidus rolls on through the Italic countryside ruled by King Daunus.[22] The landscape calls Vergil to mind, and the rage of the epic Tiberius closely parallels both the angry assault on Pallas by Turnus, Daunus's son, and the fury of Aeneas in avenging Pallas's death:

> . . . utque leo, specula cum vidit ab alta
> stare procul campis meditantem in proelia taurum,
> advolat, haud alia est Turni venientis imago.
>
> Nec iam fama mali tanti, sed certior auctor
> advolat Aeneae tenui discrimine leti
> esse suos, tempus versis succurrere Teucris.
> proxima quaeque metit gladio latumque agmen
> ardens limitem agit ferro, te, Turne, superbum
> caede nova quaerens. Pallas, Evander, in ipsis
> omnia sunt oculis, mensae quas advena primas
> tunc adiit, dextraeque datae. (*A.*10.454–56; 510–17a)
>
> [. . . as a lion leaps to the attack, when from a high lookout he spies a bull standing far off on the plains and planning battle, just so is the picture of Turnus attacking.]
>
> [Now not the rumor of such evil but a more trustworthy messenger wings its way to Aeneas, that his men are a razor's edge from death and that the time has come for him to aid the defeated Teucrians. He mows down with his sword all the troops hard nearby, and blazing, he cuts with his iron a wide swath through the battle line, seeking you, Turnus, as you gloat over your last kill. Pallas, Evander, every detail flashes before his eyes—the hospitality he first found when he came to them a stranger, and the promises exchanged.[23]]

Vergil uses the repetition of *advolat* (456, 511) to tie together Turnus's murderous attack on Pallas with Aeneas's violent retaliation. The lion Turnus flies against the bull Pallas, and the rumor of Pallas's death flies to Aeneas. The animalistic behavior of the two combatants provokes an animalistic response from Aeneas. Violence, like human parents, reproduces after its own kind. Horace combines the Vergilian sequence into one simile. The Aufidus River becomes the bull plotting its destructive charge (*tauriformis . . . meditatur,* 25–28; *meditantem in proelia taurum,* 455) and Tiberius, like Aeneas, mows through his enemy (*primosque et extremos metendo,* 31; *proxima quaeque metit gladio latumque agmen / ardens limitem agit ferro,* 513–14a). Thus the epinikion's characterization of Tiberius depends on an allusive chain: Tiberius is a second Achilles, a Turnus, and a second Aeneas bent on avenging a haughty enemy. Tiberius as Aeneas softens the negative edge caused by identifying him with Achilles and Turnus. Just before Turnus takes the belt from Pallas's armor he tersely announces that Evander's welcome of Aeneas will cost him dearly (494–95). The guest friendship of Aeneas and Evander obligates Aeneas to avenge Pallas's death, and Tiberius, too, must protect his own and his father's people.

But Horace does not allow the tension between self-destructive violence and deserved retaliation to be resolved so easily. He writes the simile backward: he reverses the *sic* and *ut* of the comparison so that the world of nature imitates the human rather than the human imitating nature, as is conventional.[24] The Aufidus acts like Tiberius, and when it does it turns into an uncontrollable animal (*tauriformis*), which violates its own nature. From spring to summer the Aufidus is at its lowest levels. Since the fields have already been cultivated, the season the simile most likely pictures is late spring to early summer when the river should be more tame, but the Aufidus rages and plots to flood Daunus's Italian countryside. The warring Tiberius within the conclusion of the metaphor turns the most important river in the South into an unnatural and destructive force against the civilization (represented in the cultivated fields) of native Italy and Horace's own Apulia.[25] The violence of even a foreign war finds its way back home.

This last simile places the epinikion in crisis. Since the panegyrist does not sufficiently suppress the notion that violence produces violence, he cannot avoid reminding audience(s) that victors may subject their own people to the violent repercussions of war. As in Vergil, a lion may be watching the attacking bull, and the attacker may become the victim. Through the ode's central stanza flows the Aufidus. Horace names the Aufidus only three other times. Although it is always a powerful and noisy river, the only other time it floods it punishes the one who lives beyond the bounds of nature (*S.*I.1.49–60).[26] Twice the Aufidus symbolizes Horace and the immortal power of his lyric (*C.*III.30.10–12; IV.9.1–4), but Pindar was the last raging torrent of poetry to flood (*C.*IV.2.5–8). Horatian lyric is slender and fat. We have come to expect from Horace a metaphor combining these two qualities, but there is no symbol of thinness to balance the fatness of this epinikion (cf. *C.*III.30.10b–11a: *qua violens obstrepit Aufidus / et qua pauper aquae Daunus*). To follow the argument of this metaphor, the attempt to immortalize Augustus through praising his sons' martial accomplishments not only opens up the *laudandi* to the implicit criticism of self-destructive violence but causes the *laudator* Horace to overflow his lyric banks and assume Pindaric and epic proportions. The epinikion presents war as a potentially hubristic act for both *laudandus* and *laudator,* and the audience is left to decide to what extent the epinikion becomes admonitory. The epinikion not too covertly argues against itself: martial praise may not be the appropriate means to immortalize Augustus.

The epinikion repeats a structural pattern familiar from the other *encomia nobilium et Augusti.* The poet fits his praise around a center that in some manner introduces dissonance (*dubia*) into the panegyric (*C.*IV.2, 4, 5, 9). Yet the tension in the second epinikion differs from the first and alters the mood of the whole piece. In c.4 Horace manipulated the similes and the secondary narrator to create ambiguity as to whether the Neros had learned nobility or military hubris over a weaker opponent. Victims vanish from c.14, and its praise reinforces the military power of the conquerors and their enemies. There is no sympathy for the weak and unsuspecting, only subjugation of the strong and rebellious. The epithets for Rome's enemies tell the story: *legis expertes Latinae / Vindelici* (7–8); *Genaunos, implacidum genus* (10); *Breunosque velocis* (11); *immanisque Raetos* (15); *devota morti pectora liberae* (18); *barbarorum . . . agmina* (29–30); *Cantaber non ante domabilis* (41); *profugus Scythes* (42); *non paventis funera Galliae* (49); *durae . . . Hiberiae*

(50); *caede gaudentes Sygambri* (51). The enemies are all objects acted upon until they pay homage to Augustus. Spirited enemies elevate the praise and give it a double edge. The nations worship Augustus, but the combination of *non ante domabilis* and *dominae Romae* (41, 44) underscores that this honor is forced compliance, a tenuous peace that would quickly evaporate if Roman might did not constrain. The sounds of battle, in the contrast of the plosives against the weaker nasals and aspirants, never die out (verses 31–32; n.b. strophes 3, 4, 7, 8, 11).

Augustus's role does not change from the first to second epinikion. He remains the teacher, but Horace assigns new pupils and curriculum. Augustus taught the Nerones; now he teaches the Vindelicians about Mars' power (8–9). The Rhaetians learn a no-holds-barred military thumping. A younger Claudius strewed the earth with their corpses—without slaughter (*sine clade*). The emotive impact of the oxymoronic *sine clade* (32) and the pun that it draws from the similar sounding *Claudius* (29) magnifies the destruction of Rome's enemies. *Victor* at the end of the verse explains the paradox: many died, just not Romans. Horace makes this graphic word picture of Rhaetian losses the transition back to his hymnic praise for Augustus and his past victories over Rome's enemies. Augustus triumphantly returns to Rome in the guise of *Fortuna* [*Redux*] bringing with him his victories (37–38),[27] a very different mode of return from the apotheosis of c.5. Therefore, as already argued, this panegyric makes the recent victories an extension of the peace won at Actium/Alexandria.

This is great praise. On the other hand, the correlation of the victory at Alexandria and over the German tribes, after the violent victory narrative for the Nerones, prompts a look back to Alexandria rather than forward from Alexandria. To view Alexandria through the conqueror/subject paradigm of these most recent victories pricks the memory that Octavian became Rome's sole ruler by willful force, just as he now controls and extends the empire. As is customary in Horatian encomia, the panegyrist promotes rather than masks the potential tensions within the praise.[28] The praise adopts the Augustan perspective, suppressing any mention of civil conflict by representing the enemy through the name of the city (*Alexandrea*, 35; cf. *RG* 1.1, *rem publicam a dominatione factionis oppressam*). Only Alexandria, however, among all the enemies enumerated, receives a truly sympathetic epithet, *supplex*. She was suppliant. The epinikion imagines Augustus conquering his enemy as she was suing for mercy. Given the Vergilian language and imagery in the ode, it is not a stretch to think that the epinikion has re-created the final drama of the *Aeneid:* Aeneas roused by vengeance and slaying Turnus, who was pleading with Aeneas to spare him. Whether such a portrait rightly represents Octavian's victories or whether Octavian in this position would be justified has fired irresolvable debate, but at this stage in the principate it would hardly be a simple uncomplicated praise for Augustus. Force and peace are always uneasy companions. Augustus knew this. The senate decreed the Altar of Peace for Augustus (13 B.C.), and Augustus built the temple of Mars Ultor (dedicated 2 B.C.).[29]

As the internal tensions of the epinikion develop, they begin to reveal the potential ambiguities in the hymn's opening question. When one has not yet read the battle narrative, it is easy to pass quickly over the introduction and think it nothing more than an exclamatory rhetorical question mimicking the panegyric trope of the small voice through which the poet honors his subjects by claiming to be incapable of praising them as they deserve.[30] Such a reading would actually be quite unconventional. Pindar and Horace do not introduce their praises with open-ended interrogatives that they leave unanswered, but both construct the poem to supply specific answers to the questions they raise.[31] In this opening question Horace foists the small voice onto the people and omits the customary foil capable of immortalizing Augustus adequately, except for himself. Horace thereby elevates himself to the task the people cannot perform. The ironic argument "I can't praise you well enough, but others can (while I am in fact praising you) becomes "Others can't, but I can, and so step aside, and I will." Reading the question in this fashion devalues the panegyric role of the Roman citizenry, which runs counter to the importance of the audience as a necessary agent in Horace's panegyric praxis; it certainly reverses c.5 where the rustic had the power through invocation to immortalize the absent princeps. Now suddenly the citizens cannot immortalize Augustus, at least not sufficiently.

Recent studies have tended to refine the leading question by emphasizing the methods by which the citizens immortalize their heroes: offices (*plenis honorum muneribus,* 2), commemorative inscriptions, and public records (*per titulos memoresque fastos,* 4). The citizens then seem comparable to the artisans of c.8. They can immortalize subjects but can never match the power of poetry, and therefore the poet offers Augustus this poem, a gift that will praise him as he deserves.[32] The contrast of the citizens' power with the poet's power to immortalize within the context of an epinikion narrows the primary interest of c.8: how would a poem be more powerful than a hard artifact, not just any poem but specifically a military praise poem, an epinikion? The answer goes to the heart of Horace's panegyric praxis and reveals just how leading the leading question may be. Since both an honorary inscription and the epinikion recount the offices and military accomplishments of the *laudandus,* the superiority of the epinikion cannot be located in factual data. Horatian panegyric praxis has already presented the praise poem as a more vibrant medium than the hard arts precisely because of its flexible interpretive value (c.8–9). Through interaction with an audience panegyric can metamorphosize, come alive, and in turn make its subjects live again. The power of a poet's praise works on and through its audiences.

The opening question remains ironic. While appearing to assign the citizens the smallest panegyric voice, the poet actually asserts their importance in the panegyric process. The tensions in the epinikion bear this out as its Pindaric and epic excesses turn introspective: Is military conquest the most suitable Augustan legacy or not? As in the ode for Lollius (c.9) and against Lyce (c.13), to be immortalized can be a blessing or a curse depending on the deeds of the *laudandus,* the character of the poet, and the perception of the audience. Perhaps Horace's epinikion would respond more closely to the question if *aeternet* were to be interpreted as a serious deliberative: What attention from the Roman citizens should immortalize Augustus? How precisely should the citizens remember him in the inscriptions and records? To refine the question further, are *patrum* and *Quiritium* purely possessive/subjective genitives, or could they contain an objective sense?[33] What care on the part of Augustus for his citizens would immortalize him? How should Augustus use his offices and by what deeds would he best secure immortal fame?[34] Once again the poet's praise through these ambiguities and tensions brings together the principal players in his panegyric agon, all of them indispensable and active agents in the creation of public memory: the *laudandus,* the *laudator,* and the audience of Roman citizens.

Equally ironic is that c.14, one of the most neglected poems in the Horatian corpus, has proven pivotal for the reception of Horace's encomiastic poetry. To immortalize Augustus according to the dictates of his own imaging sharply constrains creative authorial power. If this is all that remains of the power of the lyric bard from *Odes* I–III, then book IV represents a severe decline in poetic power, and the lyric poet can be said to have withdrawn. For such a view to be tenable, however, the poet of the epinikion must efface himself and sufficiently demean his audience so that neither the poet nor the citizens can be involved as interpretive forces that could shape or influence the panegyric. Horace's nuancing of his epinikia (his inclusion of disputes, *dubia*), far from excluding the poet and citizens, renders their participation in the interpretive process inevitable and essential. C.14 places into debate not just the mode of memory but the content of memory as well, that is, precisely how one should be remembered, and by this very question the epinikion, as complex as any other Horatian encomium, argues that the poet and the people are both together energizing agents in the formation of public identity. There is no withdrawal here. Horace's panegyric space belongs to more than just the princeps.

C.15: A Panegyric Tag[Two] — "I Really Wanted To!"

> Phoebus volentem proelia me loqui
> victas et urbis increpuit lyra,
>   ne parva Tyrrhenum per aequor
>   vela darem. tua, Caesar, aetas
>
> fruges et agris rettulit uberes   5
> et signa nostro restituit Iovi
>   derepta Parthorum superbis
>   postibus et vacuum duellis
>
> Ianum Quirini clausit et ordinem
> rectum evaganti frena licentiae   10
>   iniecit emovitque culpas
>   et veteres revocavit artis,

per quas Latinum nomen et Italae
crevere vires, famaque et imperi
    porrecta maiestas ad ortus   15
        solis ab Hesperio cubili.

custode rerum Caesare non furor
civilis aut vis exiget otium,
    non ira, quae procudit ensis
        et miseras inimicat urbis.   20

non qui profundum Danuvium bibunt
edicta rumpent Iulia, non Getae,
    non Seres infidique Persae,
        non Tanain prope flumen orti;

nosque et profestis lucibus et sacris   25
inter iocosi munera Liberi
    cum prole matronisque nostris
        rite deos prius apprecati

virtute functos more patrum duces
Lydis remixto carmine tibiis   30
    Troiamque et Anchisen et almae
        progeniem Veneris canemus.

[Phoebus, although I really wanted to sing of battles
and conquered cities, plucked a warning note on his
lyre not to launch my small sails over the Tyrrhenian
Sea. Your age, Caesar, has brought rich crops back to
the countryside, and restored to our Jove the standards
torn from the Parthian's proud temple, and closed the
doors of Janus Quirinus, announcing freedom from
wars, and has reined in lawlessness straying beyond
approved morality, and banished wrong and recalled
traditional virtues through which the Latin name and
Italic might has grown, and the empire's fame and
majesty has stretched to the rising of the sun from its
bed in the West. When Caesar keeps watch over the
state, no civil madness or violence, no rage that forges
swords and turns cities into wretched enemies will ban-
ish peace. The people who drink the deep Danube will
not break Julian commands, not the Getae, not the Seres
and the treacherous Persians, not the people born near
the river Tanais. And we on common days and festive

days with our children and our wives together surrounded by the gifts of mirthful Liber, first as we
should we will worship the gods and then as our ancestors did we will sing to the sounds of the Lydian
pipes a song of our heroes' glorious lives, of Troy and
Anchises and the offspring of nurturing Venus.]

Each book of *Odes* culminates in a declaration of Horace's own poetic achievement, a crescendo that builds from the first to third book. C.I.38 with its denunciation of Persian luxuries has been read as a rejection of poetic excess, depicted in the commonplace sympotic theme of *mediocritas*.[35] Horace is not nearly so subtle in the Swan Ode where he triumphantly sings his own metamorphosis into that melodious graceful bird and denies his own mortality (C.II.20). By the end of the third book the poet soars above the heights of the Pharaohs' pyramids (C.III.30). The expectations established by Horace's first lyric books are undone then, if *Odes* IV does not end in a similar claim of Horace's accomplishments, but instead offers an encomium for Augustus that produces little more than a scholarly yawn for its apparent lack of originality.[36]

Even more positive assessments of c.15 overlook the pattern set by the previous books and concentrate on the nature of the encomium, Augustus's peaceful as opposed to military achievements, and secondarily on Horace's sincerity. They emphasize the exaggerated polysyndeton (strophes 1–4), which unifies the string of Augustan accomplishments and leads to the extraordinary *custode rerum* (not just *Romae*) *Caesare*, in contrast to the opening *recusatio* and the poet's voice that becomes only one of the many blended together at Rome's public banquets.[37] The overt compression of convivial and political praise poetry seems to reverse the bold metapoetics of the younger Horace and to subordinate the "private" sympotic themes to the power and welfare of the state as Horace's lyric voice withdraws into the anonymous Roman crowd,[38] a retreat emphasized by the hyperbaton containing the last strophes, *nosque . . . canemus*. Augustus looms larger than life, and the poet stands in the background, winning literary fame by immortalizing his patron. It is worth asking what kind of conclusion c.15 is: climactic or anticlimactic and how? Does Horace near the end of his poetic career step back into a crowd after a rather mechanical rehearsal of the Augustan image, which avoids the types of conflicts and tensions evident in his other panegyrics, or does he continue to test the limits of panegyric convention with his own lyric genius?[39] When this final encomium (4b–24) is read within its frame, the *recusatio* (1–4a) and the Roman festival (25–32), it serves a metapoetical function as vital as each concluding ode of the previous collection. Horace in c.15 epitomizes his panegyric praxis. While insisting on the power of his lyric voice, he complicates the imperial panegyric and then concludes with an open invitation to a banquet where the poet and the Roman people will sing together praises for their founders and leaders. Here is the model for Horatian praise: the sympotic poet insisting on the preeminence of his lyric and writing a praise that lacks a definitive resolution and therefore requires an interpretive community to actively engage the song and negotiate its meaning through their voices (*nos . . . canemus*).

The *encomium Augusti* (strophes 2–6) develops from the preceding epinikion in a somewhat predictable manner. Horace questions whether the militaristic epinikion appropriately immortalizes Augustus (c.14), and consequently in the next ode (c.15) he turns from celebrating Augustus's battles to narrating the Augustan peace. Horace's praise (13–16) moves quickly through Roman history in an unbroken timeline of expanding grandeur from Rome's humble Latin origin (*Latinum nomen*) to allied power (*Italae / . . . vires*), until because of the Augustan revival her empire stretches from the rising to setting sun (15–16). The heart of the encomium thus answers back directly to the opening question of the epinikion, "What praise has the power to immortalize Augustus wherever the sun lights the inhabitable lands?" (5–6)— given the parallel, obviously the poet's praise.

Horace's panegyric narrative harmonizes with Augustus's account of his accomplishments so completely that it reads like an advance outline of Augustus's *Res Gestae,* where Augustus will report that he brought peace to Rome and her provinces (6–9; *RG* 1.1; 2; 3.1–2; 13; 25.1–2), cared for the people's sustenance and quality of life (5; *RG* 5.2; 15; 18), repaired Roman morality and reinstituted neglected rites (9–12; *RG* 6; 8.5; 19.2; 20.4; 24.1), earned the respect of Rome's subjects and even her enemies (19–20; *RG* 12; 25.2; 26–33), and restored the Republic to the senate and people (*RG* 34). Through these deeds he earned uncommon honors and political influence (*auctoritas*), encapsulated in the privilege of being named Augustus just as Horace addresses him, *Auguste . . . maxime principum* (c.14.3, 6). The point-by-point coincidence between Horace's praise and Augustus's self-imaging or, to state the argument negatively, the seeming absence of panegyric conflicts has caused this concluding ode to appear mechanical and wooden.[40] Compared to Horace's other panegyrics there does not seem to be enough poetic energy or ingenuity to excite the imagination. The grandeur of the poet's praise is the greatness of Augustus[41] —or so it appears.

However straightforward the narrative may be in which Horace lists Augustus's achievements, Horace does not suppress his lyric genius. Horace very economically presents his thesis in the first words of the encomium proper, *tua, Caesar, aetas* (4). Horace's praise is not just about Caesar but about time, and how Caesar exerts such power over time that he can possess it as his own. The organizing principle of the encomium is temporal. The movement of time in the encomium is unparalleled in convivial odes. As in c.14, Augustus is not confined within the temporal boundaries set for mortals by Horace's sympotic invitations. Anyone the poet invites to a drinking party must come immediately or lose the brief opportunity to enjoy life. The present is the only instant of time any mortal can grasp.[42] Not so for Augustus. Augustus controls both the past and future. Horace attributes the peace of the present age to Caesar because he has reestablished the past, in contrast to Aelius and the antiquarian, who stay trapped in the past and miss life's pleasures (C.III.17; 19). Augustus brought the mastery, prosperity, and peace Rome had experienced prior to the civil wars back into the present. Verbs of restoration (*fruges et agris rettulit uberes,* 5; *et signa nostro restituit Iovi,* 6; *et veteres revocavit artes,* 12) surround verbs that proclaim the Augustan achievement (*Ianum Quirini clausit,* 9; . . . *frena licentiae / iniecit,* 10–11a; *emovitque culpas,* 11b). The poem thus promulgates the position that the principate was the restoration of the *Res Publica*[43] and reverses the moral decline from age to age (*aetas*) that Horace denounced in the Roman Odes (III.6.45–48). Augustus has broken the downward cycle. Rome's present is now as good, even better than her past.

Now the sympotic poet completely reverses the *carpe diem* argument (*spem longam reseces,* C.I.11.7) and predicts the future under Augustus's protection.[44] The future dominates (*exiget,* 18; *rumpent,* 22; *canemus,* 32), while the present is confined to subordinate clauses (*quae procudit ensis / et miseras inimicat urbis*, 19b–20; *non qui profundum Danuvium bibunt*, 21). As long as Caesar's rule lasts, the future is certain—there will be neither civil nor foreign war (strophes 5–6). The same assured tone continues in the last two strophes. When Horace re-creates the *convivia*, known to Cato, and their songs of praise for Roman heroes, he imports the traditional banquets of Rome's past into the future so that Rome's future reenacts her past rituals, *nosque . . . more patrum . . . canemus*. In a real sense Rome's future becomes her past:

> Atque utinam exstarent illa carmina, quae multis saeculis ante suam aetatem in epulis esse cantitata a singulis convivis de clarorum virorum laudibus in Originibus scriptum reliquit Cato! (Cic. *Brut.* 75)

> [But would that those songs still existed that Cato recorded in his *Origines* to have been sung many years before his time at banquets, when guests in turn sang the praises of their renowned heroes!]

The evidence for such banquet songs is thin. The significant accounts can be reduced to Cicero's repetition of the above citation in *Tusc.* 1.3.1–4; 4.3.15–19, which adds only that flutes (*tibia*) provided accompaniment (also V. Max. 2.1.10), and to Varro, who reports children singing such praise (*De Vita Populi Romani* fr.84, *ap.* Non. p.77 M = p. 107 L). But whether this tradition actually existed is not the poet's concern.[45] Horace is (re)inventing it here and giving the practice a seal of authenticity (*more patrum*). Moreover, to appeal to a pre-Vergilian tradition softens the paradox of an ode that begins with a *recusatio* of epic and ends with an echo of the beginning of the *Aeneid*.

The temporal limitations that sympotic Horace prescribes for mortals clarify the extravagance of the imperial praise. Augustus, like the gods (unlike humanity), can break the barriers imposed by time both past and future. The greatness of Augustus in c.15 is his ability to unite in the present Rome's past and future, and for doing so he will be immortalized through the songs of his people. Caesar is as divine as the sympotic lyric poet could portray him without the overt use of a title.

Horace does not erase his unique lyric mark from imperial praise. Horace's clever handling of sympotic/lyric time in the encomium contradicts the notion that Horace wrote a trite poem to show Augustus how powerless the praise ordered up by a patron

could be. The temporal lyric structuring of the encomium sufficiently argues that Horace's sympotic persona influences the
quality of the poem and that the poem should not be judged dull
and hackneyed, but it proves little more. Affirming the poet's
lyric genius does not answer whether Horace has altered his
panegyric praxis at the last possible moment in the book, because
certainly he could have written a creative lyric praise that mirrors without qualification Augustus's imaging of himself. What
would place Horatian panegyric in crisis would be if Horace were
to effectively suppress any disputes or ironies in such a way as to
diminish the panegyric role for either the poet or the community.[46] I am suggesting that although this ode appears to be a
monochromatic lyric praise narrated from the viewpoint of the
laudandus, Augustus, there is, in fact, no panegyric crisis because
Horace once again complicates the praise, specifically here as in
c.1 and 9 by the frame containing the encomium: the personal singular voice of the *recusatio* (strophe 1) and the plural communal
voices of the Roman banquet (strophes 7–8). Throughout Horace
insists on the capacity of his lyric to envision and embody Roman
heroic ideals.

As is typical of the form, this *recusatio* has three basic components: (1) exclusion, in which the poet rejects certain poetic principles (typically characteristics of a particular genre); (2) subversion, namely the actual structural elements, rhetorical devices,
and themes that the author uses to contradict the exclusion; (3) inclusion, which results from the subversion and is often the appropriation of the principles that the author rejected.[47] The debate
on how to read the *recusatio* is indicative of the nature of the construct. A *recusatio* could be read seriously, that is, only on the level
of exclusion. Such a reading would keep c.15 consistent with a
stricter definition of lyric, since the poet pointedly rejects the martial heroic themes associated with *epos*. On the other hand, if the
focus shifts to the devices subverting the exclusion, the poem then
reads in an ironic fashion: the poet includes what he pretends to
exclude. On the level of inclusion the *recusatio* becomes an expansion of lyric to incorporate the themes of *epos*. This one level or
other approach (which could prove correct in a particular text)
may, however, result in an oversimplification of the *recusatio* and
the opportunities that it allows a poet to construct and communicate an idea. A poet could structure a *recusatio* that is appropriately read on both levels simultaneously: the subversion does not

totally undo the reading of the first level but rather enhances or complements it. It is not enough, therefore, to state that a *recusatio* is ironic. One must consider the relationship and interaction of the two levels to determine whether actual subversion occurs and if it does, whether or not the reading of the first level is entirely altered and the construct is totally ironic or whether the two levels offer complementary arguments.[48] Horace in his customary manner avoids either/or and in this *recusatio* plays both levels off each other so that they work together to complicate the imperial praise.

Horace's *recusatio*, as commonly observed, both recalls the exordium of Callimachus's *Aetia*,

καὶ γὰρ ὅτε πρώτιστον ἐμοῖς ἐπὶ δέλτον ἔθηκα
     γούνασιν, Ἀπόλλων εἶπεν ὅ μοι Λύκιος·
. . . .]. . . ἀοιδέ, τὸ μὲν θύ ος ὅττι πάχιστον
     θρέψαι, τὴν Μοῦσαν δ' ὠγαθὲ λεπταλέην· (fr.1.21–24 Pf.)

[For indeed, at the very moment I first placed my writing tablet on my knees, Lycian Apollo said to me, ". . . singer, tend your sacrifice to be as fat as can be, but, good poet, tend a slender Muse."]

and is also indebted to Vergil's adaptation (*Ecl.*6.3–9a):

cum canerem reges et proelia, Cynthius aurem
vellit et admonuit: 'pastorem, Tityre, pinguis
pascere oportet ovis, deductum dicere carmen.'   5
nunc ego (namque super tibi erunt qui dicere laudes,
Vare, tuas cupiant et tristia condere bella)
agrestem tenui meditabor harundine Musam:
non iniussa cano.

[As I was singing of kings and battles, the Cynthian plucked my ear and warned, "Tityrus, a shepherd should feed his sheep to be fat, should sing a finely spun song." Now I (for you will have more than enough who want to sing your praises, Varus, and to write of grim wars) mull over a rustic Muse on my thin reed pipe: I am singing my orders.]

We can be more specific. This is Horace's most precise reference to the Callimachean *dictum* and its advocacy of the compressed poetic style. Nowhere else in Horatian poetry does Apollo intervene and tell the poet to change his song. This is the job of the Muse.[49] Although Vergil in his imitation substitutes the common epithets Cynthius (3) and Phoebus (11) for the name of the god,[50]

he retains Callimachus's warning Apollo and amplifies the violence of the intervention when Apollo pulls Tityrus's ear. Vergil
further specifies the topics that Tityrus must avoid, kings and
battles (*reges et proelia*). Horace follows all these Vergilian modifi-
cations, even adopting Vergil's *proelia*. Horace makes clear from
his close interplay with Callimachus and Vergil that he is continuing the tradition of the *genus tenue* and his habit of setting his
compressed lyric style with its lighter themes in opposition to
epic praise and its themes of warring and conquest. At the level of
exclusion (C.IV.15), Horace, guided by Apollo, turns away from
martial topics and the *grande dictum* associated with *epos* (symbolized in the localizing metaphor, *Tyrrhenum per aequor*, 3; cf.
Verg. *A.*1.67: *gens inimica mihi Tyrrhenum navigat aequor*) to topics
suited to his peace-loving lyre, and accordingly the praise that
follows highlights Augustus as statesman, moral leader, and
peacemaker.

In spite of the similarities to the Callimachean and Vergilian
models, Horace changes at c.15 the primary stratagem for the *recusatio* as it was commonly deployed by Vergil and the other Augustan poets, and even by Horace himself in his other exempla.
The *recusatio* was a comic and tactful device for avoiding direct
praise. Horace's typical *recusatio* declines to praise a patron by the
pretense that his light lyrics would fall short of the patron's noble
excellence. Horace then defers to someone whose serious poetry
is more up to the task. Of course, the poet's humility is a ruse,
since the poem containing the *recusatio* proves lyric a very capable
medium for praise (e.g., C.I.6: when deferring to Varius, Horace
calls his own Muse powerful, *potens*).[51] In c.15 however, Horace
does not abandon panegyric completely as Vergil did the praise
of Varus; he, instead, continues with his praise of Augustus. He
does not refuse, even in pretense, to write praise poetry as he did
in I.6 for Marcus Agrippa; he only declines, because of Apollo's
intervention, certain aspects or topics, Augustus's military victories. This shift from refusing the act of praise to restricting its content and form reinvigorates the irony of the *recusatio*. For Horace
to pretend that he lacks the ability to praise is overly transparent
after he authored the *CS* and at the end of a poetry book containing a hymn to the divine Augustus and two epinikia. But a *recusatio* on praising military victories immediately after an epinikion
doing exactly that complicates the panegyric by reintroducing the

very question Horace posed in the epinikion. Would a rehearsal of military achievements be the best way to praise Augustus? Apollo's warning to avoid martial themes and the poet's compliance in singing of the Augustan peace and immortalizing Augustus by lyric sympotic themes can be read as a negative answer to that question. The peace-loving lyre, not war-loving epic-styled praise, best immortalizes Augustus. If Augustus did commission the two epinikia, the *recusatio* implies an answer back to the patron that risks putting Augustus at odds with his own patron deity by suggesting: 'Augustus, you have asked me to praise your military victories, and I really want to, but your own god Apollo warned me to stop.'

The drama of the *recusatio*, when viewed against the epinikia, incorporates a type of epic hierarchy for the composition of panegyric that moves from divine directive (the Muse or a god), first to the poet (the *laudator*) and only then to the patron (the *laudandus*).[52] The word order of the *recusatio* and structure of the encomium support this vatic line of authority: Apollo (divine inspiration), the poet, and then Caesar. The encomium (5–24) is arranged into a pair of two-strophe units with a central strophe. The first two strophes (5–12) focus on Augustus's success in restoring Rome's greatness and climax in the central strophe, a declaration of Rome's glory (13–16). The last two strophes (17–24) shift from the past to the future and the promise of stability that the rule of Augustus offers. Horace upsets the balance of the first and last pairs, however, by placing the beginning of the encomium proper *tua, Caesar, aetas* (4) with the end of the *recusatio*. This separation of the addressee (*Caesar*) and subject (*tua . . . aetas*) from the lead sentence of the encomium, while at the same time the caesura in line 4 falling immediately before signals that they belong syntactically with the praise that follows, transforms *tua, Caesar, aetas* as it were into an emphatic title that lauds the age of Augustus, but it also sets Caesar in contrast to Apollo at the head of the strophe. There are three players in the first strophe, Apollo, the poet, and Caesar. As the order indicates, the poet mediates between the two: *Phoebus . . . proelia me loqui . . . Caesar.*[53] Apollo and Caesar at opposing ends of the strophe, the general chiastic arrangement of subjects and objects that pins the first person of the poet in the middle, and then the abrupt switch in subject between *darem* and *tua aetas* suggest a tension between the wishes of the god and the princeps. Although the poet is pulled in opposite directions, he must heed Apollo and avoid martial praise. Apollo is the commander (*increpuit*). Caesar is the object of praise but not the inspiration, and he does not control the poetic process; he is a recipient. At the same time, Horace is not belligerent. The appeal to divine intervention, standard within the tradition of the *recusatio*, lends a playfulness to the praise: 'Augustus, I really wanted to commemorate your military victories, but Apollo would not allow me. I will at least praise you as Apollo's lyre allows.' The lyre is setting the agenda.

Horace leaves the possible conflict between Augustus and his patron deity delicately below the surface, hidden in the context and the wording of the *recusatio*. Horace never states explicitly that the epic wars were necessarily those in which Augustus was involved[54] or that Augustus had ever asked him to write an epic-styled praise poem. That such praise might please Augustus and had been requested by him is merely implied primarily by the juxtaposition of the *recusatio* on military praise with the epic-styled epinikion honoring Drusus and Tiberius. In fact, Horace in contrast to Callimachus and Vergil admits that singing about military heroism is entirely his choice. In this respect the Horatian *recusatio* is a blending of the Callimachean exemplum with a reversal of the Vergilian imitation. Apollo does not interrupt Callimachus; the god instructs him before he begins to write, while the writing tablets are on his lap.[55] Callimachus has not yet started down the wrong poetic track and does not need to be recalled, only advised positively. Vergil's Tityrus has already started his song, and Apollo has to stop him violently. The Vergilian drama does not specify whether Tityrus was willing to undertake the labor of praising Varus in the epic manner; at most, Tityrus insinuates that he is reluctant when he apologetically explains that many others will want to praise Varus, but his mind is on the pastoral muse and her slender lyric.[56] Horace, like Callimachus, has not yet begun the song, but unlike Vergil's Tityrus, Horace is one of those who desires to sing epic-styled praise. Horace compresses Vergil's two verbs describing Apollo's violent interruption (*vellit et admonuit*, plucked and warned) into a single verb and noun (*increpuit lyra*) and changes *vellit* into the homophonetic *volentem* (willing). Horace is willing to sing militaristic praise, and so far he has done just that.

Horace's imperial praise in book IV focuses almost exclusively on war: a celebration of a triumph (c.2), epinikia (c.4, 14), and a hymn to Augustus calling him back from campaigning (c.5). Now when at the very last moment the panegyrist openly declares himself in the first person, which he has not done in any imperial praise since the *intermissio* of c.4, and for the first time boldly declares that he wants to sing triumphant militaristic praise, Apollo has to stop him. The panegyrist with his propensity for martial themes must be corrected before he ever sings his final praise.[57] The punch line of the *recusatio* comes with this added twist: when Apollo instructs Horace not to sing of conquered cities, the divine imperative comes late and interrupts the panegyrist after the fact. Therefore, Horace's *recusatio* as it closes the book directly answers back to the panegyrist's warring imperial praise and actually corrects or at least redirects it to a more appropriate venue.[58] The common assumption is that Horace is simply acting out a transition, and nothing more, in the imperial image from the warring Octavian to the Augustus of Actium who brings peace to the empire.[59] Praising the great victory that Apollo had given to Augustus and the transition from (civil) foreign wars to peace would fit better in books I-III, published in 23 B.C. already almost ten years after Actium, or perhaps earlier in book IV when Horace returns to lyric, as a report on the peace of the intervening ten years between the collections, but right at the end of book IV? Perhaps Apollo's correction is not so remote in light of the Altar of Peace dedicated to honor Augustus's continued military success in the provinces and his safe return from the West (13 B.C.), and if the warring Octavian has reemerged in the invasions against the Germanic tribes. How precisely should Augustus be remembered, and whom is Apollo warning—just the poet or by inference the patron Caesar, who commissions the poet? But then again this is only a *recusatio*, and Horace is not that serious, or is he?

Horace does not take Apollo's warning too seriously. The *recusatio* has ironic edges, and at the level of inclusion Horace expands the poem's thesis by reinforcing the capacity of lyric to contain epic praise. Horace does not finish even the first strophe before he begins undermining the claim that lyric must avoid martial themes. Apollo violently plucking (*increpuit*)[60] his lyre interjects a hostile tone into the moment of inspiration and emphasizes the god's dual nature as a healer holding a lyre and a god of war carrying a bow and quiver. Horace structures Apollo's command so that it in fact assimilates epic into lyric: the chiastic word order of the symbols for lyric and epic incorporates the expansive epic sea within the confines of Horace's small lyric sails (*parva Tyrrhenum per aequor* vela, 3–4).[61] When Horace begins the encomium proper it appears he will obey the god. Apollo instructs him not to sing about conquered cities (*urbis*), and Horace signals compliance by the rhyme *urbis — uberes.* Conquered cities (*urbis*) in the age of Caesar become fertile (*uberes*) lands. But then Horace ignores Apollo's command and militarizes his praise of the Augustan peace. The Parthian king Phraates, desiring to increase his influence with Rome, in 20 B.C. peacefully returned the military standards, which the Parthians had captured and held for more than thirty years from three different Roman armies led by Crassus (53 B.C.), Decidius Saxa (40 B.C.), and Mark Antony (36 B.C.). Horace presents Augustus as the hero of a Parthian war that never was by surrounding the event with a hostile vocabulary fit for a military campaign (*derepta Parthorum superbis / postibus; clausit; iniecit; emovit; revocavit,* 6–12).[62] Caesar's guardianship of the empire (17–24) reads as a verbal reenactment of the irony in the *recusatio:* exclusion for the sake of inclusion — *non* repeated six times to cancel the effects of war. Finally, Horace closes his *Odes* with what could be a thesis statement for the *Aeneid:* "We will sing of Troy, Anchises, and the offspring of nourishing Venus" (Aeneas to Augustus). Horace, however, is not returning to the great Epic but to a pre-Vergilian tradition remembered by Cato that songs praising Rome's heroes were part of her holiday celebrations. The Horatian lyre does not give way to the weight of epic but rather gives an artful apology that the poet's chosen genre, lyric, is fully capable of the grand national themes typically associated with epic, perhaps even more so.[63] The ode is as much about the grandeur of lyric as the greatness of Augustus. From the perspective of the Horatian panegyrist the song appropriate for the heroic hymns of the banquet is not the expansive approach of epic in which the poet remains distant, but intense praise, condensed for rapid delivery, in the first person, the plural "We" not the singular "I."

The shift from the singular voice of the poet (*me . . . darem,* 1–4) to the plural of the Roman people (*nos . . . canemus,* 25–32) has been the ode's most controversial feature. It has been traditional to read the shift as an indication that Horace is losing himself (the poetic "I") in the crowd and finding anonymity among his fellow Romans.[64] Precisely what this supposed withdrawal means remains in dispute: the lyric poet is submitting to the power of Caesar, or retiring from the public stage and refusing to be the imperial poet laureate; his withdrawal is another ironic ploy to illustrate either what vacuous praise can result when the independent voice of the lyric poet is suppressed, or that the poet by his panegyrics holds the power over Augustus's immortal fame.[65] All these proposals presume that the lyric poet steps back into the crowd, but the shift from the singular voice to plural voices — more accurately the progression since Horace uses the plural early in the poem (*nostro Iovi,* 6) — need not be a withdrawal at all when the festive Bacchic conclusion of c.15 is seen as an extension of the invitations to shared lyric song (c.10–13). The assumption that Horace is retreating into community rather than inviting to community results when the chiastic structure of the book is disregarded and any connectedness between the so-called private poems and public praises is ignored so that the epinikia and the imperial praises are patched back together, as if the intervening odes are irrelevant. That the book ends with the Roman community celebrating together at a banquet and hymning their heroes is a satisfying rather than a surprising conclusion for Horace's sympotic panegyric strategy, which incorporates competing and complementary vantage points (*dubia*) and insists on the power of individuals to overcome the pains of mortality when they come together to share songs.

Horace does not resolve the ode's panegyric conflicts (*dubia*) by allowing any single voice in the *recusatio* to dominate the others no matter how powerful or necessary to the panegyric process these individuals may be: the god Apollo, the poet, or Caesar Augustus. Horatian panegyric culminates in the plural, a symposion of praise: the Dionysiac authority of the Roman community that closes the ode. This denial of heroic individualism constitutes Horace's ultimate critical *recusatio* of epic. Horace's hierarchy for the panegyric process in the poem's opening out of which all the tensions develop follows the epic model of divine inspiration, (Apollo) directing the inspired poet (Horace) to sing a particular story of the hero (Augustus): the Muse, the bard, and then the hero. By comparison the ordering of the participants at the banquet (25–32) emphasizes the power of the Roman community. *Inter* is a clever play of language and word order (26). The dramatic

scene brings together Roman citizens and places them as cele-
brants reveling together in the middle of Bacchic pleasures (*inter
iocosi munera Liberi*), whereas the structure of the poem with the
hyperbaton *nos . . . canemus* (the first and last positions) places the
god of wine among the gathered community. The god of wine
and inspiration is literally in the middle of the body of Roman citizens (*inter nos*). The inspired drunken community (*dulce est desipere loco*, C.IV.12.28) led by the lyric poet sings only for those
who have done virtuously. The community discriminates, and
thereby determines in concert whether their standards have been
met, and selects the subjects to hymn (*virtute functos more patrum
duces . . . canemus*). As is evident from the sum total of the poet's
praise and in this conclusion to the collection, Horatian panegyric
does not derive exclusively from the will of the praised and his
poet but is ultimately an interpretive act of the divinely empowered community. Horace's Roman panegyrics are sympotic and
therefore are not univocal: neither indiscriminate flattery or propaganda from a dependent *cliens*, nor one-sided criticism whether
clear or implied from a completely independent poet.[66] Horace
has claimed much more through his panegyrics than that the
poet-*cliens* is indispensable to the patron because he has the
power to immortalize the patron as the patron directs. The Horatian panegyrist fulfills a leading vatic role: he constructs the panegyric lyric agenda. The poet prescribes for the panegyric its quality (lyric mode) and content (the various deeds of the *laudandus*)
and calls together a community to join him in negotiating, creating, and re-creating Roman history and identity. The panegyrist
is both inspired and inspiring.

     With the transforming assimilation of the thesis for the *Aeneid*
into the last two lines of his lyric corpus, Horace brings book IV to
a grand conclusion every bit as bold and daring as his claims to
heroic fame in the final odes of the first collection (*Non usitata* nec
tenui *ferar / penna biformis . . . vates*, II.20.1–3a; nil parvum *aut humili modo, /* nil mortale *loquar*, III.25.17–18a; *ex humili* potens /
princeps, III.30.12b–13a)—nothing less than creating major intersections between Vergilian epic and his own lyric panegyric. In
Horace's panegyrics, as in Vergil's *Aeneid*, the will and well-being
of the community exercise a powerful hold over the ambitions of
the individual. Horace ends his epic criticism with the integration
of epic and lyric praise and thereby reconciles his lyric voice with

Vergil on Horace's own lyric terms.[67] Horace's first-person plural, "we sing" (*nos . . . canemus*), summarizes the *Aeneid*. It contains both Vergil's surprising first-person singular, "I sing" (*cano*), which immediately at the third word of his first line showcases the poet's creativity and puts epic into a lyric mode by violating the epic paradigm that the poet in the third person narrates the song of the Muse, and it contains the powerful sense of community portrayed in Aeneas's quest to found a new city. Horace has replicated in the conflicts within his own panegyrics the tensions in the *Aeneid* between individual glory, including that of the poet, and the good of the community. It is such conflict (*dubium*) that continues to make Vergil's epic and Horace's panegyric so compelling and unsettling.[68]

We have heard Horace lament Vergil's death (c.10), invite him to enjoy a symposion at Horace's house, and tell him to bring his song (c.12). At the conclusion to the whole lyric corpus Vergil finally comes to the party, and Horace the persistent lyricist has the power to add Vergil's song to his own banquet of praise. In Horace's final praise there is certainly no weakening of his lyric expression and principally no change in his manner of panegyric modeled throughout the book, which requires the *laudator*, the *laudandus*, and the Roman citizenry to add their judgments and to invest the praise with all their voices together. Horace, when he joins his voice with the Roman people, does not diminish his own. The union empowers panegyric. Horatian praise is not static or fixed but is as vibrant and alive as the Roman citizens themselves[69]—and comes alive again every time it is experienced and argued by us, Horace's most recent readers:

> non omnis moriar multaque pars mei
> vitabit Libitinam. usque ego postera
> crescam laede recens. . . . (C.III.30.6–8)

> [Not all of me will die, and most of me will avoid the Death-Goddess. Again and again I will grow modern when later generations praise me. . . .]

The Horatian panegyrist breathes (*spirat*) in from his divine source and out again upon—with—from—his own people.

Notes

1. Sympotic Horace

1. Reader beware. Horace manipulates autobiography to influence audience perception (*S.I.6; C.II.7; Epist.II.* 2.41–54); cf. McNeill (2001:1–9). For a thorough critique of Suetonius's *Vita Horati,* see Fraenkel (1957:1–23); Anderson (1995:151–64).

2. For theories on the arrangement of the *Odes,* see Dettmer (1983: 110–20, 136 n.1; Schanz-Hosius, 1935:126–27; Mutschler, 1974:132–33). The interconnectedness of the *Odes* is an essential dividing line between older and recent studies. For example, Fraenkel (1957) and Nisbet and Hubbard (N.-H., 1970:xxiii–xxiv) customarily treat an ode as an independent unit of thought. This can be a reasonable approach. An ode probably did have a life outside its poetry book. However, the focus on an ode as a self-contained presentation of one specific experience has tended to discount meaning generated by a linear reading of the collection. Kiessling (1881:48–122) first advanced the search for an element that unified Horatian poetry. After the publication of Port's study (1926:280–308, 427–68) on the Augustan poetry book, relatively little serious attention was paid to arrangement. Arguments for reading the *Odes* as a progressive and continuous dramatic movement began to gain momentum with Collinge (1961), Putnam (1986), Santirocco (1986), and Porter (1987) so that most recent studies (including Davis, 1991; Lyne, 1995; Lowrie, 1997; Oliensis, 1998; Griffiths, 2002) presume that the *Odes* can be productively studied in a holistic manner. Still, the high level of interaction between Horace's first and second lyric collection has yet to be appreciated fully.

3. Except when noted, I cite Shackleton Bailey's 1985 Stuttgart Teubner edition of Horace. Not all agree that the text is as corrupt as Shackleton Bailey's edition implies (see R. G. M. Nisbet's reviews of both

Shackleton Bailey's Teubner and its rival, S. Borzsák's 1984 Leipzig Teubner, in *Gnomon* 58 [1986] 611–15 and in *CR* n.s. 36 [1986] 227–34), but his edition calls attention to the questions critics have debated about the text, which otherwise readers would likely miss.

4. *Non sum qualis eram* (line 3) parallels *non eadem est aetas, non mens* of *Epist*.I.1.4, where just six verses later Horace resigns from lyric. Unless otherwise noted, all translations of the Greek and Roman authors are my own.

5. *Durus* is standard vocabulary for a shut-out lover (Pichon, 1902:136–82).

6. Why would Horace single out C.I.19? Lowrie (1995:44) argues that the Parade Odes extend from C.I.1–18 and consist of two series ("different lyric meters" and allusions to Horace's "lyric predecessors"). "C.1.19 brings us halfway through the first book of *Odes* . . . C.1.20 provides a new start with the address to Maecenas." Lowrie's sequencing suggests one answer. Horace by referencing c.19 recalls the structure of *Odes* I: he signals that he is now completing the first half of his lyric collection and is beginning again. One implicit question of C.IV.1 becomes, "Where has Maecenas gone?"

7. The plot is hardly original to Horace (Ibycus 287 *PMG*; Simon. fr.19–21 W.; Hunter, 2001:252).

8. Only Col. 9.2.2 (*Hyginus . . . non intermisit*).

9. Pl. *Bac*.210; *Mos*.959; Ter. *Ad*.293. Perhaps first because Propertius uses *intermissa* in his fourth book (4.80), which may have been written before C.IV.1 but published posthumously after *Odes* IV. Horace is the first poet other than Plautus (*Mos*.959; cf. [Sen.] *Oct*.731) to use the word in an erotic context. Thus Horace begins this book in satiric style by transforming a prosaic word common in the martial vocabulary of the historians into a poetic metaphor for his temporary withdrawal from Venus's wars. More will be said on the comic tone of the erotic metaphor in *intermissa, Venus, diu* later in the chapter.

10. Velleius Paterculus (2.97.1–5; 102.1–4) and Pliny (*Nat*. 9.118) rewrite Horace's praise of Lollius into blame; see c.9 in ch.2, *Encomia Nobilium*.

11. Absolute divisions between public and private (e.g., Lyne, 1995: vii; McNeill, 2001:82; cf. Ancona, 1994) are mostly artificial and result primarily not from what we really think about Horace's poetry, but from pragmatic concerns about how to present the diversity of his *Odes*. Pragmatics have often given the wrong impression (Lowrie, *CJ* 92 [1996] 295). Horace, on the other hand, places the praise for Maximus (9–28) right in the middle of a love lament for Ligurinus (1–8; 29–40). To separate the public from the private (the erotic from the political) would pull apart the introductory poem of the collection.

12. I count as sympotic not only obvious drinking songs but odes containing references to sympotic situations, although their main interest lies elsewhere (C.I.1, 4, 6, 7, 9, 11, 17, 18, 20, 27, 36, 37, 38; II.3, 5, 7, 11, 14; III.1, 6, 8, 12, 14, 15, 17, 19, 21, 28, 29; IV.1, 2, 5, 11, 12, 13, 15); cf. G. Williams (1972: 26–31). There are three major cultural distinctions between Greek drinking parties and Roman *convivia:* at *convivia* (1) women guests are alongside the men; (2) there is an emphasis on food; (3) the patron-client relationship has an influence on banquet protocol. Horace often blends the Greek and Roman, but as one could guess from the literary antecedents of each genre, the culture of the Roman banquet dominates the *Satires* and the Greek symposion the *Odes.* Maecenas wrote a *Symposion* (Bardon, 1956:16–17), and Plautus's plays prove that acquaintance with sympotic custom among the Romans was not limited to elitist Graecophiles; cf. Murray (1985:39–50).

13. Anacr. fr.36 Gent.; Mimn. 1, 2, 5 (*PLG*); Thgn. 567–70, 877–84, 1047–48, 1071–74, 1119–22 (W.); see also the numerous examples collected by Giangrande (1968:102–3, 109); Bowie (1986:13–35); Feeney (1993:41–63). Horace's originality lies in consistency. The only *carpe diem* poem without a sympotic referent is C.IV.7. The only arguable exception is C.II.16 (after the association is firmly established), but even here Horace cannot resist a convivial comment (13–16).

14. See C.I.9.9–15; 11.1–6; II.3.21–28; 11.1–17; 14.1–24; III.17.9–14; 19.1–8; 29.29–48; Commager (1957:68–80).

15. Death, which comes to every person regardless of status, and a simple lifestyle, which frees the poor from the worries enslaving the wealthy, create thematic connections between Horace's drinking songs and *Satires* (S.I.1, 2, 3, 4; II.2, 3, 5, 6). Other thematic parallels between the *Satires* and sympotic odes include the fickleness of family and friends (S.I.1.86–91; C.I.35.33–40; see Thgn. 115–16, 979–82 W.) and the rejection of epic panegyric (S.I.9; 10.40–49; II.1.10–20). The principle that bad men corrupt good morals (Thgn. 39–48 W.; Praxilla 749; 750 *PMG*) appears also in the *Satires* (I.4.105–39) but not in the sympotic odes.

16. The *Kreuzung* seriocomic as a descriptor for the sympotic should not be restricted to generic conflicts (although Horace plays genres against and with each other) but implies a game of combining contrasting moods and tones to enrich the emotional experience of the lyric moment. Martin (1931) defends the seriocomic nature of the sympotic motif, but the eccentricities of his book have caused it to be largely ignored; see Denniston's review of Martin in *CR* 45 (1931) 225–26. For the literary history of the symposion, see also von der Mühll (1976:483–505; a lecture originally delivered in 1926); Bielohlawek (1940:11–30); Giangrande (1968:91–177); Gallardo (1972:239–96; 1974:91–143); M. J. Vickers (1978). Given the arbitrary fancifulness and incompleteness of these studies, it

is not surprising that Murray still complained (1980:307): "A full study of the symposion is badly needed." This gap has been filled mostly by Murray himself (Murray, 1983a:257–72, 1983b:47–52, 1983c:195–99, 1990; Murray and Tecusan, 1995) and also by Lissarrague (1987), Slater (1991), Gowers (1993).

17. Lucius Sestius fought for Brutus in the civil wars and was proscribed. He was pardoned by Augustus, who came to respect Sestius's republican loyalties and later appointed him *consul suffectus* for the latter part of 23 B.C. (*PIR* 3.230, no.436; Lyne, 1995:73–75).

18. Horace highlights the movement of time by the synchysis of the temporal adverbs *iam* and *nunc,* which he places at the beginning of their lines, except for the first *iam,* which is postponed until after a negative (*ac neque iam,* 3; *iam,* 5; *nunc,* 9; *nunc,* 11; *iam,* 16; *nunc,* 20). Together the adverbs bring into contrast cyclical-immortal versus linear-mortal time (Lowrie, 1997:51–55). The break in the pattern (the delay of the first *iam*), obvious as the poem reaches its conclusion, brings into close relief the two pairs of negatives in the first and last stanzas (Syndikus, 1972:76). The first negatives set free the animals and farmer to enjoy spring; the last negatives imprison Sestius in the underworld outside of sympotic pleasures. The parallel is not exact because Horace pushes the negatives of the last stanza forward a line compared to stanza 1 to allow for the final "now." Horace leaves a slender moment of the present for Sestius to enjoy.

19. The secondary literature is divided between reading the poem as a pleasant spring ode (e.g., Quinn, 1980:127) or a pessimistic depiction of the brevity of life (e.g., Lyne, 1995:67). The "sudden" appearance of death (N.-H., 1970:60; Quinn, 1963:20; Lowrie, 1997:52) has brought into question the ode's structural integrity (Babcock, 1961:13; Levin, 1968:316; Lienieks, 1977:57). Death does not show up unexpectedly or suddenly. Death is a common feature in the sympotic tradition. Also, watching the seasons change (1–4) and viewing the ritual death of an animal to please an immortal god (10–11) naturally lead to thoughts of human mortality (12).

20. The best sense of lines 17–18 is that lovers' battles leave their wounds, the scratches ladies inflict on lovers' backs with their nails (see Commager, 1962:72; also Sybaris's bruises or lack of bruises, C.I.8.9–12). *Sectis* bothers critics; e.g., Peerlkamp (1834: *ad loc.*) calls these two lines a silly oxymoron. Bentley (1711: *ad loc.*) argues that *acrium* must mean the fights are real and dangerous (see Porphyrio; Orelli, 1837; K.-H., 1884: *ad loc.*). Bentley emends *sectis* to "strictis." Nisbet and Hubbard (N.-H., 1970:89) agree that the fight has to be real, but they retain *sectis.* Following Ps.-Acro they offer the meaning "the girl's nails were sharpened to a point." The problem is not *sectis* but *acrium* because violence is out of

place at a symposion, a point made elsewhere by Horace (C.I.17.21–28; 18.7–11; 27.1–8) and frequently in the Greek lyricists (see discussion later in this chapter). Still, it is unnecessary to tamper with *acrium;* its use is justified by the seriocomic interlacing that invites comparison with the heroic battles of the preceding stanzas, as well as by the common use of martial language to depict acts of love (see C.I.19; 27.9–24; II.8.13–16; III.20; IV.1.1–8, 15–18).

21. Likewise, Horace does not allow Tyndaris to forget the threats against her (C.I.17.25–28).

22. Although Horace did not invent the name (*LGPN* cites some twenty-seven examples in the Aegean islands and Cyprus alone; other instances include *IG* 1 589 [f. Εὐθύδικος], 929 [f. Ἐρεχθηίδος]; 5.1 1241 [f. Αὐρήλιος], 1424 [f. Ἀριστέας], 1436 [f. Πομπήιος]), he does use names for etymological games (e.g., Sybaris for a soft young Roman, C.I.8; Corvinus for a lover of wine, C.III.21). Given this pattern, Thaliarchus for συμποσίαρχος is credible (Orelli, 1837; K.-H., 1884:*ad loc.;* Commager, 1962:272; cf. Wickham, 1874:*proem;* Lefèvre, 1993a:147–48). That the poem is sympotic should be obvious from the thematic parallels to c.4: nature images for the passing of time; the *carpe diem* argument; a reference to the master of the feast; eroticism and dances (cf. Vessey, 1985:31; N.-H., 1970:121). Thaliarchus as symposiarch raises questions. How could Horace give orders to the *magister bibendi?* Most likely Thaliarchus is a servant, assigned that name to support the sympotic context. See Edmunds (1992:54–57); D. West (1995:43): Thaliarchus is a love interest whom the speaker is trying to win.

23. See C. II.7: in stanza 1 the soldiers Pompey and Horace risk death, and in stanza 3 Horace, imitating Archilochus 5 W., tosses away his shield. The intervening stanza 2 offers a blissful recollection of the time Horace spent drinking with his comrade. The generic implications are obvious: Horace, like the antiheroic Archilochus, would rather be at a symposion any day, sing his lyric, and avoid epic conflicts.

24. See Semon. 1.20–22a (W.).

25. See Thgn. 877–79; 983–88; 1063–68; 1129–32 (W.); Anacreontea 7, 30, 32, 34, 36, 38, 40, 42, 46 (*PLG*); Anon. fr.1009 (*PMG*); for additional parallels, see N.-H. (1970:71). Sympotic invitations in Plautus use the same rationale (*Most.*727–30; *Bac.*1195–1205). Theognis, 237–54 (W.), reverses the typical argument based on the brevity of life when he tells Cyrnus that his name will last as long as men sing at banquets (see also Ion of Chios 26.13–16 W.).

26. Also compare C.II.11.1–8, 13–17 with Thgn. 762–68 (W.). Solmsen (1948:105–9) sees Horace's influence in the third book of Propertius and its concern with the power of death. What was in Horace was readily available in the Greek lyricists.

27. Thgn. 211–12, 497–98, 499–510 (W.); Critias 6 (W.); Anacreontea 8, 47, 57 (*PLG*).

28. Some Horatian symposia are occasions for heavy drinking, often indicated by common verbs for intoxicating consumption, e.g., *potare* (*C.I.20.1*; II.11.17) and *ducere* (*C.I.17.22*; IV.12.14), or by the noun *merum*, which can denote uncut wine. The Greeks considered the practice of drinking uncut wine barbaric (the Cyclops drank unmixed wine, *Od.9.201–363*; uncut wine is a Scythian drink, Anacr. 356 *PMG*) and usually diluted their wine. There was no standard ratio of water to wine, and the strength of the mixtures varied widely (Theoc. 2.150–54; Athen. 10.429–31e). When Horace recommends drinking *merum*, he frequently uses a qualifying adjective to indicate a degree of mildness (*molli mero*, *C.I.7.19*; *quadrimum merum*, *C.I.9.7–8*; *dulci mero*, *C.III.13.2*; *lene merum*, *C.III.29.2*). Excluding ritual libations and the ecstatic celebration over the return of a lover or friend (*C.I.36.13*; II.7.6; also I.20), *merum* typically signifies the revelry associated with immoderation and drunken brawls (Postumus's heir, *C.II.14.26–27*; Lydia's lover Telephus, *C.I.13.10*; the Lapiths and centaurs, *C.I.18.8–9*; II.12.5). To place *priscus* Cato in the same company as these characters illustrates the extreme farce of Horace's hymn to his wine jar (*C.III.21.11–12*). Usually Horace omits the amount drunk or strength of the wine mixture (cf. *C.III.19.11–16*) and in general is critical of sympotic violence.

29. Thgn. 475–78, 627–28, 837–40, 873–76 (W.); also Xenoph. 1.17–20 (W.); Euenus 2 (W.).

30. Alc. 358 (L.-P.); Anacr. 356b (*PMG*), see *C.I.27*.

31. Archil. 4, 42, 120 (W.); Alc. 38A, 332 (see *C.I.37*), 335, 338, 346 (see *C.III.19*), 347 (L.-P.); Thgn. 533–34 (W.). See Bowra (1961:150–57) on the robust tone of Alcaean symposia.

32. Against violence, see Thgn. 841–44 (W.); Xenoph. 1.19–24 (W.); Dionys. Eleg. 2 (W.); Anacreontea 2, 3, 5, 42 (*PLG*). B. 13 (*PLG*) makes the sympotic setting synonymous with peace. When Diniarchus blames his act of rape on wine, Callicles responds that men should control wine and not wine control men (Pl. *Truc.*829–31; see also *Per.*795–810; *Bac.*69–72). In *C.I.27* the poet lightens the mood of a sympotic brawl with playful banter against Megylla's brother. The shift may not be as sharp as Nisbet and Hubbard think (N.-H., 1970:309), since such iambic exchanges are part of sympotic humor (Burckhardt, 1930, 4:159; M. L. West, 1974:22–39). Against reckless speech: Thgn. 295–98, 413–14 (W.); Pl. *As.*799–802; cf. Tigellius in *S.I.3*.

33. E.g., Alc. 38A (L.-P.); Thgn. 1129–32 (W.).

34. Phoc. 11 (*PLG*) prescribes both heavy drinking (οἰνοποτάζειν; see *Il.20.84*; *Od.6.309*; 20.262) and pleasant conversation. Anacreontea 38 (*PLG*) provides a more typical contrast: a lament for the brevity of life in-

terrupting an erotic symposion. The pattern can be inverted and the serious interrupted by the comic; e.g., Alc. 347 (L.-P.): cicada sweetly singing and artichoke in flower separate harsh weather (2) and oppressive heat (4–6).

35. Ion 27 (W.): religious ritual (1–6); sympotic revelry (7–10). Balancing lines: Archil. 13 (W.), Thgn. 1047–48 (W.). Couplets: Thgn. 1129–32 (W.), Euenus 2 (W.), Anacreontea 17 (*PLG*). Sections: B. 13 (*PLG*), Anacreontea 36 (*PLG*).

36. See Sapph. 1 and 94 (L.-P.); Thgn. 757–64, 765–68, 973–78 (W.); Anacreontea 7 (*PLG*).

37. Consider B. 13 (*PLG*), where ritual sacrifice (3–4) interrupts the lighter tone of wealth and songs (1–2) and youthful delights (5). The seriocomic of the sympotic setting is further depicted by the unused weapons (6–9), the erotic revels in the streets, and the boys' passionate hymns (12).

38. Compare Gerber (1970:238, 243–47) and Marcovich (1991:60–75).

39. Contrast Plato's and Xenophon's symposia. The comic in the *Symposium* is most evident in the interludes (184C4–85E5; 189A–C; 193D8–94E2; 198A–99C2; 212C4–15A3), except for the intriguing discussion, which closes the party, that the same poet ought to be able to write comedy and tragedy. Xenophon's sympotic humor is much more coarse (the antics of Philip the clown) and is more varied and visual (juggling and mimes). For a concise listing of sympotic entertainment, see Boardman (1974:209–11; 1975:218–20).

40. For the Eastern influence on Greek symposia, see Dentzer (1982); M. J. Vickers (1990:105–21); Grottanelli (1995:62–89). See Tomlinson (1990:98–100) on the date when reclining became customary at the Greek banquet (also at C.I.1.21–22; 27.8; II.3.6–7; 7.17–19; III.3.11; *Epist.*I.5.1).

41. There was an explosion of sympotic representation in the Greek archaic period; see Reitzenstein (1893). Banquet imagery has a long history in funerary art and custom. Funerary plaques often picture banquet scenes. From Thasos (5th century B.C.) there is a relief of the deceased drinking on a banquet couch (Vermeule, 1979:57–58). On Etruscan cinerary urns and sarcophagi the most common position for figures is reclining in the manner of a banqueter; e.g., a woman seated at the feet of a reclining male (Museo Archeologico, Florence 10,031); a reclining male holding a bowl (*Obesus etruscus*, Clusium 11,266); Pallottino (1955:pl. 93, 94) and von Matt (1970:pl. 137, 164–69). The death theme in literary banquets reflects perhaps on a subconscious level funerary ritual that incorporates feasting as a symbol of the afterlife. Thus feasting as a respite from warfare becomes a powerful metaphor for immortality; e.g., after Nestor and the injured Machaon retire from the fighting

and while the Greek forces suffer key losses, these two share a healing wine potion and conversation, a type of symposion surrounded by death (*Il*.11.618–803).

42. For the archaeological evidence, see Bergquist (1990:37–65).

43. On sympotic groups in the conflicts between the Greek aristocracy and democracy: Calhoun (1913:17–24, 97–147); Snell (1965:64–79); Murray (1990:149–61).

44. The melancholy Horace, consumed with thoughts of death and how he might escape it through literary fame, is a common character in Horatian criticism; e.g., Cannon (1966:86); Levin (1968:315–20). Even now this is a common impression of Horace, particularly in *Odes* IV.

45. See also Horace's martial Alcaeus combined immediately with a sympotic Alcaeus singing of Liber, the Muses, and Venus (C.I.32.5–12; Lowrie, 1995:40). Cf. Porter (1987:106): "From poems set in the artificial world of erotic sympotic poetry Horace moves back toward poems in which contemporary Roman citizens and Roman issues hold center stage." "Artificial" is a difficult description when the symposion and its poetry celebrate the essentials of life and death, eating and drinking.

46. The metaphor of returning from death to life and the heavy drinking identify Maecenas's recovery from an illness (I.20) and Horace's escape from the falling tree (III.8) with the Return Odes.

47. Horace gives no specific definition of epic beyond martial themes narrated in dactylic hexameter (*Ars* 73–74, 401–3), but when he puts forward Homer as a model, Horace highlights his swiftness (*Ars* 148–52); see Newman (1986:64). Therefore, Horace defines Homer's greatness by qualities compatible with lyric.

48. This simple characterization of the Horatian *recusatio* addresses the basic extremes of Horace's lyric to epic contrast concerning quality and motive: both the poor quality of epic praise poetry versus the refined excellence of Horatian lyric and the political pressures of epic praise versus the political freedom in lyric. Typical Horatian *recusationes* of praise poetry include C.I.6; 19.9–12; II.1; 12; IV.2; 15; *Epist*.II.1.1–4, 245–70; cf. Race's broader listing (1978:191–93). See also my discussion of the *recusatio* in C.IV.15, ch. 5.

49. Lowrie (1995:46): "It is hardly fortuitous that the poem that provides the hinge between the two parades [lyric meters and lyric predecessors, C.I.1–18] is C.I.11, the 'carpe diem' poem that defines so much of Horatian ideology." I would change 'carpe diem' to sympotic, the more inclusive signifier.

50. My view that Augustan poets accentuate the paradox of fatness within thinness has been influenced by Bing (1988), Cameron (1992:305–12; 1995: 454–83), Cody (1976), Klein (1974:217–31), Race (1978:179–86; 1988:1–34), Wimmel (1960), Davis (1991:11), and most notably Newman

(1967a; 1967b; 1974:342–60; 1986; 1990); several conversations with K. Freudenburg have helped clarify my thinking on the paradox, as well as on the likelihood that there was a mounting pressure on Augustan poets to write epic praise poetry. Whether Callimachus criticizes epic or a type of bad elegy has become a matter for intense debate (Cameron, 1995:471), but certainly Vergil, Horace, and Propertius extend Callimachus's criticism to epic's heroic themes and more specifically to epic-styled panegyric. Cameron's "principal inspiration," while fun to argue, may be impossible to identify, since the Horatian *recusationes* demonstrate that Horace is relating together and revising a variety of models.

51. Most editions retain *Onysius,* although the name is not attested. *Dionysius* seems more likely (Vaticanus lat. 3866) or *Oniscus* (Reifferscheid, 1860:*ad loc.*). There has been no adequate solution for *ut accusantem;* Bentley's "ut accusem te" (1711:*ad loc.*) or Reifferscheid's "ut excusantem" are cited most often. I translate "without faulting" to fit the general sense: Horace is sending the book to satisfy a request by Augustus, and Augustus considers his request fulfilled. The *libellum* could be *Epist.*II.1, which Augustus requested, or any other of Horace's poems.

52. I do not mean to attribute too much—or too little—literary finesse to Augustus. Whether Augustus was a careful reader is an interesting question probably without a definitive answer (cf. Suet. *Aug.*89; cf. Galinsky, 1975:211–12). Augustus's joke may be more learned than we have thought: its two comic comparisons (your book looks like you, short and fat; your scroll reminds me of a piece from a wine jar, short but well-rounded like your belly) bring together brevity and fatness with a drinking (sympotic) metaphor (even funnier if the messenger's name is Dionysius). The joke encapsulates the poetics of Horace's sympotic persona. Augustus may have already known the joke. Horace uses much the same comic routine when he tells a strong Vinnius (*vinum*) not to work up a sweat lugging Horace's heavy little books to Augustus (*Epist.*I.13). On the exact sense of *sextariolus* (the diminutive of *sextarius,* a jar of some kind; or a unit of measure; or a name brand of papyrus): Horace's poetry does not have to fit on some shard from a pot or in a pint for the joke to make sense (cf. Tovar, 1968:334–41).

53. Galinsky (1975:210–17) warns against overpoliticizing Augustan poetry; also McKeown (1984:174–78); Feeney (1992b:1–6); Kennedy (1992:35); G. D. Williams (1994:154–58). Galinsky (214): "Ovid [and Horace] writes *recusatio* poems . . . because he wants to demonstrate that he can write *recusatio* poems." This is possible, although Horace also sensitizes his audiences to the politics of his *recusationes* by imposing into his satiric and lyric to epic contrasts different motivations: satire or lyric, written for literary pleasure and excellence, compared to epic, written for profit.

54. The precise dynamics of the patron-client relationship are an open question because it is simply impossible to conceptualize fully the relationship between persons with static rules. Horace, while he presents himself as sensitive to how his social status is perceived, provides no unqualified insight. As suits the poetic occasion, he can be an intimate friend of Maecenas or an inferior dependent. For an introduction to Roman patronage, see Gold (1982, 1987); Saller (1982); Ahl (1984); Wallace-Hadrill (1989); P. White (1993); Konstan (1995); Bowditch (2001); McNeill (2001).

55. See on s.9: Salmon (1952:184–93); Anderson (1956:148–66); Fraenkel (1957:112–18); Rudd (1961:79–96; 1966:74–85); Buchheit (1968:519–55); Freudenburg (1993:209–11); J. Henderson (1999:202–27); Lefèvre (1993a:52–54); Courtney (1994:1–8). Horace's no-named *ille* has been given many names; I call him neoteric because he engages Horace in a greeting game of Catullan vocabulary and then attempts to rewrite Horace's theme of *moderatio* by manipulating a common elegiac construct (the paraklausithyron) and cleverly alluding to Horace's own satiric persona. He knows well the art of poetic compression via the learned allusion. I call him epic because like a bad epic poet he seems unlikely to go away any time soon.

56. Much of this satire depends on form, the combination of dialogue and reported narrative creating a sophisticated mode of discourse (Rudd, 1966:76). Horace thinks some responses in his head and retells them later (e.g., 11–12); others are only part of the later narrative to another person or persons (e.g., 20–21). Sometimes it is hard to tell whether Horace only thought a remark at the time, said it later, or both (e.g., 28–34). Either way the narrative strategy excludes the other poet because he never hears much of the satire, which leaves him defenseless. By manipulating the forms of speech, Horace can make the other poet seem highly intuitive (albeit usually in an obnoxious way), picking up on what Horace thinks by the way he behaves (cf. Horace, *misere discedere quaerens* [8], with the pest, '*misere cupis . . . abire*' [14])—or incredibly unaware, when, for example, nameless recommends himself for the very talents Horace despises (cf. 19, 23–25 with Horace's attacks on Lucilius, on Crispinus's absurd challenge [*S.I.4.12–13*, 16], and on Hermogenes [*S.I.3.9*]). Then again, has this other poet interested in meeting Maecenas been so disinterested in Horace, his possible ticket into the circle, that he is totally unaware of Horace's poetic tastes? He could be quoting lines back to Horace with a kind of in-your-face obstinacy. Horace's dialogue-narrative obfuscates the character of nameless.

57. *Dulcis, -e* is a standard Catullan modifier for loves and pleasures. Nothing could be "more charming and refined" (*seu suavius elegantiusve est*, 13.10) than Catullan poetry filled with Lesbia's fragrance. The dra-

matic circumstances of Catullus 13 parallel s.9. Catullus answers Fabullus that he can come to dinner at Catullus's house, if he brings the feast. Catullus's humor works well, if Fabullus has asked to enjoy Catullus's hospitality without a formal invitation—a similar situation to Horace's pest. Fabullus, though, is no pest; he is welcome as long as he brings dinner. Catullus will give him Lesbia's perfume, a metaphor for the love poems Catullus will share; see C.IV.12 when Horace orders Vergil to bring nard (song) to the party (ch.4, Songs of Mo(u)rning).

58. Cat. 10 and s.9 share a similar mode of discourse (reported conversation); see Freudenburg (1993:210).

59. My argument is a logical extension of Buchheit's (1968): Horace's satire is a literary agon touting the principle of *brevitas* (cf. van Rooy, 1972:41–46).

60. See Anderson (1956:156). Truncated epic diction = my neoteric pest of epic proportions.

61. The paraklausithyron is the sympotic revelry through the streets that ends with the κωμαστής locked out in front of a lover's door or more specifically the song the κωμαστής sings to try to gain admittance; see also C.IV.13 in ch.4.

62. This exchange (41–60) has been consistently read as a military metaphor only (except perhaps Rudd's translation of 56–58, 1966:83). Assaulting a city (Maecenas) may be the extent of the metaphor as the satirist Horace puts it in play (*contendere, victore, expugnabis, vinci, primos aditus*); the pest, however, extends the metaphor by turning the siege of Maecenas into a battle for a lover as indicated by his erotic vocabulary (*accendis, cupiam, exclusus fuero*). See C.III.15.9: Pholoë storms (*expugnat*) the homes of her young lovers. I note from P. R. Hardie's comments on Ovid's duplicity (2002:3) that the door of this satire's paraklausithyron locks certain authors (and audiences) inside and outside the text (Derrida's "threshold of writing," referenced in P. Pucci, 1978:67) either present with or absent from the poetic-political powers, either comprehending or not the satire's literary warfare.

63. K.-H. (1884:*ad loc.*) trace the pest's saying to Ps.-Phocylides 162–63 (Young, 1971) and eventually to the Branchidae oracle. The sentiment, however, is common, and the sources attributing the saying to the oracle are often inaccurate (Horst, 1978:220–21). Closer to home, the pest's immoderate credo is the exact opposite of Horace's sermonizing (S.I.1.40, 62; 2.28; 3.9, 17, 18–19; J. Henderson, 1999:214).

64. To rephrase the pest's cynicism, should Horace's friendship (*amicitia*) with Maecenas be interpreted as a euphemism for the business transactions between poet and patron (Saller, 1982:1–39; 1989:49–62; Lyne, 1995:14–16), or was theirs a genuine friendship (Suet. *Vit. Hor.*11–17; Bowditch, 2001:19–27)? Horace exploits the ambiguity. For example,

he claims Maecenas does not confide anything important to him (*S.*II.6.40–58); he had to compose poems for money, which he never would have admitted to the pest (*Epist.*II.2.49–54). Then again, Maecenas like Vergil is part of Horace's own soul (*C.*II.17.1–12; IV.11.17–20). Perhaps the pest's cynicism is a justified reaction to Horace's double-talk; cf. DuQuesnay's certainty (1984:52–53).

65. Roman civil law required a sworn witness to a forced summons to escort the litigants to the magistrate. Therefore, does Horace really escape? Mazurek (1997:1–17) thinks not. Horace may not have escaped the pest's physical presence, but in a law court the pest must speak according to prescribed standards. Horace escapes from further questions without giving any final answer.

66. Or from Lucilius (231 32 [Marx]: <*nil*> *ut discrepet ac* 'τὸν δὲ ἐξήρπαξεν Ἀπολλών' *fiat*). Because of the fragmentary condition of Lucilius's satires, reaction to Iltgen's theory (1872:19–20; see Fiske, 1920:330–36) that Lucilius's sixth book included a satire on a pest has varied widely from acceptance as a good probability to restricting Lucilian influence to Horace's first (*Ibam forte via Sacra*; cf. *ibat forte aries; ibat forte domum*, Lucil. 534 and 1142 [Marx]) and last lines; cf. Anderson (1956:148–53); and Rudd (1961:90–96). The Homeric context is as important for reading Horace's satire as the Lucilian (Porphyrio, *ad loc.*).

67. Anderson (1956:152).

68. Cf. J. Henderson's a/lert (1999:204–5): "Face it: in this modernity of rat-race cynicism, unabashed elbowing up the heap, poetry is, exactly, prostitution, snobbery, and social climbing"; also without Henderson's iambic venom, Rudd (1966:84); Zetzel (1980:71).

69. *Ultra / legem*, 1–2: Trebatius thinks Horace is concerned that some consider his poetry libelous. But Horace is addressing the art of satire, the aesthetic of invective, serious and hard-hitting versus insipid and trite (Anderson, 1984:35–42; G. Harrison, 1987:49–52). The fact that Horace's critics are divided between such extremes actually proves Horace has found the middle ground (see Freudenburg, 1990:192—the satire should not be taken too seriously). Nevertheless, the muddled boundaries between law, politics, and aesthetics and their degree of interaction is one of the satire's primary tensions (see Rudd, 1966:130–31; Leeman, 1982:160–62; 1983:209–15; Muecke, 1995:203–6).

70. On C. Trebatius Testa, see *PIR* 3.333, no.228; Fraenkel (1957:145–47); Leeman (1982:159). Horace's satire confirms that Trebatius liked to swim (Cic. *Fam.*7.10.2), enjoyed a good drinking bout (*Fam.*7.22), and possessed a keen literary mind (*Fam.*7.6; 7.12; 7.16). Cicero ribs him for his unlimited ambition and how much pleasure he takes in the status and money that comes with being the lawyer for Julius Caesar (*Fam.* 7.13.1). Trebatius has experienced the imperial rewards he is advising Horace to pursue.

71. All the components of a *recusatio* are present: the refusal to write praise, the poet's humility, and a recommendation of another poet for the task, the epicist; see Wimmel (1960:162–67); Muecke (1995:215–18). Clauss (1985:199–201) argues that Horace develops his *recusatio* from a Lucilian model (II6 fr.620, 622; earlier Fraenkel, 1957:150).

72. Lines 12b–15 (*'vires / deficiunt. neque enim quivis horrentia pilis / agmina nec fracta pereuntis cuspide Gallos / aut labentis equo describat vulnera Parthi.'*) hide a complex metrical joke. Horace is not modeling outstanding epic lines. These lines remind that even the best epic writers, even Ennius, compose some bad verses (Freudenburg, 2001: 88–92). Horace introduces his martial epic verses with the enjambed "deficient" (*vires / deficiunt*), and the end of the line, *horrentia pilis / agmina*, recalls Ennius's *sparsis hastis longis campus splendet* [*et*] *horret* (Courtney, 1993:28–29, fr.33), a line that Lucilius sarcastically corrected to *horret et al*get (fr.1190 [Marx]; Serv. *A.*11.601) and that probably was the Ennian line Horace had in mind when he defended his criticism of Lucilius with the counter-argument that Lucilius laughed at Ennius (*S.*I.10.54–55). The Ennian line has multiple gaffes, including a droning and broken disyllabic rhyming assonance that emphasizes the last syllable of every word (*-is, -is, -is, -us, -et, -et, -et*), but it is a dull verse primarily because of its complete coincidence: every word fills a foot and every beat matches the word accent (Marius Victorinus, Keil VI. p.64.31–65.13, 71.11–18, 24–32; Atilius Fortuniatianus, Keil VI. p.282.17–25, 284.12–29; Priscian, Keil III. p.460.16–23; Winbolt, 1903:70; Wilkinson, 1963:96). Horace's imitation is a perfect metrical *recusatio*. Horace draws attention to the monotony of Ennius's verse by placing the common image *horrentia pilis* in the fifth and sixth feet where coincidence is expected (13), while in the first four feet he corrects the coincidence in every foot as if he were a harsh Roman teacher disciplining a student and adding in the appropriate caesurae. Then, after Horace references the allusion with *horrentia*, his next line carries on the coincidence except in the third foot right at the word *fracta* (broken)—a howler of a joke at Ennius's expense. In short, Horace, while writing rather juvenile hexameter, demonstrates he is master of the art and has a laugh along the way. Thanks to Andrew Becker for his helpful comments on the metrics of these lines.

73. In general on II.1, I support Tatum's fine reading (1998:691–93). I only wonder whether Trebatius's advice to praise Caesar is a specific suggestion to switch to writing epic or whether Horace assumes this, and then Trebatius is a clever enough *literatus* to recognize Horace's generic subterfuge and call him on it. I rather like the idea of the lawyer, enriched by representing the imperial family, catching the poet at his literary game.

74. See Oliensis (1998:42); I would only emphasize that Horace's satiric panegyric persona is not so confident. Horace continues at least the pretense of the humble posture of the *recusatio*. He does not trust

himself to be able to speak in Caesar's ear at just the right time. Cf. C.III.25: praising Augustus is a sweet danger (*dulce periculum*).

75. *Seu fors ita iusserit, exsul* (59b) would send chills up Ovid's spine (see Oliensis, 1998:44). Horace's determined refusal to give up his satire corresponds to the persistent pest's creed to win his way in to Maecenas at exactly the same lines, 57-60.

76. On Choerilus of Iasus and his few surviving lines, see *EGF, FGrH, SH*; also *RE* 3.2361-63 s.v. *Choirilos* (5); *Der Neue Pauly* 2.1139 s.v. *Choirilos* [3]; Brink (1971:365-66; 1982:244); Cameron (1995:278-79). Alexander had at least four other poets to record his deeds: Agis of Argos, Anaximanes of Lampsacus, Pyrrho of Elis, and Cleo of Sicily. These poets became the standard for poor poetry and Choerilus the most defamed of them all (Curt. 8.5.7-8). Their critics highlight two faults: (1) falling short of Homeric *ingenium*; (2) engaging in exaggerated flattery to win Alexander's favor (Porph. on *Ars* 347; Ps.-Acr. on *Epist*.II.1.233; Aus. *Ep*.9a.11-14 [Green, 1991:201]). The criticism against the poets often incriminates Alexander for his poor literary taste (cf. Porphyrio's anecdote on Alexander's criticism of Choerilus). Cameron questions identifying Choerilus as an epic poet. What meager evidence on Choerilus's verse that survives consistently indicates a writer of epic by describing his work as long (*tanto opere*, Ps.-Acr.) and comparing him to Homer (Philodemus, *FGrH* 72 T fr.26-27 and 153 F VII fr.10-12; Fest. p.360.10-11 [Lindsay, 1913]). Horace clearly presents Choerilus as an epic poet. He compares Choerilus to Varius, Vergil, and Homer and then follows the comparison with his standard *recusatio*.

77. On Plato, see Nightingale (1995:55-59).

78. Bowditch (2001:50-53) argues that the gift economy of patronage depends on a "disequilibrium" in the value of the gifts given and received in favor of the patron so that the client never fully discharges his debt, and the relationship must be continued. Thus patronage produces social cohesion. Horace's presentation of exchange and its benefits (*amicitia*) is more balanced and mutual. His persistent emphasis on *moderatio* (aversion to such banausia) requires an equilibrium in the exchange, and therefore his "voluntarism" (Bowditch's term) or autonomy becomes less of a pretense. For instance, Horace's claim to nobility in the *Epistles* and *Odes* IV (n.b. c.3) stresses such equality. Poetry is the highest service, and Horace can name its price (C.IV.8.10b-11).

79. Horace is taking his own advice, S.I.1.118-19.

80. A reader tuned in to Horace's music could already answer my question. Horace gives away the irony behind his faltering silence with the hypermetric *cur facunda parum decoro / inter verba cadit lingua silentio?* (35-36).

81. See *scribere, Epist*.II.1.109-17, 219-28.

82. On Ovid's exilic persona (less metaphoric than Horace's or not?) Tarrant (2002:29–31) comments, "The minimalist rhetoric of these passages is painfully moving."

83. How much does *Epist.*I.17.19–22 apply to Horace?

84. Lyne (1995:9–11) and previously Armstrong (1986:255–88).

85. Horace in c.1 pulls together a variety of poetic forms (Putnam, 1986:36 n.1; Porter, 1975:nn.1–2): an epithalamium (a secondary consideration for Kiessling, 1884: *proem*; developed by Bradshaw, 1970:142–53, and Habinek, 1986:407–16); an *apopompe* for Venus (Fraenkel, 1957:410); a propempticon blessing Venus on her journey to Fabius's house; and hints of a *recusatio* (Commager, 1962:291–97; Lefèvre, 1968:166–89). This is also the closest Horace comes outside of the *Epodes* to the tone of love elegy. Moving from one form to the next with seamless transitions, Horace keeps the audience guessing what will come next.

86. *OLD* s.v. *venus*, 4; Adams (1982:57, 98, 188–89).

87. *Durus* is not a common descriptor for an erection (cf. *intendere/intentus, tendere, rigidus, tentigo*), but Juvenal, when describing how certain eunuchs are able to have an erection (6.377), refers to an adolescent just reaching manhood as *iam durum*. In such a context "hardness" likely refers to more than the roughness of a first beard.

88. Cinara, the artichoke (κινάρα; σκόλυμος), when taken with wine was thought to be an aphrodisiac (Davis, 1991:65–71; also M. Lowrie's review of Davis in *BMCR* 2, 1991:421; Nagy, 1994a:421–22). Horace misses his *Cinara* now. Stoppard's/Housman's Mr. Fry or scholarly Richard Bentley, caught in the ambiguity of *intermissa*, could not appreciate the poet's fun (see Stoppard, 1998:47–48).

89. Cf. Men. Rh. 407: the person giving a κατευναστικὸς λόγος, an encouragement to the wedding couple for sexual intercourse, should mention the guests' and his own prowess in lovemaking.

90. Maximus's father, Q. Fabius, died in 45 B.C. Maximus must have been born at least by the preceding year, 46. It is unlikely Horace wrote c.1 earlier than the *CS* (17 B.C.), which would mean Maximus could be no younger than twenty-nine, rather old for a Roman aristocrat to marry. It is speculation whether this was his first marriage (Syme, 1986:403).

91. Murray (1985:41) prefers c.15 as the proem to book IV.

2. *Encomia Nobilium* and Horace's Panegyric Praxis

1. The epigraph translation was taken from Russell and Wilson (1981: *ad loc.*).

2. Others also have doubts about Suetonius's word choice, e.g., Brink (1982:243); P. White (1993:115); Hills (2001:615–16).

3. Also Freudenburg (2002:139–40). McNeill (2001:75) reads *Epist.*II.

1.111–13 as an admission from Horace that he was writing *carmina* all the time; *versus* (111), however, is not so specific. Horace describes all poetry composed in response to societal pressures.

4. Encomia addressed to noblemen, married into the imperial family (1, 2), are balanced by two imperial praises (14, 15). C.3 and 6 (two hymns celebrating the poet's inspiration), enclosing two imperial praise pieces for Drusus and Augustus (4, 5), are grouped against another set of four odes (10–13), sympotic lyrics akin to *Odes* I–III. Left in the middle are three odes to noblemen (7–9), which have at their center (8) praise for the poet. Horace has ensured that the poet remains central.

5. Lyne (1995:30, 189–90) judges Augustus's views on literature simplistic. What we know of Augustus's literary perception and tastes derives from Suetonius, whose account indicates that Augustus knew how to modify language to fit the circumstances (*Aug*.85–89). For instance, Augustus's oratorical style and prose rhythms were moderate (as is evident in the *RG*), but he was free in his correspondence, where colloquialism would be more appropriate, to coin new expressions (e.g., *baceolus* for *stultus*). Augustus's ability to manipulate language and his use of monuments for his own imaging suggest a pragmatic and sophisticated literary sense; see Augustus's joke that Horace's poems were short and fat like their poet (ch.1).

6. Also Kennedy (1992:29).

7. On the nature of Maecenas's power in the 20s, see Brink (1982:528–30); G. Williams (1990:258–75); P. White (1991:130–38); Lyne (1995:132–38). That Maecenas lost first place in the collection is certainly significant (the break from past practice would be noticed) but is too circumstantial to confirm that Maecenas fell from Augustus's favor after he gossiped to his wife about the conspiracy of Murena (Suet. *Aug*.66.3; Tac. *Ann*.3.30). Regardless of the status Maecenas had lost in the political hierarchy at the time of *Odes* IV, Horace still honors Maecenas with an ode celebrating his birthday (c.11).

8. There is no evidence for competition between Tiberius and Maximus when c.1 was written (early 16 B.C. near the time of Maximus's marriage) and published. Maximus's career, however, continued to flourish while Tiberius's favor with Augustus declined. By the time of his exile Ovid overlooks Tiberius, mentioned in the *Fasti* in only later revisions, and turns to Maximus for help (*Pont*.1.2.113–18; 3.3.1–4, 95–108; see Syme, 1986:403, 409).

9. On Maximus's age, see ch.1; political career, *PIR*[2] 3.103–5, no. 47; *RE* 6.1780–89 s.v. *Fabius* 102; Syme (1978:135–55; 1986:124, 396, 403–20); the importance of aristocratic marriage alliances to the Fabii, Münzer (1920:98–109). The rumors about Maximus's death (Tac. *Ann*.1.5; cf. Syme) increase the irony of the love encomium for Horace's future au-

dience. Maximus, like many heroes, was ruined by his beloved. Cassius Severus's scathing epigram on Maximus (Sen. *Cont*.2.4.11–12, Håkanson [1989]) is certainly not the entire story.

10. It is unnecessary to justify Horace's praise, unless one assumes that panegyric must be entirely serious. Fraenkel (1957:413–14) argues that Horace includes verse 14 to elevate the praise to an acceptable level. Horace's attempt here, even allowing for the erotic parameters, could hardly qualify as typical praise for a nobleman. The praise of Censorinus (c.8) and Lollius (c.9) would come closer. Bradshaw (1970:142–53; see Habinek, 1986:413) attempts to temper Horace's characterization of Maximus by insisting that *commissor* lose its riotous edge ("singing a triumphal song" in the Pindaric sense of κωμάζειν) so that the eulogy is appropriate for a man courting a relative of Augustus. Even in ritual contexts Pindar's κωμάζειν does not lose its revelry.

11. The portrait of Maximus is best understood as contingent on that of the poet; e.g., Maximus's eloquence heightens the frustration of Horace's faltering tongue, 35–36; Habinek, 1986:413–14.

12. Hyperbole need not be negative (P. R. Hardie, 1986:241–92), although Horace's praise for Maximus demonstrates that panegyric is the product of imagination and that hyperbole can introduce seriocomic tensions difficult to read. Horace constantly plays with such tensions in his encomia.

13. Iullus Antonius, son of Mark Antony and Fulvia, was raised by Octavia and became a favorite with Augustus. Antonius had a fine political career (co-consul, 10 B.C., with Africanus Fabius Maximus, Paulus's brother, c.1), but he died in disgrace (2 B.C.) after he was caught in an adulterous scandal with Augustus's daughter Julia (Vell. 2.100; Plu. *Ant*.87; Tac. *Ann*.4.44; Cass. Dio 51.15; 54.26; 55.1; 55.10; *PIR*[2] 1.153–54, no. 800; Schanz-Hosius, 1935:2.273; Syme, 1986:144, 396–99). Horace's later readers could note that infidelity does not sit well after an encomium portraying Maximus as the great lyric lover while engaged to Augustus's cousin Marcia.

14. G. Williams (1990:270–72) does not consider IV.2 and 15 *recusationes*, and certainly in details they break from Horace's pattern. In c.2 there is no admonitory figure to stop the poet from singing martial themes, but only the briefest suggestion that Iullus would be better suited to sing Augustus's triumph. This would be enough to bring to mind the *recusatio* for an audience so accustomed to this Horatian tactic (parvus / *carmina fingo. / concines* maiore *poeta* plectro, c.2.31b–33; *sed neque* parvum / *carmen maiestas recipit tua*, Epist.II.1.257b–258a; *quaere modos* leviore plectro, C.II.1.40). Williams also neglects the martial Apollo of c.6 and admonitory Apollo of c.15. Cf. Race (1978:192).

15. See Davis (1991:11–30).

16. Freis (1983:27–36).

17. After his triumph over Dalmatia, Actium, and Egypt (29 B.C.), Augustus declined all others, but it is unclear when this solidified into recognized official policy; cf. DuQuesnay (1990:132 n.22). If Horace wrote his praise before he knew there would be no triumph, he certainly knew when he published it (13 B.C.). If Horace had wanted to play it safe, he could have avoided prophetic praise altogether and had Iullus sing of a clear-cut victory. A triumph that never was for a battle never fought exemplifies well Antonius's exaggerated Pindaric style (see Cicero's criticism of Greek panegyric for attributing false triumphs to their heroes, *Brut*.62). For a complete view of the debate surrounding the *clades Lolliana*, see c.9 later in this chapter. For the Sygambri as a symbol of Augustan peace, see C.IV.14.51–52. It is difficult to begin with a projected triumph over the Sygambri, call further attention to the *clades* by praising Lollius's victorious arms (IV.9.43–44), and then use with total seriousness the same tribe as the crowning example of Augustan peace (c.14); cf. Prop. 4.6.77–79.

18. Fraenkel (1957:438–39); Syndikus (1973:307–08); S. J. Harrison (1995b:123).

19. See Seager (1993:36).

20. Cf. the poet's enthusiasm over Actium (*Ep*.9.21–23). Is the second person (49) Augustus or Antonius (cf. Putnam, 1986:58 n.20; S. J. Harrison (1995b:123)? Either identification retains the incongruity between the communal praise (45–52) and Antonius's grand Pindaric praise (33–44). It is tempting to take every "you" (33, 41, 49, and 53) as the same person, Antonius, and I prefer, like Putnam, the reading of the *deteriores*, *tuque*, over the majority reading, *teque* (49). Antonius then leads the procession. Placing Antonius in such a prominent role complements the hyperbolic quality of his panegyric persona (cf. Kirby, 1992:42–50). Perhaps part of the panegyrist's fun is that he disguises who plays the lead in praising Augustus: the crowd, Iullus, or himself.

21. Horace's sources for the bee metaphor give away the mix: Pindar (*P*.10.53–54), Callimachus (*Ap*.110–12; *Aet*. fr.1.29–30 Pf.), and Vergil (*G*.4.179); cf. Putnam, (1986:55–56).

22. Cf. *Epist*.I.3.6–29.

23. Cf. Fitzgerald (1987:80–83); Kirby (1992:44–45); Nagy (1994a:416).

24. Obviously Horace does not apply his warning against competing with Pindar (c.2) to himself.

25. Verrall (1884:7 n.1); Becker (1963:180–82). Cf. Estévez (1982:279–300).

26. Fraenkel (1957:407, 410) sensed as much when he argued that c.3 and 6 were the "first fruits" of Horace's return to lyric after the success of the *CS*; Putnam (1986:74–75 n.23).

27. Horace's listing of boxing, chariot racing, and warfare (c.2; 3) introduces the epinikion (c.4), since Horace classifies epinikia by contest (*Ars* 84; see Sider, 2001:285 n.29). On the priamel form, see Race's (1982) classic.

28. Those holding this view do not necessarily think less of Horace's poetry; e.g., Putnam (1986:16–22); Lyne (1995:38–39); McNeill (2001:131–34). My arguments defend Armstrong (1997:398–401) against what McNeill labels his "overstatement" of the independent Horace. Imperial praise (see ch.3 and 5) is not as free from disputes (*dubia*) as presumed.

29. Horace's pride in the *CS* (*Epist*.II.1.132–138) should not be so belittled; see Putnam (2000) on the poet's vatic power in the *CS*.

30. Sulla: Venus (Balsdon, 1951:1–10); Julius Caesar: Venus (Weinstock, 1971:83–111); Sextus Pompeius: Neptune (Taylor, 1931:120–21); Marc Antony: Dionysus (Scott, 1929:133–41; 1933:7–49). The literature on Augustus and Apollo is vast, but the following provide an overview: Taylor (1931:118–21, 131–34); Lambrechts (1953:65–82); Gagé (1955, 1981); E. Simon (1957:30–44); Weinstock (1971:8–15); Liebeschuetz (1979:82–85); Kienast (1982); Zanker (1988:48–53); Galinsky (1969:9–10; 1992:471–72; 1996:215–20, 295–302); J. Miller (1994:99–112); Gurval (1995:87–136). On the *Aedes Apollonis Palatini*, see Carettoni (1983); Zanker (1983:21–40; 1988:85–89); Lefèvre (1989); Richardson (1992:14).

31. Horace's Apollo warns against overestimating the intentionality of Octavian's imaging, especially early in his career. Although Horace's earlier writings avoid martial themes in general, when he does address Rome's conflicts (*Ep.* 1 and 9) there is no association of Octavian with Apollo, unless perhaps in the suggestive humor behind Apollo saving Horace from the pest (*S*.I.9.78). Only once does Horace invoke Apollo as Caesar's guardian (*C.* I.21.9–16). Horace's odes for the dedication of the Palatine temple (*C*.I.31–32; Babcock, 1967:189–94) are the poet's own prayers for blessing and do not mention Augustus. However, the psychological impact of Apollo's temple, dominating the summit of the Palatine, does not require literary or numismatic support (Suet. *Aug*.29.1, 3, 31.1; Cass. Dio 53.1.3; Serv. *A*6.72; *CIL* VI.4.2 nos. 32323, 32326). Gurval (1995:102–3, 136), when he claims that Augustan poets do not make any connection between Augustus's divinity and Apollo, misses that the tandem of opening lines in c.5 and 6 (discussed fully later in this chapter) identify Apollo as Augustus's divine parent. Also at approximately the same time as these odes, fifteen years after Actium, there was an increasing interest in Actian Apollo as Gurval (89–90 n.6) notes in the numismatic evidence; cf. J. Miller (1994:99–112).

32. C.I.32.5–16: war-loving Alcaeus praises Venus with the lyre; C.III.3.69–72: Horace ends his longest retelling of the Trojan epic by disavowing the epic themes he has just written into lyric.

33. Vergil's Aeneas owes more to Venus than Apollo (*A*.1.229–53; 10.18–62; 12.18–62; J. Miller, 1994:108). For the legend of Aeneas and Troy as evidence for a collective Roman *muthos,* see Torelli (1999:65–183).

34. Niobe is a multiplex symbol (Hom. *Il*.24.596–620; Diod. Sic. 4.74; Paus. 1.21.3; 2.21.9; 5.11.2; 5.16.4; 8.2.5,7; Apollod. *Bibl*.3.5.6; Ov. *Met*.6.146–316; Hyg. *Fab*.9,11) and it is hard to judge how far Horace imagined that his audience would read his ode against other earlier accounts. Niobe represents unending grief, but Homer's Niobe facilitates the resolution of Priam's grief and Achilles' anger. Tityos seems easier since, although he is worshipped in his homeland Euboea (Strabo 9.3.14), he is a chief sinner in Hades (Hom. *Od*.11.576–81; Pi. *P*.4.90–93; Pl. *Grg*.525E; Joseph. *BJ*.2.156; Apollod. *Bibl*.1.4.1; Lucr. 3.984–94; Verg. *A*.6.595–600; Hyg. *Fab*.55). Horace also lists Tityos as one of the damned (*C*.II.14.8; III.4.77), but at *C*.III.11.21 the lyre has the power to make Tityos momentarily forget his eternal pain. Here again is the duality of Apollo: the god slew Tityos, but the god's lyre brings him relief.

35. The layout of Apollo's Palatine temple can be taken to support this view (Kellum, 1985; E. Simon, 1986; Lefèvre, 1989; cf. Gurval, 1995: 123–31). One entered the temple through doors decorated with symbols of Octavian's vengeance on Rome's enemies (Apollo slaying the Niobids and overthrowing the Gauls' attack on Delphi; Prop. 2.31.13–14) and saw Apollo not with his bow but a lyre, a symbol of Augustan peace.

36. Wimmel (1960).

37. Ross (1975:27–28 n.5).

38. Nagy (1994b:3–7) identifies in the etymology of Apollo "the god of authoritative speech, the one who presides over speech acts." The application of speech-act theory is particularly relevant to panegyric, where the words spoken or written are the very act of praising (*C*.IV.8.11–12). Apollo's governance of the propriety and impropriety of speech acts means that in a laudatory context Horace has every reason to invoke the blessing of an admonitory Apollo.

39. See the introduction.

40. Peerlkamp (1834) obelized 29–44. Others divide the ode into two: Sanadon (1728:*ad loc.;* endorsed by Shackleton Bailey, 1985); Bücheler (1859:158–60). Verrall (1884:76–82) complains about Horace's techniques but does not split the ode; cf. G. Williams (1968:64).

41. Fraenkel (1957:400–402); Reckford (1969:133–34); Cairns (1971: 440–44); Syndikus (1973:346–48); A. Hardie (1998:251–93).

42. To clarify my argument on *Ep*.9 (1997:323–27), I agree with G. Williams (1968:217) that Horace collapses the present and future, and I disagree only about whether *Ep*.9 exhibits such a structure and whether Maecenas is actually attending the party. The *carpe diem* argument would imply he is not.

43. Cairns (1971:440–44) argues that c.6 is a different song with a different occasion entirely from the *CS*. While the differences between the gods of the two songs could support Cairns, the dramatic situation of the ode is too close to the circumstances of the *CS* not to remind the reader of its composition and performance.

44. *C.*I.32: Horace asks the lyre for a song when the ode is that song he is requesting. *C.*IV.15: Horace's praise of Augustus (4–24) is the banquet song that he predicts at the end of the ode (25–32). See Lefèvre (1993b:143–57).

45. Wickham (1874:*praef.*, n.1); Fraenkel (1957:402–3). Cf. Borzsák (1976:25–36) on Apollo Agyieus, who watches over the maturation of Rome.

46. For chronologies of Augustan imaging, see P. R. Hardie (1986: 136); Zanker (1988:79–100, 167–238); McNeill (2001:89–138). C.5–6 warn that such chronologies cannot be made absolute since Augustan imperial representations place together opposing symbols (such as restoration [c.5] and vengeance [c.6]). See also Zanker's discussion (193–215) of the Forum of Augustus and its temple of Mars Ultor; Galinsky (1992: 468–75) on the Ara Pacis; the tension between the corruption and splendor of the golden age (Barker, 1996:442–46); Augustus's association with Romulus (Hinds, 1992:129–31).

47. Poets do not always distinguish the characteristics of the Muses and Graces (Hes. *Th.*915–17; Pi. *O.*14.13–17a). It would make no difference whichever Horace had in mind.

48. On Simonides, see Barchiesi (1996b:247–53). For the most extensive index on the metaphor of the fallen tree, see Nisbet (1987:243–51).

49. P. R. Hardie (1994:102) suggests that Horace also had in mind Verg. *A.*9.150–53. If he is correct, Horace to intensify Achilles' pride writes into his Achilles the image of Turnus's boastful hubris against the Trojans. Turnus does not need the deception of a Trojan horse to destroy his enemies. He is bolder than even Achilles.

50. See Thomas (1985:61–73).

51. "Potential disavowal" and "apparent reversal," because later I argue that Horace interprets the *Aeneid* as lyrical (c.12, 15). The poets are two halves of the same process: Vergil's epic incorporates lyric, and Horace's lyric incorporates epic.

52. Can the numbering 4.6 be coincidental? Propertius's Apollo, like Horace's, is Actian and sympotic (67–76). Propertius's rehearsal of Augustan victories (in particular the return of the Parthian standards in a banquet setting) harmonizes also with *C.*IV.14, 15.

53. P. White (1993:20 n.39–40) cites Verg. *G.*2.39–44; 3.42; Prop. 2.1.1–16; 3.9.52; Tib. 2.1.35–36; Ov. *Fast.*1.3–26; *Pont.*1.7.28; 2.3.78; 4.12.23; Mart. 12.3.5; Stat. *Silv.*1.4.19–36; *Laus Pis.*216–18—No Horace.

54. Compare the lyre as the advocate (σύνδικος) for Apollo and his Muses (Pi. *P*.1.1–2).

55. Richards (1942:289).

56. About Torquatus we know only that his speech defending a Moschus was still known to Porphyrio in the third century (on *Epist*.I.5.9); see *PIR* 2.329, no. 122. Torquatus may have written some light verse (Plin. *Ep*.5.3.5; Syme, 1986:396). If this Torquatus is from the *Manlia gens,* as is likely given the ascriptions of the manuscripts and the testimonia of the scholia, his limited political career may be explained. Lucius Manlius Torquatus, the family's last consul, was an Epicurean (Cic. *Fin*.1.23–25, 39), and therefore he and his sons may have gradually withdrawn from public life.

57. Housman could not resist (consciously or unconsciously?) adding back in the image of the banquet (*Diffugere Nives*): "Torquatus, if the gods in heaven shall add / The morrow to the day, what tongue has told? / *Feast then thy heart,* for what thy heart has had / The fingers of no heir will ever hold" (17–20).

58. Whether Postumus was fictitious or not (cf. Commager, 1962:285; N.-H., 1978:223; P. White, 1995:151–61), the legal meaning of his name, born too late for inclusion in a father's will, emphasizes the futility of a rich miser saving his hoard for a wanton heir.

59. Commager (1962:286).

60. Some think Horace pessimistic. Postumus, however, is neglecting the joys of life, not Horace. (Porph. *ad loc.;* Orelli, 1837:*proem;* Commager, 1962:285; N.-H., 1978:238 s.v. *dignior*). Even so, *dignior* (25) has given pause. Nisbet and Hubbard appear unruffled by the word, since it was normal for a Roman to be concerned that his heir be deserving. *Dignior,* however, cannot be understood from Postumus's viewpoint (he will be dead when the heir is drinking his wine), but can only be the opinion of the sympotic poet. A. Y. Campbell (1945:*ad loc.*) emends to "durior," turning praise for the heir into criticism. Campbell cannot be right: the rough pessimism is directed toward Postumus — otherwise, why chide him at length about the inescapability of death? See Matt. 22.8: those declining the king's invitation to his son's wedding party are οὐκ ἄξιοι.

61. This ode was written well before the untimely deaths of Augustus's heirs, except Marcellus (23 B.C.). Because Augustus was prone to illness, anyone concerned about who would succeed him could not gamble on him living as long as he did. Augustus himself began to advance his sons with early elections to offices by 24 B.C. On Augustus's efforts to create a succession, see Syme (1939:415–39); for the Augustus as republican viewpoint, see Eder (1990:120–22).

62. The Euripidean version: Phaedra falls in love with Hippolytus,

the son of her husband Theseus, and when he rejects her, she commits suicide and leaves behind a note accusing Hippolytus of raping her. Before Theseus learns the truth he curses his son, and Poseidon answers by causing Hippolytus's death.

63. For the Wissenschaftsgeschichte and complete analysis of c.8, see S. J. Harrison (1990:31–43).

64. "Theoretically" is sarcastic. S. J. Harrison (1990:34), based on *sodalibus* (2), surmises that Horace wrote this ode as a response to a personal patronage Horace had to sustain after the decline of Maecenas's influence. If Censorinus commissioned a praise ode, is this what he had in mind?

65. On Pindar in c.8, see S. J. Harrison (1990:34–36). Horace's imitation of Pindar continues from c.2 on, but likewise the force of the *recusatio*. Horace is Pindar's rival and better; see Lefèvre (1993a:276–77, 299–300). The poet's use of Pindar is part of his criticism against the nondiscriminating praise of standard panegyric.

66. The antiquarian so enamored with his own genealogy that he misses life's pleasures (C.III.19) parallels Horace's stereotype of the proud young nobleman. C.IV.8 and III.19 are two of the three odes that mention Aeacus (cf. II.13).

67. The general sense of C.III.19.11b–12, while intensely argued (Bentley, 1711; Orelli, 1837; T. E. Page, 1883:*ad loc.*; Marquardt, 1879–82: 331–36; A. Y. Campbell, 1945:*ad loc.*), relies on *commodis* (12). Either mixture, one-quarter pint of wine to a pint of water or three-quarters wine to the pint, is generously strong; but the *vates* (*attonitus*) will choose the more potent.

68. Does Horace reserve military praise in *Odes* IV for Augustus and his sons out of deference to the princeps (Syme, 1986:399; S. J. Harrison, 1990:33)? By comparison, the actual description of Drusus's military victory (c.4.17–18, 23–24) is hardly longer than the praise for Lollius's (c.9.43–44), but the epic-styled similes in the proemium, the gnome, as well as the historical narrative of c.4, lend the imperial praise a more august tone; see Lowrie (1997:76). To preview the next chapter, Horace does not change his panegyric praxis altogether and exclude disputes (*dubia*) from his epinikia. That he does not could be predicted from the *recusatio* of c.2 and the sequencing of c.3–6 that surrounds imperial praise with the poet's divine inspiration.

69. The younger Gaius Marcius (Vell. 2.102.1; Cass. Dio 55.5; *PIR*[2] 5.2.177–78, no. 222; Syme, 1986:79, 333 n.32, 395–97, 405–6; S. J. Harrison, 1990:32–33) is the more likely addressee than Lucius Marcius (cos. 39), one of the two senators who attempted to shield Julius Caesar. The encomium fits Horace's praise for up-and-coming young nobles.

70. Syme (1986:399).

71. Horace does not always differentiate poetry from the visual arts. *Ars* 361-65 likens the interpretation of poetry to painting, although the exact point of comparison is debated; Brink (1971:*ad loc.*); Trimpi (1973:1-34). Panegyric is closely related to the visual arts in that it requires the contemplation of a person or image represented by the poet. Horace in c.8, however, lessens any ekphrastic similarity to the solid arts by limiting the details of Censorinus's praise and maintaining the poem's gaze on the internal power and creativity of the poet; cf. P. R. Hardie (1993:122). Contrast the sustained pictorialism of the proemium to c.4 (discussed in ch.3) when Horace with compound ekphrastic similes directs the audience to scrutinize the imperial image.

72. See also C.IV.2.19b-20: (Pindar) *centum potiore signis / munere donat.*

73. Scholars who follow Lachmann and excise 15b-19a (*non celeres . . . rediit*) need not face this difficulty. That easy solution is tempting given the problem of *fugae, minae,* and *incendia* as the subjects of *indicant.* S. J. Harrison's (1990:32-33) proposal that the lines are an epigraphic model (also K.-H., 1884:nn.13-20; P. R. Hardie, 1993:134-35) spares all but 17 and can be defended on interpretive grounds. The weight devoted to the other arts prompts the question, Just how is poetry better? which makes for a more interesting panegyric poem and begins to explain, if only in part, why the ode is at the center of the book. One other line would have to be excised, such as 33 (Harrison), before the song would comply with Meineke's (1854) principle.

74. On the fierce competition between Horace and the visual arts, see P. R. Hardie (1993:121-39).

75. Poets (*Epist.*II.1.219-28) belittle their poetry in their search for a generous (*commodus*) patron.

76. I am not as convinced as S. J. Harrison (1990:42-43) that Augustus would appreciate the inflation of Censorinus's worth. Would he perhaps see c.8 as lowering the value of his own encomium as Horace *ponit nunc hominem, nunc deum*? The similarities between c.5 and 8 (the sympotic setting complete with *pateris,* Castor, and Hercules, c.5.33-36) are a little too close for comfort.

77. I would argue that line 28 is a principal tenet for this ode and the book, and therefore is Horatian.

78. Most editors are either satisfied by Bentley's defense or have no problem understanding Lollius as the primary subject since the appositional substantives are so far removed from *animus.* Shackleton Bailey (1985) speculates that four lines were lost after 38. To me, the progression of the metaphor seems natural enough and complements the syntax: *prudens* and *rectus* set up *vindex,* which is followed at the beginning of every other line by *consul* and *iudex.*

79. Lollius in the historians: Vell. 2.97, 102; Plin. *Nat.*9.118; Suet. *Aug.*23, *Tib.*12–13; Tac. *Ann.*1.10; 3.48; Cass. Dio 53.26; 54.6, 20. Cf. *PIR²* 5.1.83–84, no. 311; *RE* 13.1377–87 s.v. *Lollius* 11; Syme (1933:17–19; 1986).

80. Cass. Dio 54.6; see *Epist.*I.20.26–28.

81. Only Velleius directly states that Augustus replaced Lollius with Drusus. This may well have happened whatever Lollius's performance. Augustus was looking for opportunities to put forward his stepsons. Syme (1933:17–18) rejects the notion that Lollius's defeat caused any major changes in Augustus's military policy and questions the accuracy of Dio's chronology; see Woodman's (1977:110–11) convincing rebuttal.

82. Cf. Woodman (1977:110–11) and Radke (1986:768–82) on Velleius's objectivity.

83. Syme (1933:17–18).

84. Cf. Putnam (1986:168–69 n.19); Lyne (1995:205–6).

85. Admittedly "reasonable" and "some skepticism" are noncommittal. Accusations of bribery against Lollius and his tampering with Gaius, strictly in the historians, postdate Horace's ode. But rumors usually precede charges (cf. Sage, 1994:569–70), and Horace's praise betrays an uncomfortable shift between the poet's celebration of his poetics in the first half and his "apologetic" stance in the second (Woodman, 1977:110–11). This tonal shift perhaps indicates a panegyrist who imagines that praising Lollius will find a cool reception.

86. Syme (1933:17–19) discredits Velleius; six years later (1939:429) and again over fifty years later (1986:402) he defends vigorously his position.

87. [1] Reckford (1969:130–31); Syndikus (1973:375–76, 384). [2] T. E. Page (1883:*proem*); Fraenkel (1957:425–26); Garrison (1991:359 nn.43–44). [3] This is the most widely held view: Orelli (1837:*excursus*); Wickham (1874:*proem*); K.-H. (1884: *proem*); Syme (1978:153; 1939:428–29; 1986:402); Putnam (1986:168–69 n.19); S. J. Harrison (1990:33); Lefèvre (1993a:276–77). Commager (1962:321–22 n.18) and Quinn (1980:nn.34–44) argue that Horace's praise defends Lollius's reputation, but they view the encomium overall as rather perfunctory; also A. Y. Campbell (1924:228). [4] Ambrose (1965:1–10) relies heavily on Velleius's Lollius and therefore has been summarily dismissed, but there is more room for irony in the encomium than has been admitted. Seager (1993:37) refers to the encomium as "deliberate tactlessness" and a "whitewashing job," making the point that Lollius never risked his life for his fatherland; also Sage (1994:565–86).

88. Those maintaining that the encomium strengthens Lollius's reputation often read 43–44 as a metaphor that limits the victory to Lollius's civil life (suggested by Porphyrio and taken up by Orelli, Page, and Quinn). This interpretation must take *victor* as subordinate to *iudex*

and not as a parallel appositive with *animus;* otherwise, *animus-victor* could apply to military deeds. This is not the best way to interpret the nominative sequence. Granted, *vindex, consul,* and *iudex* (not *victor*) all stand in first position and follow every other verse, but *victor* balances the position of *animus* near the end of its line. Also *animus* occupies two lines as does *vindex* and *consul; animus* as *iudex* and *animus* as *victor* would maintain the two-line symmetry. It simplifies the metaphor to acknowledge that the encomium admits blame (Wickham, 1874:nn.40–44; Lyne, 1995:205–6; Seager, 1993:37).

89. See Sage (1994:566–68).

90. The ambiguity between praise and blame includes memory (*Epist.*II.1.262–63): *discit enim citius meminitque libentius illud / quod quis deridet quam quod probat et veneratur.*

91. On narrative in Horatian lyric, see Lowrie (1997:1–16, 97–137). This ode for which narrative is so vital to the overall argument is the only time Horace mentions the lyricist Stesichorus (8), whose use of narrative was exceptional (M. L. West, 1971b:302–14). Horace's *graves* is a technically appropriate designation for Stesichorus's Muses because he wrote epic myth into lyric. Horace is about to do the same.

92. *Proelia coniugibus loquenda* is contested. The *Iliad* ends in the wailing of the surviving Trojan women, which is the primary and most grievous form of praise. The cries of women for their dead husbands add a strong emotive depth to c.4 (see ch.3). Simonides' influence is evident in Horace's tones of lament (Barchiesi, 1996a:5–47; Lowrie, 1995:45, 1997:185; the articles in Boedeker and Sider, 2001, particularly Harrison, 2001:261–71). *Ceae,* line 7, also neatly designates Simonides' nephew, Bacchylides.

93. *Epist.*I.2.15–16.

94. The immediate sense of *coniugibus puerisque* is general: wives and children (K.-H., 1884:n.23). Yet there is nothing to prevent anyone from reading into the narrative further details that they know about the characters (cf. Putnam, 1986:163–64). The condition *si priores Maeonius tenet sedes Homerus* invites a comparison of the epic and lyric traditions, which in turn suggests that the narrative is designed to encourage just such over-reading, specifically a reading that compares the Homeric tale to the Horatian. See also Horace's erotic *Odyssey* in Tyndaris's lyric song, C.I.17.18–20 (Lowrie, 1995:44).

95. The identical line numbers, the negative (*nequiquam* [c.15] and *non* [c.9]) at the beginning of both scenes, and the repetition of *ferox* in c.9 at a line end (21) demonstrate how interrelated the two episodes are.

96. Horace's narrative combines characters who do not stand up well to the scrutiny of an audience invited to question whether the deeds of some merit immortal fame and not others. Teucer fought like a child hid-

ing behind its mother (Hom. *Il*.8.268–72, 312–24) and failed to offer appropriate sacrifices (*Il*.23.850–83). Idomeneus was an impetuous braggart (*Il*.13.374–82; 23.474–81), a personality Augustus did not admire (Suet. *Aug*.25). Sthenelus, Diomedes' charioteer, was often replaced at moments of crisis and left standing behind (*Il*.5.835–38; 8.98–115).

97. Compare Wickham (1874:n.21); Putnam (1986:163).

98. The Stoic principles in the encomium for Lollius also prompt the memory: it was the Stoic sage Stertinius (*S*.II.3.193–207) who argued that Agamemnon's murder of Iphigenia was every bit as much an act of insanity as Ajax's suicide.

99. On the priestly prophetic function of the poet, see Newman (1967b).

100. Ambrose (1965:5–6): *labores* is the subject of *carpere* and *obliviones* the object. Although I agree with Ambrose that the praise of the introduction is not unequivocal, it is not for the syntactical explanations he proposes (see Sage, 1994:577).

101. See Cat. 68. 41–46.

102. Orelli (1837) and Putnam (1986:164) cite *N*.7.12–13, but perhaps *O*.10.91–92 is even closer; for other parallels, see Gow (1950) on Theoc. 16.30.

103. See forgetting (*obliviscitur*) the cares of love (*Ep*.2.37–38). When faced with the obligations of his patronage, Horace himself welcomes the undisturbed state of inertia and forgetfulness (*S*.II.6.60b–62; *Ep*.14.2). Again there are implications for Horatian poetics: the Pierian Muses refresh Caesar from the fatigue of war (*C*.III.4.37–40).

104. *Carpere* as a verb of destruction: Cat. 68.35, Verg. *G*.3.215, Liv. 8.38.6, Ov. *Ars* 2.114; surprise attacks: Caes. *Civ*.1.63.2, Cat. 62.36, Liv. 6.32.11, 7.12.12, Ov. *Met*.2.781. In Horace: *S*.I.5.95; II.6.93; *C*.II.17.12 (choosing a road or direction); *S*.II.3.256; *C*.I.11.8; III.27.44; IV.2.29 (plucking); *C*.III.27.64 (carding wool). Most read *carpere* in c.9 as a synonym for *rodere*; Putnam's (1986:159) "to pluck" reflects more Horatian usage.

105. Quinn (1980:nn.45–52). This may also have been Fraenkel's position (1957:426), since he judges that the principles are not relevant to Lollius.

106. *Beatus* is the equivalent of the Stoic εὐδαιμονία, the blessings surrounding the virtuous man (Cic. *Luc*.134). For the Stoic only the wise man is truly rich. The Stoic sage as *rex* is represented here by the consulship of Lollius's upright mind; cf. Lyne (1995:145–46; 205–6).

107. Most others, including Orelli (1837:nn.51–52); K.-H. (1884: nn.45–52); Syndikus (1973:385); Putnam (1986:168); Lyne (1995:204). Wickham (1874:n.45) hedges: the maxims were meant to defend Lollius's character and make him think.

108. There may be another intertextual chain that raises questions about Horace's praise of Lollius's *moderatio*. Forms of *intereo* are infrequent in Horace: only six, and half in the *Ars* (61, 146, and 464). The future participle *interitura* (c.9.1) appears also in c.7.9–10 (*ver proterit aestas / interitura*), an ode containing in its *carpe diem* argument, as discussed earlier, a warning about greedy heirs. The language of c.7 recalls C.II.18.15–16: *truditur dies die / novaeque pergunt interire lunae*. The primary thesis of c.18 is *moderatio* and the emptiness of wealth. These are the only instances of the verb in the *Odes:* two against wealth and then the last praising the restraint of Lollius, who grew rich through provincial rule.

109. The association of c.9 with Horace's criticism of the Stoic sage in *S.I.3* and *II.3* is strengthened by shared characters (Helen, *S.I.3.107–8*; Teucer and Agamemnon, *S.II.3.187–213*) and themes (avarice, a great evil for the Stoic, *S.II.3.82*).

110. Words and their conventions constantly suffer death and rebirth, a cycle controlled by the changing force of usage (*Ars* 60–72). This is just the type of paradox Horace loves. Poetry becomes immortal when it first dies and then is reborn in an endless cycle of interpretive transformation, which Horace illustrates by renewing the metaphor of the falling leaves from Homer and Simonides (61–62; see Sider, 2001:283–85). P. A. Miller (1991:365–88) speaks of an unresolved dialogue among Horatian poems that grants to the poet, gods, and heroes their own autonomy. The same occurs within the praise poems of *Odes* IV.

3. *Encomia Augusti*, "Take One"

1. From Russell and Wilson (1981:*ad loc.*).

2. Rhaetia ran north from modern Tyrol up into Switzerland to the Danube. From west to east it extended from Lake Constance to the Inn River (Cass. Dio 54.22). Vindelicia is the northernmost area of Rhaetia along the southern bank of the Danube from the Lake to the Inn. Although Rhaetia encompasses Vindelicia, sources tend to list them separately (Bentley, 1711) and this is reflected in the wide variance among the lesser manuscript readings and scholia that remove the apposition (*Raetis* : *R[a]eti et* σχA Vollmer: *gerentem et*). Editors (excluding Shackleton Bailey, who retains *Raeti*) prefer the reading *Raetis . . . Alpibus,* but this does not solve a larger problem. Tiberius invaded from Gaul and moved east into Rhaetia (Scullard, 1959:255), while Drusus pushed up from the south. Both epinikia (c.4, 14), however, assign the victory over the Vindelici to Drusus, leader of the southern advance. Here one can worry too much. The evidence does not pinpoint all the exact movements of the two brothers (e.g., Cass. Dio, 54.22.4: Lake Garda, Geneva,

Constance?). There is no need to superimpose accurate troop movements onto Horace's epinikion, a fictive re-animation of the moment of attack and victory.

3. Shackleton Bailey's "roborat" for the strongly attested *roborant* is unconvincing. He has been led to make the change by Porphyrio's reading of *recti* as a genitive singular and the parallelism of the singular *doctrina* with *promovet*. Horace also does not use *cultus* as a plural subject. Reading *recti* as a limiting genitive with *cultus* would not alter the sense significantly, but it is difficult to read *cultus* as a singular because this removes the contrastive rhyme *roborant* . . . *indecorant* (n.b. the chiastic arrangement of lines 34, 36).

4. On the history of the text, see below later in this discussion. From the latter part of the sixteenth century (Scaliger noted in Lambinus, 1605), *Nemean* 5.16b–18 has been cited as the probable source for the digression (18–22). Add in Scaliger's favor that the two disavowals are similar in voice and content: στάσομαι' (*quaerere distuli*, 21) οὔ τοι ἅπασα κερδίων / φαίνοισα πρόσωπον ἀλάθει' ἀτρεκής· / καὶ τὸ σιγᾶν πολλάκις ἐστὶ σοφώτατον ἀνθρώπῳ νοῆσαι. Pindar's full stop is laced with the irony of the *praeteritio*. He alludes to the story of how Peleus and Telamon murdered their half brother, which he refuses to tell. He follows up his feigned silence with two interrelated metaphors illustrating his poetic power, the latter being the eagle. Horace takes up the opening of *Nemean* 5 when he develops in detail the superiority of poetry to the solid arts (c.8, 9). *Nemean* 5 then is in the background of c.4, 8, and 9.

5. For chiasmus as an organizational principle in Pindar, see Illig (1932); Hamilton (1974:56–78); Greengard (1980:17–46). The invocation-reinvocation pattern (Greengard, 54–62) does not require the same deities (Pi. *P*.8: opening prayer to Hesychia; closing prayer to Zeus).

6. A lyre lulling Jupiter's eagle to sleep and soothing Ares so that he drops his spears deepens the violence of Horace's predatory eagle (c.4) and avenging Apollo (c.6).

7. There has been consensus that c.4 has a bipartite structure. The disagreement is whether the last stanza is part of Hannibal's speech, resulting in a 10–9 split or an added conclusion so that the structure becomes 9–9–1. Reckford (1960:23–28) supports the latter view, citing the same pattern for the CS. He is probably correct, as I argue below for other reasons internal to the ode. I also find the bipartite approach somewhat limited. It disguises the intricacy of Horace's Pindaric imitation by lumping together the proemium, victory announcement, digression, and the beginning of the gnome without offering any insight into the transitions important to the sense of the whole. To accentuate a split after the ninth stanza glosses over the gnomic panel, as if it were an appendage to the opening twenty-eight lines. The gnome is more than an

eight-line thematic transition between two parts since even if it were omitted, the ode would run on naturally (*Nerones* to *Neronibus*). There is symmetry in the ode, but it is more complex than a bipartite division (Syndikus, 1973:322–23).

8. The accounts of Ganymede's abduction vary (*RE* 6.737–49; Sichtermann, 1953; Bruneau, 1962:196–210; Bremmer, 1980:286). When reading a victory ode for Drusus and Tiberius, the rape of Ganymede from the statue group in Tiberius's grotto at Sperlonga comes to mind.

9. Horace's snake is quiet compared to Vergil's, *A*.11.751–56. The coordination of sound and sense is not exclusively or even primarily Pindaric but was popular in Roman poetry in general, especially the *neoteroi*. For examples in Vergil, see Lyne (1989); S. J. Harrison (1991: 285–91); Horsfall (1995a:237–48); O'Hara (1997:241–58); Perkell (1999).

10. For a list of comparable compound similes and their effects, see Fraenkel (1957:427–28); G. Williams (1968:752–54; 1980:52, 78). On the related rhetorical device, *dicolon abundans,* see O'Hara (1997:248). Williams concludes that the victims in Horace's first simile are of secondary importance. The two similes are not so distinct. Young Ganymede, the bleating sheep, and the hissing serpent prepare the audience emotionally for the lion's attack on the roe.

11. Is the mother the roe's (Nauck, 1854; Ritter, 1857:*ad loc.;* T. E. Page, 1883:n.14; Shorey, 1898:n.14; Lowrie, 1997:329) or the lion's (Wickham, 1874:n.14; K.-H., 1884:n.13; Moore, 1902:345; Reckford, 1960:28 n.7; Quinn, 1980:nn.13–16; Putnam, 1986:83)? Those favoring the mother lioness resolve the tautology *ubere . . . lacte* by interpretation (*ubere* with adjectival force hardly avoids the harsh redundancy; cf. Quinn, Putnam) or emendation ("mane" [Bentley] or "iamque" [Shackleton Bailey] for *lacte*). Any ambiguity enriches the simile's compelling psychological drama. *Matris ab ubere* follows naturally Horace's first description of the roe, *pascuis intenta.* The flow of the line suggests that the roe, preoccupied with feeding, has wandered off from her mother's nurturing protection. *Lacte depulsum* requires the audience to adjust their sympathies to account for the natural order of the food chain, which also demands that the young lion learn from its mother to hunt down its own food. Cf. Vergil's lion simile on the bloodthirsty Mezentius (*A*.10.723–29; Putnam, 1986:87–88). Vergil arouses pity for Mezentius's victim by developing the savagery of the lion—Horace by dwelling on the youthful innocence of killer and killed. The pathos of Horace's simile lies in the unavoidability of the act—young lions learn to hunt, and roes must be wary or die. And yet the intrusion of a predator into the serene meadow directs sympathies primarily toward the unsuspecting roe.

12. The tragedy of a deer (Dido) caught unawares by the hunter's deadly arrow is compounded by a hunter (Aeneas) who does not know

he has hit his target (*A.* 4.69b–73). There will be a death, but the whole affair seems useless. The deer will die, and the hunter will never know. The tragedy of Vergil's hunt does not rely on the innocent youth of the characters, but their ignorance; cf. below Hannibal's lack of forethought in his decision to attack Rome (c.4.50–53).

13. While V. Max. saves his stronger disapproval for divorce, his attitude about adoption is mostly negative: blood relationships should always supersede the adoptive and purely legal (7.7.2; 7.7.5; Mueller, 2002:195 n.58).

14. See Vell. 2.75; 79.2; 94.1; 95.1; Suet. *Cl.*1; Cass. Dio. 48.44; Tac. *Ann.*1.10. Carcopino's review (1929:225–36) of these sources has yet to be superseded; see also Syme (1958:vol.1, 425); W. R. Johnson (1969:177 n.16).

15. W. R. Johnson (1969:176–79): Pindar's "dogma is Herrenmoral" (*O.*9.108–12; *O.*13.13; *P.*8.44–45; *N.*3.40–41; 5.40–43; 6.8–11; 10.50–54), whereas Horace, according to the conventions of Alexandrian panegyric, shifts the balance so that "*ars* (is) extolled, *ingenium* demoted." Johnson then must read the ode as an awkward flipping back and forth between nurture (Augustus) and nature (Nerones) so that somehow Augustus has the preeminence. The assumption is that, since this is Augustus's epinikion, Horace would not have him share the praise. The ode's structure requires more balance (Wilkinson, 1945:109; Reckford, 1960:24).

16. Horace's return to the animal imagery of the proemium and gnome marks the ode's primary comparisons: education — birth (30–32) and Hannibal — Rome (50); see Connor (1987:93–94). The extraordinary leap from the attacking eagle and lion to the attacked Hydra refusing to die is an indication of Hannibal's hostility to Rome (compare Collinge, 1961:13–14 with Porter, 1975:202–3). Hannibal does not read the opening similes as sympathetic to Rome.

17. Pi. *P.*4.263–69 (Fraenkel, 1957:430 n.3); Verg. *A.*2.624–31 (Putnam, 1986:96–98). Hannibal plays his deceitful game well. It appears that a triumphant Roman voice has wrested the speech from Hannibal's control and is singing unqualified praise for Rome (see Reckford, 1960:25–26, 1969:136; Lowrie, 1997:332–33). The remainder of the metaphoric chain, to which the first simile is well joined, shows the tree simile for what it is — one of Hannibal's monstrous images.

18. Putnam (1986:96 n.30).

19. These two Vergilian tree similes (2.624–31; 4.438b–46) are closely related: longevity (*antiquam . . . ornum*, 2.626; *annoso . . . robore*, 4.441), shaken treetops (*concusso vertice*, 2.629; *concusso stipite*, 4.444– 45), and the groans and shrieks from their wounds (*vulneribus . . . congemuit*, 2.630–31; *it stridor*, 4.443). Dido's death parallels the calamity of Troy's

fall, but there is no escape for her. Given the close correlation, it is unlikely that Horace, while working with the same concept of triumph and suffering, would think of the fallen tree simile and not the other unyielding tree. Vergil's simile of the unfelled tree is powerful poetry because its comparison is confused. The tree begins as a symbol for Aeneas's rejection of Dido's love, but by the end of the simile the same sinister oak reaching from heaven to hell foreshadows Dido's suicidal descent into the underworld. Horace's Hannibal mirrors the dual symbolism of Vergil's simile by coloring his seemingly complimentary image with sinister undertones.

20. Once Dido discovers that Aeneas is leaving she repeatedly calls him *perfidus*. The question is, who has been truly deceitful: Aeneas, Dido, Hannibal, the storyteller, the panegyrist?

21. Also Lyce (*nec rigida mollior aesculo*, C.III.10.17).

22. Apollod. *Bibl*.3.4.1–2.

23. See Giangrande's (1967:329–31) review of the textual criticism on 67–68 (also Maas, 1956:228; Hunt, 1974:355–56). *Geretque . . . loquenda* satisfies no one (Shackleton Bailey's cruxes). The tricolon should retain Rome as the subject and end on a grand note of praise. The tricolon falls flat, if Horace writes a parallel to the epic-styled *dicenda Musis proelia* (IV.9.21) but changes *Musis* to the obscure *coniugibus*. Some emend: *geretque proelia*] feretque praemia (A. Y. Campbell, 1945); *coniugibus*] carminibus (Peerlkamp, 1834), Pieriis (Hunt). Others explain *coniugibus*. The wives are Roman (Orelli, 1837:nn.65–68; with more reservation Wickham, 1874:n.68), and Horace is borrowing from the Spanish custom of mothers hymning their young war heroes (Orelli cites Sal. *Hist*.2.fr.92 [Maurenbrecher]). These are not Roman but Carthaginian wives (Ritter, 1857). Horace wanted to write something like *musis* or *poetis* but avoided such epic praise of the Hannibalic War so as not to offend Augustus (Giangrande). None of the proposed solutions account for the strange reversal caused when Hannibal praises such monstrosities. The tricolon is like the mythological sequence that it caps. Hannibal begins with what looks like praise for Rome, but by the time he finishes he has manipulated the images to provoke sympathy for the victims. By switching *coniugibus* for the standard *Musis*, Hannibal calls attention to the laments of Carthaginian wives for their dead husbands (see C.IV.2.21–22).

24. Does Hannibal speak the last four lines? Copyists and early commentators were divided. The present tenses of the manuscripts argue for the poet, the future tenses for a Hannibalic prophecy (Wilamowitz-Moellendorff, 1913:320–21). Porphyrio assigns the lines to the poet. Heinze changed his mind in his seventh edition (1930) and excluded the lines from the speech. Fraenkel (1957:428 n.1) argues that in the absence

of a clear marker to end the speech there is no reason to exclude the lines (also Syndikus, 1973:329; Quinn, 1980:nn.73–76; Putnam, 1986:98 n.32; Lyne, 1995:203). Since the predominant organizing principle of the epinikion is ring composition, is not *Hasdrubale interempto* (*Hasdrubal / devictus*, 38–39) a fairly clear marker? Far be it from me to try to resolve the debate and ruin the praise's ultimate dispute (*dubium*); see Lowrie (1997:335).

25. Putnam (1986:99).

26. C.4 still has more critics than admirers. Just when one thinks that the score has been settled in Horace's favor (Fraenkel, 1957:426–31; Reckford, 1960:23–28; W. R. Johnson, 1969:179–81), the same criticism resurfaces. Kiernan (1999:88) is only the most recent detractor (T. E. Page, 1883:*proem*; Wilkinson, 1945:85–86; Commager, 1962:230–31; Lyne, 1995:201).

27. W. R. Johnson (1969:171 n.3) wonders about parody; Connor (1987:95) has no doubt. Horace's Pindaric imitation in C.IV.2 poses the same difficulty. I argued for parody in chapter 2 because of the irony in the *recusatio* and the grand bucolic depiction of Horace's lyric persona (25–36).

28. Such multivalent discourse prompts Fowler (1995:248–66) to wonder whether Horace presents panegyric as incompatible with his lyric poetics. I would not be this skeptical (see the conclusion of C.IV.2, ch.2). We have too naively presumed that *our* ancient authors uniformly imagined proper panegyric as univocal praise designed to persuade their audience to the particular view of the *laudandus* (see the introduction). Horatian panegyric does not readily fit this presupposition because it does not suppress even the most obvious disputes. Horace's construction of panegyric reveals a more complex conception of praise, one that appreciates and actualizes the creative potential of the audience.

29. Crotty (1982:7) implies that this traditional reading of Pindaric epinikia is simplistic. Further investigation could prove enlightening. Horace may be original here, but it is as likely that he sensed different nuances within Pindar's praise that caused him to construct panegyric as he did.

30. Wickham (1874:nn.18–22) and Reckford (1960:28 n.8): the digression highlights the Vindelicians' violent nature to embellish Drusus's victory. Ambrose (1973:28 n.7): Drusus is slighted when Horace assigns legendary status to the Vindelici.

31. Anchises' speech intersects c.4 and c.8 at several points: the defeat of Hannibal (845–46), the importance of Roman *mores* for sustaining peace (852), and the life-giving power of the solid arts (*excudent alii spirantia mollius aera / (credo equidem), vivos ducent de marmore vultus*, 847–48).

32. This includes Tiberius's and Drusus's parents. After Perusia fell to Octavian, Livia, when she was eighteen years old and Tiberius barely two, fled with her husband Claudius Nero when he sought refuge with Sextus Pompeius in Sicily. Soon the couple left Sicily for Greece. On the hardships endured by the infant Tiberius while his parents were refugees, see Vell. 2.75; Suet. *Tib*.4–6. Not even two years later Livia was married to Octavian. Change does not erase memory.

33. Commager (1962:231); Connor (1987:95). Cf. Ambrose (1973:26–33): Horace's epinikion is a metaphor warning Augustus against pursuing a policy of expansion into Germany.

34. See Seager (1993:36–37).

35. See von Albrecht (1982–84:229–41).

36. Galinsky (1988:321–48); Perkell (1989:5–17); Feeney (1991:150).

37. The digression has been judged so prosaic and irrelevant that it is beneath Horace (Peerlkamp, 1834; Meineke, 1854; Müller, 1869; for a fuller review, see Harms, 1935:48). That lines can be removed without ruining the meter has further suggested interpolation (Fraenkel, 1957:429 n.1), which had to occur earlier than Servius, who attests to the lines (on *A*.1.243). The guilty contributor would have been as clever as Horace, since the digression is joined to the ode on multiple levels, structurally, thematically, not to mention the allusion to the sympotic Horace (discussed later in the chapter). Many let the digression stand but defend it without enthusiasm as an annoying piece of Pindaric excess (Orelli, 1837; Wickham, 1874; K.-H., 1884; A. Y. Campbell, 1924:207; Wilkinson, 1945:108–9; Commager, 1962:230; Connor, 1987:94–95). Fraenkel (1957:428–30) and W. R. Johnson (1969:172–74) deserve much credit for reversing the negative criticism. They read the digression as a type of *praeteritio*. Clearly the digression contains an element of disavowal. The question is what is its force within the epinikion; compare T. E. Page (1883:*ad loc*.) with G. Williams (1968:753–54).

38. Horace compares Drusus's behavior to the instincts of predatory animals (Connor, 1987:94).

39. Fraenkel (1957:430).

40. See Putnam (1986:88–89).

41. W. R. Johnson (1969:180).

42. Johnson (1969:171–72).

43. When Shackleton Bailey emends *vina* to "tecta," he must think that he improves the sense of *hinc*, that is, the vinedresser returns home from the countryside. He inadvertently ruins the focus on the power of ritual libation. The libation is the means by which Augustus returns to the community (discussed later in the chapter); see Syndikus (1973: 342).

44. Verg. *Ecl*.9.47; *G*.1.465–68; Suet. *Jul*.88; Plin. *Nat*.2.93–94, 98; Plu.

*Caes.*69.4–5; Obseq. 71 (Dio dates this comet to 16 B.C., 54.19.7–8); cf. Taylor (1931:89–92), Weinstock (1971:370–84), Ramsey and Licht (1997).

45. By senatorial decree (30 B.C.) libations were to be poured to Augustus's *genius* at every private and public banquet (Dio Cass. 51.19.7). The bibliography on the development of the imperial cult is extensive (see Herz, 1975:833–910; Pollini, 1990:334–35 nn.1, 3); on Horace and C.IV.5: Taylor (1931:151–53; 181–85); Nock (1947:108); Wili (1948:368); Lambrechts (1953:65–82); Doblhofer (1966:100–101); Fishwick (1969: 356–67); Fears (1977:125–30); Liebeschuetz (1979:69–70); Galinsky (1996: 300–302).

46. Cf. the apotheosis of *Epist.*II.1: the Roman citizens are performing rites to Augustus's *numen* while he is still living (*praesenti tibi*, 15). Yet the epistle does not equal the hymn's praise; the epistle has no prayer, no festival, and implies a warning that divinization for the living provokes envy (12). Note the shared vocabulary: *maturus* (c.5.3; epist.1.15) and *tuum numen* (5.34–35; 1.16).

47. See Lyne, 1995:193–217; DuQuesnay, 1995:131, 187.

48. By c.15 Lowrie (1997:350–51) finds little left of the *potens vates.* Not to give away the ending of Horace's and my book, but Horatian panegyric expresses its independence by embedding itself in a community of fellow citizens and then shaping an environment for creative dialogue between competing voices. The poet does not withdraw his lyric voice when he represents it as part of communal song (ch.5).

49. DuQuesnay (1995) provides a thorough sociohistorical study of c.5 as an occasional poem. This is precisely how DuQuesnay is limiting: the ode is solely occasional, given no life within *Odes* IV or beyond the historical moment of a single performance. Accordingly he reads the ode as univocal praise designed to persuade the audience to Augustus's viewpoint. See G. Williams (1990:275), Putnam, (1990:212–38), and McNeill (2001:89–130) on the ambiguities in Horace's earlier *encomia Augusti.* McNeill (131–38), however, reads the encomia of *Odes* IV as unqualified praise.

50. The new moral positivism, compared to the Roman Odes (especially III.3), is cited in general throughout the commentaries; most recently, Lowrie (1997:336); Oliensis (1998:117–18).

51. I have imitated the listing of the *Romanae res* in asyndeton (17–24), since it is an important rhetorical feature of the encomium. It has a wooden effect that alliteration and assonance only partly overcome. For example, the repetition *domus* and *edomuit* functions as an explanatory connective (21–22): the home is undefiled because convention and law have rid it of impiety.

52. Oliensis (1998:127): "the hymn to Augustus . . . has no space within it for Horace."

53. Noted by DuQuesnay (1995:164); cf. Lowrie (1997:336): "Horace does not say that Augustus' efforts have achieved these ends." The connection is made, but subtly.

54. Fraenkel (1957:448); Putnam (1986:113).

55. DuQuesnay (1995:164 n.190); cf. Nisbet (1989:93). Proposed emendations: 17 *rura*] prata Faber (1671); 18 *rura*] farra Bentley (1711). On retaining *rura*, see Wickham (1874) and Fraenkel (1957:443 n.5). Cf. Syndikus (1973:336–38).

56. Quinn (1980:nn.25–28).

57. The only detractor is G. Williams (1968:99–100, 163); c.5 is Fraenkel's favorite (1957:443 n.1).

58. Compared to his other hymns, the lyric poet here resists narrative (Lowrie, 1997:336–37).

59. Collinge (1961:8).

60. Oliensis (1998:117).

61. Coleman (1977:73–74 n.6).

62. It has been argued that Vergil does not have Octavian in mind; e.g., Grisart (1966:115–42); C. G. Hardie (1975:115). Although it is not necessary that the shepherd's benefactor be a historical figure, the circumstances are close enough to suggest Octavian. Even if Octavian is not here, the eclogue still establishes that the Augustan poets, like their Hellenistic predecessors, praised benefactors as gods.

63. For an overview of Vergil's proemium, his promise of an epic for Augustus, and rejection of strict neoteric *brevitas*, see Thomas (1985:61–73; 1988, 2:36–37).

64. This is similar to the narrative strategy that Horace employs when Hannibal praises Rome (c.4), except that Vergil does not tinge the prophecy with the ironic insults of an enemy like Hannibal. Horace's Hannibal advertises the deceptive possibility of panegyric storytelling; Vergil's prophet Anchises disguises it.

65. Compare *Ecl*.9.48–50 with c.5.29–32: there is rejoicing (*gauderent*, 48; *laetus*, 31), the tending of the vineyard and grafting of fruit (*duceret . . . uva colorem. / insere, Daphni, piros*, 49–50; *vitem viduas ducit ad arbores*, 30), and vineyards on the hillsides (*apricis in collibus*, 49; *collibus in suis*, 29).

66. Petr. *Sat*.17.5: *utique nostra regio tam praesentibus plena est numinibus ut facilius possis deum quam hominem invenire.*

67. Peerlkamp's (1834) "Marcellis" for the manuscripts' *Marcelli* (46) has convinced many editors. The family designation, such as Scauri, allows the reader to include the younger Marcellus, a more contemporary lead-in to the *Iulium sidus*. There is no need to emend: even if the specific reference is to the older Marcellus, it would be a natural reflex to think also of the younger (N.-H., 1970:161–62).

68. Also Tarquinius and Cato are listed with Hercules, Castor, and Pollux.

69. *Superbos / Tarquini fascis* (34b–35a) is a fine archetype for all the Etruscan kings. The first Etruscan king introduced the *fasces,* and the epithet *superbos* applies specifically to the last; see N.-H. (1970:156). Garrison (1991:nn.33–44) proposes that Horace's list imitates the statues of the *summi viri* on the right gallery of the temple to Mars Ultor (Zanker, 1988:210–15). If so, what might the poet be implying with his inclusion of Tarquin, the haughty last king of Rome, within the poetic reconstruction of a temple designed to depict the continuity of the Augustan achievement? This cannot be covered over with a general explanation of Roman prosperity under Tarquin's rule. *Rex* and *superbus,* particularly in combination, were never terms of praise in republican or imperial Rome.

70. Augustus returns once more to earth in C.III.5 (*praesens divus,* 2) and then after accomplishing heroic deeds in Spain returns like Hercules (*Herculis ritu*) to Rome (C.III.14). The poet's rotation of Augustus between heaven and earth, begun in C.I.2 and continued through the last apotheosis of the third book and into *Odes* IV (c.4, 5), reinforces his identity as an incarnate deity, *divus praesens.*

71. The manuscripts, scholiasts, and editors are evenly divided between the future *bibet* and the present *bibit.* Both make good sense. The prophetic future is so certain that the present tense explains its force, which in addition to the obvious orthographic similarities accounts for the two readings. *Bibit* has the advantage of fitting Horace's custom of portraying Augustus as a god incarnate (*divus praesens*). Cf. Wickham (1874:*ad loc.*).

72. *Fulmen* and its corresponding forms are not common in Horace (C.I.3.40; 12.60; III.3.6; 4.44, 74; 16.11; IV.4.1). There is no other occurrence of the word between C.I.12 and III.3.

73. Also C.III.5.1–4.

74. Fraenkel (1957:441–42); Syndikus (1973:331–32); Quinn (1980: nn.1–8); Putnam (1986:103); Garrison (1991:351 n.1).

75. For the role of light in Oriental, Greek, and Roman panegyric, see Meuli (1955:208 n.5); Weinstock (1971:381–84). Typically the light of the ruler eclipses all other lights or drives out darkness; see Lucretius on Epicurus (3.1042–44; 5.10b–12). The same motif continues in the writings of the early church (I Thes. 5.5–8; I John 2.8).

76. Cass. Dio 54.27.2–3; Suet. *Aug.*31. Augustus was particularly proud of his election to the office of pontifex maximus (*RG* 10). See Taylor (1931:183–85, 190–204, 245–46); Liebeschuetz (1979:71–77).

77. DuQuesnay (1995:151) classifies the ode strictly as a klētikon. It would be more accurate to see the poem as a transition between forms:

from the klētikon to the actual return. The hymn form, as I argue, bridges the gap between Augustus's absence at the beginning of the ode and his presence at the end.

78. See Maecenas's return after an illness (C.I.20); also C.I.36.10–16 (Numida), II.7.20–28 (Pompeius), and III.14.17–28 (Augustus).

79. The beauty of spring's renewal makes the party more enticing and adds urgency by symbolizing the transience of youth; also C.IV.12.1–12 and the two Faunus odes, I.4.1–12; I.17.1–16 (on Faunus and Faustitas in c.5, see Oliensis, 1998:116–18). The Parthians, Scythians, and Spanish Cantabrians are standard sympotic fare for martial conflicts that should be forgotten for the drinking party (C.II.11.1–4a; III.8.17–24; III.29.25–28).

80. Note Horace's invitation to his comrade Pompey (*ergo obligatam redde Iovi dapem*, C.II.7.17). This is the only other time Horace uses the imperative *redde* in the *Odes*, or for a sympotic invitation (cf. *S*.II.8.80; *Epist.*I.7.95; II.1.216).

81. See Wickham (1874:n.9); K.-H. (1884:n.9); Syndikus (1973:334–36).

82. Cf. Quinn (1980:nn.9–16).

83. K.-H (1884:n.9) cite the similar Oppian *Hal.*4.331–43 and posit a common lost Hellenistic source behind Oppian and Horace, perhaps Callimachus (see DuQuesnay, 1995:159 n.167; cf. Prop. 3.7, cited by Putnam, 1986:105–6).

84. DuQuesnay (1995:172–73) recognizes that the allusion to the Ennian apotheosis of Romulus at the beginning of the ode is "still in play" at the transition, that is, the Romans calmed their grief for the absent Romulus by deifying him, but DuQuesnay maintains that the peasant's celebration is a completely private occasion. Syndikus (1973:342–43) notes the obvious repetition of a ring structure in the two requests (*bone dux*, 4, 37) and complains that the speaker's situation has completely changed. It has. The lament in the allusion to Romulus sets up the peasant's invocation that enacts the apotheosis (Augustus's return), and the apotheosis (Augustus's return) in turn sets off the celebration. The poet has made the moment of apotheosis the climax that unifies the ode's two sections.

85. *Condere diem* (to pass time) from the metaphor of burying the day, is attested but not common (Lucr. 3.1090; Verg. *Ecl.*9.52; *G.*1.458; Stat. *Theb.*10.54; Plin. *Ep.*9.36.5). Although Horace uses the word in this sense only here, it is particularly apt because the vinedresser is a *conditor* according to two of the more common denotations of the word. (1) He preserves the wine (Var. *R.*1.13.6; Verg. *Ecl.*3.43; Tib. 1.10.47; H. C.I.20.3; Ov. *Ars* 2.696; *Fast.*5.269, 518); (2) he inaugurates a new dispensation (Verg. *A.*1.33; 10.35; Stat. *Silv.*4.1.37; Plin. *Nat.*7.120).

86. By "magic" I mean the power of a poet's *carmina* within a ritual occasion to transfigure and transcend physical realities (*Epist*.II.1.132–38); see Putnam (2000:132–46).

4. Songs of Mo(u)rning

1. Lyne (1995:136, 207). Since *Odes* IV culminates in imperial panegyric (c.14–15), one could speculate that the public "saps" the private.

2. Oliensis (1998:144). What are we to make of the fact that Horace berates old Lyce? Her survival and transition (and the poet's) into a decrepit hag would not be a compliment in any case.

3. The synthesis of the lyric voice and themes with encomium (c.1) suggests reconciliation as the more productive approach.

4. For an overview of funerary ritual in Greek and Roman society, see Toynbee (1971); Alexiou (1974); Reece and Collins (1977); Hopkins (1983); Flower (1996); Beissinger and Wofford (1999:189–235); Pearce and Struck (2000). Russell and Wilson (1981:xiii–xviii) trace the early literary history of the *epitaphios*. On the elaborate ceremonies of imperial funerals: Julius Caesar (App. *BC*.2.147; Suet. *Caes*.84; Dio Cass. 44.35, 51); Augustus (Tac. *Ann*.1.8; Suet. *Aug*.100; Dio Cass. 56.31–34); Septimius Severus (Hist. Aug. *Sev*.24; Hdn. 4.2).

5. In Rome mourning was not a completely private matter, since laws were passed to regulate displays of grief (V. Max. 6.3; Mueller, 2002:139–43).

6. The *epitaphios* was considered didactic (Isoc. *Evagoras* 5; Plb. 6.53.3, 9–10).

7. Cf. Bowra (1952:9–10). Cicero nearly excludes *laudatio* as a category of rhetoric because its proofs develop naturally from the character of the *laudandus,* which the audience can verify since they witnessed the life (*de Orat*.2.43–49, 65, 342–47; *Part*.71–72, 75–82; see the introduction). He logically concludes that a funerary encomium is not a proper occasion for orators to show off their talents (*de Orat*.2.341).

8. Aristotle (*Rh*.1358a36–b8) differentiates the classes of rhetoric by the function of the hearers. An audience can be a judge (κριτής) in the case of forensic and deliberative, or a spectator (θεωρός) in epideictic (see the introduction). Aristotle does not elaborate on the specific qualities of a spectator (Russell and Wilson, 1981:xix), but Isocrates also represents the panegyric writer and audience as spectators and athletes, and neither are passive (*Evagoras* 79).

9. Greene (1999:193, 195).

10. Vergil and Horace think alike, sometimes. Horace uses the question of whether a Carthaginian lament should be embraced to complicate Hannibal's speech (C.IV.4.50–72). How persuasive should

Hannibal's encomiastic lament be? Should his audience be hard like Aeneas or not?

11. The lover's lament before a rejecting beloved becomes a potent weapon when the internal and external audiences differ in their reactions to the lament. The beloved may remain unmoved, but those listening in may accept the lament and identify with the rejected lover. This is the power of the paraklausithyron. The singer then has won a new beloved, and the one rejecting has become rejected. This reversal is demonstrated in the progression of Horace's laments for Ligurinus to his curse on Lyce (c.10–13).

12. The introduction occurred seven to eight years before *S.*II.6, dated to approximately 31 B.C.; see Wickham's (1891) introduction to the *Satires*, section 2.

13. K.-H. (1884, vol.2:xxii); van Rooy (1973:87); Leach (1978:79–105).

14. Vergilius of IV.12 is the poet; see c.12 later in this chapter.

15. Each view has supporters. In spite of the long-standing debate (J. S. Campbell, 1987:314–15 nn.1–3), the primary dimensions of the problem are found in Lockyer (1967:42–45); Basto (1982:30–43); J. Pucci (1992:659–73); Thomas (2001:55–73). Elder (1952:140–58) first hinted that the propempticon might be a metaphor on poetics; then Commager (1962:119–20); Lockyer (1967); and Cairns (1972:235) more cautiously; Zumwalt (1974:455); Kidd (1977:97–103); and Basto (1982). Excepting perhaps Zumwalt, who thinks the ode takes aim at both poets, most interpret the ode as honoring Vergil. Pucci and Thomas think Horace is more critical. I agree with Pucci that Horace's propempticon contains a metaphoric critique of Vergil's new project of writing epic. His conclusion that the poets' earlier friendship was broken I find less convincing. Professional disagreements often stimulate creativity and are not necessarily an indicator of either a close or a broken friendship. Thomas sees no hard evidence that Vergil and Horace were personal friends. Does *animae dimidium meae* refer solely to the intricate intertextuality of their poetry? It does not with Maecenas (*C.*II.17.5). For positive assessments of *animae dimidium meae*, see Duckworth (1956:281–316); Schmidt (1983: 1–36).

16. Buttrey (1972:31–48) documents the mercantile vocabulary of *C.*I.3, which continues in *C.*IV.12, 21–22, 25.

17. Nisbet and Hubbard (N.-H., 1970:289) discount Donatus's account (in a late and corrupt manuscript) that a Vergilian saying lies behind Nautes' advice: "(Vergilius) solitus erat dicere nullam virtutem commodiorem homini esse patientia, ac nullam adeo asperam esse fortunam quam prudenter patiendo vir fortis non vincat" (Diehl, 1911:36). Vergil's favorite saying aside, Horace's *consolatio* uses the *Aeneid* for a lesson on moderation in lament. For a fuller discussion of the *Aeneid* in

c.24, see Putnam (1993:130–33). Khan (1967:107–17) proposes that Horace is answering a specific Vergilian elegy composed to mourn Quintilius — interesting but highly conjectural.

18. I have not singled out *Ecl.*5 randomly. Its bipartite and chiastic structure is similar to Horace's epinikion (c.4), and its combination of lament and apotheosis is a mirror image of c.5, Horace's hymn to Augustus (see ch.3). For more specific markers, see the arguments on *Ecl.*5 later in this chapter.

19. Compare Mopsus's order to inscribe a verse on the tomb (42–44) to Horace's later claim that poetry overpowers honorary inscriptions (C.IV.8; 14). Mopsus's lament for Daphnis contains multiple metaphoric referents to the death of the oral tradition: the bucolic landscape is in ruin; the hazel trees testify to Daphnis's death (21); Pales, a purely Roman deity, and the Greek god Apollo both desert the land.

20. For a full account, see Festa (1933:436–41); also N.-H. (1970:48). Horace's use of *animae* both in *S.*I.5.41–42 and *C.*I.3.8 links the expressions *alter* and *dimidium*.

21. Callimachus is the more popular source, but Meleager contains the more promising parallels. Nisbet and Hubbard (N.-H., 1970:48) conclude Horace depends on both.

22. I am not convinced that Ligurinus must be a freeborn citizen. Supporters of this view take *deciderint comae* as referring to cutting a youth's hair when he assumes the *toga virilis* (Shorey, 1898:n.3; Quinn, 1980:nn.1–5; Garrison, 1991:n.3). *Deciderint* need not be so specific. Long hair symbolizes eternal youth, for example, Apollo and Bacchus (Tib. 1.4.33–38; 2.5.121). Although attested (Cassius Ligurinus, the procurator of Moesia under Septimius Severus), the name Ligurinus is uncommon among Roman nobility. Whether Ligurinus was a real person and Horace bisexual is beside the point (compare G. Williams, 1962:38–41 with Shackleton Bailey, 1982:67–75). The name likely occurred to Horace because it suited the character's dramatic role. The Ligurians were legendary for their toughness (Cic. *Agr.* 2.95; Liv. 5.35; 22.33; 27.39; n.b. Diod. Sic. 5.39), and Horace's Ligurinus remains hard-hearted in contrast to Cycnus, a king of the Ligurians. Cycnus, while weeping beside the Po for his lost lover Phaethon, was metamorphosized into a swan. Horace's strained use of *pluma* (feathers) for Ligurinus's facial hair exploits the connection with Ligurinus's mythic past (see note 24 below). When Ligurinus's unfeeling rejection of love contradicts his mythic lineage, the poet puts old man's hair on his face, a far different metamorphosis that forces Ligurinus to face his own future of painful loneliness.

23. Propertius concludes book 3 with a similar warning to Cynthia (25.11–18). The wrinkled Cynthia before a mirror, the reversal of the *exclusus amator* (this time Cynthia will be shut out, *exclusa*, not the male

lover), and the minatory conclusion closely parallel Horace's plaint against Ligurinus. For an account of possible Hellenistic sources and a comparison of Prop. 3.25 to the threats against Lydia (C.I.25) and Lyce (C.IV.13), see K.-H. (1884:*proem*); Pasquali (1920:461); Fraenkel (1957:414 n.1); G. Williams (1968:556–57); Syndikus (1973:387–88).

24. *Pluma* is appropriate for the downy hair of a young male's first beard but is not attested in this sense elsewhere. Horace uses *pluma* for no other person except himself, when he metamorphosizes into a swan (C.II.20.12). Bentley (1711) emends to "bruma," but the association of the word with the poet's and the Ligurian king Cycnus's transformation into a swan works well in an ode in which another Ligurinus faces transformation (see note 22 above). *Pluma* also contrasts well with the thorny roughness of *hispida,* which the scholiasts gloss with *hirsuta.* Horace uses this designation in a topographical description (*hispidos . . . agros,* C.II.9.1–2), its most common denotation, but Vergil first applies it to the human form (of Triton, *A.*10.210; the Vergilian context includes the myth of Cycnus's metamorphosis, see Putnam, 1986:182 n.9). Later Silius Italicus (13.333) uses *hispida* for Pan's beard, and Martial (3.58.37) to describe a goat. Horace uses *punicea* only here and coined *involitant,* which never appears again.

25. Editions divide evenly between the majority reading *Ligurinum* and the poorly attested *Ligurine.* I prefer the lesser reading (Bentley, 1711). Not only does the vocative fit better with the direct address of the next line (*dices*) and the intransitive use of *verterit,* but it more closely conforms to the earlier lament (*sed cur, heu, Ligurine, cur,* c.1.33).

26. Enumerated earlier in this chapter.

27. Horace makes *alterum, animis, incolumes* stand out by placing them in emphatic positions and assigning them uncommon meanings. *Alter* nowhere else describes one's changed reflection in a mirror, and *incolumes* appears only here for smooth beardless cheeks (*TLL* 7.1, 979.82: *incolumis* IA1b, "audacius de genis nondum tonsis"). The precise sense of *animis* remains dubious. When *animus* refers to a state of mind, although there are instances of the plural (*OLD* s.v. 10–14), it is typically singular as in the first address to Ligurinus, IV.1.30, *iam nec spes animi credula mutui.* The plural represents more often a negative connotation, such as anger or haughtiness (courage is split between the singular and plural). Commager's translation (1962:297) dodges the problem by omission; Müller (1869:nn.6–8) suspects that the plural is a metrical accommodation (see *Epist.*I.17.40). Surely Horace could have expressed the same thought in any number of words to avoid the hiatus *animo incolumes.* Putnam (1986:183) thinks the plural signifies Ligurinus's recurrent regret. Most interpret *animis* as a synonym for *mens* and read the last two verses as repeating the lesson on the transience of desire and desir-

ability (line 7). I propose reading *his animis* in the sense of *meis amoribus* (a common gloss in the manuscripts, e.g., Reg. lat. 1703 [R] and Vat. Lat. 3257) and taking it closely with *incolumes:* "Why don't my cheeks come alive again with their passions?" *Animis* as a qualifying ablative better explains the unusual *incolumes* than a tautology of *mens.* The use of the plural allows Horace to communicate well enough his meaning and to neatly disguise the difference between *animus* and *anima* so that *alterum . . . animis incolumes* might be more easily associated with *animae dimidium meae.*

28. Such biographical interpretation (Fraenkel, 1957:415) has fallen out of vogue and has been ridiculed as simplistic (Commager, 1962:297–98; Quinn's [1980:317–18] and Putnam's [1986:179 n.3] rewriting of Fraenkel); see Nethercut's more balanced approach (in McKay, 1982:vi; cf. McNeill, 2001:4). The poet prompts biographical associations when Horace states his age (*circa lustra decem*, c.1.6). This is not to deny the conventions of the cursed lover popular in Hellenistic poetry or to insist that the poet is lamenting his own age and nothing more. I would simply say that both views are present: Ligurinus and Horace (his poetics as well) are in the mirror. Here life and poetics merge so closely that they are indistinguishable.

29. See Edmunds (2001:159–63).

30. The neglect of c.11 is "perverse" (Commager's word, 1962:302, 305). Since then several fine reviews have appeared, but they leave the relationship between the two odes relatively unexamined. The most influential include von Albrecht (1995:83–88); Argetsinger (1992:175–93); Bernays (1996:35–42); Boyle (1973:181–84); Reckford (1959:25–33); Opperman (1957:102–11). On the Hellenistic sources for C.II.4: Pasquali (1920:489–95); Cairns (1977:132–33); N.-H. (1978:66–68); in general, Syndikus (1972:365–68); Pavlock (1982:89); Davis (1991:19–22); D. West (1998:29–33).

31. Most concentrate on Horace's own black cares (*atrae . . . curae*, 35–36) and forget the startling change in the poet's persona between rejection and seduction.

32. Care must be taken not to minimize the depth of Horace's generic interplay that encompasses epic, tragedy, and particularly comedy. Specifically, when the ode moves into its second half, the comic plots familiar to the Romans from the *fabulae palliatae* of their own playwrights emerge. Credit Syndikus (1972:366–68), Cairns (1977:132), and Garrison (1991:nn.18–20) for moving the discussion in this direction.

33. Sophocles' tragedy *Ajax*, not Homer (*Il.*1.138), names Tecmessa; *Tekmessa, RE* 5A.157. Horace reserves his epic antonomasia for the more prominent character Cassandra.

34. N.-H. (1978:71 n.7), Davis (1991:22), and D. West (1998:31) limit

medio in triumpho (7) to the conflagration of Troy. Since the immediate example of Ajax has connections with Greek tragedy, the ode could also have in view Agamemnon's tragic homecoming. Although Horace applies Roman terms to foreign customs, it would be natural to assume that a *triumphus* takes place after the victorious hero returns home. We do not need to split hairs. The characters and colors of one scene (Agamemnon, Cassandra, the red fires of Troy) project the other (Agamemnon, the red beacon fires, Cassandra, the scarlet draped walk to the palace). If Agamemnon can be taken as a tragic reference, then the exempla constitute a generic ring: epic-tragedy-epic.

35. Xanthias need not be a Greek slave (D. West, 1998:33; cf. Ritter, 1857:*proem;* Quinn, 1980:nn.1–4). Horace commonly assigns characters a Greek name as part of his mixing of Greek and Roman worlds (e.g., C.I.8, *Sybaris*). Orelli (1837:*proem*) speculates that the pseudonym Xanthias protects a member of the Flavii (cf. Wickham, 1874:*proem*), but Horace could have chosen the name to exploit its comic potential (Phyllis ["leafy"], C.IV.11); see Boyle's list of names and meanings (1973:168, 186 n.18).

36. Not that love affairs with slaves were so taboo among the Romans. The poem concerns itself with supposed generic parameters rather than cultural precision (cf. N.-H., 1978:67).

37. Phocis is the district around Delphi. For the learned, the epithet adds a subtle association with the blond Apollo, a deity of conflicting characteristics (revelation-mystery; healing-affliction).

38. See D. West (1998:30–31); Davis (1991:20–21); N.-H. (1978:71 nn.6–7).

39. N.-H. (1978:72 n.10). Maybe the snob Xanthias, and epic writers in general, should notice that being too epic/heroic has dire consequences.

40. *Nescias* appears over fifty times: *ut nescias, quasi nescias,* and instances in other conditions account for the majority. *Nescias* introduces indirect questions, including alternative questions, but *nescias* as a tentative affirmative modeled on *haud scio an* or *nescio an,* as far as I can find, is unparalleled except in pseudo-Quintilian, *Decl. Maior.*16.7.9. Cf. N.-H. (1978:73 n.13).

41. That nobility births nobility is featured in the epinikion C.IV.4.29–32, and the principle again complicates the song's plot (see ch.3). For further examples of the theme, see Marcovich (1975:8).

42. Therefore, *crede* is better understood as "imagine" or "suppose;" see Pl. *As.*202; *Rud.*458; *Truc.*322; Ter. *Eu.*711; *OLD* s.v. *credo* 5, 7.

43. On *nescias, certe* cf. Cairns (1977:132, 134); N.-H. (1978:68, 73).

44. After the poet lists Phyllis's physical charms (21), *integer* (22), de-

rived from *in-tango* (untouched) and synonymous with virgin, has to be laughable.

45. Cairns (1977:132).

46. Horace dates the wine in only eight other sympotic poems (*Ep*.13; *C*.I.9; 20; III.8; 14; 21; *Epist*.I.5). Horace's strong association of the sympotic and *carpe diem* results naturally in some agreement between the dating of wines and the theme of aging. The exception is *C*.III.28.8, which dates the wine to Bibulus's consulship (59 B.C.): a double pun on the name *bibulus* (fond of drinking) and the personification of the wine jar that delays (*cessantem Bibuli consulis amphoram*), just as Bibulus delayed the plans of his co-consul, Julius Caesar.

47. I would not insist that Phyllis be the same actual individual as the Phyllis courted by Xanthias any more than her Telephus be the same as Lydia's ensnared lover (*C*.I.13). Nor is Phyllis just any name. Horace, by repeating the name Phyllis in only two odes in which she plays the part of a younger love interest for an aging poet, creates in her a symbolic location for the power of lyric over time.

48. The sympotic metaphor of girls mixing with boys pictures the eroticism of the scene (E. *Ba*.233–38); see Commager (1962:303). Kiessling and Heinze (K.-H. 1884:*ad loc*.) note that the replacement of *ancilla* with *puella* removes the distance between master and servant and creates a more seductive appeal to Phyllis. I would add that it distinguishes the poet from Xanthias, who was ashamed to love a slave girl (*C*.II.4).

49. On *vis multa*, see Putnam (1986:187–88): the ivy through enjambment (*vis / multa*) binds the stanzas together so that the leafy ivy (Phyllis) stands for the artifice of song that joins the lovers.

50. Horace achieves a dual effect with *avet*. Its meaning, "to crave" (see *S*.I.1.94; Lucr. 3.1082–84), supplies the primary sexual force for the metaphor, whereas the archaism *avet . . . spargier* increases the solemnity of the verse. The altar cannot be for the sacrifice to Maecenas's *genius* to celebrate his birth. The Romans did not practice animal sacrifices for birthday rituals (Argetsinger, 1992:187). The love altar would be very appropriate for Venus. April was her month as well as Maecenas's, a happy coincidence for the lyric poet desiring love (15–16).

51. For *trepido* in contexts of the passing of time, see *C*.II.3.12; 11.4; III.27.17; 29.32; the only exception is II.19.5, which treats the poet's Bacchic inspiration. Bentley (1711) and A. Y. Campbell (1945) conjecture "crepitant" for *trepidant*. Bentley wants to remove any darkness from the scene but leaves *sordidum . . . fumum*. Once the Horatian contexts for *trepido* are considered, the flickering flames and the dark smoke set the mood for the black cares, the end of love and life. The celebration is not without care, which fits the seriocomic pattern of Horace's symposia.

Besides, a fire-producing dirty smoke, which occurs when the flame is burning inefficiently, requires *trepidant* (wavers), not "crepitant" (crackles). Not to mention that "crepitant" would spoil the increasing instability in the progression *festinat, cursitant, trepidant*.

52. *Ater* has sinister overtones (*S*.II.7.115; *C*.II.3.16, cf. Verg. *A*.10.77; *C*.II.16.2; III.1.40; 14.13; 27.18); see N.-H. (1970, 1978:*C*. I.37.27, II.14.17 *ad loc.*).

53. The *OLD* lists *occupavit* (21) under "to seize political control or military command." Horace frequently uses the verb with a militaristic nuance (*Ep*.16.10; *C*.I.12.19; *C*.III.6.13; 24.3). The only other time Horace uses the word in book IV he plays it against Lollius. Lollius deployed his victorious arms against the enemy, but he would more rightly take possession (*occupat*) of the name blessed (9.43–47); on Lollius's loss to the Sygambri, see c.9 in ch.2.

54. Cf. Putnam (1986:193–94).

55. The pessimism can be overdone. The poet writes *alia* not *ulla*: he is attempting to convince Phyllis to accept his love by promising his fidelity as much as admitting his old age.

56. For the power of wine over cares, *C*.I.7.17–20; 17.21–22; 18.3–4; II.11.17–18; III.12.1–2; 17.14–16. The closest parallel is *C*.III.28: the poet invites Lyde to share a night of song and lovemaking, and the wine that he instructs her to bring out of storage has the power to conquer resistance (2b–4). The poet's song (wine) will win a responsive song (lovemaking) from her.

57. *Modus* denotes spatial and quantitative relationships, and therefore well describes the process of making verse in lyric rhythms (*TLL* s.v. *modus* IA1b, IA2a, b). For the use of the corresponding participle *minutus*, "insignificant," see Munro (1878:65) on Cat. 25.12.

58. On the ode's musicality: von Albrecht (1995:83–88).

59. Horace uses the language of *alterum/animae dimidium meae* and reworks *carpe diem* to comfort Maecenas — they will seize the final journey together (*supremum / carpere iter comites parati, C*.II.17.11–12). Horace compensates well for not addressing *C*.IV.1 to Maecenas by placing his birthday ode after the ode to Ligurinus where the poet remembers Vergil as his other half (see c.10 earlier in this chapter). The poet draws his inner circle of friends tightly, repeating *alteram, alterum* at the end of the sixth verse in both *C*.II.17 and IV.10, the same line where Vergil is first named in the *Odes* (I.3). On "alteram" for *altera* of the manuscripts, see N.-H. (1978:*ad loc.*).

60. Commonly cited studies on the identity of Vergilius are Wickham (1874); Bowra (1928); Fraenkel (1957); Collinge (1961); Moritz (1968, 1969); Reckford (1969); Porter (1972); Minadeo (1975); Belmont (1980); Pavlock (1982); Putnam (1986).

61. For an earlier presentation of my arguments on c.12, see *Vergilius* (T. S. Johnson, 1995b:49–66).

62. G. Williams (1968:122 n.1) without argument condemns the view that Vergilius is the poet. Lambinus (1561) and Peerlkamp (1834) do not risk any identification, although the latter (s.v. *studium lucri*) rejects the mss. *ad Vergilium negotiatorem*. Commager (1962:274–75) finds the problem distracting.

63. Quinn (1963:13–14) judges the poem an early work, since along with other imperfections the description of spring rambles. Why would a mature Horace publish such a flawed effort? Quinn's answer, an extreme extension of Suetonius, is that the ode is filler to complete a book requested by Augustus.

64. See Mayer (1985:33–46).

65. Fraenkel (1957:418 n.1) quoted by Belmont (1980:5), Minadeo (1975:161), Moritz (1969:174), Porter (1972:72 n.1), Thomas (2001:56). Others dismissing the poet: Orelli (1837:*ad loc.*); Franke (1839:222–23); Müller (1869:*ad loc.*); Wickham (1874:*proem*); T. E. Page (1883:*proem*); K.-H. (1884:*proem*); Plessis and Lejay (1924:*ad loc.*); Putnam 1986 (205–6 n.13); Clay (2002:131).

66. Bentley (1711) s.v. *nardo vina merebere:* "nam *nobiles iuvenes* quoscumque hic intelligit, qui, ut ubique usu venit, principem sui aevi poetarum clientem et sodalem sibi adsciscebant." Also Döring (1830:127–28); Bowra 1928 (165–67); A. Y. Campbell (1945:*ad loc.*); Hahn (1945: xxxii); Wili (1948:358); Collinge (1961:75–76 n.2); Quinn (1963:11–16, 1980:*proem*); Perret (1964:179); Moritz (1968:116–31); Pavlock (1982:89–94); Davis (1991:181); Thomas (2001:56–67).

67. On similarities to C.I.24, see Reckford (1969:128–29); to I.3, see Minadeo (1975:162–63). For other Vergilian parallels, especially in stanzas 1–3, see in particular Döring (1830:127–28); Bowra (1928:166–67); Hahn (1945:xxxii). For the presence of the *Aeneid* in *Odes* IV, see Fraenkel (1957:375).

68. See von Albrecht (1991:147–59).

69. Fraenkel's assessment (1957:419) that the eulogy praises a small man is out of step with the structure of the ode; see Moritz (1969:175).

70. Thus Reckford (1969:128–129) concludes that Horace is not addressing the Vergil, but remembering him. For arguments based on various ring patterns, see Belmont (1980:7–10); Minadeo (1975:162–63); Porter (1972:76–78). Note also a metrical pattern (Belmont, 5): the meter of c.12, third Asclepiadean, is used in eight other odes (I.6, 15, 24, 33; II.12; III.10, 16; IV.5), seven of which have well-known addressees (excluding only Lyce in III.10). Counting IV.12, five out of the nine poems in this meter name either Maecenas, Vergil, or Augustus.

71. Bowra (1928:165).

72. Moritz (1969:192).

73. See Collinge (1961:75–76); Moritz (1969:192); Porter (1972:87).

74. Venus (Aphrodite) often sends favorable winds like the *Favoni* of C.I.4 and renews life in spring (E. *Ba*.402–14; Lucr. 1.1–25; Ov. *Fast*.4.125–32, *Her*.16.23–24; Galinsky, 1966:231; Castriota, 1995:69, 198 nn.59–61). The Phyllis ode, just before c.12, takes place during April, the month of maritime Venus.

75. Ov. *Met*.6.424–674 tells the full story. The details of the myth vary, either Procne or Philomela being the mother of Itys and one sister or the other changed into a nightingale and swallow (Conington, 1858, on Verg. *Ecl*.6.78). Vergil does not help us with Horace. He names Philomela the server of the feast and therefore more than likely the mother transformed into a nightingale (*Ecl*.6), but then Procne is the mother transformed into a swallow (*G*.4.15) and Philomela is the sister transformed into the nightingale (*G*.4.511). The swallow is the more traditional herald of spring (*Epist*.I.7.13; Ov. *Fast*.2.853). It is difficult—and unnecessary for the sense of the ode—to pin down the specific version Horace had in mind.

76. A. Y. Campbell (1945) writes "heu" for *et*. The emendation has not won the support it deserves. Notwithstanding the poetic merits of "heu," *et* is too weak to hold the line at the critical moment. For example, Bennett's Loeb translation omits the connective altogether.

77. Unquenchable thirst is a symptom of disease and by extension a symbol of death. Wine rituals and the symposion, often closely associated with death (see *Levis et Gravis*, ch.1; also Deonna, 1939:53–81; Grottanelli, 1995:62–89), provide relief from the pain of mortality. The shift from thirst to the celebration of a symposion becomes a metaphoric transition that signals Vergil's return and lyric Horace's triumph over death.

78. See Commager (1957:68–80).

79. Cf. C.I.4.15; 11.6–7a; IV.11.25–26a, 29b–31a; also the poet's own renunciation of sympotic pleasures, IV.1.30.

80. See *Ecl*.5 in c.10 earlier in this chapter.

81. On Horace's criticism of Vergil's epic poetics (C.I.3; 24) and the theme of *animae dimidium meae*, see c.10 earlier in this chapter.

82. N.-H. (1970:41): Why was the *Aeneid* entrusted to Varius and Tucca, not to Horace? Nisbet and Hubbard are only puzzling over possibilities. Minadeo (1975:163) states directly that the friendship was broken; also Thomas (2001:58), although he omits all of Horace's allusions to Vergil in book IV except for c.12 and gives no consideration to that ode's plaintive tone. Perhaps the lyric Horace was telling the truth: he was not the one for editing epic.

83. Bowra (1928:165); Belmont (1980:13).

84. Horace uses *lucrum* positively at C.I.9.14–15; cf. Putnam, 1986:206 n.13.

85. Bowra (1928:165) cites Catullus's rough treatment of Furius and Aurelius (poem 16). Belmont (1980:12–13) takes *molle atque facetum / Vergilio annuerunt* (S.I.10.44b–45a) as a remark on Vergil's sense of humor: he knew how to take a joke (cf. Jackson, 1914:136–37). On the importance of sympotic guests being able to give and take jokes, see Slater (1990: 213–14).

86. Putnam (1986:205–6 n.13).

87. Fraenkel (1957:223 n.2) grants that Horace is joking with Maecenas, but not Horace with Vergil.

88. See Horace's Epic Criticism, ch.1.

89. Lines 67–70, Diggle (1970). The chain of allusion from Itys to Phaethon via Euripides is, at the least, finely spun. It is interesting that the nightingale's lament sounds a harmony (ἁρμονίαν).

90. Davis (1991:183–85).

91. Wili (1948:358); Porter (1972:86); Minadeo (1975:163); Davis (1991:186–87).

92. See wine toasting as a metaphor for the pleasure of sharing songs, Dionysius eleg. 1 (W.).

93. An exchange of song with Vergil foreshadows the conclusion of the sympotic theme in book IV: adopting and reworking national themes in the lyric mode (c.15).

94. See also fatness and thinness in Theoc. 6.88–100. I suspect that there are poetic qualifications behind *adduxere sitim*, 13: 'dryness' is a Callimachean aesthetic value (Batstone, 1998:125–35).

95. Cf. Castriota (1995:135).

96. Apollo's promotion of the lyric form and Horace's association of that form with national themes within the sympotic motif are one more instance of the blending of Apolline and Dionysiac symbolism in the art of the early empire (see C.II.19.25–28; III.25.1–8). For a fuller discussion with special emphasis on the Ara Pacis, see Castriota (1995:106–23).

97. Contrast Ancona's readings (1994) on how Horace uses time against lovers.

98. Horace does not make the parallels between Lydia (C.I.25) and Lyce hard to spot. Most commentators (e.g., Catlow, 1976:813–21) observe in general that I.25 and IV.13 parade some of the harshest abuse in the *Odes*. Specifically, Lydia will be like the dry leaves (*aridas frondes*, 19) that the youths discard in favor of verdant ivy (*pubes hedera virenti / gaudeat*, 17–18a); Lyce is the dry oak Cupid passes by (*aridas / quercus*, 9–10) when he lights on the cheeks of verdant Chia (*virentis . . . Chiae*, 6–7); see Davis (1991:223).

99. For examples in the epigrams, see Esler (1989:172–73 nn.1–4).

100. Catlow (1976:820); Putnam (1986:227); Connor (1987:189). On the vicious realism of the attack: Wilamowitz-Moellendorff (1913:321–22); K.-H. (1884:*proem*); Copley (1956:160 n.40).

101. E.g., Lyde (*C* III.28.6b–8).

102. This is the majority opinion: Minadeo (1982:41); Putnam (1986:224–28); Connor (1987:188–89); Esler (1989:175–76); Arkins (1993:113); Ancona (1994:97, 100); Syndikus (1995:26–27); Oliensis (1998:144).

103. According to Catlow (1976:819) the metaphor of a snow-covered head (12) adds a touch of beauty to the portrait of ugly Lyce and by echoing the same image applied generally to humanity in the Soracte ode starts the poet reflecting on the brevity of his life. Putnam (1986:222 n.3) is less pleased, citing Quintilian (8.6.17), who calls the metaphor hard (*dura*), but Putnam also is reminded of the Soracte ode and its vocabulary (*nive, virenti, canities*). There is another closer referent, *nives*, also at a verse end in an earlier ode to a Lyce (III.10.7). The storied winter weather, then not even a veiled threat of the white hair ahead for Lyce, shows its teeth as the final feature in Horace's description of Lyce's ugly face (yellow teeth, wrinkles, and snowy hair, IV.13.9–12). Threat has become reality. Horace turns a universal image for old age into a very personal attack — not very introspective and not very pretty.

104. Nisbet (1962:187–88) finds the whole psychologically unconvincing; cf. Boyle (1973:168, 184). Two remedies predominate. (1) The inconsistencies reflect the ode's emotional depth as the rejected poet struggles with an anger that brought on Lyce a result, old age and loss, that he has experienced himself and finds repulsive (Catlow, 1976:819). (2) When Horace returns to cursing at the end of his song, the empathy that he has felt causes him to mollify his threat (Fraenkel, 1957:416). Some (e.g., Catlow, 1976:820; Lyne, 1980:211; Arkins, 1993:113; cf. Putnam, 1986:227) see in Horace's representation of the youths as fiery a suggestion that they are blind to the reality that their torches, too, will one day flame out. This is little consolation for Lyce.

105. Quinn (1963:99); Lyne (1980:211).

106. So Putnam (1986:227) implies.

107. As in C.I.16.

108. See Phld. *A.P.*5.112

109. The poet's last praise to Melpomene reiterates Horace's vatic status (cf. IV.3.13–15 with I.1.35–36; IV.3.19–20 with II.20.9–12; IV.3.10–12, 24 with III.30.15b–16). See also c.3 in ch.2.

110. Rejection is the most plausible motive for the personal tone of the poet's anger.

111. The cursing of Lyce also repeats the language of another ode to Lydia (III.9). Chloë and Chia are both skilled in playing the lyre (*Chloe*

regit, / *dulcis docta modos et citharae sciens,* 9.9b–10; *virentis et* / *doctae psallere Chiae* 13.6b–7). Lydia and Lyce were happy when they were not placed after another love (*arsisti neque erat Lydia post Chloen,* / *multi Lydia nominis,* 9.6–7; *felix post Cinaram notaque et artium* / *gratarum facies,* 13.21–22a), and the fates direct the length of the rival lovers' lives (*si parcent animae* [*puero,* line 16] *fata superstiti,* 9.12; *sed Cinarae brevis* / *annos fata dederunt,* 13.22b–23). The repetitions associate the two odes to Lydia (I.25, III.9) with the two to Lyce (III.10, IV.13); on the possible implications for the paraklausithyron motif, see the discussion of lines 13–16, later in this chapter.

112. Opinions vary: the speaker is being rejected (Cairns, 1972:89); he was rejected but is no longer an *exclusus amator* (N.-H., 1970:291; Catlow, 1976:815); there is not enough detail to exclude either scenario (W. J. Henderson, 1973:59–60); the poet does not put himself into the poem but remains objective (Arkins, 1983:163). D. West's Horace (1995:117–19), a "Professor of Love," stands behind the poem's actors having a chuckle at their naïveté and "the silliness of love poets." The poem, however, has such a compelling personal edge that the supposition of someone viewing the drama with bemused or remorseful detachment seems in my opinion too remote. Of course, Horace does not solve this dilemma and allows us to read into the dramatic situation as much as we would like.

113. By the use of "singer," "poet," and "Horace," I am not implying that the singer of the ode should or may be distinguished from the voice of the poet (see the introduction to this book). Others argue this distinction primarily in C.I.25, where the first person is more hidden. The reference to Cinara, closely associated with Horace's persona as the old poet (c.1), makes it unlikely that we should imagine a singer other than the poet. This, of course, does not imply that Lyce must be a real person any more than the character played by the poet must be autobiographical.

114. Wills (1996:180–81).

115. Lyce makes an excellent stock name for a courtesan (*lupa,* the Roman equivalent for Lyce, was slang for prostitute, Liv. 1.4.7–8), but after Horace has so frequently referenced the poems of his earlier collection and immediately after the dual addresses to Ligurinus (c.1; 10) and Phyllis (c.11; II.4), it is difficult to suppress the memory of III.10, the only other ode to a Lyce. Certainly the identical name might prompt the memory of the other Lyce, even if she ultimately were to be viewed as a different character.

116. The pathetic *quo . . . quo* meant to rouse sympathy for the singer (III.10.5) will be repeated at IV.13.17–18 in an unempathetic renewal of the song's opening attack (see the later discussion of lines 17–20).

117. Rufinus *A.P.*5.76.4–6 is particularly close (gray hair, wrinkles,

and the loss of one's younger self, καὶ νῦν τῶν προτέρων οὐδ' ὄναρ οὐδὲν ἔχει; cf. *quid habes illius, illius,* 18b). The authenticity of the similar Call. epigr. 63.1330–32 is in dispute, and the author may again be Rufinus (see G.-P., 1965, vol. 2:214). The two epigrams do interact through the repetition of οὐδ' ὄναρ. A beloved not even dreaming up a pity for the lover she rejected becomes not even a dream of her former self. Refusing to admit a suitor is a type of self-destruction. Such threats are not traditionally made as an expression of empathy motivated by pity but as an attack motivated by revenge or at least by the desire to persuade the beloved to stop resisting. Horace, too, is hardly being empathetic, as the entire tone of the ode demonstrates. See also Rufin. *A.P.*5.21, 27, 28, 92, 103; Mel. *A.P.*5.204; Maced. *A.P.*5.233, 271; Jul. Aegypt. *A.P.*5.298; Agath. *A.P.*5.273; Prop. 3.25.11–14; Ov. *Ars* 2.113–120; 3.57–76; *Met.*15.232–236; *Tr.*3.7.31–44; Mart. 10.90.1–4.

118. *Epist.*I.10.5 is the only other time Horace uses the word (*vetuli notique columbi*).

119. *Sollicitare* can be positive or negative, "to stimulate" or "disturb" (*OLD* s.v. *sollicito* 1, 4, 5c). The double entendre that results from Lyce interpreting her song positively and everyone else around her interpreting it negatively insults Lyce's total lack of self-awareness (*caecus Amor sui / . . . vacuum plus nimio Gloria verticem,* C.I.18.14b–15). She thinks she arouses, but she actually bothers; cf. Lyne (1980:211).

120. The Greek lyricists well establish the seriocomic nature of the symposion; see *Levis et Gravis* in ch.1; n.b. Alcaeus (political views), Theognis, Xenophanes, Bacchylides, and the Anacreontea.

121. The notable exceptions are odes celebrating returns (I.20, 36; II.7; III.14) or Dionysiac inspiration (II.19; III.25). Slater (1990:216, C.I.27) names Horace "the most civilized of symposiasts." I would add that in general the sympotic scenes of *Odes* III are more vigorous.

122. See the *carpe diem* admonitions against entertaining excessive hope (C.I.4.15; 11.6–7; IV.11.30). Only Vergil is advised otherwise (C.IV.12.19–20).

123. *Impudens* should shock. Horace never tosses off shame words lightly. Besides Lyce only two other women are shameless. Medea is named by the metonymy *impudica Colchis* (*Ep.*16.58), and Europa declares herself *impudens* when she realizes that lust caused her to abandon her father (C.III.27.49–50). Medea, Europa, and Lyce all give in to their sexual appetites so that they violate accepted social mores.

124. No other Horatian singer has a shaky song, *cantu tremulo,* 5; see the *symposion non decorum* which Trimalchio must endure, *tremula taeterrimaque voce cantavit,* Petr. *Sat.* 70.7.3; cf. Horace's excited Dionysiac song, C.II.19.5.

125. Chia (Χία) is a common name (a Chia may have been a resident

of Horace's Apulia in the second century B.C.; see *LGPN*), but this is the only occasion Horace names a woman Chia. In Horace *Chia* is the wine, and as such the name seduces the senses. Chian is the choicest and a most expensive wine, followed by Coan, Thasian, and Lesbian (Allen, 1961:67–68; Mole, 1966:115, 137–38 n.152; Ray, 1967:158–59. Aristophanes (Athen 1.29) lists Chian as a dangerously strong aphrodisiac. The name adds erotic potency to Chia and by comparison adds insult to Lyce, whose name means she-wolf. *Doctus/a* signals excellence in music and poetry (Cat. 35.17; Prop. 3.21.28; Tib. 3.6.41; see *S.*I.10.87; *C.*I.1.29; III.9.10; *Epist.*II.1.117). Horace sarcastically calls the poetasters learned (e.g., the boor; cf. *S.*I.9 line 7 with line 51).

126. See (*C.*II.2.18–24) Horace's reliance on repeated prefixes to contrast Virtue's rejection of the rich elite (*dissidens, eximit, dedocet, deferens*) with her honor for and presence with the self-controlled (*ingentis, irretorto*).

127. The singer's raillery against Lyce recalls the language of Horace's previous paraklausithyra, specifically the odes to Lydia (I.25; III.9) and to Lyce (III.10); cf. W. J. Henderson (1973:51–67). I suggest that the final ode against Lyce completes a dramatic cycle of the motif in which two pairs of corresponding poems pose opposite resolutions, the first moving from a lover's lament to acceptance and possible renewal (*C.*I.25; III.9 to Lydia) and the second from a lover's lament to rejection and cursing (*C.*III.10; IV.13 to Lyce). Once more, c.13 demands a look back. I include as Horatian paraklausithyra any reference to the rejected lover at a closed door (*Ep.*11.19–22; *S.*I.2.64–67; II.3.259–65; *C.*I.25; II.8.17–20; III.7.29–32; 9.20; 10; 14.21–24; 15.8–10; 16.1–8; 26.6–8). The paraklausithyron offers an extensive bibliography, but Copley's work (1956), which supersedes Haight (1950), remains the most comprehensive. To the bibliographic lists cited by Copley (144 n.1) and W. J. Henderson (1973:51 nn.1–5), add Schmeling (1971:333–35) and Cairns (1972:s.v. *komos*). The literary paraklausithyron ("the song sung by the lover at his mistress's door, after he has been refused admission," Copley) developed from the *komos* after the symposion, when the drunken lover caroused the streets to the door of a beloved's house, which he found locked against him. A complete paraklausithyron (a rarity) depicts the *komos*, the rejection at the door, and the rejected lover's lament. This view of the door, of course, is only the stereotyped form of a multiplex motif (see Canter, 1920). The following citations provide a sampling (Schmeling, 1971:344–45): the open door (Ar. *Ec.*938–75; Pl. *Cur.*1–164; Prop. 1.8.27–46; 1.10.15–16; 2.14; Tib. 1.9.53–64); the ineffectual door (Cat. 67.13–14; Prop. 2.6.37–42; 4.1.135–50; Tib. 2.3.71–74); the lament to and by the door (Cat. 67; Prop. 1.16); threat prophecy (Mel. *A.P.*5.204; Rufin. *A.P.*5.76 and 103; Marc. Arg. *A.P.*5.118); voyeurism and the crack in the door (Petr. *Sat.*26); the *exclusa amatrix*

(Asclep. *A.P.*5.164; Rufin. *A.P.*5.43; on Prop. 3.25, see Pasquali's [1920: 440–61] comparison to Horace's paraklausithyra); the *inclusus/a amator/ amatrix* (Mel. *A.P.*5.184; Rufin. *A.P.*5.21; Prop. 1.3.35–36; 2.29; 3.6.19–34; Petr. *Sat.*94.7–8); *furtivus amator* (Tib. 1.2; 1.6.9–10; Ov. *Am.*1.6); *diffamatio* (Cat. 11.16–23; 17.14–22; 37.11–20; 58).

128. The transition to the paraklausithyron motif, specifically the locked-in lover, begins with *excubat* (8), a rare word in Horace, used elsewhere only once and in the noun form (*excubiae*) for the dogs guarding Danaë, who is also a locked-in lover (*C.*III.16.1–4); cf. Ov. *Am.*3.11.12.

129. See *includo* (*OLD* s.v. 8) and *condo* (*OLD* s.v. 14); Putnam (1986:224 n.7).

130. Just so that the antiquarian knows, the choicest Chian wines in the first century B.C. sold for as much as the best of the Greek wines, 400 sesterces per amphora. The average day-laborer would have to work about four months to pay for a jar of quality Chian (Mole, 1966:221).

131. The poet's negative spin on the *fasti* complicates the opening question of c.14, when the panegyrist wonders how the Romans can appropriately immortalize Augustus by such records (*memoresque fastos*, 4). The *fasti* in Horace do not guarantee immortality, although they played a prominent role in imperial panegyric: e.g., the *Fasti Capitolini Consulares et Triumphales* (Richardson, 1992:23 s.v. *Arcus Augusti*).

132. Horace's favored variation of the paraklausithyron is the *inclusa amatrix*. When the poet tells Chloris (III.15) to stop playing love games (4–5), go home, and attend the household tasks (13–14), he effectively shuts her in behind the door. Chloris's daughter Pholoë, an *exclusa amatrix*, assumes a position of power exactly the opposite of Lydia (*C.*I.25). Lydia's door closes her in; Pholoë breaks into the young men's houses. Horace retells the myth of Acrisius and Danaë in the manner of a *furtivus amor* (*C.*III.16, the first two words, *inclusam Danaen*).

133. These repetitions are cited as the primary evidence that the poet changes his curse to an empathetic expression of sorrow for Lyce's aging (e.g., Catlow, 1976:820; Ancona, 1994:100).

134. Cf. Cupid's and Venus's rejection of Lyce to Aphrodite's gracious attendance to Sappho's prayer (1 L.-P.), when the goddess grants that the fleeing lover will pursue Sappho (καὶ γὰρ αἰ φεύγει, ταχέως δι-ώξει) and the beloved rejecting Sappho's gifts will quickly change her mind and give her presents (αἰ δὲ δῶρα μὴ δέκετ᾽, ἀλλὰ δώσει).

5. *Encomia Augusti*, "Take Two"

1. First and second, earlier and later, and last and final designate order within the collection and do not imply a particular order of composition.

2. 1–9a: a dual direct address (*Auguste; maxime principum*) complemented by a relative clause stating the honorand's major deed (*quem . . . Vindelici didicere . . . quid Marte posses*); 33–35, 41–52: the repeated second-person pronoun.

3. Like Pindar, Horace sets a metaphoric tone with a number of uncommon expressions (*aeternet*, 5; *implacidum*, 10; *grave proelium*, 14; *Pleiadum choro / scindente nubis*, 21–22; *tauriformis*, 25; *vacuam . . . aulam*, 36; *beluosus*, 47); see Putnam (1986:242 n.7; 254 n.28; 257–58).

4. G. Williams (1968:79, 162, 754–55) seeded the idea of the withdrawing panegyrist. A self-reference in the river Aufidus (25) is the only sign of the poet that Williams sees. Putnam (1986:258–59) interprets the flooding Aufidus as an allusion to Pindaric praise, which does not threaten but completely erases the poet's lyric *ego*. Recent studies all follow suit to some degree (Lyne, 1995:201–2; Lowrie, 1997:342; Oliensis, 1998:150–51).

5. Fraenkel (1957:431–32).

6. Note Ovid's self-apotheosis that ends the *Metamorphoses* and its obvious echoes of *C.III.30*.

7. See *Levis et Gravis*, ch.1.

8. Only Commager (1962:260) notes the thematic similarity between the antiquarian and Aelius (*C.III.17*): both are locked in the past. Whether the poet treats Aelius more amiably, as Commager suggests, is debatable, since Aelius's ancestry proves illusory (T. S. Johnson, 1995a:131–34), a point not too subtly made by the pig with no pedigree (*porco bimestri*, 15). No doubt the silent antiquarian (*taces*, 19.8) and the silent lyre (*tacita*, 19.20) are equally useless.

9. Wine, the poet's song, has the power to remove cares (*C.IV.11.35–36*) and restore hope (*C.IV.12.17–20*). For the complete discussion of these odes, see ch.4.

10. G. Williams (1968:162) might have done better to avoid "stark" and "factual" since the poet constructs the aretalogia primarily through metaphor. These adjectives become more helpful descriptors, however, within the context of the primary gnome. Since son is like father, the victories of the sons tell about the character of their father.

11. The Gigantomachy figures prominently in Augustan praise; see Innes (1979:165–68); P. R. Hardie (1986:85–90).

12. See Verg. *A.6.582–84*; Hom. *Od.11.307–20*.

13. MacLeane (1856) and Wickham (1874:*ad loc.*) read *spectandus* as equivalent to θαυμαστὸς . . . ὅσιος. The laudatory exclamation only intensifies the effect of the qualifying *prope*.

14. T. E. Page (1883:n.20); Quinn (1980:nn.14–24). A. Y. Campbell (1945:n.20) is so put out by *prope* that he emends: "ut aqualis" for *prope qualis*.

15. Consider the equally prosaic qualifier, *aut nihil aut paulo* (Cat. 68.131; Feeney, 1992a:42).

16. Wickham (1874:n.24) brings metaphor to a sudden halt at *impiger*. Bentley (1711:*ad loc.*) accordingly emends *ignis* to "enses." Actually the sentence has been running on since at least verse 9, and metaphor has been the operative mode of expression since the Titan/Gigantomachy of the third strophe. A sudden transition would occur only if *impiger . . . medios per ignis* were unmetaphoric.

17. Collinge (1961:75–76 n.2).

18. Quinn (1980:nn.25–34); Putnam (1986:247); P. R. Hardie (1986: 288).

19. Putnam (1986:247–48) recognizes a "negative tone running through the poem's core stanzas." He presents Horace as a diplomatic *laudator* who makes Augustus both "fully and partially responsible," that is, the victory belongs entirely to Augustus, but he did not commit the actual violence. This is a difficult splitting of the argument in an epinikion stating that Tiberius and Drusus followed their father's will to the letter (*peractis / imperiis*, 39–40) and after another epinikion stressing that children follow their father's character and training.

20. On the poetics of this Horatian autobiography, see Sympotic Horace Exiled, ch.1.

21. Compare Hector, C.II.4.10–12.

22. Garrison (1991:366 nn.25–29): compounds in the Greek style are uncommon in Catullus and the *neoteroi*. The scholiasts cite *corniger* (Verg. *A*.8.77) as a model for *tauriformis*, an apt enough description for a river because of the strength and sound of its waters. In addition, *tauriformis* provides one more important touch point for the simile of the bull at *A*.10.454–56, as I argue later in this chapter.

23. In these similes Vergil is very conscious of his art. His use of *imago* stresses the ekphrastic quality of the simile (not unlike Horace's similes in his epinikia), and he breaks the narrative with an address to Turnus. The epic Vergil once more creates a more direct and personal lyric mood.

24. Noted by G. Williams (1968:755); Garrison (1991:366 nn.25–29). Garrison makes no further comment, and Williams sees the change merely as Horace's attempt to personalize the metaphor and make Tiberius's attack more vivid. So much could be said about Horace naming his native Aufidus without the switch of the particles.

25. Although the manuscripts strongly attest *indomitas . . . undas* (20), Bentley (1711) and Shackleton Bailey (1985) accept *indomitus* (*Auster*, by metaphor Tiberius), the reading of the *deteriores* (Turicensis Carolinus 6). As Bentley argues, *undas* stands for the Rhaetians, and "untamed" would hardly be suitable for a people Tiberius had worn down. *Spectan-*

dus, indomitus, impiger form an adjectival series appropriate for a heroic warrior and set the tone for the violent characterization of Tiberius. In addition to the obvious orthographic similarities that would account for the variant, a copyist who has already written verses 12 and 16 with adjective-noun combinations in first and last positions (also 36, 52), a common pattern in the fourth line of the Alcaic strophe, would be led to continue the pattern by writing *indomitas . . . undas,* especially if doing so would bring the epinikion more into line with later panegyric convention by suppressing a potential negative in the characterization of the *laudandus.*

26. *Diluvies* (*diluviem,* 28) occurs outside of Horace only at Lucr. 5.255, 6.292 and Plin. *Nat.*9.8.3. Horace uses the word only one other time, *C.*III.29.40, to contrast floods (*diluvies*) with a person who can master himself and be content with the present.

27. The altar of *Fortuna Redux* was dedicated in 19 B.C., when Augustus returned from the East; see Putnam (1986:251 n.21).

28. For a broader look at tensions contained in Horace's listings of imperial boundaries, see Horsfall (1995b:23–34).

29. Contrast Southern (1998:104): "the erstwhile image of Octavian the Triumvir . . . had to be decisively shed." This transition may be more difficult than supposed. As the history of most countries including the United States suggests, civil wars can be hard to forget.

30. Wickham (1874:nn.1, 2); T. E. Page (1883:*proem*); Quinn (1980: nn.1–6); Oliensis (1998:150).

31. Pi. *O.*2; 6; *P.*7; *I.*7; fr.29. H. *C.*I.2.25–30 (answer: Mercury and Caesar, 41–52); I.6.13–16 (answer: Varius, *scriberis* / *scripserit* from verses 1 and 14); I.12.1–4 (answer: Jupiter and Caesar, 49–60); I.31.1–3 (answer: contentment, health, and song, 15–20); see Norden (1956:152).

32. K.-H. (1884:*proem,* n.1); Putnam (1986:260); P. R. Hardie (1993: 134); Lowrie (1997:340–41).

33. *Cura* commonly occurs with an objective genitive, and the distinction between the possessive and objective is very unstable. Horatian practice displays variety: *cura* with a possessive genitive (*C.*II.8.7–8; III.21.14–15; *Ars* 85); with an objective genitive (*S.*I.6.32; *Ep.*9.37–38; *C.*I.12.49–51; *Epist.*I.5.13; *Ars* 330–31). *Epist.*I.14.6–7 makes use of the ambiguity between the possessive and objective, when *Lamiae* reads as both. Lamia's piety and care toward his brother (possessive) delays Horace because of his piety and care for his friend Lamia (objective).

34. P. R. Hardie (1993:138 n.51) cites as a possible source for the introductory question a fragment of Ennius's *Scipio* (Var. *Scipio* I, II Vahlen [3rd. ed.]; Hist. Aug. *Claud.*7.6–8): *rogo, quantum pretium est clipeus in curia tantae victoriae? quantum una aurea statua? dicit Ennius de Scipione: "Quantam statuam faciet populus Romanus, quantam columnam, quae res*

tuas gestas loquatur?" possumus dicere Flavium Claudium, unicum in terris principem, non columnis, non statuis sed famae viribus adiuvari. Trebellius Pollio quotes Ennius in his praise of M. Aurelius Claudius's victory over 320,000 barbarians who had invaded Roman territory. Claudius quickly defeated them through his inborn courage (*ingenita illa virtute*). Without any context for the Ennian fragment it is impossible to know what use Ennius made of the questions, whether they were rhetorical or were answered more specifically in the rest of the poem as in Pindar and Horace, but if Pollio gives us a clue, then we see that the power of one's reputation (*fama*), gained by protecting the state, is the means to immortality. This fits the Horatian context and suggests that Horace's questions also may incorporate a reference to Augustus's care for the citizens.

35. On c.38 as a possible symbolic restatement of the *genus tenue*, see especially Barchiesi (2001:151–54); also Fraenkel (1957:297–99); Commager (1962:117–18); Davis (1991:44, 118–26); Syndikus (1972:340–42); Fowler (1989:97); David (1991:41, 118–26). Others without belittling the ode reject a metapoetical sense (e.g., Nisbet, 1995:44–30; D. West, 1998: 65–66).

36. J. A. Harrison (1981:104): "The verse is as competent as ever but enthusiasm is lacking." Commager (1962:226) blames Augustus: "In the years after 27 B.C. there was ever more for him [Horace] to applaud, yet at the same time there was ever less to appeal to his imagination." Like Commager (34–35), Lyne (1995:31–39, 75–78, 195–98) focuses on the *recusatio*, but I suspect that he would conclude, as he does about the rest of Horace's "court poetry," that it is not the sort of poetry Horace would have produced without pressure from his patron; cf. Garrison's view (1979:40–43) that Horace was a political romantic whose political poetry lacked the irony of his other works. Also Brink (1982:525) judges that Fraenkel's high opinion of the political poems, including *Odes* IV, is "exaggerated not only on historical but on political grounds."

37. K.-H. (1884:nn.4, 17, 25); Fraenkel (1957:449–52); G. Williams (1968:162–69, 436–38); Reckford (1969:137); Quinn (1980:*proem*, nn.25–32). The elisions between *que* and *et* (14, 25, 31), the only elisions in the poem except *rectum evaganti* (10), accentuate the polysyndeton.

38. A. Y. Campbell (1924:113): the pleasures of the banquet are designed to make the political pill easier to swallow; also Ludwig (1961:8–9); Fowler (1995:257–58).

39. This question has become the question for c.15: Putnam (1986: 262–306); Fowler (1995:248–66); Lowrie (1997:343–52); Oliensis (1998: 150–53).

40. Reckford (1969:136): "What troubles us most about the political odes of Book IV, and especially *Odes* IV, 5 and IV, 15, both to Augustus,

is the absence of inner conflict;" also Commager (1962:227); Syme (1989:120). Cf. Lowrie (1997:343).

41. Fraenkel (1957:251, 452–53); Reckford (1969:136–37); Putnam (1986:286, 288–89, 307–9); Galinsky (1996:260); McNeill (2001:133–34).

42. C.I. 6, 7, 9, 11; II.3, 11, 14; III.17, 19, 29. See the discussion of Augustus's control over the past in c.14 earlier in this chapter.

43. Fraenkel (1957:450–51) identifies in *rettulit, restituit,* and *revocavit* the official position that Augustan policy was a restoration of the *Res Publica* (also G. Williams, 1968:168–69; Putnam, 1986:281). Galinsky (1996:64–65) contends that neither Augustus nor any of the poets testify to a "momentous reassertion of the republic." Strictly interpreted Horace's *re-* addresses the restoration of traditions and military prestige, not policies of governance.

44. The only sympotic invitation in which Horace reverses the *carpe diem* argument to include thought for the future is in C.IV.12 (*spes donare novas,* 19), the last sympotic invitation before c.15. Cf. Horace's hymn to the divine wine jar and its power to give hope: *tu spem reducis mentibus anxiis* (C.III.21.17).

45. Momigliano (1957:104–14) accepts the existence of these *carmina* but denies they support the ballad theory (already discredited by Mommsen), which would make the *carmina* the roots of Roman historiography. G. Williams (1968:164–65) and Zorzetti (1990:289–307, 1991: 311–29) are less convinced of the historicity of the accounts (Gel. 11.2.5); against Zorzetti's skepticism, see Horsfall (1994:50–75).

46. Lowrie (1997:342, 344–45, 351–52) observes that the subordination of the poet's lyric aesthetic to politics would constitute the ode's crisis. The question then (the question on which Lowrie ends her book) is whether the panegyric exhibits any irony, and if so, what is its effect. I propose, given the complexities of the singer's praise, that the crisis does not occur.

47. Cf. Race (1988:1–35, n.b. 3, 16–18). Davis (1991:11–77) defines the *recusatio* as a rhetorical means of assimilating the characteristics of another genre.

48. Fowler (1995) reads the small voice of the Horatian *recusatio* as both serious and ironic. If the small voice is the preferred aesthetic for lyric, the lyric mode is incompatible with the grandeur required for praise poetry, and lyric panegyric is impossible. Horace's task is to keep us from noticing, and Fowler suggests that Horace fails since visible behind the small voice is a Bacchic excess that surpasses the boundaries of the Callimachean aesthetic. But Horace fails only if we restrict his task to re-presenting solely the perspective of the *laudandus.* At least Fowler's observation acknowledges that Horatian panegyric encompasses more

concerns and tensions than our traditional conception of panegyric allows. Within *Odes* IV, lyric voice(s) make panegyric not only possible but powerful.

49. Other Horatian *recusationes* of political or laudatory poetry include *S*.II.1.10–20; *C*.I.6; 19.9–12; 26; II.1; 11; 12; III. 3; 8; 29; IV.2; *Epist*.II.1.1–4, 245–70 (cf. Race, 1978:191–93). There is a sea of work written on the *recusatio*, to borrow Horace's metaphor (c.15.3). For my listing of seminal works on the *recusatio* and its importance in Horace's epic criticism, see ch.1. For a closer analysis of Horace's inclusion of the pastoral Vergil and high epic style in Horace's *recusationes*, especially *C*.I.6, see Silk (1969); Ahern (1991:301–14); Davis (1991:33–39); Smith (1994: 502–5); Lyne (1995:31–39, 75–78); Putnam (1995:50–64); cf. Cameron (1995:454–75).

50. Cynthius and Phoebus have more positive connotations than Lycian. Mt. Cynthius on Delos, a reputed birthplace of Apollo, was long associated with a deity of fertility and procreation (Solomon, 1994:43); cf. Burkert's defense (1994:49–60) of Wilamowitz-Moellendorff's hypothesis (1903:575–86) that the worship of Apollo came to Greece from Asia Minor, specifically Lycia. Horace uses only the name Phoebus ('radiant'; see *C*.IV.6.26, 29). Horace's emphasis on Apollo as god of the sun matches his praise for Augustus as the light of Rome and the empire (*C*.IV.5.5–8; 14.5–6). Horace also, however, prefaces the warning Phoebus in his *recusatio* with an angry ode cursing none other than a woman named Lyce. Phoebus's poet means to be heard.

51. Horace goes as far as to say that Maecenas's prose would be a more appropriate medium than his own lyric for praising Augustus's battles (*C*.II.12.9–12). Horace sometimes surprises by reversing his *recusatio;* see *C*. III.3.69–72 and the poet's confusion that his Muse has allowed him to confine serious grand themes within the narrow constraints of his merry lyre. Dionysus inspires the poet to sing immortal praise for Caesar (*C*.III.25.17–18a: *nil parvum aut humili modo, / nil mortale loquar*). Horace also advises his friend Valgius to set aside his weepy elegies and join Horace in singing the triumphs of Augustus (*C*.II.9.17–20).

52. See Laird (1999:300–301).

53. Schiesaro (1997:63–89, n.b. 67) argues the same for Vergil's *Georgics.*

54. Horace may also have been influenced by Propertius's *recusationes* (2.1; 3.3 and 9); see Fraenkel (1957:449 n.6); Commager (1962:34–35); Wimmel (1960:290–91 n.2, 1965:88–91); Syndikus (1973:422); Putnam (1986:266–71); Lyne (1995:33–38). Although the commonly accepted publication date for Propertius's third book is sometime in the late 20s B.C., well before Horace composed his fourth book, determining

exactly who influenced whom among contemporaries is always difficult. Besides using similar metaphors for the epic to lyric contrast (a
stream, *tali . . . flumine*, 3.3.15; expansive sea, *vastum . . . aequor*; and large
sails, *grandia vela*, 3.9.3–4), Propertius follows up his *recusationes* with
praise for many of Rome's heroes (3.3.1–12; 9.21–56), whom Horace
leaves unnamed (*duces*) in the last strophe of c.15. Propertius's vision of
himself resting in the lap of his lover and watching Caesar's triumph
(3.4.11–22) contains several parallels to the Horatian *recusationes* of book
IV: captured cities (verse 16; c.15.2); the offspring of Venus (verse 19;
c.15.32); the poet cheering from the crowd (verse 22; c.2.45–48). Given
the high degree of correspondence between the poets' *recusationes* and
Propertius's specific refusal to sing the praises of Caesar Augustus, it is
reasonable to assume that the battles Horace refuses to praise are also
Caesar's.

    55. Cameron (1995:454).

    56. Cf. *Ecl*.8.6–13 where Vergil wants to sing Pollio's praise.

    57. The last time Apollo stepped in on the poet, he saved him from
the patronizing pest (*S*.I.9.78). Perhaps the god does the same in the *recusatio* c.15. The question again is who exactly is the pest, since Horace
in c.15 is the one wanting to sing of Augustus's military glories. Apollo
even more clearly in c.15 saves the poet from himself. The typical *recusatio* focuses on the will of the warning deity (C.II.12.13–14: Horace's
Muse desired, *voluit*, that Horace sing sweetly for Licymnia). The *recusatio* of *Epist*.II.1.257 is the closest to c.15: Horace states that he desires to
sing grand praises for Caesar, and the *recusatio* comes after the fact, at
the end of a letter that begins by honoring Augustus as a god on the
earth (15–17). Otherwise in *Epist*.II, Horace reverts to his earlier pattern
of pretending that the task is beyond the ability of his plain poetry, and
to prove his alleged inability he deflates the praise by pedantically listing off Caesar's accomplishments among the epic topics that he is not up
to writing (252–56).

    58. Lowrie (1997:345) also observes that Apollo warns Horace just
after he has finished such martial praise in an epinikion, but she does not
make the application to any praises before c.14. This reference to c.14
would be enough to carry my argument.

    59. See Fraenkel (1957:449); Commager (1962:225); G. Williams (1968:
169); Putnam (1986:269–71, 284, 285); McNeill (2001:131–35); Holzberg
(2002:41). More specifically, Syndikus (1973:420–24) and Lyne (1995:38–
39): the historical shift from war to peace removes the tension behind the
conventional *recusatio*. Horace does not have to sing of epic battles because Augustus has brought peace. In effect, irony erases panegyric conflict since the playfulness of the *recusatio* is that now Horace's lyric voice
aligns with the Augustan achievement. Lowrie (1997:345–46) assesses

the implications well: it would be a violent anticlimax (a collapse of the lyric persona) if Horace really subordinates his poetics to the political vacillations of war and peace. However, this supposedly clear shift away from civil war to the peace and mastery of the empire dramatized by the *recusatio,* as it is commonly read, projects an ideal not entirely compatible with the Horatian encomia of c.14–15, which do not distinguish Octavian victorious in the civil wars from Augustus's subjugation of rebellious foreigners, the foreign being an extension of the civil. Augustus, by contrast, rewrites the civil as foreign war, which is evident from the careful crafting of the opening of his *Res Gestae.* Augustus casts himself as a defender of the Republic against outside attack and omits the names of all rivals and civil enemies (as well as basically anyone else but himself; see Ramage, 1987:21–28). Throughout the *Res Gestae* emphasis remains on foreign wars. Both the epinikion (14.34–40) and its panegyric tag (15.17–24) tie together as one Octavian's victory in the civil wars and his pacification of the provinces. Bluntly put, Horace does not allow Augustus much of a cover-up in the negative *non,* when he follows *custode rerum Caesare* immediately by *furor civilis* (17–18); see Gruen (1985:51–72). In this song of peace, Horace does not completely abandon martial vocabulary and imagery.

60. *Increpare* commonly denotes the sounds of war: arms clashing (Liv. 1.25.4); the twang of the bow (Prop. 4.3.66); ships crunching together (Sil. 17.276). Thus as a verb of warning it connotes a hostile menacing tone (Liv. 22.28.9; 29.3.1; 45.23.19; Tac. *Hist.*2.44.9–10).

61. Ovid expands the fatness recommended by the Callimachean dictum and launches his elegy onto an epic voyage (*Fast.*2.1–4). Ovid announces the journey by juxtaposing *carmine crescit.* He then expands Horace's small sails (*parva vela*) and inverts Horace's word order by incorporating elegy within the parameters of the epic image (*velis, elegi, maioribus*). Whereas Horace includes epic themes within the slenderness of lyric, Ovid will broaden elegy, its meter and themes, to epic proportions. See Newlands (1995).

62. Horace's praise is not original here (*Epist.*I.12.27–29 describes the fruitfulness of Italy in the context of military victories). Interrelated depictions of war and peace are common in Augustan Rome, as the images of the Ara Pacis and the Forum of Augustus attest (Galinsky, 1992:468–75; 1996:111). The standards held by the Parthians had been a longstanding disgrace. Their return immediately became a primary symbol of Augustan power and influence (Liv. *peri.*139; Vell. 2.91.1; 94.4; Suet. *Aug.*21.3; *Tib.*9.1; Cass. Dio 54.8.1–3; 9.4–5; Tac. *Ann.*2.1–3) and was celebrated as a great military victory (Cass. Dio: καὶ αὐτοὺς ἐκεῖνος ὡς καὶ πολέμῳ τινὶ τὸν Πάρθον νενικηκὼς ἔλαβε; also Ov. *Fast.*5.579–98;

*Tr.*2.225–36). Sacrifices were held; Augustus placed the standards in a small shrine to Mars Ultor on the Capitoline and then moved them to the temple of Mars Ultor in his forum when it was ready in 2 B.C.; Augustus celebrated an *ovatio*, riding into the city on horseback, and was honored with a triumphal arch. Cf. Chaumont (1976:73–84) and Gruen (1985:63–67, n.b. 65).

63. Collinge (1961:114): "To be sure, either Phoebus is disregarded, or else the correction of subject lies merely in giving a 'Julian' slant to it: otherwise it is hard to distinguish the last stanza's *virtute functos duces* and *Troiam* from the first's *proelia* and *victas urbis.*" It is not the 'Julian' slant, but the *potens lyra* slant.

64. *Nos* does not mean either that Horace is speaking on behalf of the Roman people or using a literary plural to focus attention on generic distinctions as in C.I.6 (see Fraenkel, 1957:251, 448, 452; Lowrie, 1997:347 n.43). The singing is convivial and by definition a communal experience involving more than one individual voice.

65. I am not exhausting all the possibilities; for example, Horace so fully embraces the public stage that he must adjust the singularity of his lyric voice. Oliensis (1998:152–53) interprets Horace's withdrawal as an act of "self-obliteration," but she proposes, as does Quinn (1980:*proem*) that Horace maintains some authority by refusing to posture as the poet laureate. Lyne (1995:38–39 n.15) is thankful that such sympotic praise songs ("ghastly monstrosities") were only promised and never written. On the poet's power to immortalize, see Putnam (1986:265, 291–306); Galinsky (1996:260). Lowrie (1997:349–52) leaves open the implications of the poet's absorption into community, but she posits that the withdrawal of the poetic "I" puts into play the question whether creative poetry is compatible with the increasing autocracy of post-Augustan Rome. For Lowrie the irony is that Horace has staged his own panegyric failure (so Fowler argues, 1995), which would be the poet's ultimate act of control. There is much in Lowrie's reading that is perceptive; a retreat to community may be self-affirming for the poet, not self-effacing. I would argue, based on Horace's panegyric praxis and its consistent emphasis on the experience of song shared among multiple voices, that the *ego-nos* progression represents not a dichotomy between the poet and the community, as if the two were in opposition, but a combination of both where the multiple voices brought together by the sympotic poet produce the vitality of panegyric.

66. The symposion is dialogic, that is, a communal moment comprising multiple voices and shared experiences; Leach (1998:51–52).

67. The assimilation of epic into lyric makes sense out of the opening *recusatio* and its obfuscation of the conventional tensions of epic to lyric,

war to peace, expansive to small. Horace's conclusion is so successful that even those who wonder whether there is any room in the communal song for the lyric *ego* still find themselves drawn to its power; Oliensis (1998:153); Lowrie (1997:351).

68. Cf. Thomas (2001:69).

69. *Spirat,* breathing in and out, is Horace's word throughout book IV for lyric power (*quod spiro et placeo, si placeo, tuum est,* 3.24; . . . *spirat adhuc amor* [*Aeoliae puellae*], 9.10; note Lyce's loss of power: *quae* [Lyce] *spirabat amores,* 13.19).

Works Cited

Commentaries, Concordances, Dictionaries, Editions, Lexica

Adams, J. N. 1982. *The Latin Sexual Vocabulary.* Baltimore: Johns Hopkins Univ. Press.

Bentley, R., ed. 1711. *Q. Horatius Flaccus, ex recensione et cum notis atque emendationibus Richardi Bentleii.* Leipzig. 3rd ed. Reprint, New York: Garland, 1978.

Bergk, T., ed. 1843. *Poetae Lyrici Graeci.* 3 vols. Leipzig: Teubner.

Borzsák, S., ed. 1984. *Q. Horati Flacci Opera.* Leipzig: Teubner.

Brink, C. O. 1971. *Horace on Poetry II: The Ars Poetica.* Cambridge: Cambridge Univ. Press.

———. 1982. *Horace on Poetry III: Epistles Book II.* Cambridge: Cambridge Univ. Press.

Campbell, A. Y., ed. 1945. *Q. Horati Flacci Carmina cum Epodis.* London: Hodder & Stoughton.

Coleman, R., ed. 1977. *Vergil: Eclogues.* Cambridge: Cambridge Univ. Press.

Conington, J., ed. 1858, 1863, 1871. *Publi Vergili Maronis Opera.* 3 vols. London. Rev. by Nettleship: vol. 1-2, 4th ed. 1881, 1884; vol. 3, 3rd ed. 1883.

Courtney, E., ed. 1993. *The Fragmentary Latin Poets.* Oxford: Clarendon.

Diehl, E., ed. 1911. *Die Vitae Vergilianae und ihre antiken Quellen.* Bonn: E. Marcus & E. Weber.

Diggle, J., ed. 1970. *Euripides: Phaethon.* Cambridge: Cambridge Univ. Press.

Döring, F. W., ed. 1830. *Quinti Horatii Flacci Carmina.* Turin: Joseph Pomba.

Faber, T., ed. 1671. *Quinti Horatii Flacci Opera.* Saumer, France.

Fraser, P. M., and E. Matthews, eds. 1987– . *A Lexicon of Greek Personal Names*. Oxford: Clarendon.

Garrison, D. H., ed. 1991. *Horace: Epodes and Odes, A New Annotated Latin Edition*. Norman: Univ. of Oklahoma Press.

Gentili, B., and C. Prato, eds. 1979, 1985. *Poetarum elegiacorum testimonia et fragmenta*. 2 vols. Leipzig: Teubner.

Gow, A. S. F., ed. 1950. *Theocritus*. 2 vols. Cambridge: Cambridge Univ. Press. 2nd ed., 1952. Reprint, 1965.

Gow, A. S. F., and D. L. Page, eds. 1965. *The Greek Anthology: Hellenistic Epigrams*. 2 vols. Cambridge: Cambridge Univ. Press.

Green, R. P. H., ed. 1991. *The Works of Ausonius: Edited with Introduction and Commentary*. New York: Oxford Univ. Press.

Håkanson, L., ed. 1989. *L. Annaeus Seneca Muior: Oratorum et Rhetorum Sententiae, Divisiones, Colores*. Leipzig: Teubner.

Hardie, P. R., ed. 1994. *Virgil: Aeneid Book IX*. Cambridge: Cambridge Univ. Press.

Horst, P. W. van der, ed. 1978. *The Sentences of Pseudo-Phocylides*. Leiden, Netherlands: Brill.

Jacoby, F., ed. 1923–58. *Die Fragmente der griechischen Historiker*. Berlin: Weidmann.

Keil, H., ed. 1855–80. *Grammatici Latini, ex recensione Henrici Keilii*. 8 vols. Leipzig. Reprint, Hildesheim: G. Olms, 1961.

Kiessling, A., ed. 1884. *Q. Horatius Flaccus*. Berlin: Weidmann. Rev. by Heinze. Vol. 1: *Oden und Epoden*, 5th ed. 1908, 9th ed. 1958; vol. 2: *Satiren*, 6th ed. 1957; vol. 3: *Briefe*, 5th ed. 1957.

Kinkel, G., ed. 1877. *Epicorum Graecorum Fragmenta*. Leipzig: Teubner.

Klingner, F., ed. 1939. *Q. Horati Flacci Carmina*. Leipzig: Teubner.

Lambinus, D. ed. 1561. *Q. Horatius Flaccus, Ex fide, atque auctoritate decem librorum manu scriptorum, opera Dionys. Lambini Montroliensis emendatus: ab eodemque commentariis copiosissimis illustratus, nunc primum in lucem editus*. Lyon: I. Tornaesium. 6th ed. 1605.

Lindsay, W. M., ed. 1913. *Sexti Pompei Festi de verborum significatu quae supersunt cum Pauli epitome*. Leipzig: Teubner. Reprint, Hildesheim: G. Olms, 1965.

Lloyd-Jones, H., P. J. Parson, et al., eds. 1983. *Supplementum Hellenisticum*. Berlin: de Gruyter.

Lobel, E., and D. L. Page, eds. 1955. *Poetarum Lesbiorum Fragmenta*. Oxford: Clarendon.

MacLeane, A. J., ed. 1856. *The Works of Horace with English Notes*. Cambridge: J. Bartlett. Rev. by R. H. Chase, 20th ed., Boston: Allyn & Bacon.

Marx, F., ed. 1904, 1905. *C. Lucilii Carminum Reliquiae*. 2 vols. Leipzig: Teubner. Reprint, Amsterdam: Hakkert, 1963.

Maurenbrecher, B., ed. 1891, 1893. *C. Sallusti Crispi Historiarum Reliquiae.* 2 vols. Leipzig: Teubner.

Meineke, J., ed. 1854. *Q. Horatius Flaccus.* Berlin: G. Reimer.

Moore, C. H., ed. 1902. *Horace: The Odes and Epodes.* New York: American Book.

Müller, L., ed. 1869. *Q. Horatius Flaccus.* Leipzig: Teubner.

Nauck, K. W., ed. 1854. *Des Q. Horatius, Oden und Epoden, für den Schulgebrauch.* Leipzig: Teubner.

Nisbet, R. G. M., and M. Hubbard. 1970. *A Commentary on Horace: Odes Book I.* Oxford: Clarendon.

———. 1978. *A Commentary on Horace: Odes Book II.* Oxford: Clarendon.

Orelli, J. C., ed. 1837, 1838. *Q. Horatius Flaccus.* 2 vols. Turici. Rev. by I. G. Baiter, 3rd ed., 1850, 1852.

Page, D. L., ed. 1962. *Poeti Melici Graeci.* Oxford: Clarendon.

Page, T. E., ed. 1883. *Q. Horatii Flacci: Carminum Libri IV, Epodon Liber.* London: Macmillan. Rev. ed., 1895. Reprint, New York: St. Martin's Press, 1977.

Peerlkamp, P. H., ed. 1834. *Q. Horatii Flacci Carmina.* 2nd ed., Amsterdam: F. Müller, 1862.

Pfeiffer, R., ed. 1949, 1953. *Callimachus.* 2 vols. Oxford: Clarendon.

Plessis, F., and P. Lejay, eds. 1911, 1924. *Q. Horati Flacci Opera: Oeuvres d' Horace.* 2 vols. Paris: Hachette.

Quinn, K., ed. 1980. *Horace: The Odes.* London: Macmillan.

Reifferscheid, K. W. August, ed. 1860. *C. Suetoni Tranquilli praeter Caesarum libros Reliquiae.* Leipzig: Teubner.

Richardson, L., Jr. 1992. *A New Topographical Dictionary of Ancient Rome.* Baltimore: Johns Hopkins Univ. Press.

Ritter, F., ed. 1857. *Q. Horatius Flaccus in usum scholarum brevi annotatione instruxit Franciscus Ritter.* Leipzig: Engelmann.

Russell, D. A., and N. G. Wilson, eds. 1981. *Menander Rhetor.* Oxford: Clarendon.

Sanadon, Noël Etienne. 1728. *Les poésis d'Horace, disposées suivant l'ordre cronologique, et traduites en François, avec des remarques et des dissertations critiques.* Paris.

Schanz, M. von. 1935. *Geschichte der römischen Literatur bis zum Gesetzgebung des Kaisers Justinian, zweiter Teil: Die römische Literatur in der Zeit der Monarchie bis auf Hadrian.* Rev. by C. Hosius, 4th ed., Munich: C. H. Beck.

Shackleton Bailey, D. R., ed. 1985. *Q. Horati Flacci Opera.* Stuttgart: Teubner.

Shorey, P., ed. 1898. *Horace, Odes and Epodes.* Boston: B. H. Sanborn.

Skutsch, O., ed. 1985. *The Annals of Q. Ennius: Edited with Introduction and Commentary.* Oxford: Clarendon.

Syndikus, H. P. 1972. *Die Lyrik Des Horaz, Eine Interpretation der Oden: Band I, Erstes und zwietes Buch*. Darmstadt: Wissenschaftliche Buchgesellschaft.

———. 1973. *Die Lyrik Des Horaz, Eine Interpretation der Oden: Band II, Drittes und viertes Buch*. Darmstadt: Wissenschaftliche Buchgesellschaft.

Thomas, R. F., ed. 1988. *Virgil: Georgics*. 2 vols. Cambridge: Cambridge Univ. Press.

Vahlen, J., ed. 1854. *Ennianae Poesis Reliquiae*. Leipzig: Teubner. 3rd ed., 1928.

Vollmer, F., ed. 1907. *Q. Horati Flacci Carmina*. Leipzig: Teubner.

West, M. L., ed. 1971, 1972. *Iambi et Elegi Graeci ante Alexandrum Cantati*. 2 vols. Oxford: Clarendon. 2nd ed., 1989, 1992.

Wickham, E. C., ed. 1874, 1891. *Quinti Horati Flacci Opera Omnia: The Works of Horace with a Commentary*. 2 vols. Oxford: Clarendon. Vol. 1, 3rd ed., 1896.

Woodman, A. J., ed. 1977. *Velleius Paterculus: The Tiberian Narrative (2.94-131)*. Cambridge: Cambridge Univ. Press.

Young, D., ed. 1971. *Theognis. Ps.-Pythagoras. Ps.-Phocylides. Chares. Anonymi Aulodia. Fragmenta Teliambicum*. 2nd ed., Leipzig: Teubner.

Other References

Ahern, C. F., Jr. 1991. "Horace's Rewriting of Homer in *Carmen* I. 6." *CPh* 86: 301-14.

Ahl, F. 1984. "The Rider and the Horse: Politics and Power in Roman Poetry from Horace to Statius." *ANRW* II.32.1: 40-110.

Albrecht, M. von. 1982-84. "Horazens Römeroden." *AAntHung* 30: 229-41.

———. 1991. "Natur und Landschaft in der römischen Lyrik dargestellt an Frühlingsgedichten (Catull, 46; Horaz, *Carm*. 1,4; 4,7; 4,12)." *Ktèma* 16: 147-59.

———. 1995. "Orazio e la musica." In Setaioli, 1995: 83-88.

Alexiou, M. 1974. *The Ritual Lament in Greek Tradition*. Cambridge: Cambridge Univ. Press.

Allen, H. W. 1961. *A History of Wine: Great Vintage Wines from the Homeric Age to the Present Day*. London: Horizon Press.

Ambrose, J. W., Jr. 1965. "The Ironic Meaning of the Lollius Ode." *TAPhA* 96: 1-10.

———. 1973. "Horace on Foreign Policy: *Odes* 4.4." *CJ* 69: 26-33.

Ancona, R. 1994. *Time and the Erotic in Horace's* Odes. Durham, NC: Duke Univ. Press.

Anderson, W. S. 1956. "Horace, the Unwilling Warrior: *Satire* I, 9." *AJPh* 77: 148–66.

———. 1984. "Ironic Preambles and Satiric Self-Definition in Horace *Satire* 2.1." *Pacific Coast Philology* 19: 35–42.

———. 1995. "*Horatius Liber,* Child and Freedman's Free Son." *Arethusa* 28: 151–64.

Argetsinger, K. 1992. "Birthday Rituals: Friends and Patrons in Roman Poetry and Cult." *ClAnt* 11: 175–93.

Arkins, B. 1983. "A Reading of Horace, *Carm.* 1.25." *C&M* 34: 161–75.

———. 1993. "The Cruel Joke of Venus: Horace as Love Poet." In Rudd, 1993: 106–19.

Armstrong, D. 1986. "*Horatius eques et scriba.*" *TAPhA* 116: 255–88.

———. 1997. "Some Recent Perspectives on Horace." *Phoenix* 51: 393–405.

Babcock, C. L. 1961. "The Role of Faunus in Horace, *Carmina* 1.4." *TAPhA* 92: 13–19.

———. 1967. "Horace *Carm.* 1.32 and the Dedication of the Temple of Apollo Palatinus." *CPh* 62: 189–94.

Balsdon, J. P. V. D. 1951. "Sulla Felix." *JRS* 41: 1–10.

Barchiesi, A. 1994. *Il poeta e il principe: Ovidio e il discorso augusteo.* Rome: Laterza. Published in English as *The Poet and the Prince: Ovid and Augustan Discourse.* Berkeley: Univ. of California Press, 1997.

———. 1996a. "Poetry, Praise, and Patronage: Simonides in Book IV of Horace's *Odes.*" *ClAnt* 15: 5–47.

———. 1996b. "Simonides and Horace on the Death of Achilles." *Arethusa* 29: 247–53.

———. 2001. *Speaking Volumes: Narrative and Intertext in Ovid and Other Latin Poets.* London: Duckworth.

Bardon, H. 1956. *La Littérature Latine Inconnue: L'Époque Impériale.* Paris: C. Klincksieck.

Barker, D. 1996. "'The Golden Age Proclaimed?' The *Carmen Saeculare* and the Renascence of the Golden Race." *CQ* n.s. 46: 434–46.

Bartsch, S. 1994. *Actors in the Audience: Theatricality and Doublespeak from Nero to Hadrian.* Cambridge, MA: Harvard Univ. Press.

———. 1998. *Ideology in Cold Blood: A Reading of Lucan's Civil War.* Cambridge, MA: Harvard Univ. Press.

Basto, R. 1982. "Horace's *Propempticon* to Vergil: A Re-examination." *Vergilius* 28: 30–43.

Batstone, W. 1998. "Dry Pumice and the Programmatic Language of Catullus 1." *CPh* 93: 125–35.

Becker, C. 1963. *Das Spätwerk des Horaz.* Göttingen: Vandenhoeck & Ruprecht.

Beissinger, M., J. Tylus, and S. Wofford, eds. 1999. *Epic Traditions in the Contemporary World: The Poetics of Community*. Berkeley: Univ. of California Press.

Belmont, T. E. 1980. "The Vergilius of Horace, *Ode* 4.12." *TAPhA* 110: 1–20.

Bergquist, B. 1990. "Sympotic Space: A Functional Aspect of Greek Dining-Rooms." In Murray, 1990: 37–65.

Bernays, L. 1996. "Zur Interpretation des Horaz—*Ode* 4.11." *Prometheus* 22.1: 35–42.

Bielohlawek, K. 1940. "Gastmahls- und Symposionslehren bei griechischen Dichtern (Von Homer bis zur Theognissammlung und Kritias)." *WS* 58: 11–30.

Bing, P. 1988. *The Well-Read Muse: Present and Past in Callimachus and the Hellenistic Poets*. Hypomnemata 90. Göttingen: Vandenhoeck & Ruprecht.

Boardman. J. 1974. *Athenian Black Figure Vases*. New York: Oxford Univ. Press.

————. 1975. *Athenian Red Figure Vases: The Archaic Period*. London: Thames & Hudson.

Boedeker, D., and D. Sider, eds. 2001. *The New Simonides: Contexts of Praise and Desire*. New York: Oxford Univ. Press.

Borzsák, S. 1976. "*Dive quem proles Niobea . . .* Ein Interpretationsversuch zu Hor. C. IV, 6." *Grazer Beiträge* 5: 25–36.

Bowditch, P. L. 2001. *Horace and the Gift Economy of Patronage*. Berkeley: Univ. of California Press.

Bowie, E. L. 1986. "Early Greek Elegy, Symposium and Public Festival." *JHS* 106: 13–35.

Bowra, C. M. 1928. "Horace, *Odes* IV.12." *CR* 42: 165–67.

————. 1952. *Heroic Poetry*. London: Macmillan.

Boyle, A. J. 1973. "The Edict of Venus: An Interpretive Essay on Horace's Amatory Odes." *Ramus* 2: 163–88.

Bradshaw, A. T. von. 1970. "Horace, *Odes* 4.1." *CQ* n.s. 20: 142–53.

Bremmer, J. 1980. "An Enigmatic Indo-European Rite: Paederasty." *Arethusa* 13: 279–98.

Bruneau, P. 1962. "Ganymède et l'aigle: images, caricatures et parodies animales du rapt." *Bulletin de Correspondance Hellénique* 86: 193–228.

Bücheler, F. 1859. "Zur Kritik und Erklärung: Zu Horaz' Oden IV, 6." *RhM* 14: 158–60.

Buchheit, V. 1968. "Homerparodie und Literaturkritik in Horazens *Sat.* I, 7 und I, 9." *Gymnasium* 85: 519–55.

Burkert, W. 1994. "Olbia and Apollo of Didyma: A New Oracle Text." In Solomon, 1994: 49–60.

Burckhardt, J. 1930. *Griechische Kulturgeschichte.* 4 vols. Stuttgart: Deutsche Verlags-Anstalt.

Buttrey, T. V. 1972. "Halved Coins, the Augustan Reform, and Horace, Odes I.3." *AJA* 76: 31–48.

Cairns, F. 1971. "Five 'Religious' Odes of Horace (I, 10; I, 21 and IV, 6; I, 30; I, 15)." *AJPh* 92: 433–52.

———. 1972. *Generic Composition in Greek and Roman Poetry.* Edinburgh: Edinburgh Univ. Press.

———. 1977. "Horace on Other People's Love Affairs (*Odes* I 27; II 4; I 8; III 12)." *QUCC* 24: 121–47.

Calhoun, G. M. 1913. *Athenian Clubs in Politics and Litigation.* Austin: Univ. of Texas Press. Reprint, New York: B. Franklin, 1970.

Cameron, A. 1992. "Genre and Style in Callimachus." *TAPhA* 122: 305–12.

———. 1995. *Callimachus and His Critics.* Princeton: Princeton Univ. Press.

Campbell, A. Y. 1924. *Horace: A New Interpretation.* London: Methuen.

Campbell, J. S. 1987. "*Animae Dimidium Meae:* Horace's Tribute to Vergil." *CJ* 82: 314–18.

Cannon, M. 1966. "Turbulence and Horace." *CB* 42: 85–87.

Canter, H. V. 1920. "The Paraclausithyron as a Literary Theme." *AJPh* 41: 355–68.

Carcopino, J. 1929. "Le mariage d'Octave et de Livia et la naissance de Drusus." *Revue historique* 161: 225–36.

Carettoni, G. 1983. *Das Haus des Augustus auf dem Palatin.* Mainz: P. von Zabern.

Castriota, D. 1995. *The Ara Pacis Augustae and the Imagery of Abundance in Later Greek and Early Roman Imperial Art.* Princeton: Princeton Univ. Press.

Catlow, L. W. 1976. "Horace, *Odes* I, 25 and IV, 13: A Reinterpretation." *Latomus* 35: 813–21.

Chaumont, M.-L. 1976. "L'Arménie entre Rome et l'Iran. I. De l'avènement d'Auguste a l'avènement de Dioclétien." *ANRW* II.9.1: 73–84.

Clauss, J. J. 1985. "Allusion and Structure in Horace's Satire 2.1: The Callimachean Response." *TAPhA* 115: 197–206.

Clay, J. S. 2002. "Sweet Folly: Horace, Odes 4.12 and the Evocation of Virgil." In Paschalis, 2002: 129–40.

Cody, J. V. 1976. *Horace and Callimachean Aesthetics.* Collection Latomus 147. Brussels.

Collinge, N. E. 1961. *The Structure of Horace's Odes.* New York: Oxford Univ. Press.

Commager, S. 1957. "The Function of Wine in Horace's Odes." *TAPhA* 88: 68–80.

———. 1962. *The Odes of Horace: A Critical Study.* New Haven, CT: Yale Univ. Press.

Connor, P. 1987. *Horace's Lyric Poetry: The Force of Humour.* Victoria, Australia: Aureal.

Copley, F. O. 1956. *Exclusus Amator: A Study in Latin Love Poetry.* Madison, WI: American Philological Assoc.

Courtney, E. 1994. "Horace and the Pest." *CJ* 90: 1–8.

Crotty, K. 1982. *Song and Action: The Victory Odes of Pindar.* Baltimore: Johns Hopkins Univ. Press.

Davis, G. 1991. *Polyhymnia: The Rhetoric of Horatian Discourse.* Berkeley: Univ. of California Press.

Dentzer, J.-M. 1982. *Le Motif du banquet couché dans le Proche Orient et les monde grec du septième au quatrième siècle avant J.-C.* Paris: Boccard.

Deonna, W. 1939. "Croyances funéraires: La soif des morts.—Le mort musicien." *Revue de l'Histoire des Religions* 119: 53–81.

Dettmer, H. 1983. *Horace: A Study in Structure.* Hildesheim: G. Olms.

Diggle, J., J. B. Hall, and H. D. Jocelyn, eds. 1989. *Studies in Latin Literature and Its Tradition in Honor of C. O. Brink.* CPhS Suppl. 15. Cambridge, UK: Cambridge Philological Society.

Doblhofer, E. 1966. *Die Augustuspanegyrik des Horaz in formalhistorischer Sicht.* Heidelberg: C. Winter Universitätsverlag.

Duckworth, G. E. 1956. "*Animae Dimidium Meae:* Two Poets of Rome." *TAPhA* 87: 281–316.

DuQuesnay, I. M. Le M. 1984. "Horace and Maecenas: The Propaganda Value of *Sermones* I." In Woodman and West, 1984: 19–58.

———. 1995. "Horace, *Odes* 4. 5: *Pro Reditu Imperatoris Caesaris Divi Filii Augusti.*" In Harrison, 1995a: 128–87.

Eder, W. 1990. "Augustus and the Power of Tradition: The Augustan Principate as Binding Link between Republic and Empire." In Raaflaub and Toher, 1990: 71–122.

Edmunds, L. 1992. *From a Sabine Jar: Reading Horace, Odes I.9.* Chapel Hill: Univ. of North Carolina Press.

———. 2001. *Intertextuality and the Reading of Roman Poetry.* Baltimore: Johns Hopkins Univ. Press.

Elder, J. P. 1952. "Horace, *C.* I, 3." *AJPh* 73: 140–58.

Esler, C. C. 1989. "Horace's Old Girls: Evolution of a Topos." In Falkner and de Luce, 1989: 172–82.

Estévez, V. A. 1982. "*Quem Tu, Melpomene:* The Poet's Lowered Voice (*C.* IV 3)." *Emerita* 50: 279–300.

Falkner, T. M., and J. de Luce, eds. 1989. *Old Age in Greek and Latin Literature.* Albany: State Univ. of New York Press.

Fantham, E. 1999. "Two Levels of Orality in the Genesis of Pliny's *Panegyricus.*" In MacKay, 1999: 221–37.

Fears, J. R. 1977. *Princeps a Diis Electus: The Divine Election of the Emperor as a Political Concept at Rome*. Rome: American Academy.

Feeney, D. C. 1991. *The Gods in Epic: Poets and Critics of the Classical Tradition*. Oxford: Clarendon.

———. 1992a. "'Shall I Compare Thee . . . ?' Catullus 68B and the Limits of Analogy." In Woodman and Powell, 1992: 33–44.

———. 1992b. "*Si licet et fas est*: Ovid's *Fasti* and the Problem of Free Speech under the Principate." In Powell, 1992: 1–25.

———. 1993. "Horace and the Greek Lyric Poets." In Rudd, 1993: 41–63.

Feeney, D. C., and A. J. Woodman, eds. 2002. *Traditions and Contexts in the Poetry of Horace*. Cambridge: Cambridge Univ. Press.

Festa, N. 1933. "Animae dimidium meae." *Sophia* 1: 436–41.

Fishwick, D. 1969. "*Genius* and *Numen*." *HThR* 62: 356–67.

Fiske, G. C. 1920. *Lucilius and Horace: A Sudy in the Classical Theory of Imitation*. Madison: Univ. of Wisconsin Press.

Fitzgerald, W. 1987. *Agonistic Poetry: The Pindaric Mode in Pindar, Horace, Hölderlin, and the English Ode*. Berkeley: Univ. of California Press.

Flower, H. I. 1996. *Ancestor Masks and Aristocratic Power in Roman Culture*. Oxford: Clarendon.

Fowler, D. P. 1989. "First Thoughts on Closure: Problems and Prospects." *MD* 22: 75–122.

———. 1995. "Horace and the Aesthetics of Politics." In Harrison, 1995a: 248–66.

———. 1997. "On the Shoulders of Giants: Intertextuality and Classical Studies." *MD* 39: 13–34.

———. 2000. *Roman Constructions: Readings in Postmodern Latin*. New York: Oxford Univ. Press.

Fraenkel, E. 1957. *Horace*. Oxford: Clarendon.

Franke, K. L. 1839. *Fasti Horatiani*. Berlin: William Besser.

Freis, R. 1983. "The Catalogue of Pindaric Genres in Horace *Ode* 4.2." *ClAnt* 2: 27–36.

Freudenburg, K. 1990. "Horace's Satiric Program and the Language of Contemporary Theory in Satires 2.1." *AJPh* 111: 187–203.

———. 1993. *The Walking Muse: Horace on the Theory of Satire*. Princeton: Princeton Univ. Press.

———. 2001. *Satires of Rome: Threatening Poses from Lucilius to Juvenal*. Cambridge: Cambridge Univ. Press.

———. 2002. "*Solus Sapiens Liber Est*: Recommissioning Lyric in Epistles 1." In Feeney and Woodman, 2002: 124–40.

Gabba, E., ed. 1983. *Tria Corda: Scritti in onore di Arnaldo Momigliano*. Como, Italy: Edizioni New Press.

Gagé, J. 1955. *Apollon romain: essai sur le culte d' Apollon et le développement du 'ritus Graecus' à Rome des origines à Auguste*. Paris: Boccard.

————. 1981. "Apollon impérial, Garant des 'Fata Romana.'." *ANRW* II.17.2:561–630.

Galinsky, G. K. 1966. "Venus in a Relief of the Ara Pacis Augustae." *AJA* 70: 223–43.

————. 1969. *Aeneas, Sicily, and Rome.* Princeton: Princeton Univ. Press.

————. 1975. *Ovid's Metamorphoses: An Introduction to the Basic Aspects.* Oxford: Basil Blackwell.

————. 1988. "The Anger of Aeneas." *AJPh* 109: 321–48.

————. 1992. "Venus, Polysemy, and the Ara Pacis Augustae." *AJA* 96: 457–75.

————. 1996. *Augustan Culture: An Interpretive Introduction.* Princeton: Princeton Univ. Press.

Gallardo, M. D. 1972. "Los Symposios de Luciano, Ateneo, Metodio y Juliano." *Cuadernos de Filologia Classica* 4: 239–96.

————. 1974. "El Simposio Romano." *Cuadernos de Filologia Classica* 7: 91–143.

Garrison, D. H. 1979. "*Quo Musa Tendis?* Horace's Augustan Patriotism." *CB* 55: 40–44.

Gerber, D. E. 1970. *Euterpe: An Anthology of Early Greek Lyric, Elegiac, and Iambic Poetry.* Amsterdam: Hakkert.

Giangrande, G. 1967. "Two Horatian Problems." *CQ* n.s. 17: 327–31.

————. 1968. "Sympotic Literature and Epigram." In *L'Épigramme grecque,* 91–177. Fondation Hardt: Entretiens sur l' antiquité classique 14. Geneva.

Gold, B. K., ed. 1982. *Literary and Artistic Patronage in Ancient Rome.* Austin: Univ. of Texas Press.

————. 1987. *Literary Patronage in Greece and Rome.* Chapel Hill: Univ. of North Carolina Press.

Gowers, E. 1993. *The Loaded Table: Representations of Food in Roman Literature.* Oxford: Clarendon.

Greene, T. M. 1999. "The Natural Tears of Epic." In Beissinger, Tylus, and Wofford, 1999: 189–202.

Greengard, C. 1980. *The Structure of Pindar's Epinician Odes.* Amsterdam: Hakkert.

Griffiths, A. 2002. "The Odes: Just Where Do You Draw the Line?" In Feeney and Woodman, 2002: 65–79.

Grisart, A. 1966. "Tityre et son Dieu: Des identifications nouvelles." *LEC* 34: 115–42.

Grottanelli, C. 1995. "Wine and Death—East and West." In Murray and Tecusan, 1995: 62–89.

Gruen, E. S. 1985. "Augustus and the Ideology of War and Peace." In Winkes, 1985: 51–72.

Gurval, R. A. 1995. *Actium and Augustus: The Politics and Emotions of Civil War*. Ann Arbor: Univ. of Michigan Press.

Habinek, T. N. 1986. "The Marriageability of Maximus: Horace, *Ode* 4.1.13-20." *AJPh* 107: 407-16.

———. 1998. *The Politics of Latin Literature: Writing, Identity, and Empire in Ancient Rome*. Princeton: Princeton Univ. Press.

Habinek, T. N., and A. Schiesaro, eds. 1997. *The Roman Cultural Revolution*. Cambridge: Cambridge Univ. Press.

Hägg, R. 1983. *The Greek Renaissance of the Eighth Century B.C.: Tradition and Innovation*. Stockholm: Swedish Institute in Athens.

Hahn, E. A. 1945. "Horace's Ode to Vergil." *TAPhA* 76: xxxii.

Haight, E. H. 1950. *The Symbolism of the House Door in Classical Poetry*. New York: Longmans Green.

Hamilton, R. 1974. *Epinikion: General Form in the Odes of Pindar*. The Hague: Mouton.

Händel, P., and W. Meid, eds. 1983. *Festschrift für Robert Muth: zum 65. Geburtstag am 1. Januar 1981*. Innsbruck: Amœ.

Hardie, A. 1998. "Horace, the Paean and the Roman *Choreia* (*Odes* 4.6)." *Papers of the Leeds International Latin Society* 10: 251-93.

Hardie, C. G. 1975. "Octavian and *Eclogue* 1." In Levick, 1975: 109-22.

Hardie, P. R. 1986. *Virgil's Aeneid: Cosmos and Imperium*. Oxford: Clarendon.

———. 1993. "*Ut pictura poesis*? Horace and the Visual Arts." In Rudd, 1993: 120-39.

———. 2002. *Ovid's Poetics of Illusion*. Cambridge: Cambridge Univ. Press.

Harms, E. 1935. *Horaz in seinen Beziehungen zu Pindar*. Marburg, Germany: H. Bauer.

Harrison, G. 1987. "The Confessions of Lucilius (Horace *Sat.* 2.1.30-34): A Defense of Autobiographical Satire?" *ClAnt* 6: 38-52.

Harrison, J. A. 1981. *Horace in His Odes*. Bristol: Bristol Classical Press.

Harrison, S. J. 1990. "The Praise Singer: Horace, Censorinus and Odes 4.8." *JRS* 80: 31-43.

———. 1991. *Vergil: Aeneid 10*. Oxford: Clarendon.

———, ed. 1995a. *Homage to Horace*. Oxford: Clarendon.

———. 1995b. "Horace, Pindar, Iullus Antonius, and Augustus: Odes 4. 2." In Harrison, 1995a: 108-27.

———. 2001. "Simonides and Horace." In Boedeker and Sider, 2001: 261-71.

Heller, J. L., and J. K. Newman, eds. 1974. *Serta Turyniana: Studies in Greek Literature and Palaeography in Honor of Alexander Turyn*. Urbana: Univ. of Illinois Press.

Henderson, J. 1999. "Be Alert (Your Country Needs Lerts): Horace, *Satires* 1.9." In Henderson, *Writing down Rome: Satire, Comedy, and Other Offences in Latin Poetry*, 202–27. Oxford: Clarendon. Originally published in *PCPhS* 39 (1993): 67–93.

Henderson, W. J. 1973. "The Paraklausithyron Motif in Horace's *Odes*." *AClass* 16: 51–67.

Herz, P. 1975. "Bibliographie zum römischen Kaiserkult (1955–1975)." *ANRW* II.16.2: 833–910.

Hills, P. D. 2001. "Ennius, Suetonius, and the Genesis of Horace, *Odes* 4." *CQ* 51: 613–16.

Hinds, S. 1992. "*Arma* in Ovid's *Fasti*, Part 2: Genre, Romulean Rome and Augustan Ideology." *Arethusa* 25:113–53.

———. 1998. *Allusion and Intertext: Dynamics of Appropriation in Roman Poetry*. Cambridge: Cambridge Univ. Press.

Holzberg, N. 1998. *Ovid: Dichter und Werk*. Munich: C. H. Beck. Published in English as *Ovid: The Poet and His Work*. Ithaca, NY: Cornell Univ. Press, 2002.

Hopkins, K. 1983. *Death and Renewal*. Cambridge: Cambridge Univ. Press.

Horsfall, N. 1994. "The Prehistory of Latin Poetry: Some Problems of Method." *RFIC* 122:50–75.

———. 1995a. *A Companion to the Study of Virgil*. Leiden: Brill.

———. 1995b. "Orazio e la conquista del mondo: problemi di ideologia e di metaforica." In Setaioli, 1995: 23–34.

Hunt, J. M. 1974. "Cinq explications de texte." *L'Antiquité Classique* 43: 355–57.

Hunter, R. 2001. "The Poet Unleaved: Simonides and Callimachus." In Boedeker and Sider, 2001: 242–54.

Illig, L. 1932. *Zur Form der pindarischen Erzählung: Interpretationen und Untersuchungen*. Berlin: Junker & Dünnhaupt.

Iltgen, J. J. 1872. *De Horatio, Lucilii aemulo*. Montabaur.

Innes, D. C. 1979. "Gigantomachy and Natural Philosophy." *CQ* n.s. 29: 165–71.

Jackson, C. N. 1914. "Molle Atque Facetum." *HSPh* 25: 117–37.

Johnson, T. S. 1995a. "Horace, *C.* III.17: A Flawed Genealogy." *ICS* 20: 131–34.

———. 1995b. "Vergilius at the Symposion." *Vergilius* 40: 49–66.

———. 1997. "Sympotica Horatiana: Problems of Artistic Integrity." *Philologus* 141: 321–37.

Johnson, W. R. 1969. "Tact in the Drusus Ode: Horace, Odes 4.4." *California Studies in Classical Antiquity* 2: 171–81.

Kellum, B. 1985. "Sculptural Programs and Propaganda in Augustan Rome: The Temple of Apollo on the Palatine." In Winkes, 1985: 169–76.

Kennedy, D. F. 1992. "'Augustan' and 'Anti-Augustan': Reflections on Terms of Reference." In Powell, 1992: 26–58.

Khan, H. A. 1967. "Horace's Ode to Virgil on the Death of Quintilius: 1, 24." *Latomus* 26: 107–17.

Kidd, D. A. 1977. "Virgil's Voyage." *Prudentia* 9: 97–103.

Kienast, D. 1982. *Augustus: Prinzeps und Monarch.* Darmstadt: Wissenschaftliche Buchgesellschaft.

Kiernan, V. G. 1999. *Horace: Poetics and Politics.* New York: St. Martin's Press.

Kiessling, A. 1881. "Horatius: I. Zur Chronologie und Anordnung der Oden." *Philol. Untersuchung* 2: 48–122.

Kirby, J. T. 1992. "Textual, Structural, and Interpretive Issues in Horace *Carm.* 4.2." *Antichthon* 26: 42–50.

Klein, T. M. 1974. "The Role of Callimachus in the Development of the Concept of the Counter-genre." *Latomus* 33: 217–31.

Konstan, D. 1995. "Patrons and Friends." *CPh* 90: 328–42.

Laird, A. 1999. *Powers of Expression, Expressions of Power: Speech Presentation and Latin Literature.* New York: Oxford Univ. Press.

Lambrechts, P. 1953. "La politique 'apollinienne' d'Auguste et le culte impérial." *La Nouvelle Clio* 5: 65–82.

Leach, E. W. 1978. "Vergil, Horace, Tibullus: Three Collections of Ten." *Ramus* 7: 79–105.

———. 1998. "Personal and Communal Memory in the Reading of Horace's *Odes,* Books 1–3." *Arethusa* 31: 43–74.

Leeman, A. D. 1982. "Rhetorical Status in Horace, *Serm.* 2, 1." In B. Vickers, 1982: 159–63.

———. 1983. "Die Konsultierung des Trebatius: Statuslehre in Horaz, *Serm.* 2.1." In Händel and Meid, 1983: 209–15.

Lefèvre, E. 1968. "*Rursus Bella Moves?* Die literarische Form von Horaz, c. 4, 1." *RhM* 111: 166–89.

———. 1989. *Das Bild-Programm des Apollo-Tempels auf dem Palatin.* Konstanz: Universitätsverlag.

———. 1993a. *Horaz: Dichter im augusteischen Rom.* Munich: C. H. Beck.

———. 1993b. "Waren horazische Gedichte zum 'öffentlichen' Vortrag bestimmt?" In Vogt-Spira, 1993: 143–57.

Levick, B., ed. 1975. *The Ancient Historian and His Materials: Essays in Honor of C. E. Stevens on His Seventieth Birthday.* Westmead, UK: Gregg International.

Levin, D. N. 1968. "Horace's Preoccupation with Death." *CJ* 63: 315–20.

Liebeschuetz, J. H. W. G. 1979. *Continuity and Change in Roman Religion.* Oxford: Clarendon.

Lienieks, V. 1977. "Spring and Death in Horace." *CB* 53: 57–61.

Lissarrague, F. 1987. *Un flot d'images: un esthétique du banquet grec.* Paris:

A. Biro. English trans. by Andrew Szegedy-Maszak. *The Aesthetics of the Greek Banquet: Images of Wine and Ritual*. Princeton: Princeton Univ. Press, 1990.

Lockyer, C. W. 1967. "Horace's *Propempticon* and Vergil's Voyage." *CW* 61: 42–45.

Lowrie, M. 1995. "A Parade of Lyric Predecessors: Horace C. 1.12–1.18." *Phoenix* 49: 33–48.

———. 1996. "Conflict in Horace." *CJ* 92: 295–301.

———. 1997. *Horace's Narrative Odes*. Oxford: Clarendon.

Ludwig, W. 1961. "Die Anordnung des vierten Horazischen Odenbuches." *MH* 18: 1–10.

Lyne, R. O. A. M. 1980. *The Latin Love Poets: From Catullus to Horace*. Oxford: Clarendon.

———. 1989. *Words and the Poet: Characteristic Techniques of Style in Vergil's Aeneid*. Oxford: Clarendon.

———. 1995. *Horace: Behind the Public Poetry*. New Haven, CT: Yale Univ. Press.

Maas, P. 1956. "Korruptelen in Horazens Oden." *SIFC* 27/28: 227–28. Reprinted in *Kleine Schriften*, 603–4. Munich: C. H. Beck, 1973.

MacCormack, S. G. 1981. *Art and Ceremony in Late Antiquity*. Berkeley: Univ. of California Press.

MacKay, E. A., ed. 1999. *Signs of Orality: The Oral Tradition and Its Influence in the Greek and Roman World*. Leiden: Brill.

Marcovich, M. 1975. "A New Poem of Archilochus: *P. Colon*. inv. 7511." *GRBS* 16: 5–14.

———. 1991. "Xenophanes on Drinking Parties and Olympic Games." In *Studies in Greek Poetry*. ICS Suppl. 1, 60–84. Atlanta: Scholars Press.

Marquardt, J. 1879–1882. *Das Privatleben der Römer. Handbuch der römischen Altertümer*, vol. 7. Leipzig: S. Hirzel. 2nd ed., 1886. Reprint, Darmstadt: Wissenschaftliche Buchgesellschaft, 1990.

Martin, J. 1931. *Symposion: Die Geschichte einer literarischen Form*. Paderborn, Germany: F. Schöningh.

Martindale, C., ed. 1997. *The Cambridge Companion to Virgil*. Cambridge: Cambridge Univ. Press.

Matt, Leonard von, M. Moretti, and G. Maetzke. 1969. *Terra e arte degli Etruschi*. Genoa: Stringa. English trans. by Peggy Martin. *The Art of the Etruscans*. New York: H. N. Abrams, 1970.

Mayer, R. 1985. "Horace on Good Manners." *PCPhS* 31: 33–46.

Mazurek, T. 1997. "Self-Parody and the Law in Horace's *Satires* 1.9." *CJ* 93: 1–17.

McKay, A. G., ed. 1982. *Vergilian Bimillenary Lectures 1982*. *Vergilius* Suppl. 2. College Park, MD: Vergilian Society.

McKeown, J. C. 1984. "*Fabula Proposito Nulla Tegenda Meo:* Ovid's *Fasti* and Augustan Politics." In Woodman and West, 1984: 169–87.

McNeill, Randall L. B. 2001. *Horace: Image, Identity, and Audience.* Baltimore: Johns Hopkins Univ. Press.

Meuli, K. 1955. "Altrömischer Maskenbrauch." *MH* 12: 206–35.

Miller, J. 1994. "Virgil, Apollo, and Augustus." In Solomon, 1994: 99–112.

Miller, P. A. 1991. "Horace, Mercury, and Augustus, or the Poetic Ego of Odes 1–3." *AJPh* 112: 365–88.

Minadeo, R. 1975. "Vergil in Horace's *Odes* 4.12." *CJ* 71: 161–64.

———. 1982. *The Golden Plectrum: Sexual Symbolism in Horace's Odes.* Amsterdam: Rodopi.

Mole, W. 1966. *Gods, Men, and Wine.* London: Wine & Food Society.

Momigliano, A. 1957. "Perizonius, Niebuhr, and the Character of Early Roman Tradition." *JRS* 47: 104–14.

Moritz, L. A. 1968. "Some 'Central' Thoughts on Horace's *Odes.*" *CQ* n.s. 18: 116–31.

———. 1969. "Horace's Virgil." *G&R* ser. 2, 16: 174–93.

Muecke, F. 1995. "Law, Rhetoric, and Genre in Horace, *Satires* 2.1." In Harrison, 1995a: 203–18.

Mueller, H.-F. 2002. *Roman Religion in Valerius Maximus.* London: Routledge.

Mühll, Peter von der. 1976. "Das griechische Symposion." In *Ausgewählte kleine Schriften,* 483–505. Basel: Friedrich Reinhardt.

Munro, H. A. J. 1878. *Criticisms and Elucidations of Catullus.* Cambridge, UK: Deighton, Bell.

Münzer, F. 1920. *Römische Adelsparteien und Adelsfamilien.* Stuttgart: J. B. Metzler. English trans. by Thérèse Ridley. *Roman Aristocratic Parties and Families.* Baltimore: Johns Hopkins Univ. Press, 1999.

Murray, O. 1980. *Early Greece.* Sussex, UK: Harvesters Press. 2nd ed., Cambridge, MA: Harvard Univ. Press, 1993.

———. 1983a. "The Greek Symposion in History." In Gabba, 1983: 257–72.

———. 1983b. "Symposion and Männerbund." In Oliva and Frolíkova, 1983: 47–52.

———. 1983c. "The Symposion as Social Organization." In Hägg, 1983: 195–99.

———. 1985. "Symposium and Genre in the Poetry of Horace." *JRS* 75: 39–50.

———, ed. 1990. *Sympotica: A Symposium on the Symposion.* Oxford: Clarendon, 1990.

Murray, O., and M. Tecusan, eds. 1995. *In Vino Veritas.* London: British School at Rome.

Mutschler, F.-H. 1974. "Beobachtungen zur Gedichtanordnung in der ersten Odensammlung des Horaz." *RhM* 117: 109–33.

Nagy, G. 1994a. "Copies and Models in Horace *Odes* 4.1 and 4.2." *CW* 87: 415–26.

———. 1994b. "The Name of Apollo: Etymology and Essence." In Solomon, 1994: 3–7.

Newlands, C. E. 1995. *Playing with Time: Ovid and the Fasti*. Ithaca, NY: Cornell Univ. Press.

Newman, J. K. 1967a. *Augustus and the New Poetry*. Collection Latomus 88. Brussels.

———. 1967b. *The Concept of Vates in Augustan Poetry*. Collection Latomus 89. Brussels.

———. 1974. "Callimachus and the Epic." In Heller and Newman, 1974: 342–60.

———. 1986. *The Classical Epic Tradition*. Madison: Univ. of Wisconsin Press.

———. 1990. *Roman Catullus and the Modification of the Alexandrian Sensibility*. Hildesheim: Weidmann.

Nightingale, A. W. 1995. *Genres in Dialogue: Plato and the Construct of Philosophy*. Cambridge: Cambridge Univ. Press.

Nisbet, R. G. M. 1962. "Romanae Fidicen Lyrae: The Odes of Horace." In Sullivan, 1962: 181–218.

———. 1987. "The Oak and the Axe: Symbolism in Seneca, *Hercules Oetaeus* 1618ff." In Whitby, Hardie, and Whitby, 1987: 243–51.

———. 1989. "Footnotes on Horace." In Diggle, Hall, and Jocelyn, 1989: 87–96.

———. 1995. "Tying Down Proteus." In S. J. Harrison, ed. *Collected Papers on Latin Literature*, 414–30. Oxford: Clarendon.

Nock, A. D. 1947. "The Emperor's Divine *Comes*." *JRS* 37: 102–16.

Norden, E. 1956. *Agnostos Theos: Untersuchungen zur Formengeschichte religiöser Rede*. 4th ed. Darmstadt: Wissenschaftliche Buchgesellschaft. 1st ed., Leipzig: Teubner, 1916.

O'Hara, J. 1997. "Virgil's Style." In Martindale, 1997: 241–58.

Oliensis, E. 1998. *Horace and the Rhetoric of Authority*. Cambridge: Cambridge Univ. Press.

Oliva, P., and A. Frolíkova, eds. 1983. *Concilium Eirene XVI: Proceedings of the 16th International Eirene Conference Prague 31.8–4.9 1982*. Prague.

Opperman, H. 1957. "Maecenas' Geburtstag (Horat. c. IV 11)." *Gymnasium* 64: 102–11.

Pallottino, M. 1955. *Art of the Etruscans*. London: Thames & Hudson.

Pasquali, G. 1920. *Orazio lirico*. Florence: Le Monnier. Reprint, 1966.

Paschalis, M., ed. 2002. *Horace and Greek Lyric Poetry*. Rethymon Classical Studies 1. Univ. of Crete.

Pavlock, B. 1982. "Horace's Invitation Poems to Maecenas: Gifts to a Patron." *Ramus* 11: 79–98.

Pearce, J., M., Millett, and M. Struck, eds. 2000. *Burial, Society, and Context in the Roman World.* Oxford: Oxbow.

Perkell, C. 1989. *The Poet's Truth: A Study of the Poet in Virgil's Georgics.* Berkeley: Univ. of California Press.

———, ed. 1999. *Reading Vergil's Aeneid: An Interpretive Guide.* Norman: Univ. of Oklahoma Press.

Pernot, L. 1993. *La rhétorique de l'élogie dans le monde greco-romain.* 2 vols. Paris: Institut d'études augustiniennes.

Perret, J. *Horace.* 1964. English trans. by Bertha Humez. New York: New York Univ. Press.

Pichon, René. 1902. *De sermone amatorio apud latinos elegiarum scriptores.* Paris: Hachette.

Pollini, J. 1990. "Man or God: Divine Assimilation and Imitation in the Late Republic and Early Principate." In Raaflaub and Toher, 1990: 334–63.

Port, W. 1926. "Die Anordnung in Gedichtbüchern augusteischer Zeit." *Philologus* 81: 280–308, 427–68.

Porter, D. 1972. "Horace *Carmina*, IV, 12." *Latomus* 31: 71–87.

———. 1975. "The Recurrent Motifs of Horace, *Carmina* IV." *HSPh* 79: 189–228.

———. 1987. *Horace's Poetic Journey: A Reading of Odes 1–3.* Princeton: Princeton Univ. Press.

Pöschl, V., ed. 1983. *2000 Jahre Vergil: Ein Symposion.* Wolfenbütteler Forschungen 24. Wiesbaden.

Powell, A., ed. 1992. *Roman Poetry and Propaganda in the Age of Augustus.* London: Bristol Classical Press.

Pucci, J. 1992. "Horace and Virgilian Mimesis: A Re-Reading of *Odes* 1.3." *CW* 85: 659–73.

Pucci, P. 1978. "Lingering on the Threshold." *Glyph* 3: 52–73.

Putnam, M. C. J. 1986. *Artifices of Eternity: Horace's Fourth Book of Odes.* Ithaca, NY: Cornell Univ. Press.

———. 1990. "Horace, *Carm.* 2.9: Augustus and the Ambiguities of Encomium." In Raaflaub and Toher, 1990: 212–38.

———. 1993. "The Languages of Horace's *Odes* 1.24." *CJ* 88: 123–35.

———. 1995. "Design and Allusion in Horace, *Odes* I.6." In Harrison, 1995a: 50–64.

———. 2000. *Horace's Carmen Saeculare: Ritual Magic and the Poet's Art.* New Haven, CT: Yale Univ. Press.

Quinn, K. 1963. *Latin Explorations: Critical Studies in Roman Literature.* London: Routledge.

Raaflaub, K. A., and M. Toher, eds. 1990. *Between Republic and Empire:*

Interpretations of Augustus and His Principate. Berkeley: Univ. of California Press.

Race, W. H. 1978. "*Odes* 1.20: An Horatian *Recusatio.*" *California Studies in Classical Antiquity* 11: 179–96.

——. 1982. *The Classical Priamel from Homer to Boethius. Mnemosyne* Suppl. 74. Leiden: Brill.

——. 1988. *Classical Genres and English Poetry.* London: Croom Helm.

Radke, G. 1986. "Le *carmen Lollianam* d'Horace." *Latomus* 45: 768–82.

Ramage, E. S. 1987. *The Nature and Purpose of Augustus' "Res Gestae."* Stuttgart: F. Steiner.

Ramsey, J. T., and A. Lewis Licht. 1997. *The Comet of 44 B.C. and Caesar's Funeral Games.* Atlanta: Scholar's Press.

Ray, C. 1967. "Wines of Italy." In Λ. L. Simon, 1967: 151–266.

Reckford, K. 1959. "Some Studies in Horace's Odes on Love." *CJ* 55: 25–33.

——. 1960. "The Eagle and the Tree (Horace, *Odes* 4.4)." *CJ* 56: 23–28.

——. 1969. *Horace.* New York: Twayne.

Reece, R., and J. Collins, eds. 1977. *Burial in the Roman World.* London: Council for British Archaeology.

Reitzenstein, R. 1893. *Epigramm und Skolion: Ein Beitrag zur Geschichte der alexandrinischen Dichtung.* Giessen: Ricker'sche Buchhandlung. Reprint, Hildesheim: G. Olms, 1970.

Richards, G. 1942. *Housman, 1897–1936.* New York: Oxford Univ. Press.

Rooy, C. A. van. 1972. "Arrangement and Structure of Satires in Horace, *Sermones* Book I: Satires 9 and 10." *AClass* 15: 37–52.

——. 1973. "'Imitatio' of Vergil, *Eclogues* in Horace, *Satires,* Book I." *AClass* 16: 69–88.

Ross, D. 1975. *Backgrounds to Augustan Poetry: Gallus, Elegy and Rome.* Cambridge: Cambridge Univ. Press.

Rudd, N. 1961. "Horace's Encounter with the Bore." *Phoenix* 15: 79–96.

——. 1966. *The Satires of Horace: A Study.* London: Cambridge Univ. Press.

——, ed. 1993. *Horace 2000: A Celebration, Essays for the Bimillennium.* Ann Arbor: Univ. of Michigan Press.

Sage, P. W. 1994. "Vatic Admonition in Horace *Odes* 4.9." *AJPh* 115: 565–86.

Saller, R. P. 1982. *Personal Patronage under the Early Empire.* Cambridge: Cambridge Univ. Press.

——. 1989. "Patronage and Friendship in Early Imperial Rome: Drawing the Distinction." In Wallace-Hadrill, 1989: 49–62.

Salmon, E. T. 1952. "Horace's Ninth Satire in Its Setting." In M. E. White, 1952: 184–93.

Sandel, M. J. 1996. *Democracy's Discontent: America in Search of a Public Philosophy.* Cambridge, MA: Harvard Univ. Press.

Santirocco, M. S. 1986. *Unity and Design in Horace's Odes*. Chapel Hill: Univ. of North Carolina Press.

———. 1995. "Horace and Augustan Ideology." *Arethusa* 28: 225–43.

Schiesaro, A. 1997. "The Boundaries of Knowledge in Vergil's *Georgics*." In Habinek and Schiesaro, 1997: 63–89.

Schmeling, G. 1971. "The *Exclusus Amator* Motif in Petronius." In *Fons Perennis: Saggi critici di Filologia Classica raccolti in onore del Prof. Vittorio D' Agostino*, 333–57. Turin.

Schmidt, E. A. 1983. "Vergils Glück: Seine Freundschaft mit Horaz als ein Horizont unseres Verstehens." In Pöschl, 1983: 1–36.

Scott, K. 1929. "Octavian's Propaganda and Antony's *De Sua Ebrietata*." *CPh* 24: 133–41.

———. 1933. "The Political Propaganda of 44–30 B.C." *MAAR* 11: 7–49.

Scullard, H. H. 1959. *From the Gracchi to Nero: A History of Rome*. New York: Praeger. 5th ed., London: Methuen, 1982.

Seager, R. 1993. "Horace and Augustus: Poetry and Policy." In Rudd, 1993: 23–40.

Setaioli, A., ed. 1995. *Orazio: umanità, politica, cultura: Atti del Convegno di Gubbio, 20–22 ottobre 1992*. Perugia: Università di Perugia.

Shackleton Bailey, D. R. 1982. *Profile of Horace*. Cambridge, MA: Harvard Univ. Press, 1982.

Sichtermann, H. 1953. *Ganymed, Mythos und Gestalt in der antiken Kunst*. Berlin: Mann, 1953.

Sider, D. 2001. "'As Is the Generation of Leaves' in Homer, Simonides, Horace, and Stobaeus." In Boedeker and Sider, 2001: 272–88.

Silk, E. T. 1969. "Bacchus and the Horatian *Recusatio*." *YCS* 21: 195–212.

Simon, A. L., ed. 1967. *The Wines of the World*. New York: McGraw-Hill.

Simon, E. 1957. *Die Portlandvase*. Mainz: Römisch-Germanisches Zentralmuseum.

———. 1986. *Augustus: Kunst und Leben in Rom um die Zeitenwende*. Munich: Hirmer.

Slater, W. J. 1990. "Sympotic Ethics in the *Odyssey*." In Murray, 1990: 213–20.

———, ed. 1991. *Dining in a Classical Context*. Ann Arbor: Univ. of Michigan Press.

Smith, R. A. 1994. "Horace Odes 1.6: *Mutatis Mutandis*, a Most Virgilian *Recusatio*." *Gymnasium* 101: 502–5.

Snell, B. 1965. *Dichtung und Gesellschaft: Studien zum Einfluß der Dichter auf das soziale Denken und Verhalten im alten Griechenland*. Hamburg: Claassen.

Solmsen, F. 1948. "Propertius and Horace." *CPh* 43: 105–9.

Solomon, J., ed. 1994. *Apollo: Origins and Influences*. Tucson: Univ. of Arizona Press.

Southern, P. 1998. *Augustus*. London: Routledge.

Stoppard, T. 1997. *The Invention of Love*. London: Faber & Faber. Reprint, New York: Grove Press, 1998.

Sullivan, J. P., ed. 1962. *Critical Essays on Roman Literature: Elegy and Lyric*. Cambridge, MA: Harvard Univ. Press.

Syme, R. 1933. "Some Notes on the Legions under Augustus." *JRS* 23: 14–33.

———. 1939. *The Roman Revolution*. Oxford: Clarendon.

———. 1958. *Tacitus*. 2 vols. Oxford: Clarendon.

———. 1978. *History in Ovid*. Oxford: Clarendon.

———. 1986. *The Augustan Aristocracy*. Oxford: Clarendon.

———. 1989. "Janus and Parthia in Horace." In Diggle, 1989: 113–24.

Syndikus, H. P. 1995. "Some Structures in Horace's Odes." In Harrison, 1995a: 17–31.

Tarrant, R. 2002. "Ovid and Ancient Literary History." In P. R. Hardie, ed. *The Cambridge Companion to Ovid*, 13–33. Cambridge: Cambridge Univ. Press.

Tatum, W. Jeffrey. 1998. "*Ultra Legem:* Law and Literature in Horace, *Satires* II 1." *Mnemosyne* Ser. 4, 51: 688–99.

Taylor, L. R. 1931. *The Divinity of the Roman Emperor*. Middletown, CT: American Philological Assoc.

Thomas, R. F. 1983. "Callimachus, the *Victoria Berenices* and Roman Poetry." *CQ* n.s. 33: 92–113.

———. 1985. "From *Recusatio* to Commitment: The Evolution of the Vergilian Programme." *Papers of the Liverpool Latin Seminar* 5: 61–73.

———. 2001. *Virgil and the Augustan Reception*. Cambridge: Cambridge Univ. Press.

Tomlinson, R. A. 1990. "The Chronology of the Perachora *Hestiatorion* and Its Significance." In Murray, 1990: 95–101.

Torelli, M. 1999. *Tota Italia: Essays in the Cultural Formation of Roman Italy*. Oxford: Clarendon.

Tovar, A. 1968. "Augustus Ridicules Horace's Shortness: A Comment on the Word *Sextariolus*." *AJPh* 89: 334–41.

Toynbee, J. M. C. 1971. *Death and Burial in the Roman World*. Ithaca, NY: Cornell Univ. Press.

Trimpi, W. 1973. The Meaning of Horace's *Ut pictura poesis*." *Journal of the Warburg and the Courtauld Institute* 36: 1–34.

Vermeule, E. 1979. *Aspects of Death in Early Greek Art and Pottery*. Berkeley: Univ. of California Press.

Verrall, A. W. 1884. *Studies, Literary and Historical, in the Odes of Horace*. London: Macmillan. Reprint, New York: G. E. Stechert, 1924.

Vessey, D. W. T. 1985. "From Mountain to Lover's Tryst: Horace's Soracte Ode." *JRS* 75: 26–38.

Vickers, B., ed. 1982. *Rhetoric Revalued: Papers from the International Society for the History of Rhetoric*. Medieval and Renaissance Texts and Studies 19. Binghamton, NY: Center for Medieval and Early Renaissance Studies.

Vickers, M. J. 1978. *Greek Symposia*. London: Joint Assoc. of Classical Teachers.

———. 1990. "Attic *Symposia* after the Persian Wars." In Murray, 1990: 105–21.

Vogt-Spira, G., ed. 1993. *Beiträge zur mündlichen Kultur de Römer*. Script-Oralia 47. Tübingen: Grunter Narr.

Wallace-Hadrill, A., ed. 1989. *Patronage in Ancient Society*. London: Routledge.

Weinstock, S. 1971. *Divus Julius*. Oxford: Clarendon.

West, D. 1995. *Horace Odes I: Carpe Diem*. Oxford: Clarendon.

———. 1998. *Horace Odes II: Vatis Amici*. Oxford: Clarendon.

West, M. L. 1971b. "Stesichorus." *CQ* n.s. 21: 302–14.

———. 1974. *Studies in Greek Elegy and Iambus*. Berlin: de Gruyter.

Whitby, Mary, ed. 1998. *The Propaganda of Power: The Role of Panegyric in Late Antiquity*. Leiden: Brill.

Whitby, Michael, P. Hardie, and Mary Whitby, eds. 1987. *Homo Viator: Classical Essays for John Bramble*. Bristol: Bristol Classical Press.

White, M. E., ed. 1952. *Studies in Honour of Gilbert Norwood*. Toronto: Toronto Univ. Press.

White, P. 1991. "Maecenas' Retirement." *CPh* 86: 130–38.

———. 1993. *Promised Verse: Poets in the Society of Augustan Rome*. Cambridge, MA: Harvard Univ. Press.

———. 1995. "Postumus, Curtius Postumus, and Rabirius Postumus." *CPh* 90: 151–61.

Wilamowitz-Moellendorff, U. von. 1903. "Apollon." *Hermes* 38: 575–86.

———. 1913. *Sappho und Simonides: Untersuchungen über griechische Lyriker*. Berlin: Weidmann.

Wili, W. 1948. *Horaz und die Augusteische Kultur*. Basel: Benno Schwabe.

Wilkinson, L. 1945. *Horace and His Lyric Poetry*. Cambridge: Cambridge Univ. Press.

———. 1963. *Golden Latin Artistry*. Cambridge: Cambridge Univ. Press.

Williams, G. 1962. "Poetry in the Moral Climate of Augustan Rome." *JRS* 52: 28–46.

———. 1968. *Tradition and Originality in Roman Poetry*. Oxford: Clarendon.

———. 1972. *Horace*. Greece and Rome, New Surveys in the Classics 6. Oxford: Clarendon.

———. 1980. *Figures of Thought in Roman Poetry*. New Haven, CT: Yale Univ. Press.

———. 1990. "Did Maecenas 'Fall from Favor'? Augustan Literary Patronage." In Raaflaub and Toher, 1990: 258–75.

Williams, G. D. 1994. *Banished Voices: Readings in Ovid's Exile Poetry.* Cambridge: Cambridge Univ. Press.

Wills, J. 1996. *Repetition in Latin Poetry: Figures of Allusion.* Oxford: Clarendon.

Wimmel, W. 1960. *Kallimachos in Rome: Die Nachfolge seines apologetischen Dichtens in der Augusteerzeit.* Hermes Einzelschriften 16. Wiesbaden.

———. 1965. "Recusatio-Form und Pindarode." *Philologus* 109: 83–103.

Winbolt, S. E. 1978. *Latin Hexameter Verse.* London: Methuen, 1903. Reprint, New York: Garland.

Winkes, R., ed. 1985. *The Age of Augustus: Interdisciplinary Conference Held at Brown University, April 30 – May 2, 1982.* Providence, RI.

Woodman, A. J., and D. West, eds. 1984. *Poetry and Politics in the Age of Augustus.* Cambridge: Cambridge Univ. Press.

Woodman, A. J., and J. Powell, eds. 1992. *Author and Audience in Latin Literature.* Cambridge: Cambridge Univ. Press.

Zanker, P. 1983. "Der Apollontempel auf dem Palatin: Ausstattung und politische Sinnbezüge nach der Schlacht von Actium." In *Città e Architettura nella Roma Imperiale,* 21–40. Analecta Romana Instituti Danici Supplementum 10. Copenhagen, 1983.

———. 1988. *The Power of Images in the Age of Augustus.* Ann Arbor: Univ. of Michigan Press.

Zetzel, J. E. G. 1980. "Horace's *Liber Sermonum:* The Structure of Ambiguity." *Arethusa* 13: 59–77.

Zorzetti, N. 1990. "The *Carmina Convivalia.*" In Murray, 1990: 289–307.

———. 1991. "Poetry and the Ancient City: The Case of Rome." *CJ* 86: 311–29.

Zumwalt, N. K. 1974. "Horace C.1.34: Poetic Change and Political Equivocation." *TAPhA* 104: 435–67.

General Index

Achilles, 8, 19, 30, 32–33, 58–59, 61–62, 64–66, 88, 137, 149–50, 190–92, 234n.34, 235n.49
Actium, 20, 56, 63, 110, 122, 195, 209, 232n.20, 233n.31, 235n.52
adoption, 245n.13
Aeneas, 59, 73, 106, 110, 122, 137, 139, 190–93, 234n.33, 244–45n.12. *See also* Vergil: the *Aeneid* in Horace
Aeneid. See under Vergil
Agamemnon, 88–89, 149–50, 241n.98, 257–58n.34
aging lover, abuse of, 134, 142–43, 168–71, 174–80, 264n.103. *See also* invective
agon, 20, 98, 225n.59; as a metaphor for panegyric, xiv, xvii, 95, 109, 197–98
Agrippa, M., 8, 163, 206
Alcaeus, 11, 222n.45. *See also* Index Locorum
Alexander the Great, 23–25, 164, 228n.76
Alexandria, 186, 188, 195–96
Alexandrian poetry. *See* neotericism
Algidus, Mount, 107
Altar of Peace, 63, 196, 209, 235n.46, 263n.96, 276n.62
alter poeta. See animae dimidium meae
amicitia, 19, 22. *See also* patronage

Anchises, 110, 122, 247n.31, 250n.64
animae dimidium meae, 138–39, 141–44, 157, 163–64, 254n.15, 255n.20, 256–57n.27, 260n.59. *See also* Vergil: relationship to Horace
animal similes, 98–103, 105, 110, 192–94, 243n.6, 244–45nn.9–12, 245n.16, 248n.38
Antonius, Iullus, xv, 41, 42, 48–50, 70, 189, 231n.13
Antonius, M., 189, 231n.13, 233n.30
Apelles, 25
Apollo: Apollo's Palatine Temple, 56, 63, 68, 117, 233nn.30–31, 234n.35; poet's defender, 19–20, 41, 51–52, 56, 64–68, 71, 99; in the *recusatio*, 14–15, 60, 166, 205–10, 231n.14, 275nn.57–58; relationship to Augustus, xv, 20, 56–58, 60–61, 122–23, 124, 187, 207–8, 233nn.30–31, 274n.50; symbol of transition from war to peace, 57–59, 63, 206–7, 234n.35, 275n.59
apopompe, 229n.85
aporia, xvi–xvii. *See also* disputes in panegyric
apotheosis, 78, 116, 118, 121, 122–29, 132–33, 141, 145, 147, 163, 252n.84. *See also* Augustus: divinity of; *divus praesens*

301

Apulia, 67, 194
Arcadia, 161–62, 165
archives. See *Fasti*
arete. See virtue, poetic
Aristotle, views on rhetoric, xiv, 94,
253n.8. *See also* banausia; Index Locorum
arrangement of the *Odes*, 41–42, 67,
99–100, 118, 134–35, 181–82, 200,
215n.2, 230n.4, 237n.68
audience, xiii–xiv, xvii, 16, 22, 25–26,
29–30, 38, 86, 109, 114, 136–37, 181,
198, 200–201, 210–13
Aufidus, 192–94, 269n.4, 270n.24
Augustus: address to, 45, 48, 117, 120,
124, 130–33, 197, 200–211, 269n.2;
divinity of, 58, 60, 78, 116–30, 132–
33, 186–87, 195, 196–97, 202–3,
249n.46 (*see also* apotheosis; divine
right of kings; *divus praesens*);
family of, xv, 48, 60, 71, 128,
231n.13, 236n.61; as father, 102–4,
109–12, 119, 186, 187–88, 193,
239n.81, 248n.2, 270n.19; Forum of,
276–77n.62; moral legislation of,
201; as patron, xiii, 30–31, 40–41,
43, 94, 163, 208–9, 222–23nn.50–51,
261n.63; as reader, 15–16, 22, 41,
223n.52, 230n.5; triumphs of, xvii,
49, 71, 94, 208–9, 232n.17, 274n.51;
warnings to, 60, 73, 209, 248n.33.
See also Altar of Peace; *Pax Augusta*
autobiography, Horace's, 28–39, 169,
215n.1, 257n.28, 265n.113. *See also*
patronage: Horace's

Bacchus. *See* Dionysus
ballad theory, 273n.45
banausia, 23–24, 31, 160, 164, 166,
228n.78
banquet couch, 12–13, 221nn.40–41.
See also symposion
Barchiesi, A., xvii, xix
Bellerophon, 155
Bentley, R., 79, 160
blame, xiv, 74, 89–92, 181, 216n.10,
240n.90. *See also* invective

boor, the, 16–21, 224nn.55–56, 266–
67n.125
Bowra, C. M., 160–61
Branchidae oracle, 225n.63
brevitas in lyric, 8, 13, 15, 23, 31–33,
50–51, 62, 165–66, 194, 206, 208,
210, 272n.35. *See also* Callimachus;
neotericism
Brutus, Marcus Iunius, 218n.17
burial customs, 136, 253n.4

Callimachus, xv–xvi, xviii–xix, xx,
14–15, 28, 40, 50–51, 60, 67, 141,
205–6, 208, 252n.83, 273–74n.48,
276n.61. See also *brevitas* in lyric;
neotericism; Index Locorum
Cameron, A., xvi
Carmen Saeculare, xiii, xviii–xix, 4, 27–
28, 48, 57–61, 63–64, 68, 118, 121,
206, 232n.26, 233n.29, 235n.43,
243n.7
carpe diem, 6–7, 9, 40, 62, 65–66, 68, 70–
73, 90, 155, 164, 166, 168, 175–76,
181, 187, 202, 217n.13, 219n.22,
234n.42, 241n.104, 242n.108,
259n.46, 260n.59, 266n.122,
273n.44
Cassius Dio, 239n.81. *See also* Index
Locorum
Castor. *See* Dioscuri
catharsis, 137
Cato the Elder, 125, 203, 210, 220n.28,
251n.68
Catullus, 15–18, 28, 169, 191, 270n.22.
See also Index Locorum
Censorinus, C. Marcius, 42, 71, 74–79,
231n.10, 237n.64, 237n.69
Chia, lover's name, 171, 174–79,
266n.125
Chian wine, 176, 177, 266–67n.125,
268n.130
Choerilus of Iasus, 23–25, 164,
228n.76
Cicero, xiv–xv, 89, 94, 203, 253n.7. *See
also* Index Locorum
Cinara, 27, 38–39, 135, 170–71, 174,
179–80, 229n.88, 265n.113

civil wars, 3–4, 30–31, 33, 38, 57, 107, 111, 131, 192, 196, 202–3, 209, 218n.17, 271n.29, 275–76n.59
clades Lolliana, 82, 232n.17. *See also* Lollius, M.
Claudian line, 103–4, 106, 108–11
Cleopatra, 13–14, 123, 176, 186, 189
Collinge, N. E., 121, 191
comedy, 148–53, 155–56. See also *fabulae palliatae*
compound simile, 105, 107, 244n.10
Crotty, K., 109
Cupid, 174–78
curse. *See* invective
Cycnus, 155, 255n.22, 256n.24

Daedalus, 47, 50, 165
Danaë, 268n.132
Deiphobus, 87–88, 89
Diana, 59, 66, 76
Dido, 106, 137, 244–45n.12, 245–46nn.19–20
Dionysus, xvii, 13, 30, 77–78, 117, 122–23, 125, 162–63, 176, 211–12, 233n.30, 263n.96, 266n.121, 274n.51
Dioscuri, 76–77, 125–26, 128, 238n.76
disputes in panegyric, xv–xix, 42–43, 45, 50, 61, 84, 86, 92–93, 94, 109, 113, 119, 121, 128–29, 185, 190, 194, 196–98, 201–2, 213, 233n.28, 237n.68, 246–47n.24, 247n.28, 249n.49
divine right of kings, 123. *See also* Augustus: divinity of
divus praesens, 119, 124, 127, 132, 186, 251nn.70–71. *See also* apotheosis; Augustus: divinity of
Drusus, Nero Claudius, xv, 40–41, 82, 84, 98–114, 118, 181, 184–95, 237n.68
dubia. See disputes in panegyric
DuQuesnay, I. M. Le M., 117–18, 121
durus, 32, 35, 107, 216n.5, 229n.87. *See also* paraklausithyron

Edmunds, L., xvi–xvii
education: Horace's, 29–33. *See also* nature and nurture

ekphrasis, 101, 110, 189, 238n.71, 270n.23
elegy, 19, 36, 122, 173, 178, 222–23n.50, 224n.55, 229n.85, 254–55n.17, 274n.51, 276n.61
Ennius, 21–22, 85, 127–28, 227n.72, 271–72n.34. *See also* Index Locorum
epic poetry, criticism of, xix, 8, 14–39, 48, 50–51, 58, 66, 71, 85, 149–51, 164–66, 194, 204–10, 222n.48, 223n.53, 258n.39, 273n.47. *See also* Vergil: criticism of
Epicurus, Epicureanism, xviii–xix, 26, 123, 236n.56, 251n.75
epinikion, xv, xvi, 40, 42, 48–49, 60, 94–114, 118, 181–98, 206–8, 233n.27, 237n.68, 255n.18
epitaphios, 253n.4, 253n.6
epithalamium, 34, 45, 151, 229n.85
epos. See epic poetry
Euripides, 165, 236n.62
exclusus amator (exclusa amatrix), 173, 181, 255n.23, 265n.112, 268n.132. *See also* paraklausithyron
exile, as metaphor, 26, 30–39, 41

Fabius Maximus, Paulus, xv, 5, 34–35, 37, 42, 43–45, 49, 70–71, 142, 153, 160, 176, 229n.90, 230–31nn.8–13
fabulae palliatae, 151, 257n.32. *See also* comedy
Fasti, 177, 197, 268n.131
Fasti Capitolini Consulares et Triumphales, 268n.131
Faunus, 8, 252n.79
Faustitas, 121, 252n.79
Forum of Augustus. *See under* Augustus
Fowler, D., xvi, xix
Fraenkel, E., xviii, 62, 135, 160

Ganymede, 101, 103, 110, 244n.8
genius, 117, 129. *See also* Augustus: divinity of
genre, 3, 135, 148–49, 151, 166, 204
genus tenue. See brevitas in lyric

gift-exchange, 24, 76–79, 84, 144, 165, 228n.78
Gigantomachy, 139, 188–91, 269n.11, 270n.16
Greene, T., 137

Hannibal, 76–77, 104–8, 110–12, 114, 185–86, 190, 244–45n.12, 245n.17, 250n.64, 253n.10
Harrison, S. J., 77
Hasdrubal, 104, 108
Hector, 19, 87–88, 149–50
Heinze, R., 62
Helen, 87–89, 138
Hercules, 76–78, 122–23, 125–26, 128, 238n.76, 251n.70
Hinds, S., xvi
Hippolytus, 73, 236–37n.62
Homer, 8, 19, 23, 28, 48, 50, 67, 74, 86, 88–89, 228n.76, 240n.94, 242n.110. *See also* Index Locorum
Housman, A. E., 69, 229n.88, 236n.57
hyperbaton, 88, 155, 200, 212
hyperbole, 49, 78, 121, 190, 231n.12

iambic poetry, 3, 38, 171
iambic tone, 17, 20, 169, 220n.32. *See also* invective
immortality, 68, 76, 79, 89–90, 109, 159, 162–63, 169–70, 180, 242n.110. *See also* symposion: sympotic time
inclusa amatrix, 177–78, 268n128, 268n.132. *See also* paraklausithyron
intention, authorial, xvi–xvii
intertextuality, 5–6, 66–67, 242n.108
invective, 134, 142, 169–74, 226n.69. *See also* aging lover, abuse of; iambic tone
Itys, 159, 163
Iulium sidus, 117, 123, 250n.67
Iullus. *See* Antonius, Iullus

Johnson, W. R., 114
Julian line, 104, 106, 108–11, 277n.63
Julius Caesar, 60, 117, 123, 124, 226n.70, 233n.30, 237n.69, 253n.4, 259n.46

Jupiter, symbol of Augustan power, 98, 102, 108, 109, 124–27, 189

Kiessling, A., 62
klētikon, 130–32, 251–52n.77
komos, 225n.61, 267n.127. *See also* paraklausithyron

lament, xx, 36–37, 87, 108, 131–33, 134–37, 139, 141, 143–45, 147, 161–66, 167, 170–72, 180, 213, 216n.11, 240n.92, 246n.23
Lares, 117, 129. *See also* Augustus: divinity of
Lepidus, M. Aemilius (*triumvir*), 129
Leuconoë, 9, 11, 113, 155, 168
Liber. *See* Dionysus
Ligurinus, 27, 35–36, 41, 107, 134, 138–45, 146–47, 153, 155, 157, 162–64, 169, 178–80, 216n.11, 254n.11, 255n.22, 265n.115
litotes, 76, 180
Livia, 104, 248n.2
Lollius, M., 42, 71, 74, 79–92, 197, 216n.10, 231n.10, 237n.68, 239nn.79–81, 239n.85, 242n.108, 260n.53. See also *clades Lolliana*
Lowrie, M., xix, 118
Lucceius, Lucius, xv
Lucilius, 22, 62, 224n.56, 227n.72. *See also* Index Locorum
Lucretius, 26, 123. *See also* Index Locorum
Ludi Saeculares, 117. See also *Carmen Saeculare*
Ludi Victoriae Caesaris, 117
lustrum, 152
Lyce, 40, 134–35, 139, 167–80, 181, 197, 253n.2, 254n.11, 255–56n.23, 274n.50
Lydia, 5, 40, 168, 173–74, 180, 255–56n.23, 263n.98, 264–65n.11, 268n.132
Lyne, R. O. A. M., xviii, 84, 117–18, 135, 171
Lysippus, 25

Maecenas: circle of, xiii, 16, 18–21, 25, 54, 139, 157, 217n.12; friendship with Horace, 43, 154, 156–57, 160, 216n.6, 224n.54, 225–26n.64, 230n.7, 259n.50. *See also* patronage: Horace's

magic, xix, 132, 253n.86

magister bibendi, 6, 37, 76, 172, 219n.22. *See also* symposion

Marcia, xv, 34, 44, 231n.13

Mars, 122, 124, 185–86, 195; temple of Mars Ultor, 196, 235n.46, 251n.69. *See also* Augustus: Forum of

Medea, 266n.123

Melpomene, 41, 51–54, 71, 98, 99, 264n.109

Menander Rhetor, xv, 40, 94. *See also* Index Locorum

Mercury, 62, 124, 271n.31

merum, 44, 72, 117, 120, 220n.28

metathesis, 150

mirror images, 138–39, 178, 255n.18

Moritz, L. A., 161

nature and nurture, 102–5, 108, 112, 119, 195, 245n.15, 258n.41. *See also* Augustus: as father

neotericism, 16–19, 224n.55, 225n.60, 244n.9, 250n.63, 270n.22. See also *brevitas* in lyric; Callimachus

Nero, C. Claudius, 104, 108

Nero, Tiberius Claudius, xv, 104, 248n.52

Niobe, 58–59, 65, 234n.34

numen, 117, 123. *See also* Augustus: divinity of

Octavian. *See* Augustus

Odysseus, 8, 32–33

Oliensis, E., xviii, 121, 135

Ovid, xvi–xvii, xix, 68, 225n.62, 228n.75, 229n.82, 269n.6. *See also* Index Locorum

Pallas, 192–93

Parade Odes, 216n.6, 222n.49

paraklausithyron, 18–19, 174, 177–78, 224n.55, 225n.62, 254n.11, 264–65n.111, 267n.127. See also *durus; exclusus amator; inclusa amatrix; komos*

Paris, 87–88

parody, 40, 48–50, 109, 149, 247n.27

Parthian(s), 82, 122, 210, 235n.52, 252n.79, 276–77n.62

patronage: definition of, 19, 57, 78–79, 163, 224n.54, 228n.78; Horace's, xiii, 6, 16–22, 28–33, 54, 57, 63–64, 68, 118, 208, 211–13, 237n.64, 241n.103. *See also* Augustus: as patron

Pax Augusta, 110, 167, 195, 200–202, 207, 210, 232n.17

Phaethon, 155, 165, 255n.22, 263n.89

Philomela, 163

Phyllis, 66, 138, 145–56, 161, 165, 169–71, 176, 180, 259n.47, 265n.115

Phoebus. *See* Apollo

Pindar, as Horace's rival, xvii–xviii, 48–51, 53–54, 62, 64, 68, 70, 98–100, 104, 106, 109–11, 125, 185, 189, 194, 196–97, 232n.17, 232n.24, 237n.65, 243n.7, 247n.27, 247n.29. *See also* Index Locorum

Plato, xvi, 24. *See also* Index Locorum

Plautus, 101, 121, 149, 217n.12. *See also* Index Locorum

Pliny the Younger, 82–83. *See also* Index Locorum

Poe, Edgar Allan, 3, 169

Pollux. *See* Dioscuri

Pompeius, Sextus, 233n.30, 248n.32

Porphyrio, 4, 161, 239n.88, 243n.3, 246n.24

praeteritio, 248n.37

priamel, 38, 53–54, 62, 76, 125–26, 233n.27

pro/anti-Augustan, xviii, 60

Procne, 159, 162

propaganda, xviii, 40, 57–61, 63

propempticon, xiii, 139, 141, 144, 174, 176–77, 229n.85, 254n.15

Propertius, xvi, 28, 67–68, 122–23, 219n.26. *See also* Index Locorum

Pseudo-Acro, 4, 143, 161
Putnam, M. C. J., xiii, 108, 135, 164,
    192

Quinn, K., 171, 191

recusatio, xiii, 14–16, 21, 24–25, 27–28,
    33, 41, 45, 48–50, 64, 66–67, 71, 94,
    125, 166, 196, 201, 203–11, 222n.48,
    222–23n.50, 223n.53, 227nn.71–72,
    228n.76, 229n.85, 231n.14, 237n.65,
    237n.68, 247n.27, 273–74nn.47–49,
    274–75n.54
Res Gestae, 201–9, 230n.5, 275–76n.59.
    See also Augustus in Index Loco-
    rum
Return Odes, 13, 49, 130–32, 176,
    222n.46, 266n.121
Rhaetian(s), xv, 112, 188–92, 194–95,
    242n.2
rhetoric, xiv, 94, 253nn.7–8
Roman Odes, 111, 119, 202, 249n.50
Romulus, 78, 125, 127–28, 129,
    235n.46, 252n.84
ruler cult, 129, 133, 249n.45. *See also*
    Augustus: divinity of

Sallustius Crispus, 43
Sappho, 28, 68, 84, 87, 89, 135, 179,
    182. *See also* Index Locorum
seriocomic, xx, 3–12, 15, 45, 58, 64, 92,
    113, 119, 154, 155–56, 159, 175,
    217n.16, 218–19n.20, 220–22nn.34–
    41, 259n.51. *See also* symposion
Sestius, Lucius, xiii, 7–8, 11, 14, 90,
    161, 164, 218n.17
Simonides, 28, 240n.92, 242n.110. *See
    also* Index Locorum
slaves, in comedy, 148, 150–52, 155,
    258nn.35–36, 259n.48
Socrates, 33
solid arts, Horace's rivalry with, 76–
    79, 197, 238n.71, 238n.74, 243n.4,
    247n.31, 255n.19
soliloquy, 171
speech acts, 234n.38
sphragis, 57, 64, 67

Stoic(ism), 91–92, 241n.98, 241n.106,
    242n.109
story, storytelling, xiv, xvii, 42, 67,
    105, 118
Suetonius, xiii, xviii, 3, 40–41, 82, 86,
    104, 117, 229n.82, 261n.63. *See also
    Vita Horati;* Index Locorum
Sygambri, xv, 48–49, 82, 195, 232n.17
symposion: in the Greek lyricists, 9–
    12, 166, 175, 219–21nn.23–37; mod-
    eration in, xix, 10–11, 19, 72, 77,
    154, 155, 175–76, 200, 220n.32; poli-
    tics in, 12–14, 181, 217n.12,
    222n.43; revelry at, 11, 44, 153,
    220n.28; ritual, 12, 44, 130, 132–33,
    154, 248n.43; in satire, 7, 217n.15;
    sympotic time, 7, 71–73, 84, 113,
    153–54, 156, 159, 161–63, 169–72,
    175, 187, 202–3, 218n.18, 259nn.46–
    47. *See also carpe diem;* seriocomic

Tacitus, 82. *See also* Index Locorum
Telephus, 153, 155, 168, 259n.47
Thalia, 66–67
Theocritus, 67. *See also* Index Loco-
    rum
thirst, as a stylistic metaphor, 77,
    262n.77, 263n.94
Tiberius Caesar, xv, 40–41, 43, 82, 84,
    99, 181, 184–95, 230n.8, 237n.68
Torquatus, 68, 70–73, 138, 236n.56
tragedy, 148–53
Trebatius Testa, 21–22, 226n.70
triumphs. *See under* Augustus
Trojan War, 59, 66–67, 86–90, 149–50,
    166, 190–93, 233n.32, 240n.92
Turnus, 192–93, 235n.49

Varius Rufus, xiii, 8, 18, 24–26, 33, 48,
    50, 228n.76
Varro, 203
vates, xiii, 51, 57, 67, 133, 147, 165, 180,
    182, 207, 212, 233n.29, 237n.67,
    241n.99, 249n.48, 264n.109. *See also*
    virtue, poetic
Velleius Paterculus, 82–83. *See also* In-
    dex Locorum

Venus, symbol of lyric power, 3–5, 27–28, 34–39, 68, 107, 142, 152–53, 169, 176, 178–79, 216n.9

Vergil: the *Aeneid* in Horace, 48, 66–67, 105–6, 111, 114, 139–40, 165–66, 196, 203, 210, 212–13, 235n.51, 254–55n.17, 261n.67; criticism of, 14–15, 24–26, 40, 67, 139–40, 154, 160, 163–66; *imitatio* of, 50, 60, 122, 160–61, 190–94, 205–6, 208, 213, 224–25n.57, 245–46n.19, 250n.64, 253n.10; relationship to Horace, xiii, 139–45, 157, 158–66, 225–26n.64, 262n.82 (see also *animae dimidium meae*). *See also* Index Locorum

Vindelician(s), xv, 101, 102–3, 110–13, 186, 188–90, 194–95, 242n.2

virtue, poetic, 71, 78–79, 84–85, 89–90, 98–99, 109, 113

Vita Horati, 15, 30, 40, 118, 215n.2. *See also* autobiography, Horace's.

wine, as metaphor for the pleasure of sharing songs, 156–57, 162–63, 165, 211–12, 260n.56, 263n.92

Index Locorum

Agathias, *Epigrammata* (*Anthologia
    Palatina*)
    5.273: *265–66n.117*
Alcaeus (Lobel and Page [L.-P.])
    38A: *220n.31, 220n.33*
    332: *220n.31*
    335: *220n.31*
    338: *220n.31*
    346: *220n.31*
    347: *220n.31, 220–21n.34*
    358: *175, 220n.30*
Anacreon
    eleg. 2.1–2 (West [W.]): *11*
    fr. 36 (Gentili [Gent.]): *217n.13*
    356 (Page [*PMG*]): *220n.28*
    356b (Page [*PMG*]): *175–76,
    220n.30*
Anacreontea (Bergk [*PLG*])
    2: *220n.32*
    3: *220n.32*
    5: *220n.32*
    7: *219n.25, 221n.36*
    8: *220n.27*
    17: *221n.35*
    30: *219n.25*
    32: *219n.25*
    34: *219n.25*
    36: *219n.25, 221n.35*
    38: *219n.25, 220n.34*
    40: *219n.25*

    42: *219n.25, 220n.32*
    46: *219n.25*
    47: *220n.27*
    57: *220n.27*
Anonymous, *Fragmenta* (Page [*PMG*])
    fr. 1009: *219n.25*
Apollodorus, *Bibliotheca*
    1.4.1: *234n.34*
    3.4.1–2: *246n.22*
    3.5.6: *234n.34*
Appian, *Bella Civilia*
    2.147: *253n.4*
Apuleius, *Florida*
    18.142: *157*
Archilochus (West [W.])
    4: *220n.31*
    5: *219n.23*
    13: *221n.35*
    42: *220n.31*
    120: *220n.31*
Aristophanes, *Acharnenses*
    243: *150*
Aristophanes, *Aves*
    656: *150*
Aristophanes, *Ecclesiazusae*
    938–75: *267n.127*
Aristotle, *Ethica Nicomachea*
    1107b, 1122a–b, 1123a: *24*
Aristotle, *Politica*
    1258, 1337b4–22: *24*

Aristotle, *Rhetorica*
  1358a36–1358b8: *xiv, 253n.8*
  1358b38–1359a5: *xiv*
  1362b29–1363a16: *xiv*
Asclepiades, *Epigrammata* (*Anthologia Palatina*)
  5.164: *267–68n.127*
Athenaeus, *Deipnosophistae*
  1.29: *266–67n.125*
  10.429–31e: *220n.28*
Augustus, *Res Gestae*
  1.1: *195, 201*
  2: *201*
  3.1–2: *110, 201*
  5.2: *201*
  6: *201*
  8.5: *201*
  10: *251n.76*
  12: *201*
  13: *201*
  15: *201*
  18: *201*
  19.2: *201*
  20.4: *201*
  24.1: *201*
  25.1–2: *201*
  26–33: *201*
  34: *201*
Aulus Gellius, *Noctes Atticae*
  11.2.5: *273n.45*
Ausonius, *Epistulae* (Green)
  9a.11–14: *228n.76*

Bacchylides (Bergk [*PLG*])
  13: *220n.32, 221n.35, 221n.37*

Caesar, *de Bello Civili*
  1.63.2: *241n.104*
Callimachus, *Aetia* (Pfeiffer [Pf.])
  I. fr. 1.13–30: *14*
  I. fr. 1.21–24: *205–6, 208*
  I. fr. 1.29–30: *232n.21*
  IV. fr. 110: *xvi*
Callimachus, *Epigrammata* (Gow and Page [G.-P.])
  63.1330–32: *265–66n.117*

Callimachus, *Epigrammata* (Pfeiffer [Pf.])
  41: *141*
Callimachus, *Fragmenta* (Pfeiffer [Pf.])
  fr. 384: *xvi*
  fr. 400: *141*
Callimachus, *Hymnus in Apollinem*
  110–12: *232n.21*
Cassius Dio
  44.35, 51: *253n.4*
  48.44: *245n.14*
  51.1.3: *233n.31*
  51.15: *231n.13*
  51.19.7: *249n.45*
  53.26: *239n.79*
  54.6: *239nn.79–80*
  54.8.1–3: *276n.62*
  54.9.4–5: *276n.62*
  54.19.7–8: *248–49n.44*
  54.20: *239n.79*
  54.22: *192, 242n.2*
  54.26: *231n.13*
  54.27.2–3: *251n.76*
  55.1, 10: *231n.13*
  55.5: *237n.69*
  56.31–34: *253n.4*
Catullus
  1: *17–18*
  10: *17, 225n.58*
  11.16–23: *267–68n.127*
  13.10: *224–25n.57*
  16: *263n.85*
  17.14–22: *267–68n.127*
  25.12: *260n.57*
  35.17: *266–67n.125*
  37.11–20: *267–68n.127*
  44: *17*
  58: *267–68n.127*
  62.36: *241n.104*
  64: *66, 191*
  67: *267n.127*
  68: *241n.101, 241n.104, 270n.15*
Cicero, *de lege Agraria*
  2.95: *255n.22*
Cicero, *Brutus*
  62: *xv, 232n.17*
  75: *203*

Cicero, *Epistulae ad Atticum*
  4.6: *xv*
Cicero, *Epistulae ad Familiares*
  5.12.2–4: *xv*
  7.6, 12, 16, 22: *226n.70*
  7.10.2: *226n.70*
  7.13.1: *226n.70*
Cicero, *de Finibus Bonorum et Malorum*
  1.23–25, 39: *236n.56*
Cicero, *de Inventione*
  1.7: *xiv*
Cicero, *Lucullus*
  134: *241n.106*
Cicero, *de Oratore*
  2.43–49, 65, 342–47: *xiv, 89, 253n.7*
  2.341: *xiv, 253n.7*
Cicero, *Partitiones Oratoriae*
  70: *xiv*
  71: *xiv, xv*
  71–72: *xiv, 89, 253n.7*
  73–74: *xiv*
  75–82: *xiv, 89, 253n.7*
Cicero, *Tusculanae Disputationes*
  1.3.1–4: *203*
  4.3.15–19: *203*
Columella, *de Re Rustica*
  9.2.2: *216n.8*
Critias (West [W.])
  6: *220n.27*
Curtius
  8.5.7–8: *228n.76*

Diodorus Siculus
  4.74: *234n.34*
  5.39: *255n.22*
Dionysius Chalcus (West [W.])
  1: *263n.92*
  2: *220n.32*
Dioscorides
  5.57: *165*

Ennius, *Annales* (Skutsch)
  105–9: *127–28*
Ennius, *Fragmenta* (Courtney)
  fr. 33: *227n.72*
Euenus (West [W.])
  2: *220n.29, 221n.35*

Euripides, *Bacchae*
  233–38: *259n.48*
  402–14: *262n.74*
Euripides, *Phaethon* (Diggle)
  67–70: *165, 263n.89*

Festus (Lindsay)
  p. 360.10–11: *228n.76*

Herodian (Historicus)
  4.2: *253n.4*
Hesiod, *Theogony*
  915–17: *235n.47*
Homer, *Iliad*
  1.138: *257n.33*
  5.835–38: *240–41n.96*
  6: *87*
  8.98–115: *240–41n.96*
  8.268–72: *240–41n.96*
  8.312–24: *240–41n.96*
  11.618–803: *221–22n.41*
  13.374–82: *240–41n.96*
  13.389–93: *66*
  16.480–86: *66*
  19.409–14: *66*
  20.84: *220n.34*
  20.443: *19*
  22.226–46: *88*
  22.358–60: *66*
  23.474–81: *240–41n.96*
  23.850–83: *240–41n.96*
  24.476–551: *137*
  24.596–620: *234n.34*
Homer, *Odyssey*
  6.309: *220n.34*
  9.201–363: *220n.28*
  11.307–20: *269n.12*
  11.576–81: *234n.34*
  20.262: *220n.34*
  24.39–40: *66*
Horace, *Ars Poetica*
  55: *139, 160*
  60–72: *242n.110*
  61: *242n.108*
  73–74, 401–403: *222n.47*
  84: *233n.27*
  85: *271n.33*

Horace, *Ars Poetica* (*continued*)
   146: *242n.108*
   148–52: *222n.47*
   322: *31*
   330–31: *271n.33*
   347: *228n.76*
   354–65: *23*
   361–65: *238n.71*
   438: *138*
   464: *242n.108*
Horace, *Carmina*
   I.1: *xiii, 38, 52, 54, 62, 66, 68, 138,*
     217n.12, 221n.40, 222n.49,
     264n.109, 266–67n.125
   I.2: *xiii, 119, 123–25, 138, 251n.70,*
     271n.31
   I.3: *xiii, 138, 139, 140, 141, 144, 160,*
     163–65, 251n.72, 254n.16,
     255n.20, 260n.52, 260n.59,
     261n.67, 262n.81
   I.4: *xiii, 7–8, 11, 14, 36, 90, 161, 164,*
     217n.12, 252n.79, 262n.74,
     262n.79, 266n.122
   I.5: *xiii, 168*
   I.6: *xiii, 7, 8, 21, 33, 48, 71, 206,*
     217n.12, 222n.48, 261n.70,
     271n.31, 273n.42, 274n.49,
     277n.64
   I.7: *7, 8–9, 36, 58, 90, 107, 217n.12,*
     220n.28, 260n.56, 273n.42
   I.8: *218–19n.20, 219n.22, 258n.35*
   I.9: *7, 9–10, 11, 12, 36, 113, 161,*
     217n.12, 217n.14, 220n.28,
     259n.46, 263n.84, 273n.42
   I.10: *62*
   I.11: *7, 9–10, 11, 36, 62, 90, 113, 138,*
     154, 161, 168, 187, 202, 217n.12,
     217n.14, 222n.49, 241n.104,
     266n.122, 273n.42
   I.12: *31, 58, 62, 117, 123, 125–26,*
     127, 251n.72, 260n.53, 271n.31,
     271n.33
   I.13: *11, 62, 168, 220n.28, 259n.47*
   I.15: *87–88, 138, 240n.95, 261n.70*
   I.16: *264n.107*
   I.17: *11, 62, 66, 168, 217n.12, 218–*
     19n.20, 220n.28, 252n.79, 260n.56

   I.18: *7, 11, 132, 217n.12, 218–19n.20,*
     220n.28, 222n.49, 260n.56,
     266n.119
   I.19: *5, 216n.6, 218–19n.20, 222n.48,*
     274n.49
   I.20: *7, 13, 160, 163, 216n.6, 217n.12,*
     220n.28, 222n.46, 252n.78,
     252n.85, 259n.46, 266n.121
   I.21: *58, 233n.31*
   I.24: *138, 139–40, 144, 160, 161,*
     163–64, 254–55n.17, 261n.67,
     261n.70, 262n.81
   I.25: *36, 169, 170, 173–74, 180, 255–*
     56n.23, 263n.98, 265n.113,
     267n.127, 268n.132
   I.26: *107, 274n.49*
   I.27: *7, 11, 217n.12, 218–19n.20,*
     220n.30, 220n.32, 221n.40
   I.30: *138*
   I.31: *68, 233n.31, 271n.31*
   I.32: *62, 138, 222n.45, 233n.31–32,*
     235n.44
   I.33: *261n.70*
   I.35: *7, 13, 217n.15*
   I.36: *13, 217n.12, 220n.28, 252n.78,*
     266n.121
   I.37: *13, 36, 217n.12, 220n.31*
   I.38: *7, 13, 66, 138, 200, 217n.12,*
     272n.35
   II.1: *222n.48, 231n.14, 274n.49*
   II.2: *43, 267n.126*
   II.3: *7, 10, 11, 14, 66, 164, 217n.12,*
     217n.14, 221n.40, 259n.51,
     273n.42
   II.4: *138, 147–53, 259n.48, 265n.115,*
     270n.21
   II.5: *66, 217n.12*
   II.7: *13, 49, 62, 66, 90, 163, 215n.1,*
     217n.12, 219n.23, 220n.28,
     221n.40, 252n.78, 252n.80,
     254n.15, 266n.121
   II.8: *174, 218–19n.20, 267n.127,*
     271n.33
   II.9: *256n.24, 274n.51*
   II.10.17–20: *58*
   II.11: *7, 11, 66, 155, 164, 217n.12,*
     217n.14, 219n.26, 220n.28,

252n.79, 259n.51, 260n.56, 273n.42, 274n.49

II.12: 220n.28, 222n.48, 261n.70, 274n.49, 274n.51, 275n.57

II.13: 237n.66

II.14: 7, 11, 14, 72–73, 217n.12, 217n.14, 220n.28, 234n.34, 266n.121, 273n.42

II.16: 10, 217n.13, 260n.52

II.17: 157–58, 219n.21, 225–26n.64, 240n.94, 241n.104

II.18.15–16: 242n.108

II.19: 263n.96, 266n.121

II.20: 31, 34, 50, 51–52, 98, 200, 212, 256n.24, 264n.109

III.1: 189, 217n.12, 260n.52

III.2: 91–92, 156–57

III.3: 58, 123, 126–27, 221n.40, 233n.32, 251n.72, 274n.49, 274n.51

III.4: 58, 188–89, 234n.34, 251n.72

III.5: 251n.70, 251n.73

III.6: 111, 202, 217n.12, 260n.53

III.7.29–32: 267n.127

III.8: 7, 11, 13, 160, 164, 217n.12, 222n.46, 252n.79, 259n.46, 274n.49

III.9: 5, 264–65n.111, 266–67n.125, 267n.127, 267n.127

III.10: 138, 169, 173, 246n.21, 261n.70, 264n.103, 264–65n.111, 265n.116, 267n.127

III.11.21: 234n.34

III.12: 168, 217n.12, 260n.56

III.13.2: 220n.28

III.14: 13, 62, 131–32, 217n.12, 251n.70, 252n.78, 259n.46, 260n.52, 267n.127

III.15: 4, 26, 36, 173–75, 176, 217n.12, 225n.62, 267n.127, 268n.132

III.16: 251n.72, 261n.70, 267n.127, 268n.128, 268n.132

III.17: 7, 177, 201, 217n.12, 217n.14, 260n.56, 260n.59, 269n.8, 273n.42

III.19: 4, 7, 36–37, 62, 76, 78, 138,

177, 187, 217n.12, 217n.14, 220n.28, 220n.31, 237n.n.66–67, 266n.124, 273n.42

III.20: 218–19n.20

III.21: 217n.12, 219n.22, 220n.28, 259n.46, 271n.33

III.22: 138

III.23.9: 107

III.24.3: 260n.53

III.25: 13, 212, 227–28n.74, 263n.96, 266n.121, 274n.51

III.26: 5, 168, 267n.127

III.27: 241n.104, 259n.51, 260n.52, 266n.123

III.28: 7, 66, 168, 217n.12, 259n.46, 260n.56, 264n.101

III.29: 7, 36, 164, 217n.12, 217n.14, 220n.28, 252n.79, 259n.51, 271n.26, 273n.42, 274n.49

III.30: 31, 34, 51–52, 84, 98, 194, 200, 212, 213, 264n.109, 269n.6

IV.1: xv, xvii, xvii, 4, 26–28, 32, 34–38, 41, 42, 43–45, 51, 64, 68, 71, 74, 92, 99–100, 114, 136, 137, 139, 142–43, 146, 152–54, 170, 172, 176–77, 180, 204, 216n.6, 216n.9, 216n.11, 217n.12, 218–19n.20, 229n.85, 256n.25, 256n.27, 257n.28, 260n.59, 262n.79, 265n.113, 265n.115

IV.2: xv, xvii, xviii, 41, 42, 43, 45–51, 52, 53, 54, 62, 64, 71, 92, 94, 99–100, 117, 131, 172, 189, 194, 209, 217n.12, 222n.48, 232n.24, 233n.27, 237n.65, 237n.68, 238n.72, 241n.104, 246n.23, 247n.27, 274n.49, 274–75n.54

IV.3: xiv, xv, xvii, xviii, 41, 51–54, 56, 62, 67–68, 71, 92, 98, 165, 172, 179, 182, 228n.78, 232n.26, 233n.27, 237n.68, 241n.103, 264n.109, 278n.69

IV.4: xv, xvii, xviii, xx, 40–41, 51, 56–57, 60–61, 67–68, 71, 78, 92, 95–114, 118–19, 127, 131, 181, 184–85, 188, 189–90, 194, 209, 233n.27, 237n.68, 238n.71,

Horace, *Carmina* (*continued*)
 240n.92, 250n.64, 251n.70,
 251n.72, 255n.18, 258n.41
 IV.5: *xvii, xviii, xx,* 40–41, 51, 56–57,
  58, 59–61, 67–68, 71, 78, 92, 99–
  100, 114–33, 163, 181, 184, 186–
  87, 194, 195, 209, 217n.12,
  235n.46. 237n.68, 238n.76,
  255n.18, 261n.70, 272–73n.40,
  274n.50
 IV.6: *xv, xvii, xviii,* 41, 51, 52, 54–68,
  71, 90, 92, 99–100, 165, 181, 191–
  92, 231n.14, 232n.26, 235n.46,
  237n.68, 243n.6, 274n.50
 IV.7: *xviii,* 36, 66, 68, 69–73, 83,
  99–100, 138, 181, 217n.13,
  242n.108
 IV.8: *xviii,* 28, 42, 68, 70, 71, 74–79,
  83, 84–85, 87, 90, 92, 99, 114,
  165, 181, 185, 197, 228n.78,
  231n.10, 234n.38, 243n.4,
  247n.31
 IV.9: *xv, xviii,* 42, 68, 70, 71, 74, 79–
  92, 99, 114, 135, 138, 179, 181,
  182, 194, 197, 204, 231n.10,
  232n.17, 237n.68, 243n.4,
  246n.23, 260n.53, 278n.69
 IV.10: *xvii, xviii, xx,* 41, 70, 99–100,
  134–36, 138–45, 147, 153–54,
  155, 162–64, 167, 169–70, 172,
  178–79, 181, 211, 213, 253n.10,
  260n.59, 265n.115
 IV.11: *xvii, xviii, xx,* 36, 41, 66, 70,
  99–100, 134–36, 138, 145–47,
  152–58, 162–63, 167, 169–72,
  176–77, 181, 211, 217n.12, 225–
  26n.64, 230n.7, 257n.30, 258n.35,
  262n.79, 265n.115, 269n.9
 IV.12: *xvii, xviii, xx,* 36, 41, 70, 99–
  100, 134–36, 139, 140, 141, 145,
  154, 155, 158–66, 167, 169–72,
  181, 191, 211, 212, 213, 217n.12,
  220n.28, 224–25n.57, 235n.51,
  252n.79, 254n.16, 261n.70,
  266n.122, 269n.9, 273n.44
 IV.13: *xviii, xx,* 36, 41, 70, 99–100,
  134–36, 138, 145, 167–80, 181,

 197, 211, 217n.12, 225n.61, 255–
 56n.23, 263n.98, 264n.103,
 278n.69
 IV.14: *xvii, xviii, xx,* 40–41, 99–100,
  110, 118, 136, 166, 180, 181–98,
  202, 209, 232n.17, 235n.52,
  242n.2, 253n.1, 275n.58, 275–
  76n.59
 IV.15: *xv, xvii, xviii, xx,* 6, 20, 21,
  40–41, 58, 62, 66, 74, 99–100,
  118, 136, 166, 180, 181, 198–213,
  217n.12, 222n.48, 229n.91,
  231n.14, 235n.44, 235n.51,
  235n.52, 249n.48, 253n.1,
  263n.93
Horace, *Epistulae*
 I.1: 26, 40, 78, 216n.4
 I.2.15–16: 240n.93
 I.3.6–29: 232n.22
 I.5: 70, 73, 138, 221n.40, 236n.56,
  259n.46, 271n.33
 I.7: 252n.80, 262n.75
 I.10.5: 266n.118
 I.12.27–29: 276n.62
 I.13: 223n.52
 I.14.6–7: 271n.33
 I.17: 229n.83, 256n.27
 I.20.26–28: 239n.80
 II.1: 21, 23, 24–25, 40, 60, 78, 139,
  160, 164, 179, 222n.48, 223n.51,
  228n.76, 229n.81, 229–30n.3,
  231n.14, 238n.75, 240n.90,
  249n.46, 252n.80, 253n.86, 266–
  67n.125, 274n.49, 275n.57
 II.2: 5, 26–34, 37–38, 40, 192, 215n.1,
  225–26n.64
Horace, *Epodes*
 1: 233n.31
 2.37–38: 241n.103
 8: 171
 9: 232n.20, 233n.31, 234n.42,
  271n.33
 11.19–22: 267n.127
 12: 171
 13: 259n.46
 14.2: 241n.103
 16: 260n.53, 266n.123

Horace, *Sermones*
  I.1: *38, 194, 217n.15, 225n.63,*
     228n.79, 259n.50
  I.2: *217n.15, 225n.63, 267n.127*
  I.3: *90, 91–92, 217n.15, 224n.56,*
     225n.63, 242n.109
  I.4: *62, 217n.15, 224n.56*
  I.5: *xiii, 62, 138, 139, 140, 141, 144,*
     160, 241n.104, 255n.20
  I.6: *18, 54, 78, 139, 160, 215n.1,*
     271n.33
  I.9: *16–20, 22, 217n.15, 233n.31,*
     266–67n.125, 275n.57
  I.10: *18, 20–21, 139, 160, 217n.15,*
     227n.72, 263n.85, 266–67n.125
  II.1: *21–22, 23, 24–25, 164, 217n.15,*
     274n.49
  II.2: *78, 217n.15*
  II.3: *91, 217n.15, 241n.98, 241n.104,*
     242n.109, 267n.127
  II.5, *217n.15*
  II.6: *54, 217n.15, 225–26n.64,*
     241n.103, 241n.104, 254n.12
  II.7.115: *260n.52*
  II.8: *78, 252n.80*
Hyginus, *Fabulae*
  9, 11: *234n.34*
  55: *234n.34*

Ibycus (Page [*PMG*])
  287: *216n.7*
Ion of Chios (West [W.])
  26.13–16: *219n.25*
  27: *11, 221n.35*
Isocrates, *Evagoras*
  5: *253n.6*
  79: *253n.8*
Isocrates, *Helena*
  11–15: *xiv*

Josephus, *Bellum Judaicum*
  2.156: *234n.34*
Julianus Aegyptius, *Epigrammata*
     (*Anthologia Palatina*)
  5.298: *265–66n.117*
Julius Obsequens
  71: *248–49n.44*

Juvenal
  6.377: *229n.87*

Laus Pisonis
  216–18: *235n.53*
Livy
  1.4.7–8: *265n.115*
  1.25.4: *276n.60*
  5.35: *255n.22*
  6.32.1: *241n.104*
  7.12.12: *241n.104*
  8.38.6: *241n.104*
  22.28.9: *276n.60*
  22.33: *255n.22*
  26.8–9: *107*
  27.39: *255n.22*
  29.3.1: *276n.60*
  45.23.19: *276n.60*
  peri 139: *276n.62*
Lucilius (Marx)
  231–32: *226n.66*
  II6 fr. 620, 622: *227n.71*
  fr. 1190: *227n.72*
  534, 1142: *226n.66*
Lucretius
  1.1–25: *262n.74*
  3.938–39: *26*
  3.984–94: *234n.34*
  3.1040–44: *123, 251n.75*
  3.1082–84: *259n.50*
  3.1090: *252n.85*
  5.7–54: *123, 251n.75*
  5.255: *271n.26*
  6.24–28: *123*
  6.292: *271n.26*

Macedonius, *Epigrammata* (*Anthologia
     Palatina*)
  5.233, 271: *265–66n.117*
Marcus Argentarius, *Epigrammata*
     (*Anthologia Palatina*)
  5.118: *267n.127*
Martial
  3.58.37: *256n.24*
  10.30.6: *107*
  10.90.1–4: *265–66n.117*
  12.3.5: *235n.53*

Meleager, *Epigrammata* (*Anthologia Palatina*)
    5.184: *267–68n.127*
    5.204: *265–66n.117, 267n.127*
Meleager, *Epigrammata* (Gow and Page [G.-P.])
    81: *141*
Menander Rhetor
    368.1–8: *xiv, 94*
    398.1–6: *40*
    407: *229n.89*
Mimnermus (Bergk [*PLG*])
    1, 2, 5: *217n.13*

New Testament
    Matthew 22.8: *236n.60*
    I. Thessalonians 5.5–8: *251n.75*
    I. John 2.8: *251n.75*
Nicolaus, *Progymnasmata*
    48.20: *xiv*

Oppian, *Halieutica*
    4.331–43: *252n.83*
Ovid, *Amores*
    1.6: *267–68n.127*
    3.11.12: *268n.128*
Ovid, *Ars Amatoria*
    2.113–20: *265–66n.117*
    2.114: *241n.104*
    2.696: *252n.85*
    3.57–76: *265–66n.117*
Ovid, *Epistulae ex Ponto*
    1.2.113–18: *230n.8*
    1.7.28: *235n.53*
    2.3.78: *235n.53*
    3.3.1–4, 95–108: *230n.8*
    4.12.23: *235n.53*
Ovid, *Fasti*
    1.3–26: *235n.53*
    2.1–4: *276n.61*
    2.853: *262n.75*
    4.125–32: *262n.74*
    4.949–54: *129*
    5.269, 518: *252n.85*
    5.579–98: *276n.62*
Ovid, *Heroides*
    16.23–24: *262n.74*

Ovid, *Metamorphoses*
    2.781: *241n.104*
    6.146–316: *234n.34*
    6.424–674: *262n.75*
    15.232–36: *265–66n.117*
Ovid, *Tristia*
    2.225–36: *276–77n.62*
    3.7.31–44: *265–66n.117*

Pausanius
    1.21.3; 2.21.9; 5.11.2; 5.16.4; 8.2.5, 7: *234n.34*
Petronius Arbiter, *Satyricon*
    17.5: *250n.66*
    26: *267n.127*
    70.7.3: *266n.124*
    94.7–8: *267–68n.127*
Philodemus, *Epigrammata* (*Anthologia Palatina*)
    5.112: *264n.108*
Philodemus, *Fragmenta* (Jacoby [*FGrH*])
    72T fr. 26–27: *228n.76*
    153F VII fr. 10–12: *228n.76*
Phocylides (Bergk [*PLG*])
    11: *220n.34*
Ps.-Phocylides (Young)
    162–63: *225n.63*
Pindar, *Fragmenta*
    29: *271n.31*
Pindar, *Isthmian Odes*
    4.43–47: *98*
    7: *271n.31*
Pindar, *Nemean Odes*
    3: *98, 245n.15*
    5: *98, 243n.4, 245n.15*
    6.8–11: *245n.15*
    7.12–13: *90, 241n.102*
    10.50–54: *245n.15*
Pindar, *Olympian Odes*
    2: *125, 271n.31*
    6: *271n.31*
    9.100a, 108–12: *104*
    9.108–12: *245n.15*
    10.91–92: *90, 241n.102*
    13.13: *245n.15*
    14.13–17a: *235n.47*

Pindar, *Paeanes*
  6: *62, 66*
Pindar, *Pythian Odes*
  1: *98, 100, 236n.54*
  4: *234n.34, 245n.17*
  5.111–12: *98*
  7: *271n.31*
  8: *104, 243n.5, 245n.15*
  10.53–54: *232n.21*
Plato, *Gorgias*
  525E: *234n.34*
Plato, *Leges*
  801e–2a, 829c–e, 957d–e: *xvi*
Plato, *Respublica*
  396b–d, 401b: *xvi*
  590a8–c: *24*
Plato, *Symposium*
  184C4–85E5, 189A–C: *221n.39*
  193D8–94E2, 198A–99C2: *221n.39*
  212C4–15A3: *221n.39*
Plautus, *Asinaria*
  202: *258n.42*
  799–802: *220n.32*
Plautus, *Bacchides*
  69–72: *220n.32*
  210: *216n.9*
  1195–1205: *219n.25*
Plautus, *Curculio*
  1–164: *267n.127*
Plautus, *Menaechmi*
  143–46: *101*
Plautus, *Mostellaria*
  727–30: *219n.25*
  959: *216n.9*
Plautus, *Persa*
  795–810: *220n.32*
Plautus, *Rudens*
  458: *258n.42*
Plautus, *Truculentus*
  322: *258n.42*
  829–31: *220n.32*
Pliny the Elder, *Naturalis Historia*
  2.93–94, 98: *248–49n.44*
  7.120: *252n.85*
  9.8.3: *271n.26*
  9.118: *82–83, 216n.10, 239n.79*
Pliny the Younger, *Epistulae*

5.3.5: *236n.56*
9.36.5: *252n.85*
Plutarch, *Antonius*
  87: *231n.13*
Plutarch, *Julius Caesar*
  69.4–5: *248–49n.44*
Polybius
  6.53.3, 9–10: *253n.6*
Praxilla (Bergk [*PLG*])
  749, 750: *217n.15*
Propertius
  1.3.35–36: *267–68n.127*
  1.8.27–46: *267n.127*
  1.10.15–16: *267n.127*
  1.16: *267n.127*
  2.1: *235n.53, 274–75n.54*
  2.6.37–42: *267n.127*
  2.14: *267n.127*
  2.29: *267–68n.127*
  2.31: *68, 234n.35*
  3.3: *274–75n.54*
  3.4: *122, 274–75n.54*
  3.6.19–34: *267–68n.127*
  3.7: *252n.83*
  3.9: *235n.52, 274–75n.54*
  3.21.28: *266–67n.125*
  3.25: *255–56n.23, 265–66n.117, 267–68n.127*
  4.1.135–50: *267n.127*
  4.3.66: *276n.60*
  4.4.80: *216n.9*
  4.6: *xvi, 67, 122–23, 232n.17, 235n.53*

[Quintilian], *Declamationes Maiores*
  16.7.9: *258n.40*
Quintilian, *Institutio Oratoria*
  8.6.17: *264n.103*

Rufinus, *Epigrammata* (*Anthologia Palatina*)
  5.21: *265–66n.117, 267–68n.127*
  5.27: *265–66n.117*
  5.28: *265–66n.117*
  5.43: *267–68n.127*
  5.76: *265–66n.117, 267n.127*

Rufinus, *Epigrammata* (*continued*)
   5.92: *265–66n.117*
   5.103: *265–66n.117, 267n.127*

Sallust, *Historiae* (Maurenbrecher)
   2. fr. 92: *246n.23*
Sappho (Lobel and Page [L.-P.])
   1: *221n.36, 268n.134*
   94: *221n.36*
Scriptores Historiae Augustae, Claudius
   7.6–8: *271–72n.34*
Scriptores Historiae Augustae, Severus
   24: *253n.4*
Semonides (West [W.])
   1.20–22a: *219n.24*
Seneca the Elder, *Controversiae*
   2.4.11–12: *230–31n.9*
[Seneca], *Octavia*
   731: *216n.9*
Servius, *in Vergilium Commentarius*
   1.243: *248n.37*
   6.72: *233n.31*
   11.601: *227n.72*
Silius Italicus
   12.536: *107*
   13.333: *256n.24*
   17.276: *276n.60*
Simonides (West [W.])
   fr.11.1–2: *66*
   fr. 19–21: *216n.7*
Statius, *Silvae*
   1.4.19–36: *235n.53*
   4.1.37: *252n.85*
   4.4.16: *107*
Statius, *Thebais*
   10.54: *252n.85*
Strabo
   4.6.8: *192*
   9.3.14: *234n.34*
Suetonius, *Augustus*
   21.3: *276n.62*
   23: *82, 239n.79*
   25: *240–41n.96*
   29.1, 3: *233n.31*
   31: *233n.31, 251n.76*
   62, 69: *103*
   66.3: *230n.7*

   85–89: *230n.5*
   89: *25, 223n.52*
   100: *253n.4*
Suetonius, *Claudius*
   1: *245n.14*
Suetonius, *Julius Caesar*
   84: *253n.4*
   88: *248–49n.44*
Suetonius, *Tiberius*
   4: *103*
   4–6: *248n.32*
   9.1: *276n.62*
   12–13: *239n.79*
Suetonius, *Vita Horati*
   15: *225–26n.64*

Tacitus, *Annales*
   1.5: *230n.9*
   1.8: *253n.4*
   1.10: *82, 239n.79, 245n.14*
   2.1–3: *276n.62*
   3.30: *230n.7*
   3.48: *239n.79*
   4.44: *231n.13*
Tacitus, *Historiae*
   2.44.9–10: *276n.60*
Terence, *Adelphi*
   293: *216n.9*
Terence, *Eunuchus*
   711: *258n.42*
Theocritus
   2.150–54: *220n.28*
   6.88–100: *263n.94*
   16.30: *241n.102*
Theognis (West [W.])
   39–48: *217n.15*
   115–16: *217n.15*
   211–12: *220n.27*
   237–54: *219n.25*
   295–98: *220n.32*
   413–14: *220n.32*
   475–78: *176, 220n.29*
   497–510: *220n.27*
   533–34: *220n.31*
   567–70: *217n.13*
   627–28: *220n.29*
   757–64: *221n.36*

762–68: *219n.26*
765–68: *221n.36*
837–40: *220n.29*
841–44: *220n.32*
873–76: *220n.29*
877–84: *217n.13, 219n.25*
973–78: *11, 221n.36*
979–82: *217n.15*
983–88: *219n.25*
1047–48: *11, 217n.13, 221n.35*
1063–68: *219n.25*
1071–74: *217n.13*
1119–22: *217n.13*
1129–32: *219n.25, 220n.33, 221n.35*
Tibullus
    1.2: *267–68n.127*
    1.4.33–38: *255n.22*
    1.6.9–10: *267–68n.127*
    1.9.53–64: *267n.127*
    1.10.47: *252n.85*
    2.1.35–36: *235n.53*
    2.3.71–74: *267n.127*
    2.5.121: *255n.22*
    3.6.41: *266–67n.125*

Valerius Maximus
    2.1.10: *203*
    6.3: *253n.5*
    7.7.2, 5: *245n.13*
Varro, *Res Rusticae*
    1.13.6: *252n.85*
Varro, *de Vita Populi Romani*
    fr. 84: *203*
Velleius Paterculus
    2.75: *245n.14, 248n.32*
    2.79.2: *245n.14*
    2.94.1: *245n.14*
    2.91.1: *276n.62*
    2.94.4: *276n.62*
    2.95.1: *245n.14*
    2.97: *82–83, 216n.10, 239n.79*
    2.100: *231n.13*
    2.102: *82–83, 216n.10, 237n.69,*
       239n.79
Vergil, *Aeneid*
    1.1–3: *105*
    1.33: *252n.85*

1.67: *206*
1.229–53: *234n.33*
2.17–19a: *66*
2.238–39a: *66*
2.624–40: *106, 245n.17, 245–*
    46n.19
4.69b–73: *244–45n.12*
4.314: *137*
4.384: *166*
5.1: *137*
5.446–49: *66*
5.710: *140*
6.466, 469: *137*
6.582–84: *269n.12*
6.595–600: *234n.34*
6.789–807: *122*
6.851–53: *110*
7.638–39b: *191*
8.77: *270n.22*
9.150–53: *235n.49*
10.18–62: *234n.33*
10.35: *252n.85*
10.77: *260n.52*
10.210: *256n.24*
10.454–56: *192–93, 270n.22*
10.494–95: *193*
10.510–17a: *192–93*
10.723–29: *244n.11*
11.186: *166*
11.751–56: *244n.9*
12.18–62: *234n.33*
12.82–97, 332–37: *191*
Vergil, *Eclogues*
    1: *30, 122*
    2: *139, 144*
    3.43: *252n.85*
    4.55: *140*
    5: *139, 140–42, 144, 163, 255n.18*
    6: *14–15, 20, 60, 67, 154, 160, 166,*
       205–6, 208, 262n.75
    8.6–13: *275n.56*
    9: *30, 122, 248–49n.44, 250n.65,*
       252n.85
Vergil, *Georgics*
    1.40–42: *122*
    1.458: *252n.85*

Vergil, *Georgics* (*continued*)
  1.465–68: *248–49n.44*
  2.39–44: *235n.53*
  3. *proem.*: *122*
  3.215: *241n.104*
  3.42: *235n.53*
  4.15: *262n.75*

4.179: *232n.21*
4.511–15: *160, 262n.75*
Vitruvius, *de Architectura*
  1. *proem.*: *123*

Xenophanes (West [W.])
  1: *12, 220n.29, 220n.32*

WISCONSIN STUDIES IN CLASSICS

General Editors
Richard Daniel De Puma and Patricia A. Rosenmeyer

E. A. THOMPSON
Romans and Barbarians: The Decline of the Western Empire

JENNIFER TOLBERT ROBERTS
Accountability in Athenian Government

H. I. MARROU
A History of Education in Antiquity
Histoire de l'Education dans l'Antiquité, translated by GEORGE LAMB

ERIKA SIMON
Festivals of Attica: An Archaeological Commentary

G. MICHAEL WOLOCH
Roman Cities: Les villes romaines by Pierre Grimal, translated and edited
by G. Michael Woloch, together with A Descriptive Catalogue of
Roman Cities by G. Michael Woloch

WARREN G. MOON, editor
Ancient Greek Art and Iconography

KATHERINE DOHAN MORROW
Greek Footwear and the Dating of Sculpture

JOHN KEVIN NEWMAN
The Classical Epic Tradition

JEANNY VORYS CANBY, EDITH PORADA, BRUNILDE
SISMONDO RIDGWAY, and TAMARA STECH, editors
Ancient Anatolia: Aspects of Change and Cultural Development

ANN NORRIS MICHELINI
Euripides and the Tragic Tradition

WENDY J. RASCHKE, editor
The Archaeology of the Olympics: The Olympics and Other Festivals in Antiquity

PAUL PLASS
Wit and the Writing of History: The Rhetoric of Historiography in Imperial Rome

BARBARA HUGHES FOWLER
The Hellenistic Aesthetic

F. M. CLOVER AND R. S. HUMPHREYS, editors
Tradition and Innovation in Late Antiquity

BRUNILDE SISMONDO RIDGWAY
Hellenistic Sculpture I: The Styles of ca. 331–200 B.C.

BARBARA HUGHES FOWLER, editor and translator
Hellenistic Poetry: An Anthology

KATHRYN J. GUTZWILLER
Theocritus' Pastoral Analogies: The Formation of a Genre

VIMALA BEGLEY and RICHARD DANIEL DE PUMA, editor
Rome and India: The Ancient Sea Trade

RUDOLF BLUM AND HANS H. WELLISCH, translators
Kallimachos: The Alexandrian Library and the Origins of Bibliography

DAVID CASTRIOTA
Myth, Ethos, and Actuality: Official Art in Fifth Century B.C. Athens

BARBARA HUGHES FOWLER, editor and translator
Archaic Greek Poetry: An Anthology

JOHN H. OAKLEY and REBECCA H. SINOS
The Wedding in Ancient Athens

RICHARD DANIEL DE PUMA and JOCELYN PENNY SMALL, editors
Murlo and the Etruscans: Art and Society in Ancient Etruria

JUDITH LYNN SEBESTA and LARISSA BONFANTE, editors
The World of Roman Costume

JENNIFER LARSON
Greek Heroine Cults

WARREN G. MOON, editor
Polykleitos, the Doryphoros, and Tradition

PAUL PLASS
The Game of Death in Ancient Rome: Arena Sport and Political Suicide

MARGARET S. DROWER
Flinders Petrie: A Life in Archaeology

SUSAN B. MATHESON
Polygnotos and Vase Painting in Classical Athens

JENIFER NEILS, EDITOR
Worshipping Athena: Panathenaia and Parthenon

PAMELA WEBB
Hellenistic Architectural Sculpture: Figural Motifs in Western Anatolia and the Aegean Islands

BRUNILDE SISMONDO RIDGWAY
Fourth-Century Styles in Greek Sculpture

LUCY GOODISON and CHRISTINE MORRIS, editors
Ancient Goddesses: The Myths and the Evidence

JO-MARIE CLAASSEN
Displaced Persons: The Literature of Exile from Cicero to Boethius

BRUNILDE SISMONDO RIDGWAY
Hellenistic Sculpture II: The Styles of ca. 200–100 B.C.

PAT GETZ-GENTLE
Personal Styles in Early Cycladic Sculpture

CATULLUS
DAVID MULROY, translator and commentator
The Complete Poetry of Catullus

BRUNILDE SISMONDO RIDGWAY
Hellenistic Sculpture III: The Styles of ca. 100–31 B.C.

ANGELIKI KOSMOPOULOU
The Iconography of Sculptured Statue Bases in the Archaic and Classical Periods

SARA H. LINDHEIM
Mail and Female: Epistolary Narrative and Desire in Ovid's Heroides

GRAHAM ZANKER
Modes of Viewing Hellenistic Poetry and Art

ALEXANDRA ANN CARPINO
Discs of Splendor: The Relief Mirrors of the Etruscans

TIMOTHY S. JOHNSON
A Symposion of Praise: Horace Returns to Lyric in Odes IV